REGIONAL ANALYSIS

Volume I
Economic Systems

STUDIES IN ANTHROPOLOGY

Under the Consulting Editorship of E. A. Hammel,
UNIVERSITY OF CALIFORNIA, BERKELEY

Andrei Simić, THE PEASANT URBANITES: A Study of Rural-Urban Mobility in Serbia

John U. Ogbu, THE NEXT GENERATION: An Ethnography of Education in an Urban Neighborhood

Bennett Dyke and Jean Walters MacCluer (Eds.), COMPUTER SIMULATION IN HUMAN POPULATION STUDIES

Robbins Burling, THE PASSAGE OF POWER: Studies in Political Succession

Piotr Sztompka, SYSTEM AND FUNCTION: Toward a Theory of Society

William G. Lockwood, EUROPEAN MOSLEMS: Economy and Ethnicity in Western Bosnia

Günter Golde, CATHOLICS AND PROTESTANTS: Agricultural Modernization in Two German Villages

Peggy Reeves Sanday (Ed.), ANTHROPOLOGY AND THE PUBLIC INTEREST: Fieldwork and Theory

Carol A. Smith, REGIONAL ANALYSIS, Volume I: Economic Systems, and Volume II: Social Systems

in preparation

Frank Henderson Stewart, FUNDAMENTALS OF AGE-GROUP SYSTEMS

Raymond D. Fogelson and Richard N. Adams (Eds.), THE ANTHROPOLOGY OF POWER: Ethnographic Studies from Asia, Oceania, and the New World

REGIONAL ANALYSIS

Volume I
Economic Systems

EDITED BY

Carol A. Smith

Department of Anthropology
Duke University
Durham, North Carolina

ACADEMIC PRESS   New York   San Francisco   London

A Subsidiary of Harcourt Brace Jovanovich, Publishers

ACADEMIC PRESS, INC.
111 Fifth Avenue, New York, New York 10003

United Kingdom Edition published by
ACADEMIC PRESS, INC. (LONDON) LTD.
24/28 Oval Road, London NW1

Library of Congress Cataloging in Publication Data

Main entry under title:

Regional analysis.

    (Studies in anthropology)
    Includes bibliographies and index.
    CONTENTS: v. I.   Economic systems.—v. II.   Social
systems.
    1.   Underdeveloped areas—Commerce—Congresses.
2.   Central places—Congresses.   3.   Social systems—
Economic aspects—Congresses.   I.   Smith, Carol A.
HF1413.R428   380.1'09172'4   75-30474
ISBN 0—12—652101—8 (v. I)

Contents

Section A   INTRODUCTION: THE REGIONAL APPROACH TO ECONOMIC SYSTEMS

Section C **SPATIOECONOMIC ORGANIZATION
IN COMPLEX REGIONAL
SYSTEMS**

Contents

List of Contributors

Numbers in parentheses indicate the page on which the authors' contributions begin.

Gordon Appleby (147), Department of Anthropology, Stanford University, Stanford, California, and Institute for Scientific Analysis, 210 Spear Street, San Francisco, California

Raymond J. Bromley (91), Department of Social Administration, University College of Swansea, Swansea, Wales

Lawrence W. Crissman (183), Department of Anthropology, University of Illinois at Urbana-Champaign, Urbana, Illinois

William O. Jones (303), Food Research Institute, Stanford University, Stanford, California

Klara Bonsack Kelley (219), Department of Anthropology, University of New Mexico, Albuquerque, New Mexico

Stuart M. Plattner (69), Department of Sociology and Anthropology, University of Missouri—St. Louis, St. Louis, Missouri

Brian Schwimmer (123), Department of Anthropology, University of Manitoba, Winnipeg, Manitoba, Canada

G. William Skinner (327), Department of Anthropology, Stanford University, Stanford, California

Carol A. Smith (3, 255), Department of Anthropology, Duke University, Durham, North Carolina

Preface

More than a decade ago G. William Skinner proposed that the way in which regional settlement systems organized and structured social intercourse in traditional China shaped cultural as well as economic institutions in that society. Since then much has happened to deepen and widen certain aspects of the approach he pioneered, an approach we term here *regional analysis*. Economic geography, the home of the spatial models which undergird the approach, has had a veritable renaissance, reflected in its newly sophisticated methodology and techniques of analysis. Central-place theory, which provided the spatial models basic to geographers' conceptualization of regional systems and also basic to Skinner's socioeconomic analysis, has been questioned, clarified, and revised, and alternative spatial models have been fashioned from it. Careful field studies of markets and regional economies carried out in different parts of the world have identified regional patterns not predicted by central-place theory or any of the other standard locational theories, thereby stimulating the development of new regional system theories. In addition, social scientists other than geographers, economists, and regional scientists now evince interest in the implications of rural–urban relations and regional settlement patterns, among them social anthropologists, archeologists, sociologists, and political scientists.

In short, regional models today are much more sophisticated than they were 15 years ago; and, on the basis of interest, regional analysis now holds promise as a general integrating framework for many of the social sciences. Yet little work has been done to relate the new theories of regional settlement systems to types and levels of socioeconomic systems, the other major element of regional analysis. And this must be done before its general promise can be realized.

In light of the growing disparity between the specialized and the generalized versions of regional analysis, I organized a conference for the purpose of discussing ways to bring the two together again. Scholars from several disciplines who had utilized locational or other territorial models to investigate either economic or social processes in real-world systems constituted the conference group. All had done field work in non-Western areas and together represented many parts of the world and many types of societies. The plan was to concentrate on various regular and irregular patterns of settlement-system organization uncovered by field work, and to discuss them as living, growing systems in order to discover the manner in which they influenced and were influenced by sociocultural systems.

The conference was held in Santa Fe, New Mexico in the fall of 1973, and most of the papers in these two volumes were first drafted for it. The effect of interaction and discussion at the conference and afterward was significant enough, however, that none of the final essays in either of the volumes bears close resemblance to its conference draft. I encouraged general theoretical formulations, which most of the essays now display; and to round out the presentation of our findings, I solicited additional papers from others whose field work was more recent than that of most of the conferees (Adams and Kasakoff, Appleby, Bromley, Olsen, Verdery). As they presently stand, the studies in these two volumes represent the most current thinking about the general applications of the regional framework for analyzing socioeconomic systems.

The two volumes are linked by a general interest in exploring the interconnectedness of economic and social systems as they exist and develop in territorial–environmental systems, but each has a different emphasis. Most of the studies in Volume I concentrate on developing and refining models of trade and urban evolution. While this concern places Volume I squarely within the realm of economic geography, the focus on evolutionary models and the relationship between economic and political subsystems in the developmental process makes it relevant to almost any student of the economy. The studies in Volume II are concerned with social systems; primary emphasis is given to showing the interrelationships among the institutional components of complex societies, including marriage and kinship, political organization, the formation of ethnic and cultural–territorial groups, and stratification systems—all as they are affected by regional–environmental variables. Hence, those who would be interested in Volume I are likely to be interested in Volume II as well; in addition, Volume II should be relevant to anyone concerned with complex sociocultural systems and the relationships among the organizational subsystems within them.

Many people and institutions were instrumental in the preparation and publication of these studies. The conference was supported by the Mathematics in the Social Sciences Board of the National Science Foundation; I would like to thank Roy D'Andrade for putting me in touch with them. The University of New Mexico gave additional assistance in holding the conference, primarily in the form of organizational help. The conference also benefited from the presence of several people from the University of New Mexico, especially Del Dyreson, Henry Harpending, and Robert Hitchcock. Duke University provided ample secretarial and copying services for preparing many of the manuscripts, tables, and figures; I am particularly grateful for the help given by Dina Smith and Sylvia Terrell. Dina Smith deserves special thanks for the exceptional work she did setting up and typing the tables, as does Ronald Smith who drew many of the figures. I am most grateful to the contributors to these volumes; all of them made useful suggestions to one another and to me and withstood cheerfully my novice editorship.

Contents of Volume II

Section C RELIGION, POLITICS, AND STRATIFICATION

Section D POLITICAL ECONOMY: SOCIAL ASPECTS OF ECONOMIC SYSTEMS

REGIONAL ANALYSIS

Volume I
Economic Systems

Section A

INTRODUCTION: THE REGIONAL APPROACH TO ECONOMIC SYSTEMS

How might a territorial system be efficiently organized for commerce, and how might its organization vary depending on the strength of different economic and political forces? What are the sizes, numbers, and distributions of economic institutions that affect the use of space? How do these institutions evolve and form systems, and how do they affect economic behavior? Some of the principal models developed by economic geographers in answer to these questions are discussed in the following essay, in which I introduce both the major theories of economic location and the studies presented in this volume. For reasons of space, my review of geographical theories is selective, focused on those most useful for cross-cultural and sociological analyses of economic systems.

I begin with the first full-fledged locational theory, one for production systems, and move along in roughly historical order to consider theories of retail, wholesale, and periodic marketing systems; the rank–size distribution of urban centers and urban primacy; and anomalous or irregular settlement systems. The standard locational models are described, illustrated, and evaluated, special attention being given to the assumptions and weaknesses that led several contributors to this volume to develop alternative versions of them. Special attention is also given to the necessary economic *and social* conditions for the development of the various regional patterns and for market evolution in general—two central issues in this volume that have been largely neglected in economic geography. My primary concern is to point out the relevance of locational analysis for social scientists concerned with whole social systems, not just their economic parts, and to show what can be learned from them about human behavior.

Chapter 1

Regional Economic Systems: Linking Geographical Models and Socioeconomic Problems

Carol A. Smith
Duke University

Scholars concerned with "the economy" as a cross-cultural institution traditionally approach it from one of two very different perspectives. Some proceed inductively to describe and explain economic relations as they exist in a particular observable context, which in practice is almost always a relatively narrow context—a community, a market, or the like—and then devise models showing patterns of economic relations in it—relations that are necessarily specific rather than general. And some proceed deductively to define the basic or inherent constraints in all economic systems and then devise models showing patterns of economic relations in them— relations that are necessarily ideal rather than real. The first approach, associated with those students of economics who are not economists, has the virtue of uncovering features of economic relations that economists, who use the second approach, fail to consider. It also allows one to move with facility from questions concerning the economy to questions concerning the place of the economy in society. Its weakness lies in the fact that specifically focused empirical studies (and the explanations fashioned for them) are ineffective for generating theories of general economic behavior applicable to a broad range of contexts. Hence, practitioners of the first approach, who tend to find fault with many of the assumptions used by

economists, rarely develop their own economic theories;[1] and perhaps
because of this their findings are usually ignored by economists.

Economists, by contrast, always use or develop general theories to
describe how variation in one set of economic variables systematically
affects variation in another set of economic variables. These theories may
or may not be capable of describing or explaining what one encounters in
the real world. But economists are loathe to give up a good theory just
because it fails the test of empirical prediction—for the logical relations
posited by a general model are not necessarily falsified if behavior in a
real system does not meet expectations. In fact, most economists use their
theories to determine how economic systems can be made more efficient
(or how economic actors can or should better their performance) and then
attempt to change the *real* system—engineer it—so that it more faithfully
reflects some theory of a perfect economy. The weakness of this approach,
a normative rather than a descriptive one, is that one can never be sure if
the problem is in the system or in the theory; data are rarely used, in
many cases cannot be used, to test the adequacy of the theory—general
theories stand or fall on logic alone. In addition, the most widely accepted
economic theories do not grapple with social relations in the economy;
such things are not easily put into an economic model or engineered out of
a system (if indeed they should be). Thus, when the theory fails to account
for behavior in a system, one can at best discern which economic assumption has been violated—sometimes not even that—but one cannot discern
why it has been violated. For this reason alone, general economic theories
are not very helpful to students of real economic behavior, who perhaps
for this reason are frequently suspicious about the very process of theory
construction.

Relations between economists and other students of the economy are not
strained simply because one group tends to particularization and the other
to generalization; rather, this usual tension is exacerbated by the fact that
each school tends to deal with different levels of the economy. Virtually all
economic models make assumptions that cannot be justified at an individual or a local level, as even economists recognize to be true. But many
such assumptions *can* be justified at the systemic level to which
economists are usually committed. The assumption of profit maximization, for example, is found to be faulty as a description of most economic
"firms" anywhere (almost all field workers point this out, some expecting
it to revolutionize economic theory). This assumption is, however,
perfectly justifiable for competitive market economies in which those who

---

[1] The best-known and perhaps only general economic theory put forward by the inductive
school is that developed by Polanyi and several of his associates (Polanyi *et al.* 1957). This,
however, is less an independent economic theory than an assertion that standard economic
theory is inadequate to describe and analyze premodern economies; its content is almost
entirely descriptive.

do not maximize are culled from the system or so strongly penalized that to survive they must behave as if they were maximizing profit—if only by emulating the most successful firms. (So, of course, the finding does not revolutionize economic theory, even in the cases in which it should.) It may even be reasonable to assume that economic behavior in nonmarket economies will adapt to meet such economic constraints as scarcity in the pattern assumed by the standard economic theory of price—supply and demand allocating the scarce resource—so that individual motivation or knowledge of pricing need not be an important consideration in analyzing the system. In short, because of the difference that level of analysis makes, economists and noneconomists often talk past one another.

On the other hand, some local-level processes do have important effects on the economy, market or nonmarket, and therefore cannot be assumed away. Yet how does one integrate into a general economic theory the finding that peasants in some communities prefer to meet their subsistence requirements before producing for a market even though they might make a much larger profit by producing only for the market? Economists might argue that this behavior violates a certain assumption in the general theory of the perfect economy and that it will therefore produce an effect posited from the workings of the perfect system in which the assumption is not violated. But precisely what effect? And how will it affect the rest of the economy other than to make it "imperfect" (which violations of other assumptions also do)? More important, is there something about the system itself that produces this particular behavior? There *are* hypotheses to answer these questions, but without data garnered from more than a community of farmers, without economic models designed to explain imperfect systems, and without general theories that incorporate noneconomic variables, one may select whichever hypothesis one likes.

Neither I nor the contributors to this volume have devised a full solution to such problems. But we do propose a fresh approach to them that should allow the strengths of both induction and deduction to be more usefully fitted to one another. The approach involves utilization of regional–spatial models of economic systems to understand the workings of particular real-world systems for which there are empirical data, and it involves refashioning theory where necessary to account for the kinds of economic relations and behavior found. Our model-building goals are not unusual, but they are rarely achieved for the reasons I have mentioned. What gives us the ability to develop general models from specific cases is the regional approach to economic systems: using the specific models of regional economies recently developed in economic geography to bring theory *down* to a level relevant to data on empirical cases and using field data gathered on regional economies to bring data on empirical cases *up* to a level relevant to economic theory. Through matching theory and data, one can account for novel findings by proposing new models rather than attacking old ones, and one can systematically incorporate sociological variables into the economic models.

I claim much for the regional approach to economic problems: that it mediates between the local-level and macro-level approaches, thereby complementing each; that it allows concrete conceptualization of systemic economic problems; and that it attends to noneconomic variables. I must now give some substance to the approach, so that its uses and potential uses can be more fully evaluated. I begin with a brief description of the analytical features common to all regional models.

As developed and elaborated in economic geography, the units of regional analysis are these: regions, exchange systems, central places, systemic levels, and locational relations. Regions can be defined formally or functionally, the former placing emphasis on the homogeneity of some element within a territory, the latter placing emphasis on systems of functional relations within an integrated territorial system. We use the latter definition, assuming that economic systems are formed by exchange relations wherein communities or settlements in a territory are interrelated by their ties to one another through either a simple network or a hierarchical arrangement with at least one central place. (In this volume we are concerned with economic systems and exchanges, but the exchanges that define the reach of a regional system may be political, social, or ideological as well as economic.) A central place is a settlement or an aggregation of economic functions that is the hub of a hierarchical system which includes other settlements or communities relating to it on a regular basis; that is, a central place becomes the hub of a region because goods, people, and information flow primarily between it and its less differentiated hinterland. A complex regional system includes more than a single central place, each of the centers a node for systems at different levels within the larger system; the smaller systems nest within the hinterlands of larger systems, and the largest central place under consideration encompasses the regional system in question. Analysis of locational relations among the centers and their hinterlands provides the methodological framework whereby regional systems and the systemic levels within them are delimited, described, and to some extent explained. Because one is concerned with a complex economic system, *place* within the system is an important economic variable.

How different systems nest within others and how different centers are related to each other and affect the regional integration of the economy are considered to be empirical questions. But the way in which the system is integrated is assumed to influence the operation of the economic system as a whole as well as the operation of its elements—the central places, their hinterlands, and the economic actors whose behavior forms the regional system. Thus, while the "economy" is seen to be rooted in the system rather than in its elements (and as any economist will attest, this changes the nature of an economic analysis considerably), one does not lose sight of the local-level processes when dealing with the system. Moreover, because the systems analyzed are empirical, noneconomic variables remain important elements in them: Such variables as regional physiography, ecology, and demography are obvious candidates; but political organization, class stratification, and cultural differentiation within the region are also naturally involved.[2]

I will now describe the specific models with which we have worked, how they developed, and how we use them. My treatment of the economic models will be elementary for geographers and economists, but they may find useful my discussions of their sociological implications. The same holds in reverse for other social scientists with interests in economic problems.

THE THÜNEN MODEL OF LAND USE

In 1826 Thünen published a treatise on the laws of agricultural production, setting forth certain basic principles critical to modern locational geography (Thünen 1966). Thünen's thesis was a simple one: The pattern of land use is a function of the different prices of agricultural goods and of their different costs of production, and distance to a market center is a significant determinant of cost. But the simplicity of the model should not belie its power. For by introducing location into economic theory, Thünen not only independently invented the theory of marginal cost but also developed an economic model with specific real-world predictions that were measurable. Like most economic theories, it is a normative theory; but unlike many economic theories, it can be generalized to many different levels of an economy. The method of theory construction, familiar to any economist, warrants close attention by those interested in economic problems but unfamiliar with the basic techniques of economists.

[2] From this, the regional approach may appear limited in application to the economies of complex societies. This is not the case, and it is regrettable that an analysis of a simpler system could not be included here. At least one simple (nonhierarchical) economic system has been analyzed from a regional perspective, however: the *kula* trade ring of Melanesia (Brookfield with Hart 1971; Uberoi 1962). This case deserves special mention here because it shows how interpretation of local events can be changed by considering the larger system. Using a regional framework, Uberoi was able to show how political organization and stratification in the Trobriand Islands (a local system) were structured by the relationship of the Trobriand economy to a broader economy, made up of the dozens of islands involved in *kula* trade. His argument rests on the crucial role that regional trade played in the distribution of certain scarce resources, a point that Brookfield elaborates by using spatial and ecological measures common to the methodology used here. Most anthropologists now recognize Uberoi's interpretation of both the *kula* trade and Trobriand social organization as more valid than that of the community ethnographer, Malinowski. I suggest that the greater sophistication and more general insight provided by Uberoi's analysis stem from his use of a regional framework.

In order to assess the effect of distance on systems of production, Thünen assumed other relevant variables away. He assumed there was no variability in transport cost except that imposed by distance (which required producers to be located on an isotropic, or physically undifferentiated, plain with equal access to the same means of transport); he assumed prices to be determined in the market center by the normal operation of supply and demand; and he assumed no barriers to trade or production other than price- and cost-determined ones—no tariffs, no price fixing, no labor immobility, no farmer irrationality, and so forth.

Under these conditions, transport cost rises monotonically with distance from the market center and is the major variable factor of production. Increasing transport costs have the effect of lowering the farm gate price of any good produced further away from the market center, lowering the return to extra (marginal) inputs of labor and capital in its production; therefore, the rational producer intensifies production (as measured by labor and capital input per unit area) near the center and uses land less intensively as he moves (or lives) further away from the center. That is, in the absence of variability in land fertility or transport ease in all directions from the center and in the absence of competing market centers, one should find a pattern of land use typified by concentric zones of production intensity: high labor–capital inputs put into high-priced (or heavy) agricultural goods in the inner zones, where marginal productivity is highest, and low labor–capital inputs put into lower-priced (or lighter) agricultural goods in the outer zones, where marginal productivity is lower. Figure 1 shows what an optimal land-use system looks like, given Thünen's assumptions, a small competing center, and a particular agricultural regime.[3]

Because of its stringent assumptions, Thünen's model of the ideal or "isolated" state does not describe many real economies well enough to be a guide for practice. And since Thünen was concerned to develop economic laws relevant to actual problems of agricultural production, he developed the abstract model only to modify it. His modifications were made by inference from deliberately introduced (and equally abstract) changes in the ideal landscape: a special transport route, a competing market center, varying fertility in different plots of land at varying distances from the market center, different combinations of agricultural products, and so forth. By measuring the hypothetical effect of these changes, Thünen was ultimately able to describe a rational procedure for farming a particular and real Austrian estate. But the modifications Thünen introduced are much less significant than the ideal model he developed, for the modifica-

---

[3] Thünen's model does not predict agricultural regimes; it predicts only the general pattern of land use, given the local factors of production. The general pattern will be similar whatever the regime, however, because labor intensity of production will vary for different crops in all agrarian economies.

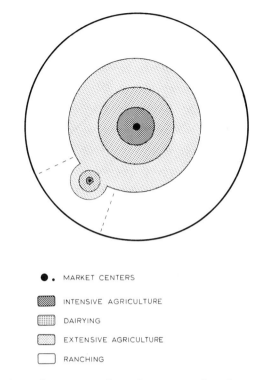

Figure 1. Thünen's model of land use under a specific agrarian regime.

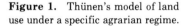 MARKET CENTERS

INTENSIVE AGRICULTURE

DAIRYING

EXTENSIVE AGRICULTURE

RANCHING

tions are applicable only to nineteenth-century Austrian estate-farming practices, while the ideal model is timeless and applicable to many different levels of analysis: the individual farmer with his various plots of land at varying distances from his home; the estate manager with laborers in different parts of a single-centered organization; the region with many individual peasant producers relating to a single dominant town; the world with different concentrations of market centers in its different parts (Chisolm 1962). Thünen's method is also timeless: developing a "normative" economic model—one that predicts certain consequences under ideal conditions, knowledge of which allows an economic "maximizer" to maximize—and then deliberately perturbing it—changing its assumptions to find the real consequences when either the conditions are not ideal or the producer is not maximizing. Hence, unlike some modern theorists, Thünen was perfectly well aware of his economic assumptions and their limitations as well as strengths.

Inasmuch as Thünen's model must be taken into account in any treatment of the space economy, all of the papers in this volume deal with it. Unfortunately, however, none addresses the model directly, although some depend in great measure on it (cf. Chapter 2, Figure 3, p. 79). In Chapter 2 Plattner, concerned with regions with a single dominant market center and the effect of distance from this center on rural demand for urban products distributed by peddlers, shows that Thünen's model, even in its ideal unperturbed state, can explain a good deal of variability in peasant commercialization in certain agrarian economies (in this case, highland Chiapas, Mexico). This should not be surprising, since, after all, many uncommercialized economies do approximate the conditions that the model assumes, and, as Chisolm points out, the larger the scale to which the model is applied, the smaller the distortion created by local topographic variability.[4] But Plattner's study should suggest to those who regard the model as hopelessly outdated that much of economic behavior in the undeveloped real world, especially that which appears to lack market motivation, can be explained by simple locational models such as Thünen's.

After 150 years of examination and use, there is little doubt that Thünen's theory of production can explain the pattern of land use and marketing in many contexts, at least where there are few widely spaced (noncompetitive) market centers and where one can assume or approximate isotropic landscape conditions (production and transport uniformity). Today, however, disturbances created by multiple market centers and changing transport patterns are so great in most marketing economies, even simple ones, that the general principle has lost much of its utility for predicting land use (Haggett 1966; Henshall 1967). Production in most modern market economies has shifted from primary sectors (agriculture and mining) to secondary (industry) and tertiary (services and commerce) sectors, and to describe and explain the present situation, geographers have had to develop other kinds of locational models. One of the most elaborate and elegant of these newer models is central-place theory, which endeavors to explain the location of market centers themselves.

CENTRAL-PLACE THEORY

Among the assumptions of central-place theory is that the location of market centers will be determined by the competitive features of the market economy, so that all areas of demand are serviced proportional to demand. This moves us from Thünen's isolated-state model, where the producers adjust, to a competitive state with multiple centers, where the centers adjust. One might see the more complex system evolving out of an isolated state as follows.

[4] For this reason I was able to apply the model with considerable success to western Guatemala (Smith 1975b). This region resembles an isotropic plain about as closely as a sphere resembles a triangle, but it is large enough (about 10,000 square miles) that topographical variation did not swamp the distance effect.

Imagine a featureless plain with two unconnected areas of population aggregation, each with its own market center (see Figure 2, part a). It makes little difference at this point how the population is distributed—people can live within the centers or can be dispersed in degrees of concentration around them. Each market center is surrounded by concentric zones of production undisturbed by the other center. With gradual population increase, one would expect out-migration from around the two initial centers to unclaimed territory and the development of smaller market centers. At some point in the process, there would be sufficient demand at the midpoint between the two initial centers to support a third major market center (Figure 2, part b). With further population increase, the plain would eventually be filled, farms or villages moving into all unclaimed spaces and by this same process spacing themselves evenly throughout. (Perfectly even distribution leads to a hexagonal lattice of settlements, a feature of location that has intrigued central-place theoreticians and that will become important later in this paper.)

At some point in the development process, it would become advantageous for the two initial population aggregates, along with others that have formed, to specialize in production and to trade with one another through the midpoint center that is located in a position to articulate trade throughout the region (Figure 2, part c). Note that at this point a *system* of central places has evolved with three levels of market centers, hierarchically arranged, and that all points on the plain are within a reasonable distance from some market center. (Note also that at this point the Thünen system of concentric zoning would become considerably less salient in determining production decisions.) Here we have the essentials of a central-place system as described by Christaller (1966) in the 1930s and as independently elaborated by Lösch (1954) in the 1940s. We have observed it grow in a fashion analogous to that proposed by G. W. Skinner more recently (1965). We must now take a closer look at the elements that

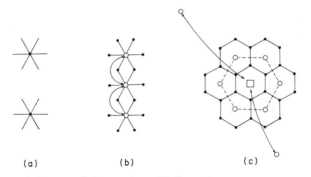

(a)   (b)   (c)

Figure 2.   An evolving central-place system with three stages.

make up the system and the theoretical postulates that have given it this form. We begin with Christaller.[5]

The Classical Theory of Central Places

Like Thünen, whose work he knew, Christaller assumed that spatial regularities can be perceived only if idiosyncratic variability in the landscape is ignored, so he assumed an isotropic landscape—an unvarying one. He made another equally unrealistic assumption to develop the model: that population is homogeneous in income and tastes and is evenly dispersed, the last of which requires that the resources utilized by the population be nonlocalized. (About the only resource that comes close to meeting this requirement is farmland.) Then Christaller considered this population as consumers of certain retail goods whose suppliers do not depend on differentiated supply sources. (He considered neither firms that buy from farmers nor firms that supply retailers; and since his retail firms must not be dependent on localized resources, his favorite example was a physician—that is, someone relatively independent of particular sources of supply.) The problem to which he sought a solution was the optimal location of these suppliers—retail firms—given those constraints. In his own words:

> I thus followed exactly the opposite procedure that Thünen did: he accepted the central city as already having been furnished, and asked how the agricultural land was utilized in the surrounding area, whereas I accepted the inhabited area as already having been furnished, and subsequently asked where the city must be situated, or, more correctly, where should the cities then be situated [1972:608].

Christaller approached the problem by considering the amount of business a retail firm could expect to get from distant consumers—the *range* of the good or service provided. He defined the range of a good as the circular area beyond which buyers would not be willing to travel for the good, given need (elasticity of demand), price, transport cost (which is added to price), and frequency of use. For instance, consumer demand for medical services is inelastic; hence, consumes go far for a physician's services. But regardless of need, consumers must have money to go to a physician, so demand is affected by cost; and cost will equal the physician's price plus transport cost. Therefore (as in Thünen's model), at a certain distance from the physician, consumers simply have insufficient means for the cost and thus no demand for the service. That point defines consumer range for a phy-

[5] The following literature gives more complete and technical reviews of central-place theory: Berry (1967), Crissman (1973), Garner (1967), Haggett (1966), and Marshall (1969). In addition, I have reviewed the recent literature in geography and marketing studies elsewhere (Smith 1974).

sician. (See Figure 1, Chapter 2, p. 72.) Christaller also had to consider the supplier and the amount of business he needs to stay in business—his economic *threshold*. This threshold was defined as the circular area containing sufficient consumer demand of a good to meet the supplier's requirements for survival in business. Physicians, for instance, can expect clients to come from a long distance; but since consumers need physicians with low frequency, each physician must command the custom of a large area in order to have enough business to meet his threshold, or minimum income requirements. The size of the area will be determined by the physician's price, population density, and local demand for his services. (It follows from these principles that for any viable retail firm, the distance that defines the firm's *threshold* must be equal to or less than the distance that defines the *range* of the firm's good.)

From these two principles, one can model consumer and supplier behavior in interaction with each other. That is, given consumer density, needs, and incomes (which add up to demand), and given supplier price and income requirements (which add up to his ability to supply), plus knowledge of transport costs, one should be able to predict how many physicians a given area can support, the actual physical distance from which consumers will come to utilize a physician, and the actual physical area that would meet the physician's threshold. From all of that, one could estimate the appropriate—most economic—spacing of physicians on the landscape. While such a prediction would be quite a feat, Christaller was even more ambitious. He wanted to explain the distribution of *all* retail firms in a region, from grocery stores to physicians to rare-book stores. His model, therefore, basically attends to various *levels* of centers (central places) and their distributions—to the spatial patterns of central-place *systems*.

Central-place systems can be built from the top down or from the bottom up; Christaller worked from the top down. He began with suppliers of a high-order good (one for which demand is so low or infrequent that it requires many consumers), assuming that as many suppliers as possible attempt to locate in a region to saturate all demand, and uncovered an optimal locational pattern for them, as follows. Each supplier will attempt to locate as far as possible from the other suppliers in order to dominate as many consumers as possible; thus, each supplier begins with a circular demand area. But when the numerous suppliers saturate a region up to their absolute minimum thresholds, the circles will overlap. Packing of circles (from competition), and consumer choice of the closest supplier with the lowest price (consumer rationality), will bisect the areas of overlap, ultimately leading to hexagonal market areas for each supplier, as well as to the minimum supplier price. Both supplier threshold and consumer range will thus be minimized. (It should be noted that this process assumes maximizing behavior by both supplier and consumer as well as perfect competition.)

Then Christaller took suppliers of a lower-order good (one for which demand is more frequent) and attempted to place them on the same landscape. He assumed that these suppliers would also be in competition and would choose locations in terms of greatest advantage, as follows. They would first locate in the centers that provided higher-order goods (first-level centers), thus inveigling business that was attracted to the higher-order goods. But since demand for the goods of this second group was sufficient to give them a lower threshold than the first suppliers, they would next locate at the interstices between the packed higher-order suppliers, thereby meeting the greatest possible demand and the least possible competition. This would provide second-level centers between first-level centers. The process would be the same for suppliers of a third order and of lower orders of goods that would produce even lower-level centers, between first- and second-level centers, and then between second- and third-level centers, and so on.

The consequences of this particular locational process are as follows. The high-level centers would become larger and more widely spaced than lower-level centers. All higher-level centers would supply both high- and low-order goods, and low-level centers would provide only low-order goods and nest in the trade areas of high-level centers. This results in a pattern such as that shown in Figure 2, part c. From the point of view of the consumer, who is providing the demand that influences supplier decisions about location, this pattern has many advantages. It provides many small centers that carry items needed frequently, so that no consumer is very far from one of them. It also provides larger centers that carry items of less frequent demand together with items needed more often, so that on the rare occasions that one might need a funeral parlor, say, one could also buy the weekly groceries and thus spread transport costs over the several items. Finally, it provides for competitive pricing by suppliers. Should any supplier charge a much higher price than another, he would lose the custom at the boundaries of his hinterland, because the most distant consumers in his "natural" trade area could afford the extra transport cost of utilizing another supplier with the savings from a lower price. Hence, suppliers' price should stabilize close to their margins, the distant consumers disciplining what would otherwise be the topological monopoly of each supplier.

Christaller's solution to the problem of central-place location thus eventuates in an arrangement that is quite satisfactory from the point of view of both consumer and supplier. But since it is based on a "fixed" nesting pattern,[6] each supplier of lower threshold always locating at the

---

[6] Each different K value is associated with different ratios of numbers of centers in successive orders. $K = 3$ runs $1:2:6:18:54:162$; $K = 4$ runs $1:3:12:48:172$; and $K = 7$ runs $1:6:42:294:2058$. Christaller assumed that any region has one fixed pattern and that one can discover which it is by examining the numbers in each order or level within the system. Most geographers now question this assumption.

midpoint between existing suppliers of high-order goods, it normally allows excess profits. That is, in a fixed nesting pattern some suppliers of second-order goods would be very likely to have thresholds too high to allow them to locate between the highest-level centers, but lower than those of the suppliers of first-order goods. They would remain in the high-level centers and thereby accrue a surplus above "normal" profits. Under these circumstances, some suppliers would be forced out of business before demand was fully saturated even as others made higher profits than they should. Christaller was aware of this problem, but he assumed that the convenience of centrality assured by the fixed nesting pattern would prevent the marginal suppliers from seeking a more competitive locational solution.

Lösch, who worked from the bottom up to build a central-place hierarchy, attempted a solution that did not give excess profits. This has each higher-order supplier locating precisely in terms of his threshold relative to the centers that supply lower-order goods. But the resulting pattern allows high-order suppliers to exist in centers without low-order suppliers—automobile distributorships without grocery stores—which appears not to happen very often. Those who have attempted to scale the items found in a system of central places (Appleby, Chapter 5; Crissman, Chapter 6; and Kelley, Chapter 7, in this volume) have always found a near perfect Guttman scale of items, major centers providing almost all the low-order as well as high-order goods to be found in the system. (See Chapter 5, Table 7, p. 164 for an example of such a scale.) This suggests that the real world may be far from competitive, even when organized in a relatively "efficient" manner. It also suggests that the real world is more Christallerian than Löschian.

Nonetheless, with the notions of threshold and range, both Christaller and Lösch were able to develop models for central-place systems that in certain respects describe the basic constraints that shape real-world systems. There are a number of serious problems with some of their assumptions, but before considering them, let us look at another situation that requires the application of the theoretical elements of threshold and range.

Periodic Centers and Mobile Traders

One notable feature of the classical central-place patterns is that they seem to be more often found in agrarian societies, where central places are periodic and traders mobile. On consideration, this is not surprising. Agrarian societies tend to have dispersed populations utilizing nonlocalized resources (farmland), periodic markets are more easily established and shifted for purely economic reasons than are permanent towns, and, most important, full-time mobile traders who utilize time as well as distance in meeting demand can locate themselves in centers with other suppliers more directly with respect to their thresholds than can full-time permanent traders. Strength of demand (which determines the firm's threshold) regulates the frequency of trader visits instead of dictating a single fixed location for the trader.

The relationship between range of a good and supplier threshold that would lead to trader mobility (and market periodicity) was first explored by Stine (1962). Stine's basic thesis is that mobile traders can enlarge the physical area that encompasses their thresholds by moving from place to place (see Figure 2, Chapter 2, p. 74). (Plattner, following Stine, defines "threshold" as the minimum range of a good.) Stine proposed that suppliers typically are mobile when the range of a good (distance that consumers will travel for it) is smaller than the suppliers' threshold (distance that encompasses sufficient demand for their survival), which one would expect to occur in uncommercialized areas. With commercialization, demand will rise, increasing consumer range and thus allowing the trader to become sedentary. At this point permanent central places come into existence. Until demand is sufficient to support permanent traders, however, markets are periodic, so that demand builds up sufficiently for the mobile trader and so that "the consumer, by submitting to the discipline of time, is able to free himself from the discipline of space [Stine 1962:70]." Lately, there has been considerable discussion in geographical circles about things traders and consumers might do besides those proposed by Stine. Plattner considers these alternative suggestions in Chapter 2 and finds that with some refinement Stine's basic thesis still holds up fairly well as far as trader mobility is concerned.

In Chapter 3 Bromley considers the other side of Stine's theory, market periodicity, and asks: Why are some places periodic and not others? What is the relationship between market periodicity and market centrality? What conditions the timing of periodicity in particular systems? How does market periodicity relate to trader mobility? He also touches on another question of general interest: What might one expect in terms of scheduling in a Christallerian nested pattern of central places if these central places are also periodic? The first solution to these questions was given by Skinner (1964) based upon empirical findings from China. Timing of periodicity seemed to be governed by demand density as measured by population density. Smaller centers were periodic, while larger ones were permanent; and as markets grew in size they simply added days to their schedule. Finally, in systems of central places that were periodic, scheduling was arranged so that smaller centers never met on days that were in conflict with major days of major centers in order that traders could move between market levels with ease. On the other hand, given a limited number of possible meeting times, smaller centers were in conflict with one another. Skinner suggested that this did not create inconvenience because the people who frequented small centers (Chinese peasants) did not visit all the neighboring markets but met their basic needs at only one—their "standard market center." Upon occasions that demanded goods not supplied locally, the peasant visited a higher-level center, designed (for traders) to be on a different schedule. This also facilitated the dual marketing pattern of local gentry, who visited both lower-level and higher-level centers regularly.

After Skinner's solution was proposed, a number of geographers working in other parts of the world found that it does not always work.[7] Skinner provided the rational solution, but some central-place systems seem not to be so rational. In particular, there is a large group of cases in which periodicity is "fixed" (all or most market centers meet once a week, regardless of size); scheduling among different centers of a system hardly exists at all (all market centers meet on the same day); and in consequence traders must be part-time rather than mobile. Bromley describes one such case in Chapter 3—that of highland Ecuador. Here *most* centers are periodic; even major urban centers with populations in the hundreds of thousands have periodic markets and marked weekly variation in shop attendance. More remarkably, most centers meet on the same day—Sunday. Bromley shows that market articulation has improved recently, due largely to changes in schedules by the major market centers—although it is still far from the kind of schedule articulation that Skinner found for China—and offers hypotheses to account both for the improvement and for the generally poor state of articulation. (In addition, Bromley discusses several new techniques he has developed for measuring and comparing schedule articulation, methods that should prove useful for any future investigation of periodicity.) In Chapter 5 Appleby describes a similar case, focusing on a whole chain of events that led to better market articulation in Puno, Peru, after World War II—about the same time that major shifts occurred in highland Ecuador.

An interesting feature of these poorly articulated systems—as measured by scheduling—is that their poor articulation seems to have been deliberately brought about by Spanish colonial policy in many parts of the New World (R. D. F. Bromley and R. J. Bromley 1975; Kaplan 1965). Why would any administration want a poorly articulated marketing system? One possibility, suggested but not fully exploited by either Bromley or Appleby, is that they did so to control trade, so that it would take place only in their terms—that is, political–administrative terms. Trade of various sorts was the economic underpinning of the Spanish colonial empire, and much of it was carried out directly by colonial administrators. Even after independence from Spain was achieved, a

---

[7] I review the market periodicity controversies in Smith (1974), arguing, as does Plattner here, that much of it seems to be misguided.

legacy had been established in many places whereby control of trade and
markets provided the incomes of a large bureaucratic class. There are
many ways in which trade and markets can be controlled, but one of the
most effective would be control of periodicity. When all market centers
meet on the same day, peasants, who provide food to the centers, can still
attend them—although they are restricted in their ability to seek other
markets with better prices. But an indigenous class of traders who arbitrage goods between centers, thereby breaking town monopolies over price,
could not develop when trade is possible only one day in seven. It seems a
likely possibility, therefore, that the type of poor schedule articulation
described by Bromley and Appleby is the product of a central-place
system designed for other than commercial purposes—designed to control
rather than facilitate trade. (See Smith, Chapter 12, Volume II, for
further development of this point.) In the next section I discuss Christaller's view of this type and other types of central-place systems.

Types of Central-Place Hierarchies

There are a number of ways in which the hierarchical–spatial ordering
of central places may be implemented (in addition to the pattern shown in
Figure 2c) that are compatible with the principles outlined earlier, and
each has distinctive economic consequences. Figure 3 shows just a few of
them—the five smallest hexagonal trade areas in an economic landscape,
in this case imposed on a basic $K = 3$ hexagonal grid. The K numbers
indicate the particular nesting pattern, referring to the amount of territory
in the hinterlands of lower-level centers that is encapsulated by the hinter-

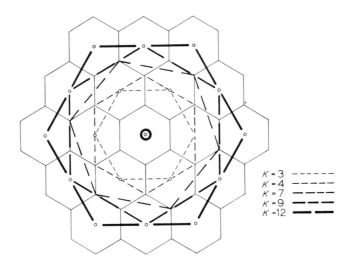

Figure 3.   Nesting arrangements of K systems.

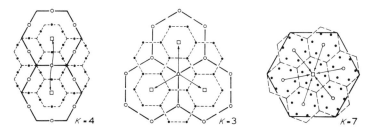

Figure 4. The three classical central-place arrangements developed by Christaller.

land of the next-higher-level center. $K = 3$ is the system that puts down more levels in the hierarchy, per number of centers, than any other—each higher-level center encompassing what sums to only three lower-level-center hinterlands: its own lower-level hinterland (remember the supplier of lower-order goods who locates in the high-level centers); and one-third share of the hinterlands of the six surrounding lower-level centers [$1 + (\frac{1}{3} \times 6) = 3$]. $K = 4$ takes its own lower-level hinterland and *half* of the hinterlands of the six surrounding lower-level centers [$1 + (\frac{1}{2} \times 6) = 4$]. Other K numbers can be similarly calculated.[8]

Christaller developed three of these models ($K = 3$, $K = 4$, $K = 7$) and described their economic characteristics. Lösch elaborated on the scheme, describing other, larger K systems, and Crissman (Chapter 6, this volume) has calculated K systems up to 84. (It is unlikely that one would find an economically organized landscape at the highest levels, however, because so many centers would be encompassed by the next-highest-level center that the amount of commerce in the region would have to be Thünen-like.) Skinner found $K = 19$ to be the modal system of the Chinese standard marketing community, and Crissman found $K = 16$ and $K = 21$ modal for a region of Taiwan. These have characteristics similar to those of the three smallest systems ($K = 19$ resembling $K = 7$, $K = 16$ resembling $K = 4$, and $K = 21$ resembling $K = 3$), as do most if not all of the other K systems.[9] Hence, I concentrate on the three types of landscape systems explained by Christaller, which have the most complete economic explanations, seem to crop up regularly, and are probably the most interesting from an empirical cross-cultural perspective. (See Figure 4.)

[8] As the K value increases, so does the size of the hexagonal net to encompass more centers. The general formula for computing the numbers of centers in successive orders for each particular K value is $N_t = K^t$, where N is the number of dependent places and t the level in the hierarchy (Haggett 1966:118–122).

[9] This is demonstrated in Haggett (1966) and Crissman (1973). The critical attribute that differentiates the three smaller K systems from one another is the number of higher-level centers (one, two, or three) to which lower-level centers orient. Larger K systems share this attribute, except that *some* lower-level centers are closer to one larger center than others are and will therefore orient to only one higher-level center, while others may orient to two or three of them.

What are some of the differences in these patterns, which Christaller termed the *marketing* landscape ($K = 3$), the *transport* landscape ($K = 4$), and the *administrative* landscape ($K = 7$)? The marketing landscape maximizes consumer travel efficiency and central-place competition by locating each lower-level center between *three* higher-level centers. This pattern seems to occur mainly when a significant portion of the consuming population is dispersed in rural settlements and when transport means are both costly and primitive. The traffic or transport arrangement of central places locates each lower-level center between *two* higher-level centers, thus minimizing the number of connecting paths between centers. This arrangement seems to be most advantageous when a significant portion of the consuming population is located in the central places themselves and when the goods marketed come from industrial or specialized farm centers rather than from dispersed rural areas and move along the established roads connecting major centers. (Skinner has suggested that one might expect to find it in mountainous areas where road building is particularly costly, because it minimizes the number of roads linking centers.) The administrative organization, in contrast to others, has no centers located on hinterland boundaries; territories are divided up discretely, with all lower-level centers orienting to *one* and only one higher-level center. Thus, it abandons the principle of interlocking competition in which lower-level centers are serviced by two or more competing higher-level centers—although competition between the higher-level centers is retained and provides for their regular lattice distribution (with hexagonally shaped hinterlands)—and it creates undivided but hierarchically organized compartments. Since divided loyalties, by either centers or citizens, would be anathema to any administrator, this principle is admirably suited to dividing up administrative areas.

A brief normative characterization of the three contrasting arrangements could be the following. The marketing pattern is most efficient for rural consumers and for the distribution of rurally produced goods. The transport pattern is most efficient for urban distributors and for the distribution of urban goods, especially those of high weight and value. And the administrative pattern is most efficient for urban-based bureaucrats or monopolists who are attempting to control a region—it is not well suited, from the point of view of the consumer, for the distribution of any economic commodities. As Skinner has pointed out (1964, Chapter 10 of this volume), an efficient administrative organization of regions is incompatible with an efficient economic organization of regions. If both organizations are to be effective, major economic centers will not always be major political centers and vice versa.

The three systems are not mutually exclusive, for a large region can combine several of the principles of organization. Figure 5 shows a composite picture of western Guatemala that in fact combines all three. At the

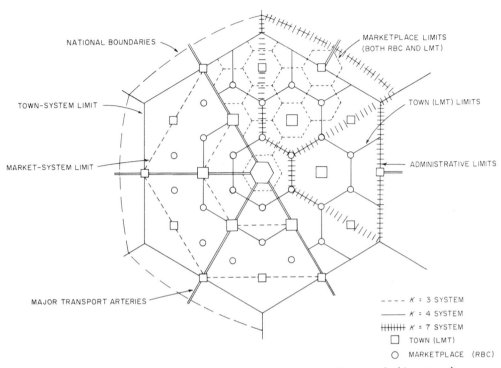

Figure 5. An abstract representation of an empirical case with three interlocking central-place patterns. Based on western Guatemala (Smith 1975a).

lowest level, peasant marketplaces (RBCs) are oriented toward urban centers (LMTs) by, appropriately enough, the marketing principle. The urban centers, on the other hand, are oriented toward one another by the traffic principle, this also appropriate because urban centers have large populations and frequently ship goods to one another along major roads. Finally, the biggest urban centers—of which there are only seven—are organized by the administrative principle, each being the political capital of territories that encompass the whole region.[10] As explained elsewhere (Smith 1975a), the congruence of major commercial and administrative centers in western Guatemala leads to inefficiency in certain aspects of commerce but fits the requirements of "administered commerce" quite well. It is precisely this kind of organization that one would expect to find in certain dualized economies where high-level commerce is administered by an elite class but where peasant marketing is competitive. (These notions are developed more fully in Chapter 12 of Volume II.) Some other features of mixed hierarchies are detailed by Skinner in this volume.

[10] Only 7 of the 10 administrative centers in western Guatemala "fit" the model, although I believe the anomalous cases can be explained (see Smith 1972).

It is quite unusual to find real economic systems displaying the nesting regularity shown for western Guatemala in Figure 5—even that required considerable transformation of actual, if not relative, locations. However, relationships between central places *are* almost always patterned, and it is rarely difficult to distinguish among landscapes organized by one of the three basic principles—administrative, transport, and economic—in the real world. (There also seem to be patterned and easily discernible distortions of central-place systems with their own economic explanations, described later in this paper.) Presumably, these different landscape systems reflect and may even structure the organization of diverse political economies in the real world. While to date little has been done to demonstrate causal or consequential correspondence between the struc-. tures and the functions of central-place systems, one need not assume that the exercise of Christallerian logic is therefore useless. The following example suggests how judicious use of it may enlighten scholarly analysis in several problem areas.

Skinner found that the modal Chinese standard marketing community fit the $K = 19$ distribution—an administrative organization. That is, there are 18 dependent villages for each market center, ideally arranged in two concentric rings (6 in the first ring, 12 in the second), with no overlap into the territories of surrounding standard markets. Independent of this, Skinner observed that most Chinese peasants utilized a *single* market center— as one expects in administratively organized landscapes. This has important implications for Chinese peasant culture, some of which Skinner detailed in his early marketing articles (1964, 1965). The "standard marketing community" *is* a community. Although tied to the broader economy and polity of China through its standard marketplace, which interlinks with other centers in other fashions ($K = 3$ and $K = 4$), being a discrete entity, it preserves for peasants the quality of a distinct, separately organized system. Skinner suggested that because of this it is the locus of the Chinese "little tradition," it bounds most peasant social interaction, and it tends to be endogamous. (The endogamy hypothesis is discussed in Volume II by Crissman and by Adams and Kasakoff.) These findings have had an important impact on students of agrarian societies, who now at least consider units other than village and nation when analyzing peasant economies.

Another implication might be drawn from the modal Chinese central-place pattern. China was notable as an empire system of immense size that showed steady, long-term economic growth and political integration, despite periods of turmoil that temporarily wiped out technological and economic advances and replaced particular ruling elites. But according to Elvin (1973), it was caught in a "high-level equilibrium trap" toward the end of its history as an empire, wherein technological advance only kept up with population growth and the general economy was unable to break out of a negative feedback process. The organization of China's central-place system may give us a clue both to its durability as an empire and to its declining evolutionary potential as a modern economy. On the one hand, the organization of high-level central places allowed intensive trade and movement across local systems by classes directly involved in administration and commerce. And the integrity of the peasant communities provided by their "administrative" ($K = 19$) organization allowed them to withstand periods of turmoil and yet be able to open during periods of reintegration, always available to be tapped by an efficient administration for surplus (Skinner 1971). But on the other hard, the $K = 19$ organization of many peasant communities may have also prevented their full integration into a national economy, pushing them at the "high-energy" level toward an involutionary economic adaptation. For while open to economic exploitation, the modal peasant standard marketing communities may not have tied into a competitive marketing network (that is, one of the competitive or "economic" hierarchical patterns) in such a way that would have allowed them to become part of a fully commercialized economy. This is not to say that the boundaries around such communities were impenetrable, but perhaps they did not easily fall to the forces of commercialization given that the boundaries also provided mechanisms for the peasant community's own protection (Skinner 1971).

These last speculations of mine may not withstand the scrutiny of China specialists, but they suggest the kinds of problems to which analysis of central-place patterns may be turned, which until now few people other than Skinner have exploited. This volume presents a number of such studies. In particular, Crissman, Kelley, Appleby, and I make some headway on the determinants of "alternative" or irregular central-place patterns, and we all detail the economic implications of these systems quite fully. (In Volume II, Appleby and I discuss some of the social implications of these irregular patterns.) Finally, Skinner goes even further in his analysis of patterns by which higher-level and lower-level centers were articulated in late traditional China, proposing a number of theories about the causes and consequences of the differences.

Modern Modifications of
Central-Place Theory

As noted earlier, central-place theory makes a number of unrealistic assumptions in order to propose some general relationships. Because of these assumptions, real-world systems are never precisely what the models predict for ideal systems. Most economists understand the difference between ideal models and real systems and would never throw out a theory just because some of its assumptions are rarely met—or they would long ago have thrown out all of the market models that assume perfect competition. But a number of geographers (e.g., Isard 1975; Webber 1971) have begun to question the usefulness of a theory that cannot predict, especially one that utilizes quite untenable assumptions. Among the assumptions that trouble them are an isotropic landscape, perfect competition among suppliers, threshold governance of supplier location, single suppliers of each good at each center, and single-purposed trips by consumers.[11] The first two assumptions are obviously "unreal" ones that assume away the variability that interferes with basic theory construction. The others are similar simplifying assumptions, but ones that lead to greater theoretical difficulty.

It is a generally recognized empirical fact that suppliers are attracted to one another, so that one usually finds not only all lower-order goods in a high-order center (Christaller's but not Lösch's assumption), but also multiple suppliers of the same item. It is also true, but not incorporated into central-place theory, that suppliers of goods are also consumers of goods. Clearly, these are related phenomena. Some suppliers locate in a center not just to provide goods to the rural hinterland but to supply goods to the suppliers. In fact, town suppliers should be among the first to appear in a system, since they reach highly concentrated demand. But as Isard has pointed out, central-place theory assumes away concentrated demand, so the very centers that appear on an isotropic plain to service a rural hinterland violate the basic assumptions of the theory (1956:270–273). Obviously, this is a problem to which solutions can be found (see, e.g., Parr and Denike 1972; Webber and Symanski 1973); the spatial consequences of these solutions have yet to be described, however.

It is also a well-known empirical fact that most consumers buy more than a single item in a trip, so that the range of *multiple* items determines their willingness to travel and their ability to give custom to any particular supplier. This not only makes the classic assumption of single-purposed consumer trips quite unrealistic but also makes unrealistic the assumption of strict threshold governance of supplier location. For if located in a central place rather than where actual threshold dictates, a more distant supplier may draw more consumers than a nearer one. The consumer who can buy several items in one trip in a more distant center can spread transport costs among the several items, so the cost of the trip may be

[11] Webber (1971) is also troubled by the assumption of supplier and consumer rationality. If one assumes perfect competition, one need not be concerned with supplier rationality—one can expect the market to discipline merchants *into* rationality. Consumer rationality is not so easily resolved. The weight of evidence about peasant consumers, however, is that they carefully measure costs in all economic aspects of their lives (e.g., Tax 1953). On the other hand, there do seem to be cases in which market attendance is not determined by economic factors (Bohannan and Bohannan 1968; Hodder and Ukwu 1969). I expect this to create difficulties only in economies in which consumers have considerable leisure; and these economies are precisely those in which one does not expect to find a central-place marketing system anyway (for reasons discussed later in this essay).

lower than that to a nearer place with a single supplier. Classical central-place theory may be accommodated by relaxing both assumptions so that one consumer inconvenience—that of having some suppliers more widely spaced than their thresholds warrant—is canceled out by a greater consumer convenience—that of buying several items at once. Excess profits that such spacing allows may be canceled out by the existence of more than a single supplier of each good in most central places or by suppliers offering an array of goods rather than a single item.[12] While a series of such relaxed assumptions may provide a more realistic solution to the locational determinants of central places, by violating the classic assumptions they leave undetermined the spatial consequences; that is, many more realistic assumptions have been suggested, but few of the spatial solutions to the changed assumptions have been provided.

Crissman is one of the few to provide a spatial solution to a changed assumption in his paper here (and more fully in his dissertation, from which this paper is drawn). Building a central-place system as Christaller did, from the top down, he makes the assumption that consumers make multipurpose trips. Also as Christaller did, Crissman allows some excess profits by locating suppliers in centers rather than strictly according to threshold. (As noted earlier, most empirical studies have supported Christaller over Lösch in this, finding all lower-order goods to be in higher-level centers.) The spatial organization of the landscape Crissman uncovers by changing this assumption is not unlike those proposed by Christaller except that larger centers have larger hinterlands than predicted by strict K number (Christallerian threshold) governance, changing the way that lower-level centers nest within them. Crissman makes an important contribution to central-place theory by following out the spatial implications of a changed assumption. While he does not provide solutions that include multiple suppliers of the same items in the higher-level centers, this should follow from other features of his model.

It is notable that Crissman's study and other empirical studies generally support Christaller over Lösch with respect to the importance of central-place determination of supplier location rather than vice versa. In some respects Lösch provided a more consistent theory of supplier location, but Christaller's models, in which supplier location and central-place develop-

---

[12] Vance observes that for wholesaling, "there is a greater tendency for competition to emerge *within* the initially important city than in some advanced spot closer to an outlying part of the market [1970:149; emphasis added]." I suspect that there is a tendency for competition to emerge within centers in retailing as well—certainly the empirical evidence points this way. If this is true, it means that classical central-place theory, which does not take supplier agglomeration into account, does not explain much of supplier behavior. This does not necessarily vitiate the theory as an explanation of retail settlement patterns—the marginal supplier in the larger center is doubtless the one who locates in the new, smaller center—but the implications of this feature of supplier behavior need attention if the theory is to stand as a general explanation of supplier–consumer interaction.

ment are interactive, seem more descriptive of real-world systems. On one point, however, the empirical evidence seems to support Lösch over Christaller. One virtually never finds a perfect Christallerian, stepwise distribution of first-level, second-level, and third-level centers, each level an exclusive category. Rather, one typically finds a rank–order distribution of centers in a system, each center slightly smaller than the next higher center, supplying only a few less specialized goods (Berry 1967). One might expect this on Löschian grounds, given a system that supplies multiple goods, each of the goods with slightly overlapping ranges. Yet larger centers empirically also have suppliers of all of the lower-order goods. So it seems this finding is not related to strict threshold governance of supplier location so much as it is related to the uneven growth of central-place systems and their adaptation to landscapes that are not isotropic (Berry and Garrison 1958). I will take up the discussion of rank–size distributions and the developmental process later. But first I would like to discuss the whole question of the relationship between the "ideal" central-place models and "real" empirical systems that some modern geographers find problematic.

Empirical studies made so far,[13] including most in this volume, generally support the notion that market economies are made up of hierarchically organized central places that are interrelated in patterned ways. The most "deviant" cases described here (by Kelley, Smith, and Appleby) show strong hierarchical organization and display many of the predicted regularities. All of these studies provide evidence that the economic organization of a region is dependent on some kind of hierarchical arrangement of central places. They also show that the economic development of a region can be measured to some degree by observing the elaboration of hierarchy and the spatial integration implied by a particular central-place arrangement. All of these studies, however, deal with systems that are uncomplicated by modern industrial developments. And studies of industrialized parts of the world show few of the predicted regularities. This suggests that the "false" assumption of dispersed demand, which does not allow for supplier location in terms of other suppliers, leads to less distortion in simpler market economies than in industrialized ones. In an industrial society most suppliers locate to supply concentrated industrial workers and other suppliers, and the theory works very poorly to predict industrial settlement distribution and location. Both Christaller and Lösch anticipated these findings by their assumptions. Evidence from industrialized regions, therefore, in no way detracts from the power of a theory for suppliers not dependent on localized resources.

---

[13] I reviewed the empirical studies of central-place patterns throughout the world in Smith (1974); and an excellent annotated bibliography of marketplace studies now exists (R. J. Bromley 1974). Regular hexagonal patterns are rarely found—which should come as no surprise to anyone acquainted with the stringent requirements for them. But hierarchical patterning along one of the several lines described here is uncovered in most of the cases.

On the other hand, it would certainly be useful to develop or amplify central-place theory, enabling it to handle cases in which demand is necessarily concentrated. There is no getting around its deficiencies in this regard. I would like to emphasize, however, that the theory has not been disproved by empirical cases that fail to live up to its predictions when the cases did not fit the assumptions.[14] I would also like to emphasize that while the assumptions are unrealistic for some cases, they do fit a broad set of empirical cases, most of them in agrarian societies.

But what of the fact that all empirical cases show distortions from the ideal patterns because the assumed conditions are never fully met in the real world? Crissman and I attempt to answer that question in our papers. Crissman points out the difference between all models and reality, emphasizing the importance of simplifying assumptions (such as an isotropic landscape) for the construction of any theory. He notes that central-place theory is not designed to predict location but to explain spatial relationships. Any model that could predict location in a particular case would be so specific that it would be useless for comparison. Many good models, like the probability model of the law of gases, cannot predict the movement (or location) of particular features (gas molecules), but they can provide a framework for understanding the general phenomenon. Crissman argues that central-place theory provides such models and relates its insights to a particular case in Taiwan, moving between an "ideal" model of the region and a "real" map of the region. The ideal system that Crissman constructs from the logic of central-place theory is not exactly what he finds empirically, but it provides a logical system by which he can *explain* what he does find empirically. This is precisely what models are meant to do.

In my paper I claim that the most unrealistic assumption of central-

---

[14] This point was made clear to me when I undertook an examination of the central-place hierarchy of western Guatemala (Smith 1972). After carefully following the methodology of central-place measurement and analysis provided by Marshall (1969), I found no regularities in the spatial patterns of high-level and low-level market centers. In fact, some high-level centers were closer to one another than they were to low-level centers, which not only flies in the face of central-place theory but in the face of common sense. Concerned more by the latter than the former problem, I began analyzing the regional flow of commodities in order to see how the strange system worked; from that I found that I had lumped retail and wholesale markets together in my classification. (Central-place theory is applicable to retail markets but not to wholesale markets.) When wholesale market functions were eliminated from consideration, I found a fairly regular central-place pattern for retail markets (Figure 5). This experience, together with discovery of the fact that few students of central-place patterns have carefully separated out retail functions in their examination of hierarchical patterns (many even ignore the inevitable distortions created by industrial agglomeration), convinces me that central-place theory is much more robust than many geographers assume. One cannot expect to find a Christallerian system in a system of centers where the hierarchy is measured by population, gross numbers of businesses, and the like; one will find a Christallerian system only when one is careful to meet the specifications of Christaller's theory, one of which is that it predicts *only* retail center distribution.

place theory is the assumption of perfect competition. But that assumption, common to many economic models, does not invalidate the theory. On the contrary, a theory of perfect markets allows one to detect and measure imperfect markets, and a theory of an ideal central-place system based on a perfect market allows one to detect and measure abnormal market conditions. On these grounds, I have attempted to discover in systematic fashion what effects abnormal market conditions have on an ideal central-place system, testing whether or not the structure of a system is directly related to its function. With data from western Guatemala, three "abnormal" market conditions are modeled and compared to the 12 subsystems of that region; two-thirds of the subsystems show various predicted symptoms of abnormality in both structure and function, and one-third are "normal." Moreover, the various normal and abnormal structures are found to predict certain consequences for the subsystem economies. Vance (1970) and E. A. J. Johnson (1970) have also developed models of irregular central-place systems by deliberately altering the classical assumptions of Christaller and Lösch, which several contributors to this volume have found useful (Kelley, Appleby, Smith, and Schwimmer). But before turning to the irregular patterns that "abnormal" market conditions produce, let us look at an irregular pattern produced by a "normal" process, growth.

URBAN CENTRAL-PLACE PATTERNS

Two general distributions of central-place orders are empirically common, neither of which conforms to the idealized patterns predicted by central-place theory. One distribution is called the rank–size ordering or the lognormal distribution of central places; in it, the product of the rank of each center (taking all centers in a region or nation together irrespective of location) remains constant. (As noted earlier, Christaller's central-place theory posits a stepwise progression of related centers for any one of the K value patterns instead of the smooth linear progression found in the lognormal distribution.) The other common but "irregular" pattern is called primacy or the primate city pattern; in it, the primary or first-level center or several of the major centers are considerably larger than predicted by the rank–size rule.[15] The two questions raised by these

---

[15] Primacy was first recognized as a deviation from the rank–size rule; primate centers are defined as those that are much more than twice the size of the secondary central place in their region. Central-place theory does not specify the sizes of different central places, only that they be discretely stratified. It is increasingly recognized, however, that primacy distorts "normal" central-place patterns (Berry and Horton 1970). On the basis of Crissman's work and my own in Guatemala, I suggest that the main distortion is suppression of intermediate-level centers.

"irregular" patterns are these: Where and why do they occur? What relationship, if any, do they have to "regular" central-place patterns?

The Rank-Size Rule

In a comprehensive review of the world-wide distribution of aggregate central-place patterns, Berry (1961) observed that the rank–size distribution usually occurs in mature, large-scale, highly urbanized, stratified, or complex economies. (Examples are the United States, India, China, and West Germany.) In a later publication (1971), Berry attempts to specify the conditions that give rise to the rank–size distribution of urban centers. He suggests a diffusion mechanism of economic growth, where impulses of economic change are transmitted simultaneously along three planes: "(a) outward from heartland metropoli to those of the regional hinterlands; (b) from centers of higher to centers of lower level in the hierarchy, in a pattern of 'hierarchical diffusion'; and (c) outward from urban centers into their surrounding urban fields [1971:116]." When growth diffuses in this pattern, it will satisfy the "law of proportionate effect" in which growth of cities is proportional to their size; that is, each center, its size affected in many ways, will grow at about the same rate, this being the only systematic influence on size. Growth is presumed to stem from major centers in the system, the focal places for all economic development, and then to trickle down equally in all directions. The mechanism for trickling down is the operation of the urban labor market. Major centers will pay higher wages, forcing some industries out to seek areas with lower wage rates. Eventually, industry will shift from larger to smaller centers, and multiplier effects of shifts in industry will push the process continually forward. Two things are necessary for this effect, however: a sustained rate of growth over a relatively long period of time and competition among firms for factors and labor as well as for markets.

What is the relationship between the rank–size distribution and the "normal" central-place hierarchy? In an important theoretical paper on the problem, Berry and Garrison (1958) showed how rank–size regularity of urban populations could be consistent with the stepwise pyramiding of central-place functions predicted by central-place theory. They hypothesized that population density and demand could vary across a broad region such that centers of similar rank in different subsystems varied in population and in some urban functions, even though they had very similar positions in the regional exchange system. Later, the hypothesis that the rank–size rule might obtain at a broad system level at the same time that smaller local systems show stepwise pyramiding was empirically confirmed (Marshall 1969; Smith 1972). In effect, disturbances created by any number of nonisotropic conditions—variation in population density or demand, landscape irregularities, differential distribution of transport facilities, and the like—would shift centers out of line with one another, even though they might be identical with respect to regional central-place functions. Given that rank–size is typically determined by urban population (rather than urban central-place functions) and that many factors other than retail service functions affect urban populations in "mature" economies, it is hardly surprising that broad national systems of centers should fall out of line with respect to their central-place tier. What is surprising is that they should fall into such a neat lognormal line when they are affected by random forces.[16]

What, then, can the lognormal distribution tell us? On the basis of where it is found (mature, industrial, wealthy countries) and the presumed beneficial effects of systemic growth, many experts assume that it is evidence of a healthy economy, equating it with social systems that are well integrated, mature, responsive, homogeneous, harmonious, and so forth. However, there is some evidence that it completely masks local system variation. E. A. J. Johnson (1970) points out that India, for instance, has a rank–size distribution of urban centers nationally but frequently displays the primate pattern at the regional level. In my study of western Guatemala, discussed earlier, I found that while the broad regional system displays rank–size regularity, two-thirds of the local systems display clear irregularities. It appears that careful local system analysis is required to explain what rank–size regularity means in any given instance.

Primate Systems

The primate city pattern is somewhat easier to interpret. It can occur at any system level, seems to result from fewer specific forces, and is a probable indicator of imperfect competition within the economy. The essential feature of primate patterns is that all parts of a region are not equally serviced, as they are with stepwise (or even most lognormal) distributions of places. Single or selected centers draw more than their share of suppliers and consumers, monopolizing the tributary area and leaving a relatively poorly serviced distant hinterland. What one has, in effect, is the Thünen arrangement, but this time with small market centers in the periphery dominated by a single large center. One would therefore expect the Thünen consequences: commercialization and intensification near the primate center, with increasing self-sufficiency and extensive production away from the center. It should be remembered, however, that Thünen's model is a normative model and cannot predict adaptations where economic factors are not flowing freely. For example, Kelley shows in

---

[16] Zipf (1949), the first to note the rank–size distribution of urban centers, is unclear about the determinants of the pattern. Berry (1971) argues that it is not random forces that give rise to it but rather the operation of the urban wage market. He bolsters his argument with a mathematical proof. Simon (1973) argues otherwise, showing how the rule operates in many other contexts of size distributions. I find it difficult to choose among the arguments.

Chapter 7 that when there are no viable economic alternatives to producers distant from major market centers, they will intensify production to meet population growth. Under competitive conditions this would lead to the development of market centers in the periphery. But if transport networks, capital, and industry are concentrated in primate centers, intensified production in the periphery may simply lead to lower prices for the peripheral product.

In highly industrialized, capital-intensive economies, primacy seems to result from economies of scale in agglomeration, particularly for the industrial sector. [Or, following Frank (1967), one could put it this way: In mature capitalistic systems unrestrained by political controls, competition and economies of scale lead to concentration and monopoly expressed in primacy or the development of metropoles.] Mera (1973) provides some confirmation for these notions in his careful study of primacy in Japan. He points out that while primacy results in regional inequities of income opportunities, service distribution, and the wage rate, the marginal returns for investment for capital-intensive industry in even extremely "swollen" cities are almost always significantly higher. Most highly developed nations today have a lognormal distribution at the national level (a number of countries, including Japan and Britain, excepted), but many of them display the primate pattern at the regional level. Moreover, urban agglomeration and primacy tend to increase with further industrialization. The trend may be dampened at present only because many of the presently developed countries have evolved from broadly articulated agrarian bases, where the classical central-place patterns seem to flourish. But if the trend is there, it has important implications for regional income distribution and economic opportunity, as well as for ecological equilibrium.

More interesting to students of cross-cultural patterns, primacy on a national scale is usually observed in immature, small-scale, underdeveloped, and simple economies, where a strong agrarian base for development never evolved but where peasant marketing systems often exist. (Examples are Peru, Guatemala, Thailand, Ceylon, Ghana, Uganda.) The primate pattern itself seems to have something to do with the form of development in these countries. Colonial and former colonial states (together with empire capitals—London, Lisbon, Paris, Madrid) exhibit the highest degrees of primacy.[17] In these states a single primate

[17] An early observer noted the following about primacy: "the lower the degree of closure, i.e., the more the system is inherently dependent on other systems to maintain its ecological stability, the higher can be expected the degree of primacy of the city (or cities) which establishes the link between the given area and the external world [Feldt, summarized in Owen and Witton 1973:326]." Colonial or former colonial states as well as their empire capitals exhibit the lowest form of closure a system can experience while still maintaining some identity. According to Berry and Horton, "primate cities are either 'orthogenetic' political and administrative capitals, 'heterogenetic' capitals of emerging nations, or empire capitals [1970:73]."

city is typically the national capital, the cultural and economic center, the chief port that links the country to the outside world, and the focus of national identity. The colonial rulers or a newly established national elite usually live in the primate center, isolated from the supporting rural hinterland made up of a traditional peasantry. It follows that economic and political dualism usually takes its most extreme form in primate systems.

From a number of cross-sectional and a very few longitudinal studies, Berry (1971) suggests that primacy may be a natural stage in the evolution of a mature economy. He observes that primacy is very rare in the least developed economies, develops in the "takeoff" stage, and disappears thereafter. But the use of national rather than regional data may be misleading. For one thing, almost all of the nations presently near or at the takeoff stage have been colonized, so primacy may simply be a side effect of the colonial impact on development. Second, if we limit the countries counted as fully developed strictly, it is not at all clear that primacy disappears, Japan and England being notable cases in point. Finally, primacy disappears into the rank–size distribution—that being counted as "normal"—and, as mentioned before, the rank–size distribution does not tell us a great deal about the real organization of local-level economic systems.

Berry seems to have a point when he argues that the concentration of capital and administration in a primate center is the surest and quickest way of "reducing entropy" or economic disorganization. From an organizational perspective it seems that primacy performs an important service. But Berry's developmental model does not account for cases of sustained primacy. In Latin America many countries have displayed strong primacy since their conquest—that is, for some 450 years. I would argue that primacy reflects the political administration of an economy in which competitive forces, necessary to a regular commercial central-place hierarchy, are minimized. In this light, primacy is not seen as preparation for economic takeoff nor as a creature of colonialism, but as the product of a particular kind of noncompetitive economy. This helps us understand primacy historically, for most premodern states, whether colonial or not, were usually characterized by a considerable degree of primate development. Primacy in them disappeared not when the economy was "modernized" in the sense of industrial development, but when it broke out of administrative control, becoming competitive. (See Smith, Chapter 12, Volume II.)

RURAL MARKETING SYSTEMS— SOME IRREGULAR TYPES

Although economic specialists once argued that a broad national agrarian base is not necessary for development (holding to the trickle-down theory), modern specialists, aware of dualized development patterns in much of the contemporary world, take the opposite position (see, e.g., Johnston and Kilbey 1972). E. A. J. Johnson (1970), especially concerned with agrarian marketing systems in highly aggregated economies, shows the pernicious effects of inadequate rural marketing structure in primate systems. He has also identified some peasant-market side effects of primacy. They are either underdeveloped peasant marketing systems where the village to market-town ratios are very low—particularly true of India, which has an average ratio of 300:1—or dendritic marketing systems (described below), found where peasant marketing is developed, but very poor and inefficient.

Two other types of rural marketing arrangements seem not to fit the classical central-place patterns for markets. They are known as solar systems (Nash 1966; Wolf 1966) and network systems (Bohannan and Bohannan 1968; Hodder and Ukwu 1969). The solar system is one in which a network of markets is organized by a single articulating center, typically urban, which creates a simple two-level hierarchy. From this description, the solar system could simply be part of a regular central-place system; but if each hierarchical (solar) unit were relatively independent of several other like units in the same region to facilitate "the traditional interaction of customary monopolies in a closed regional system [Wolf 1966:41]," they would not be part of a regular central-place system. The network system, on the other hand, has no central places—in it small rural markets are regularly interrelated by trade, but the flows are primarily horizontal, between equivalent centers or between peasants. This kind of system may be found in regions where marketing is disassociated from urban provisioning, or it may involve a kind of trade irrelevant to urban centers. Both kinds of systems are found in poor agrarian economies where marketing has social as well as economic functions. Perhaps for this reason they are often considered to result from specific cultural preferences or values—despite the fact that there is a regular cross-cultural pattern in the distribution of such systems.[18] In the following sections I attempt to show that they and dendritic systems are predictable responses to particular economic forces.

[18] Nash, for example, argues that the solar marketing system is "an aspect of general cultural differentiation" in which "whole communities have cultural traditions which vary from each other in endless small ways [1966:66–67]," and Wolf (1966) seems to go along with him. Bohannan and Bohannan (1968) and Hodder and Ukwu (1969) are explicit about their beliefs that Nigerian network or "ring" systems are culturally based. Peasant marketing systems and peasant cultural traditions undoubtedly influence, even mirror, each other (Skinner 1964), but to say that markets simply reflect cultural traditions seems to be going too far. Nash and Wolf seem especially struck by the fact that in many solar systems peasant communities will each specialize *as communities* is some market commodity and use this as evidence for the cultural priority argument. In my paper in Volume II, I attempt to demonstrate how this adaptation can be explained by the structure and economic features of solar systems.

Dendritic–Mercantile Systems

Johnson's (1970) description of dendritic marketing systems rests heavily on the description of Haitian marketing structure provided by Mintz (1960). In the Haitian system one finds almost more petty market traders than market commodities; and notwithstanding the fierce competition of multiple traders to provision a few urban markets, the Haitian economy displays unfavorable terms of trade to farmers, inefficient movement of commodities, and a static kind and rate of commodity production. According to Johnson, the morphology of the marketing system in Haiti, which is dendritic (see Figure 6), has a great deal to do with the backward features of the economy: Peasant-produced goods flow directly from rural areas to urban centers or major ports and in the process leave the domestic or peasant economy poorly serviced and undersupplied.

Johnson does not specify the chief attributes of the dendritic marketing system from the point of view of central-place theory, but they appear to be the following. Lower-level centers are tributary to one and only one higher-level center. (In most central-place hierarchies, lower-level centers are located between at least two higher-level centers toward which they orient.) And centers become progressively smaller with distance from the major or primary center. (In the $K = 7$ system, which the dendritic system most resembles by the first criterion, large centers are spaced further apart than small centers, and regular tributary areas are retained.) Because lower-level centers are not interstitially placed in dendritic systems, as they are in all regular central-place systems, tributary areas would presumably be spherical rather than hexagonal.

The economic implications of the dendritic spatial arrangement of markets should be obvious. Lower-level centers are controlled by higher-level centers, for the buyers in the former cannot choose among two or three equivalent high-level centers—that is, shop for the best price. The high-level center is therefore able to set a low buying price for rural goods and a high selling price for the specialized goods it provides to the rural area. At the same time, all lower-order centers are (ultimately) in competition to provide the primary (or primate) center with the goods it requires from them. The end result is that the terms of trade for agriculture are

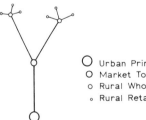

O Urban Primate Center
O Market Town
o Rural Wholesale Market
o Rural Retail Market

Figure 6. A dendritic central-place system.

determined in urban centers, while the major urban centers have no true competition in their service functions. The system is especially inefficient in distributing rural goods to rural consumers, since all goods must first flow to and from the primate center. Horizontal (peasant-to-peasant) trade is possible, as Mintz documents for Haiti, but each rural area is dependent on the supply and demand fortunes of its local area, since trade with other rural regions becomes most unwieldy—and costly. In brief, the dendritic pattern, like most primate patterns in general, suggests for marketing what Thünen's model suggests for production. Peasants in the inner zone (near the primate center) are advantaged in their production–marketing operations, while peasants in the outer zones (serviced only by small feeder markets) are seriously disadvantaged. Kelley details other disadvantages associated with dendritic marketing patterns in Chapter 7.

While Johnson is quite graphic and detailed about the structure and function of dendritic systems, he is not so clear on the determinants of the pattern. Vance (1970), however, describes a marketing structure that is similar to the dendritic system and provides a fuller explanation for its occurrence. Vance's mercantile model is based on the importance of wholesale trade in immature regions. He describes the evolution of central places in the United States with the model, noting the dominance of wholesale considerations in market (urban) location in the development of most of the western portion of the nation. According to Vance, the determinants and consequences of wholesale market orientation, which the mercantile model is designed to explain, are quite different from the determinants and consequences of retail market orientation, which central-place theory is designed to explain.

Kelley develops the mercantile theory further by showing more explicitly than Vance how export production and wholesaling lead to the linear organization described by the dendritic model. She observes that when a linear arrangement of markets is coupled with transport efficiency differentials among levels of suppliers, the major suppliers will dictate the terms of trade all the way down the line and thereby control the regional economy. She then applies the dendritic–mercantile theory to data she collected on the traditional Navajo economy, demonstrating not only the fit between her model and the case but also the power of the theory to explain several otherwise inexplicable features of the Navajo economy. Another study presented here gives added weight to Kelley's findings. Appleby describes the evolution of two marketing systems in a region of Peru, one that seems to conform more to that predicted by central-place theory and one that is consistent with the dendritic–mercantile theory. Notably, the "regular" system is based on retail trade, while the "irregular" system is based on wholesale trade. In my paper I suggest two variants of dendritic–primate systems. Imperfect competition is found to be a determinant of both variants in western Guatemala, but the organization of export production and wholesale trade determines whether the system takes a classically dendritic form or a simple primate form.

Despite the apparent utility of the dendritic–mercantile theory, certain serious reservations about its general theoretical status remain. G. W. Skinner and W. O. Jones argued (in the conference that led to this volume) that it does not distinguish between normal and abnormal conditions of growth. In addition, Jones noted that structure cannot predict function (but see my paper in this volume for a contrasting view); and Skinner observed that dendritic–primate systems would be quite normal in riverine economies or in bounded regions where a full complement of central places cannot develop on the periphery. These are cogent criticisms which most of the papers that posit dendritic systems do not fully counter. Yet the dendritic–mercantile theory seems to have considerable explanatory power for some systems that simply refuse to display normal central-place attributes even though they might meet most physical prerequisites for a normal central-place system. Moreover, some theoretical construct like that provided by the dendritic–mercantile theory seems necessary on logical grounds. Export trade and wholesaling clearly follow market channels that differ from those of retail trade; and the assumption of perfect competition is rarely met in real-world systems. These may be expected to distort "normal" central-place patterns in patterned ways. In addition, one commonly encounters peasant marketing systems that seem poorly articulated with major urban centers and that display certain structural peculiarities for which the dendritic–mercantile theory seems able to account. Finally, the evolution of primacy is not addressed by central-place theory; and primacy, a nearly dominant world-wide pattern typical of most dendritic–mercantile systems, is found in many of the regional systems described here whether or not the regional system is physically bounded.

Without question, the models of dendritic–mercantile systems utilized and developed here will be modified in the future. Theoretical advances or new data may, in fact, require entirely different formulations. But no matter how well the several versions developed here fare in the long run, they make an important contribution to present-day regional analysis by describing alternative patterns that call for explanation, by defining a new set of problems that concerns imperfect economies, and by developing some of the theoretical elements that will explain regional patterns not accounted for by central-place theory.

Solar Marketing Systems

Solar marketing systems seem to be commonplace. As described earlier, the hub of each system is a large (primate) urban center with both economic and political functions; the urban centers are widely spaced because political forces are the only ones that generate town building. Peasant markets in the hinterlands of each center are usually periodic and meet in very small rural towns or occasionally in entirely "rural" areas, and peasant communities in their hinterlands each specialize in a distinctive market commodity. What distinguishes the type from other central-place arrangements is that no intermediate-sized towns or market centers exist in the region to articulate rural trade among a number of high-level urban centers; that is, each urban center has a relatively autonomous marketing hinterland. As mentioned earlier in the context of market periodicity and urban primacy, this description actually fits that for $K = 7$ central-place systems, the "administrative" arrangement designed for political–territorial control of an area. But while the $K = 7$ pattern is the expected arrangement for any system of administrative centers, it is not the expected arrangement for market centers that should be in competition in order to be "economic." If the polity captures and defines the economic arrangements in a region, trade will not flow freely as price dictates. The observation that solar marketing systems and administrative settlement patterns resemble each other, however, is a useful insight, for solar marketing systems seem to flourish where the polity *does* control the market economy—where trade is *deliberately* prevented from flowing freely. Traditionally, much of highland South America, described here by Bromley and Appleby, fits this description and almost certainly for the reasons suggested here (cf. pp. 17–18).

The importance of identifying the political features of solar marketing systems is that it allows one to interpret market behavior in them without blaming it on peasant irrationality or conservatism. From a political perspective, a region made up of solar marketing systems would resemble one covered by feudal principalities (see Chapter 9, Map 2b, p. 314), and it would not be much better integrated. Trade and production at the local level would be Thünen-like. And at the regional level one would find what Jones in Chapter 9 terms the gold-point distribution system, in which the flow of goods among different systems in response to prices is erratic and unpredictable—"all prices in the system may influence all other prices but . . . only after much delay . . . [which] weakens the allocative efficiency of the system . . . [pp. 321–322]." The sluggish price response found in systems characterized by gold-point distribution systems, Jones points out, cannot be attributed to traditional economic behavior on the part of peasants; in West Africa, anyway, he found that both traders and producers are responding to trends in market price if and when they can. But high transport costs, coupled with inefficient communication of price information in such systems, mean that they do so with considerable risk; hence, peasant conservatism would be a rational response if indeed it *is* the response.

Solar systems need not be directly associated with *political* market control, but I expect them to be associated with some curtailment of pure market competition. In Nigeria, which has a well-developed and basically entrepreneurial marketing system, Jones found some commodities distributed by a two-level (solar) system, while others are distributed through a redistributive (central-place) hierarchy. That is, different goods flow through the *same* system in *different* ways: The solar pattern describes the distribution of subsistence goods produced and stored throughout the countryside, which therefore have an urban rather than a rural market; the redistributive pattern describes the distribution of goods produced in concentrated areas, which thus have both urban and rural markets. (It is important to note that the Nigerian redistributive hierarchy has not been demonstrated to be a competitive market hierarchy—the redistributive flow could in fact be dendritic.) As Jones points out, this demonstrates that one cannot predict from the structure of a system how people will use a system—solar systems *can* be nested in a regular central-place hierarchy.

I found the same dual pattern of commodity distribution in western Guatemala, which also has a well-developed and basically entrepreneurial marketing system. My explanation was that rural producers who *could* produce their own food supply *would* produce it because of their reluctance to depend on urban markets for redistribution of necessities— based on their experience with urban monopoly prices for other commodities (Smith 1972). (When they did so, of course, there would be little tendency for goods to flow among different urban systems because each center would be supplied by its local hinterland—hence the solar pattern.) While not the most efficient system, or a system that would cull inefficient producers, it would prevent urban monopolies from influencing rural prices of subsistence goods. It is interesting that Jones does note an urban monopoly in the distribution of one of the goods (cowpeas), which is produced in a concentrated area and distributed through the hierarchical redistribution system (Jones 1972:97). It is also relevant that prices would always be better articulated in a monopolistic redistributive flow pattern than in a competitive solar flow pattern. The fact that Nigerian marketing shows both patterns of distribution through the same markets, therefore, indicates to me that most rural Nigerian producers of basic subsistence goods are conservative, which would be true for one of three reasons: Traditional patterns of production have worked in the past, and Nigerians are reluctant to try something new; urban markets would not reward a rural division of labor because the system is too poor and immature to support a great deal of specialization; or there is a grounded and realistic fear in rural areas of urban monopolies. Jones does not espouse any of the theories, but he does explicitly reject the first and give some evidence that the second is not true.

Whatever the explanation for the present Nigerian pattern, I suggest that solar marketing systems will always develop in "administered" economies where either an administrative elite or an urban coalition of monopolists controls aspects of market location and function and where a vast socioeconomic gulf separates the rural and urban classes; and that this will produce certain traditional patterns of peasant market production (for an elaboration of this argument, see Chapter 12 in Volume II). Given the Nigerian situation, however, I cannot preclude the possibility that other things might also create solar systems of distribution.[19]

Network Marketing Systems

Jones, Bromley, Appleby, and Plattner all deal with some aspects of what I have termed solar systems in this volume. Unfortunately, however, no one examines network systems that are also amenable to regional analysis. I therefore give them special attention here, using a case described by Paul and Laura Bohannan (1968). They describe the network markets of the Tiv from both local and regional perspectives but focus on the local-level pattern in their analysis. I will attempt to demonstrate how a regional analysis can aid one's interpretation of the pattern and its economic concomitants.

The Tiv are a large tribal group in Nigeria, unified by an egalitarian kinship system rather than a centralized political system. At the local level Tiv markets are organized by a network of "rings," each market in the ring having its special day in five and each ring overlapping with other rings (see Figure 7). The markets are more or less equivalent with respect to meeting local needs, and this seems related to the fact that the Tiv are economically unstratified and relatively uncommercialized; yet Tiv visit most of the markets in their ring with some regularity, perhaps for social reasons. Each marketplace seems to fit anyone's definition of what a market should be: It is a regular, regulated occurrence, where all-purpose money is used and prices are set by local supply and demand. But according to the Bohannans, the market principle operates only in the marketplace and does not organize the Tiv economy at a broad level:

> The market was contained among Tiv because they do not—or, in the past, did not—confuse marketing with trading. Marketing means selling one's products and then buying one's requirements. Trading, on the other hand, means transporting goods for a distance with the overt intention of making a

[19] The original basis for solar marketing systems in Nigeria, especially in the Yoruba region, may have been the division of the country into small independent kingdoms that were frequently at war with one another. In addition, many peasant cultivators lived in the Yoruba urban centers; hence markets were naturally held primarily in urban rather than rural places. Lillian Trager (personal communication) has been working on this problem and upon completion of her study may be able to explain the solar marketing system in the Yoruba area more fully.

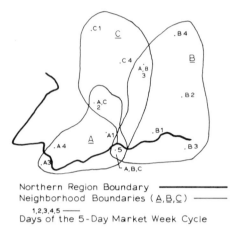

Figure 7. A network system: Tiv markets as perceived by the Tiv. [Adapted with permission from Paul Bohannan and Laura Bohannan, *Tiv Economy* (Evanston, Ill.: Northwestern Univ. Press, 1968), p. 196, Figure 24.]

Northern Region Boundary ─────────
Neighborhood Boundaries (A̲,B̲,C̲) ───────
1,2,3,4,5 ───
Days of the 5-Day Market Week Cycle

profit—buying in the cheaper market and selling in the dearer. Indigenously, Tiv are marketers, not traders.[20]

Tiv markets, then, do not regulate the Tiv organization of production, and on these grounds the Bohannans argue, first, that Tiv culture is relatively immune to the market principle and, second, that where one finds physical marketplaces the regional economy will usually lack the market principle—price-setting functions that regulate production and allocate the factors of production.[21] These claims seem much too broad; the commercial effects of marketing, the penetration of the market principle to the local level, might well be determined by the systemic, regional organization of Tiv markets. Taking my lead from Jones, I suggest that Tiv production decisions are not regulated by the market because of the way in which prices are set in network marketing systems like theirs. That is, on the basis of what Jones finds for two-level marketing systems, I suggest that markets in network (one-level) systems will respond to prices no faster than people can move through a random assortment of places on a periodic schedule. The price information they communicate on a week-to-

[20] Reprinted with permission from Paul Bohannan and Laura Bohannan, *Tiv Economy* (Evanston, Ill.: Northwestern Univ. Press, 1968), p. 241.

[21] The hypothesis that the marketing principle will be lacking in economies that support physical marketplaces was first put forward in Bohannan and Dalton (1965). This hypothesis has been severely criticized by Hill (1963) and Dupre and Rey (1973), who find little empirical support for it. It would seem that the hypothesis is tenable only if one assumes that the market principle was realized for the first time with the industrial revolution which destroyed the peasantry (the primary utilizers of physical marketplaces) as a class. Not only is the evidence for this position thin, but the very formulation of it seems ethnocentric in the extreme. Many preindustrial societies (that is, agrarian societies *with* marketplaces) price land and labor as well as market commodities.

week basis will be even later and spottier than that communicated in solar marketing systems—making it virtually useless. It follows that market prices in network systems *cannot* articulate a broad division of labor; they should not even affect a rational producer's production decisions about staple foodstuffs. Producers who depend on price information from them will be left with surpluses or shortfalls; moreover, they will not be able to obtain necessities from the marketing system will regularity or certainty.

Given a network system, then, how should Tiv respond to the market? They should first produce for their households (to achieve basic self-sufficiency), regardless of market prices in subsistence goods, and then market any surplus for necessities that can be obtained only with cash. If subsistence goods do not provide sufficient cash, cash crops selected in terms of compatibility with the subsistence farming operation as well as market price should also be grown. They should check prices in all local markets (while socializing) to sell when and where most reasonable but should not go far afield, because transport costs for agricultural goods would make selling in distant markets difficult and risky. Finally, they should never alienate land or labor, by selling them to the highest bidder, unless certain that the local market will deliver them what they need, when they need it, and at a reasonable price. Since this is precisely what Tiv do, according to the Bohannans, one could argue that it is the *presence* rather than the absence of the market principle in Tiv culture that accounts for Tiv economic behavior. But the market principle is not the real issue. By explaining the "noneconomic" behavior of the Tiv in terms of the economic characteristics of network marketing systems, one can understand the primary claim of the Bohannans—that Tiv value self-sufficiency—without recourse to their theory that Tiv are uniquely unresponsive to economic opportunity because of primordial cultural values that are incompatible with the market principle.

This explanation nicely side-steps the bootless issue of whether Tiv are economic men or not, but it is circular in that it does not explain why Tiv have not developed a better marketing system. One could use the Bohannan argument, that Tiv do not value marketing, but I prefer the following explanation. Indigenously, Tiv markets were founded and controlled by Tiv chiefs or big men who used the centralizing and economic power of a market to underwrite their own local control of people. But, indigenously, there was no class of chiefs or hierarchy of chiefs, and thus no mechanism by which a stable hierarchy of markets could have been created. Nor was there need for one. The means of production were plentiful in Tivland, so there was no class of nonfood producers (Tiv chiefs were food producers) and no scarcities in basic resources that would engender a local division of labor. Hence, indigenously, the Tiv, like most tribal (unstratified) groups, supported no economic hierarchy or diversity that would have made a market hierarchy useful.[22] This condition no longer holds today, when Tiv must pay taxes and deal in a cash economy. But when Tiv production had become sufficiently developed to support a hierarchical marketing system, local development of a hierarchy was precluded by the fact that an external hierarchy had already developed.

Viewed from the outside rather than internally, Tiv market rings appear to be the unstructured peripheral ends of a broader dendritic marketing system (see Figure 8, based on a figure in the Bohannan study). The critical nodes, undistinguished by the Tiv but not by outsiders, are the points where Tiv goods are bulked for distribution to the outside and national goods are fed into the Tiv system. Other tribal groups, Hausa and Ibo, operate at the interface of the Tiv and national marketing systems; these "foreign" traders have ties to buyers and sellers in Nigerian cities and considerably more market expertise than Tiv. Like Plattner's peddlers, they have gone out from urban centers seeking markets for urban goods and sources of foodstuffs that command high urban prices. This external system, however, is not clearly perceived by most Tiv:

> There is no formal system of [Tiv] roles that parallels the [dendritic] system of markets. . . . Although Tiv recognize that there are good places to buy various commodities and to sell others, they do not perceive the existence of the [dendritic] system. This system does not coincide with any other [Tiv] institution. Although Tiv marketplaces are overtly institutionalized, the market *system* is not [emphasis added].[23]

In other words, the Tiv perceive and operate within a *network* system, although outsiders have created and operate within a *dendritic* system in the same places. Notably, Tiv blame the outsiders, particularly the Ibo, who specialize in wholesale export of Tiv goods, for "spoiling" the market; it seems that the uncommercialized Tiv do rather poorly with respect to the broader marketing system that ultimately connects to Nigerian cities, as one would expect at the end of a dendritic system.

According to the Bohannans, Tiv elders feel helpless to stop the flow of staple crops from their farms (a flow clearly motivated by the market principle), which leaves Tiv producers vulnerable to forces they do not

---

[22] The evidence about precolonial Tiv markets is murky. They seem to have had few market centers and no local currency; and the markets that existed seem to have facilitated foreign or external trade rather than domestic exchange, as is still the case in the remoter parts of Tivland (at least in the 1950s, when the Bohannans conducted their study). Hence, one could argue that the Tiv did not support a local marketing *system* before the colonial period, but rather a few isolated markets. The fact that market names and day names are terminologically the same in Tivland does not necessarily imply that Tiv have always had markets; the five-day market cycle is common in Nigeria, which has been urbanized for centuries (Hodder and Ukwu 1969).

[23] Reprinted with permission from Paul Bohannan and Laura Bohannan, *Tiv Economy* (Evanston, Ill.: Northwestern Univ. Press, 1968), p. 219.

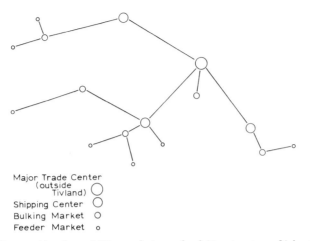

Major Trade Center
 (outside
   Tivland) ◯
Shipping Center ◯
Bulking Market O
Feeder Market o

Figure 8. The outside view of Tiv markets: a dendritic structure. [Adapted with permission from Paul Bohannan and Laura Bohannan, *Tiv Economy* (Evanston, Ill.: Northwestern Univ. Press, 1968), p. 215, Figure 25.]

control. They blame the "spoiled" market on the all-purpose money introduced from outside. It is, of course, the whole economic relationship of the Tiv to the outside that is to blame, and a clearer perception of the problem by the Tiv elders would probably not change it. Because external rather than internal demand determined the present hierarchical organization of Tiv markets, the system is poorly suited for articulating a *local* distribution of exchange goods. Trade with strangers in the dendritic marketing system carries off the local surpluses that might otherwise be used to support internal market diversification. Accordingly, Tiv markets remain internally organized into simple networks for local exchange purposes, thereby having a very limited ability to regulate production decisions for local needs and unable to sustain a local division of labor.

The external view of Tiv markets suggests that lagging Tiv response to marketing opportunity (if indeed it is a lagging response) is better explained by the place of the Tiv economy in the national economy than by the unusual strength of indigenous Tiv values. It also suggests that network marketing systems will be found in one of two environments: unspecialized economies in which there is no scarcity of the basic means of subsistence or unspecialized economies penetrated by highly specialized ones with strong demand for large quantities of either raw materials or foodstuffs that require little in the way of specialized production. There will be no need for a centralized marketing apparatus unless internal scarcities or external demand generates a local division of labor. This brings up a related question: What generates markets or a division of labor in the first place? This question is treated by several contributors to this volume, so I devote the next section to it.

In this section I hope to have demonstrated that much more work must be done to relate studies of peasant marketing systems to studies of regional or national marketing systems. Most local-level studies fail to appreciate the outside forces that determine the organization and character of local-level systems, while most national studies mask the local-level processes that must be understood in order to interpret the broader national patterns. In addition, primary attention has been given to whether or not peasants engage in marketing, this considered to be the crucial variable explaining peasant economic behavior. But it should be clear that it is not the *presence* of markets that explains the economic response of peasants but rather the *type* of market that is present.

THE ORIGIN AND EVOLUTION OF MARKETS AND CENTRAL-PLACE SYSTEMS

Most scholars, unfortunately, consider it important to take a position in the debate about the origin and universality of *market trade* in order to explain the evolution of *marketing systems* (e.g., Adams 1974; Berry 1967; Meillassoux 1971). I say "unfortunately" because the debate about market origins centers around the relative importance of social versus economic causal forces, and those caught up in it therefore tend to neglect the *interrelations* of social and economic forces in market evolution. In addition, proponents of one or the other side are often led to simplistic views of systemic development—trade once put into motion by the causal force, the system taking care of itself. The few scholars interested in central-place development cannot be accused of this oversight, but they neglect other issues, being for the most part quite cavalier about the motivating forces of development. The essays in this volume are able to combine an interest in the genesis of market trade with an interest in systemic development only by putting the debate about origins to one side and concentrating on the conjunction of social and economic forces in both market and central-place development. Since this approach to the problem is on the face of it oblique, in that it appears to duck the main issue, I will attempt to show in some detail here some of the difficulties one encounters when beginning from one of the standard positions on market or central-place origins.

The two standard views of market origins can be briefly summarized as follows.[24] One school, which I term the Adam Smith school, holds that market trade is universal in that scarce goods are always allocated by some system in which supply and demand are brought into equilibrium by the relative values attached to goods of different scarcity. Because scholars

[24] The two standard views of market origins are reviewed more fully in Berry (1967), Meillassoux (1971), and Polanyi *et al.* (1957).

of this persuasion assume a basic human propensity to truck and barter, they do not consider the development of marketing systems a problem; market exchange will develop or intensify because natural differences in resource distribution or some kind of pressure on resources, usually from population growth, will create scarcities that compel specialization and full-fledged institutions of exchange. Marketing systems arise, then, as a society becomes larger, denser, or more pressured; the initiating conditions are largely internal to the system. Because all simple economies are in the process of developing into some standard version of a "modern" economy, variation in economic or marketing systems can be explained in terms of developmental stages.

The second school, associated with the Polanyi reaction, considers market trade a rather "unnatural" human activity that requires certain specific conditions to develop—forces exogenous to the domestic economy. It originates in long-distance trade between "stranger" groups where economic maximization by the parties to exchange will not rend the social fabric. And it is expected to remain compartmentalized in preindustrial societies—to be a carefully controlled, circumscribed activity that takes place among strangers under the careful eyes of political watchdogs. Thus, the way in which the market, and the economy in general, is instituted in a society is assumed to be determined by cultural or political rather than economic variables, and no evolutionary sequence is projected for market development—although all developed market economies are held to be similar. True market economies, those permeated by the market principle, developed only once, when the economy took over society during the great social transformation of the industrial revolution, which made man and nature (labor and land) into economic commodities for the first time (Polanyi 1944). Hence, marketing *systems* are necessarily postindustrial phenomena.

The argument about the natural or unnatural aspects of market trade is destined to be unresolved—it is a philosophical rather than scientific question. And once resolved, what do we know? Can we assume that if Adam Smith is right, a full-fledged marketing system will be instituted once population density reaches a critical level, say, 60 per square mile? Or can we assume that if Polanyi is right, marketplaces will spring up and a partial market economy (with some systemic features) will be instituted once two political or cultural systems come into contact? Neither of these situations is found to be *either* a necessary *or* a sufficient condition for market development. In fact, the findings in this volume repudiate both of the standard views of market development—or, to put the best face on it, show them to be complementary rather than mutually exclusive. Systemic market exchange (something more than a sporadic event or series of events) is seen to be rooted in an internal economic differentiation that juxtaposes both "stranger" communities and political–economic strata,

each with different economic resources, abilities, and pressures upon
them. The differentiation of economic strata provides the mechanism
whereby the differentiation of economic communities becomes meaningful
and operable. Thus, regular market relations between suppliers and
consumers are found to be stimulated either by external economies or by
an organizing system that is initially more political than economic in
character—support for the Polanyi position. But the internal forces of an
elaborated exchange system are found capable of economizing land and
labor, that is, of providing a full price mechanism, without even the
faintest prospect that the economy will soon be industrialized—support for
the Adam Smith position. In addition, the important initiating condition
or mechanism that propels market exchange is found to be something that
neither side considers: the growth of hierarchical institutions *within* the
internal or domestic economy that provide the regular concentrated
demand that generates rural specialization and the local ability to supply.
That is, central places are found to develop long before an internal marketing system—they are the *causes* rather than the *consequences* of
market development.[25]

If market evolution is directly tied to the growth of nucleated settlements or to the whole constellation of central-place development—not an
especially startling idea but a neglected one—what explains central-place
evolution? Only one complete model of central-place evolution has been
worked out before now, that of Skinner (1965). But three theories of
development can be deduced from the logical models of Christaller, Lösch,
and Vance, each of which embodies an implicit causal theory. Christaller,
it will be remembered, worked from the top down to build a central-place
hierarchy; suppliers move out from an established center as demand rises
to create new centers in a region that presumably began as a Thünen-like
isolated state (as shown in Figure 2). How does Christaller's central-place
market arise in the first place, and why do smaller centers evolve around
it? Appleby suggests that Christaller's model assumes (or is best understood as assuming) a basic "class" division to underlie market exchange,
the classes being rural and urban classes, each with different goods to offer
and needs to be met in a market; with this assumption, new markets are
seen to evolve as the nonfood-producing urban class grows, compelling
rural specialization and exchange. Christaller did not actually propose an
evolutionary model, of course, but let us call the model that assumes the
following Christaller's model: Class differentiation generates market
exchange; urban growth generates rural markets; the first center is a
major urban center; and smaller centers are added to the landscape

[25] The Tiv case may seem to contradict this argument, but I suggest that the Tiv did not
have a marketing *system* until their local markets were connected to the Nigerian national
system, which supported urban centers. Before then, they had at best a few, poorly articulated trade gatherings whose locations and functions were variable and unstable (see note 22
and Bohannan and Bohannan 1968:146–219).

around it concentrically as the system grows. Polanyi's sociopolitical forces create the conditions for the system, but Adam Smith's invisible hand propels its growth.

Vance suggests that the usual motivating force for central-place development is mercantile trade between local systems. Merchants seeking new markets and sources of goods establish centers at the edges of local systems and push central-place development forward along a linear path. The first center is an entrepôt city or unraveling point, the next places are either points of attachment (in new areas) or depots of staple collection (in settled areas). Then, from a system with at least *two* major central places, connected by smaller wholesale centers, a retail system will evolve between and around them, in much the same fashion as that postulated by Christaller. The major difference is that the initial stimulus to trade is seen as *external* rather than internal, and the first stage shows a *linear* rather than concentric pattern of settlement or urban development. Thus, Adam Smith's invisible hand generates the system, but Polanyi's sociopolitical variables provide the proper environment for the system to flourish.

Lösch, unlike Christaller and Vance, began from the bottom and worked up to develop a central-place hierarchy. Small centers that provide basic necessities are the first to be established in a region, and larger ones are created as demand intensifies, locating in new interstitial places. Lösch did not propose this as an actual evolutionary sequence. But Skinner proposed a very similar one, also beginning from the bottom and working up. Skinner, the only one who should in fact be credited with an evolutionary model, begins with a region that supports only small peasant markets. (Why they are there in the first place he never attempts to explain.) Population growth gives commercial impetus to the region, requiring peasants to specialize in order to meet subsistence needs and providing for more market centers whose flows must be articulated. But rather than siting larger markets that develop as the central places for smaller ones in *new* locations (as Lösch did), Skinner sites them in old centers where possible. In one of the two sequences he works out, this stimulates the growth of small markets in places that lacked a settlement altogether; in the other it stimulates an eventual transformation of all smaller centers into larger ones. In both sequences the process is one of gradual filling in, small centers arising on the landscape between already established centers. Fissioning of market or central-place levels occurs in spurts, a single market that initially supported many villages suddenly becoming the hub for the smaller markets that develop within some of the villages, each of which then supports relatively few villages. In Skinner's model, then, urban centers would develop only as a result of rural market intensification. And while the origins of market trade are not considered in detail by Skinner, it would seem that Adam Smith's invisible economic hand both generates and propels systemic development.

Until recently, none of these theories has been put to the test (on data other than those that generated the models). Therefore, the studies of central-place and market evolution in this volume—which do put these various theories to the test—are of some importance. Let us now look at the evidence presented here; later we shall consider the logic of the arguments.

Schwimmer uses data from a newly settled region of Ghana to test the evolutionary theories of Vance and Skinner. He finds that the initial impetus to trade came from outside the local system in that external centers provided the first goods and the concentrated demand that generated internal market production and exchange (supporting Vance's position). But he also finds that the first centers to develop within the evolving system were local exchange markets rather than smaller entrepôts for import-export trade and that these evolved into a regular hierarchical system with intensification of trade (supporting Skinner's position). At first the centers for internal and external exchange diverged in function and location; but with the development of a local urban center, the two exchange systems were integrated into a single central-place hierarchy. Given a region newly settled for commercial purposes, then, Schwimmer's sequence begins with an external market, next adds small local markets, then adds a local urban center, and finally ends with the establishment of intermediate markets, displaying a regular central-place hierarchy.

Appleby uses data from Puno, Peru, to examine the evolutionary arguments of Skinner and Christaller. His evidence basically supports Christaller in that urban demand played the critical role in generating market trade. From this Appleby argues that a socioeconomic differentiation between food producers and nonfood producers (when the latter are concentrated in urban agglomerations for political-administrative purposes) creates the sufficient condition for regular instituted marketplaces. But while this is a sufficient (if not the only) condition for *marketplaces*, it is not sufficient for systemic market organization. In Puno, anyway, it produced only a group of undifferentiated, unrelated marketplaces—a solar system. What generated systemic market organization was the development of an urban hierarchy and sufficient demand in some centers to require commercial movement of rural goods throughout a system of urban centers; this stimulated specialized rural production and necessitated regional articulation of trade. Since growth and differentiation in the urban hierarchy were brought about by wholesale trade and mercantilism—the stimulus of external demand for Puno products—Appleby's case would appear to support Vance's model over Christaller's. But rural markets in the developing urban area evolved in a concentric rather than linear pattern (the linear pattern appeared in another zone) and were affected by urban demand for *food,* not urban demand for exports. The Puno sequence, then, begins with several urban marketplaces in administrative centers, next develops an urban hierarchy (stimulated by external wholesale trade), then adds small local markets, and finally emerges with a regular central-place hierarchy as intermediate-level centers are added.

Plattner and Crissman also describe the process of rural market evolution in regions that had urban centers before smaller centers, but in these cases the impetus to rural development may have been internal to the region. Neither is explicit about the origins of the urban centers: Crissman's Taiwanese towns and Plattner's Mexican town seem to have had both economic and political functions from the beginning. But inasmuch as both regions were frontier colonies (as was Puno, Peru), they may have been established as political–military centers that developed economic functions because the nonfood producers in them had to be fed by the surrounding territory—as Appleby postulates for Puno. In Plattner's case, commerce was literally carried outward from the town by peddlers who stimulated demand in rural areas to the point that small rural market centers are now developing—in a concentric pattern. Plattner's sequence, therefore, has only two stages: first a large urban center with both political and administrative functions, then several small local markets. A central-place system has not developed. In Crissman's case commercial intensification was stimulated primarily by endogenous rather than exogenous forces, population growth and internal diversification. Yet Crissman finds a linear pattern of market growth—small centers developing between already established towns. It may be relevant that periodic marketplaces never did develop in Taiwan; small towns developed along relatively modern roads as the region became more commercialized. The major towns at the beginning of the sequence, however, were major towns at the end, presumably because their initial locations determined the subsequent development of roads and minor centers. Crissman's sequence, as far back as he can take it, is the only one to show intermediate-level places developing in tandem with small local centers; but the sequence does begin with several urban centers.

All of the developing systems described here, then, *begin* with one or more urban centers and only later develop smaller rural markets or towns. Thus, no one in this volume has found Skinner's evolutionary sequence fully satisfactory. This is not to say that Skinner's models have been found to be incorrect in their particulars. On the contrary, the sequences found by Schwimmer and Appleby show that *rural* market intensification follows the predicted pattern quite closely—smaller centers develop first and are promoted to a higher level in the hierarchy as new markets develop. [Crissman found a slightly different pattern, although one that supports Skinner's modernization sequence (1965:211–221); on the other hand, Crissman's region never did support rural periodic marketplaces, and this may be relevant.] But Skinner attempted to deal with rural market evolution without considering the related problem of urban market evolution, and for that reason his theory of the initiating circumstances for market development—population growth and the "obvious" advantages of commercialization—is not convincing. Skinner seems to have ignored urban development deliberately, for heuristic purposes—almost every region of China from which he draws evidence to bolster his arguments about the evolutionary sequence did, in fact, support one or more urban centers before periodic marketplaces appeared on the landscape (Skinner 1976b). In doing so, of course, he could not consider the effect of urban centers—an effect that is presumably sociopolitical—on rural markets, and this seems to be the general problem with the unmodified Adam Smith view.

We have not resolved the problem of urban origins. In some cases it is fairly clear that urban centers were established for commercial reasons (Schwimmer), in others for political–administrative purposes (Appleby). And since each region has been colonized in the recent past and has had extensive external trade contacts at the same time urban centers and demand for rural products have grown, there is no way to select between Christaller's and Vance's models of development. Because external trade seems always to be involved, it may seem that Vance has the better theory; yet I find it as difficult to account for his mercantile trader as to account for Christaller's first town—that is, Vance does not explain the genesis of the colonizing system any better than Christaller (or Appleby) explains the genesis of rural–urban differentiation. To explain these, of course, one must go to the historical or prehistorical record.

There has been considerable archeological (Cowgill 1975; Flannery 1972; Hodder and Hassall 1971; G. A. Johnson 1973; Sabloff and Lamberg-Karlovsky 1975; Wright and Johnson 1975) and some historical (Rozman 1973, 1976; Russell 1972; Skinner 1976a, 1976b; T. C. Smith 1973) work on the problem of late. The near universal preurban pattern found is one with many small undifferentiated settlements whose "market" status is uncertain, followed by a pattern of extreme urban primacy.[26] In

[26] Although this pattern occurs in the overwhelming majority of cases, it does not seem to have been the pattern in western Europe (Russell 1972; T. C. Smith 1973). Russell found a normal rank–size distribution of urban centers in most but not all of the regions he identifies for the preplague medieval period. He found the primate pattern mainly in regions where the central city was spatially central to a highly productive agrarian hinterland. The lognormal pattern was found in the "trading" regions where the central city was located at the edge of its system. I am not sure how to interpret Russell's findings, which seem to suggest that lognormalcy is common to dendritic–mercantile trading systems, whereas primate dominance occurs in economies whose dynamic is internal trade. Our findings have been quite the opposite. It could be, however, that during Europe's medieval period the primate systems were the usual solar arrangements one expects in administered economies (and Russell's evidence supports this); while the trading regions were connecting with other trading regions, none of which was dominant, unlike the modern pattern. The evolution of trade and markets in Europe seems distinctive on several counts and deserves further investigation.

none of these studies is it clear whether the initial generating force for urban development was political centralization or commercial extension. But when stated this way it becomes clear again that the problem of "origins" is a nonproblem—political centralization and commercial extension are simply two aspects of the same phenomenon. The archeologists, at any rate, seem to be reaching this conclusion. Most now argue that one should not seek a single causal factor (e.g., Cowgill 1975; Flannery 1972; Wright and Johnson 1975), but rather seek and consider the interaction among all the potentially causal factors—that it is the feedback process among population growth, commercial expansion, and political centralization that generates new forms of economic organization. The evidence from the cases examined here also supports that position. These "modern" cases, however, support another, perhaps complementary, view as well: The development, distribution, and constitution of economic classes within a regional economy provide a powerful mechanism for explaining *variation* in the institutionalization of marketing systems.

Most of the evidence, then, seems to point to the following characteristics of market and central-place evolution. Market exchange occurs sporadically in all kinds of societies, but integrated marketing systems occur only in stratified societies with a distinct class of nonfood producers who are situated in urban or at least nucleated centers. The centers and the elite class may arise as a result of either endogenous or exogenous forces that transform the local social order, but in any event the internal market system is instituted by an elite class that requires regular and efficient food provisioning. The attractiveness of this theory is that it accords with the present consensus that rural producers will intensify production and specialize only if they have to—that is, if their "surpluses" are forcibly withdrawn by an elite (Wolf 1966). Adam Smith notwithstanding, the main beneficiaries of rural intensified production and specialization for the market are usually not the rural producers (see, e.g., Geertz 1963; Tax 1953). And Polanyi notwithstanding, internal marketing systems that display considerable development of the market principle are not restricted in distribution to the developed capitalistic economies (see, e.g., Skinner 1965; Tax 1953; and most contributors to this volume). Another attractive feature of this theory is that it can account for variability in developed and underdeveloped marketing systems with the variability in the size, distribution, and organization of the elite urban class.

ECONOMIC DEVELOPMENT

Economic development as a process has already been considered; economic development as an outcome will be considered here. What I mean by "outcome" is the assessment of an economy as developed, undeveloped, or underdeveloped—the normative view of the process. While the standard views of the development process do not allow for variation in "developed" marketing economies, most of the essays in this volume do. We have found developed—or at least relatively stable equilibrium states—for normal central-place systems, for dendritic systems, and for primate systems (modern solar systems). These findings are worthy of consideration by students of economic development, especially in light of a growing theoretical school that argues that variable patterns like these—each at different levels of development—cannot be considered stages but rather stable elements in the present organization of the world economy (e.g., Baran 1957; Dos Santos 1973; Frank 1967, 1969; Furtado 1964; Myint 1964).

Immanuel Wallerstein (1974), one of the most forceful voices for this school, suggests that the very genesis of modern marketing systems rests on the interaction of economies at different levels of development. He observes that the economic system of the sixteenth century that generated modern industrial capitalism was made up of three interdependent parts: a developed core in western Europe, a partially developed semiperiphery in southern and eastern Europe, and an underdeveloped periphery in most of the rest of the world. From this he argues persuasively that the dynamic of capitalism (or of a fully developed market economy) is based on the structural imbalance created by integrating regional economies at different levels of development into a "world-system" that allows concentration of capital in one part of it. There are probably few who would quarrel with this part of the formulation—although its neglect as a serious theory of economic development by economists is certainly one of the more interesting occurrences in modern intellectual history. The question that is open to debate is the degree to which this imbalance tends toward permanence—the degree to which "underdevelopment" develops *along with* development to become a relatively stable economic adjustment.

None of the development studies in this volume has sufficient time depth to assess the question of permanence with empirical data, nor do they attempt to do so. But many of them show the same process that Wallerstein posits for the world at a smaller, regional scale and may contribute to the larger formulation in other ways. Appleby and I, for example, document core–periphery relations in the regions we have examined—Puno, Peru, and western Guatemala (see also Smith 1975a, 1975b). In both regions competitive, interlocking central-place hierarchies have developed in the core areas and tie into peripheral areas through dendritic extensions. The peripheral areas provide raw materials, labor, or markets that seem to be necessary for funding the development of the core areas. (Peripheral markets are important sources of demand for core area products in both regions; in addition, the Puno periphery provides wool for the international market, and the Guatemalan periphery provides labor for export enterprises.) Markets are springing up in both core and periphery and becoming better integrated; moreover, peasants are increasingly drawn into a cash economy, involved in a regional or even world division of labor. Yet the development taking place has not materially altered the regional standard of living for the better. This suggests, on the one hand, that peripheral regions of the world are not economically stagnant or resistant to change—they develop the same differentiation and dynamic that impelled the evolution of world capitalism. But it suggests, on the other hand, that replication of the world development pattern in peripheral regions does not necessarily lead to local development, if this is to be measured in economic benefits.

Why? The problem is usually tackled as follows. The nonindustrial regions of the world have not developed because they have failed to meet the preconditions for it—a market mentality, local economic differentiation, "modern" sociocultural institutions receptive to economic entrepreneurship. But none of these holds in western Guatemala and Puno, Peru, where there is no lack of entrepreneurship and little in the way of social or cultural impediments to growth. The most common alternative explanation is that the "surplus" necessary to endogenous growth is being drained in export–import trade with more developed systems. This seems a more plausible explanation, but it ignores the substantial amount of accumulation that does take place in the underdeveloped parts of the world—funded by export–import trade. The problem is not that capital cannot be accumulated but that local investment opportunity for it is poor because of the very process *by which* it is accumulated. That is, capital must be concentrated in the local system if local specialization and industry are to develop; but to the degree it is concentrated—profits from export–import trade flowing to a few entrepreneurs rather than dispersed among export producers—the local market for goods is restricted. Producing for the alternative market—an external or world market—is no solution because industries in the developed countries provide powerful competition, which can be met only by severe limits on local wage and profit levels, which will also restrict local growth. Let me illustrate the dilemma with a hypothetical example.

In the beginning the agrarian region is undeveloped, its economy static, its markets administered. The administrative system hinders economic expansion, but it also provides the first necessary condition for growth by systematically encouraging the institutionalization of markets to feed the urban administrative centers and thereby allowing for the development of an urban merchant class. The merchant class attempts to develop trade and markets in peripheral areas (as in the situation described by Plattner), but the self-sufficiency of most rural producers limits endogenous trade activity and profit to a very low level. This can be termed the traditional undeveloped economy—it may be growing, it may even be entrepreneurial, but its surplus is going into political rather than economic expansion.

Then the low-energy cycle of the undeveloped system is dramatically broken by world demand for one or more of its products. Cash provided to producers of these products generates a growing market for the urban traders, made all the more dynamic by ensuing rural market dependence. (Producers of cash crops cannot maintain the same level of subsistence goods production.) The forces of growing external trade thus reduce the economic self-sufficiency of rural producers; give the local merchants seemingly unlimited opportunity for expansion and, through this, political power; and thereby break the local administrative hold over the economy. Once the political hold over the economy is broken, the economy becomes competitive, and traders seek out all the possible niches opened by growing demand. But because the economic stimulus is external, the development process in the region is not even. Most of the wealth generated by export–import trade is concentrated in a few urban centers, usually port cities, and it is they that call forth the development of production for local consumption and rural markets to facilitate it—around them. Since export goods are destined for markets outside the region, they flow along wholesale or dendritic routes to the exporting centers. Producers for export trade cannot also specialize for local demand; their markets, therefore, are provisioned by merchants from the core who are best served by the direct routes provided by the export system—that is, by dendritic market development. Hence the development of an interlocking (competitive) central-place system in the core of the region with dendritic (noncompetitive) extensions to the periphery.

During the period of "primitive accumulation" and growing "merchant capitalism" (Levine 1975), then, virtually all accumulation takes place in the core area of the region (the area close to the expanding urban markets supported by profits from external trade) through the efforts of merchants who dominate the markets in the periphery as well as in the core. A situation of near perfect competition may obtain in the core marketing system—stimulating innovation in production and expansion of trade— while a situation of near perfect monopoly may obtain in the peripheral marketing systems—with the opposite effects. The core and periphery will be equally developed in terms of market dependence, but the core area becomes much more developed in terms of market infrastructure: public services, producing units larger than a family, and trading units larger than an individual. Industries develop in the core on the foundation of profits derived from control of external trade and exploitation of the periphery. We are now ready for the "takeoff" of the regional economy.

Again the world economy and the situation of the undeveloped system in it enters in. If entrepreneurs in the periphery of the developing system were able to find their own peripheral markets and use their profits from trade to support the industries of the core, or if the core industries could find a world market, the developing endogenous system could continue to expand. But there is no periphery left for either to exploit and thus no possibility for an expanding market for core area goods. Therefore, traders from the core remain in control of all the region's markets because it is their main source of income and because they have all the advantages of scale, efficient transport, and accumulated capital. Hence the development of a semipermanent dendritic system in the periphery.[27] By preventing the economic growth and diversification of the periphery (a natural if not farsighted tendency of entrepreneurs who must "accumulate, accumulate"), however, the core area merchants doom their own incipient industries to failure: Low wage rates and market prices given to residents of the periphery will restrict the regional market, lowering core area profits; and the consequent low rate of capitalization for core area firms prevents them from competing with the heavily capitalized industries of the developed countries. In western Guatemala, for example, specialized core area production is viable today only because of the market for "ethnic" goods— clothing and household effects that are traditional features of Indian ethnic identity in the region and that have always been produced by Indian craft specialists. The market for these is now booming because of the increased Indian cash incomes from wage labor in export enterprises. But as more and more Indians abandon these traditional markers of their distinctive status in Guatemalan society (because they are costly, among other reasons), and they are doing so, the developing core industries will also die. Thus, an indigenous industry or specialized production system will not flourish here as it did in Europe, even though the local preconditions for it are met.

Trade remains important in the region, however, and through it the process of "underdevelopment" begins. As demand for the costly goods produced by local firms falls, the producers reduce wages and profit margins, reducing local demand all the more; ultimately they fail. But core area traders do not stand idly by watching their own profit margins dwindle. Being good economic men facing considerable local competition, they seek cheaper goods for the limited regional market from the already developed countries whose scale of production permits them to charge low prices while maintaining high profits even with added transport costs. Thus, in the long run, the efforts of the core area merchants to concentrate

[27] It is argued here that there is no advantage to backwardness when an underdeveloped economy is directly tied to a developed one. That is, Gerschenkron's model of development (1962), which finds advantage in backwardness, may work in semiautonomous regional systems because commercial stimulus from the outside can work directly without the kind of intervention one would expect in a "developed" administered economy (Schwimmer's study supports this view); but *dependent* backward economies have no such advantage because imported technology is not owned by residents of the underdeveloped system.

capital by controlling a limited market will provide for increasing concentration in the world industrial areas rather than for local development; that is, given the entrepreneurial process, which tends to dampen demand unless the market is virtually unlimited, they have no choice but to become wholesale agents for external firms. Hence the development of a region entirely dependent on external trade and production—the development of underdevelopment, if you will—through the efforts of individuals who might otherwise have funded or become a local bourgeoisie. My point here is that underdevelopment is a dynamic, active process, not a passive, receiving one, that depends upon the "collusion," knowing or unknowing, of entrepreneurs in both developed and underdeveloped economies (cf. Dos Santos 1973). Yet the "villains" in this drama would be the heroes in other circumstances; for the concentration of capital that generates underdevelopment in one instance can generate development in another instance.

I have based the preceding argument on the modern economic situation in the world. But might not traditional economies with limited internal markets display a similar pattern? Skinner's study in this volume is relevant to this point. He undertakes a broad study of entrepreneurship, both economic and political, in late traditional China, asking whether or not the place of an individual within a regional system affected his mobility chances or success rate. Place is defined in terms of several characteristics of China's regional systems: position in the economic central-place hierarchy, position in the administrative central-place hierarchy (the two were not identical in China), and position within the national long-distance trade network. Successful bureaucratic-degree candidates tended to come from systems that were the "cores" of both economic and administrative hierarchies; and successful traders and financiers tended to come from systems that were strategically placed with respect to long-distance trade. Both groups systematically plundered peripheral regions for the benefit of their own regions. Skinner thus demonstrates that entrepreneurship is shaped by the regional economy and by the place of the potential entrepreneur in it; he also shows that the tendency for concentration exists in traditional as well as modern economies. Elsewhere, he (1976a, 1976b) and Elvin (1973) observe that while modern market institutions and endogenous trade flourished in late traditional China and while the technological preconditions for industrialization were also met, the limited internal market and lack of an external market (due to imperial policy) prevented systematic expansion of the economy. The peripheral regions remained economically underdeveloped, the Chinese "world-system" was never fully integrated, and the Chinese economy never took off.

What these various locational studies of economic development demonstrate is that no subsystem of an economy can be understood in isolation from other subsystems and, furthermore, that no national economy can be understood without understanding the relationship among its regional subsystems. Nonetheless, development economists usually ignore regional variability. Most are concerned only with general production inputs and outputs, with the problems and likely effects of removing labor from agriculture, with market adjustments among different sectors of "the" economy—the economy always a national one and the sectors defined as agriculture, industry, and so forth rather than as spatial or even rural–urban subsystems. (See, e.g., Wharton 1969, especially the article by Jorgenson, which represents one of the more enlightened attempts at describing the development process.) And in attempting to manipulate the balance between disembodied sectors of the economy to produce development, this usually measured at an aggregate rather than a regional level, they pay relatively little if any attention to regional effects. To be sure, agricultural economists put the rural–urban dimension of a national economy into their development models (e.g., Johnston and Kilbey 1972; Kelley, Williamson, and Cheetham 1972). They are concerned, moreover, with the problem of robbing rural producers of the purchasing power necessary to sustain industrial growth. But because they see the rural sector as an undifferentiated one, they can consider only the trade-off between rural and urban growth. If the rural sector is seen as regionally differentiated, however, one can then begin to consider trade-offs between the regional systems. That is, if each regional system has its own specialty for the general economy, its own centers of concentrated capital, and so forth, then growth of the urban and rural markets within each region might complement each other so that each provides demand for the other; and this might provide the dynamic tension necessary to promote sustained growth throughout the economy.

An undifferentiated or aggregate view of economic development is not only misleading but can be pernicious. For it is often the case that the efforts of development experts concerned with speedy results enrich certain regions of a national economy, usually the most urbanized, at the expense of others, almost always the remote rural areas. Such efforts may indeed lead to rising total output and average income, but these gains cannot be sustained without internal diversification and growth in the poor rural regions. That is, they can be sustained only with massive economic operations in the developing country by external firms (whose wealth may be measured in the assessment of gains even though it eventually flows to the already developed country); and this, presumably, is not the development goal. It follows that if development efforts are aimed at alleviating poverty and the gap between the industrialized and the underdeveloped worlds, the goal expressed by most, it will not be realized without attention to the regional development process. A choice for equitable development may involve a choice for slower development because capital will not be as quickly concentrated and invested. But then, of what use is promoting the ability to produce if one does not also promote the ability to consume?

I have described the problem but have proposed no solution. I have no solution, but I can suggest several approaches that should be abandoned on the basis of what we have found. Many development theories depend heavily on the role of the entrepreneur in motivating systemic economic growth, blaming lack of development on lack of entrepreneurship. This seems to be an extremely rare problem; in fact, we find that entrepreneurs as agents of world trade may actually promote underdevelopment. It seems important, therefore, to go beyond the problem of "motivating" economic development—the problems seem to be more often structural than cultural, political, or even narrowly economic. Others see traditional political systems as hindrances. Again this seems to be rare, and it could be argued that untrammeled economic processes do more damage than not—that the polity should be strengthened vis-à-vis the economy to direct the growth process toward more equitable goals. Still others see international trade as the villain, arguing for stiff tariffs and the like. But in much of the world, expanding external trade is the only hope for development—the only means by which self-sustaining static economies can develop an internal dynamic, as the Chinese example illustrates. A world division of labor, moreover, is no less sensible now than when Adam Smith proposed it; but it cannot subvert internal diversification either—each regional economy must have its internal dynamic as well as the dynamic of world trade to feed upon. The balance must be finely tuned in each instance. Finally, most development experts argue for very rapid concentration of capital in the developing country to fund the internal diversification process. But as I hope to have illustrated, concentration should not be so speedy that it vitiates local demand, or else it will undermine its own achievement. I argue, in short, that economic development should be seen as the process whereby rural or undifferentiated parts of an economy become increasingly specialized in production requiring more efficient *and* equitable exchange articulation among the parts— increasing hierarchical *and* vertical market integration. The solution, then, may rest on promoting several urban centers or "growth poles" in the developing region or nation, which will individually concentrate capital but will also provide competition and markets for one another, thereby providing the necessary internal dynamic for sustained growth.

SUMMARY AND CONCLUSIONS

Some of the most basic questions about economic systems are dealt with in this volume: How do economic systems evolve? What role does social organization play in economic development? Why do rural producers display "conservative" economic behavior, or do they? When and where can entrepreneurial activity be expected, and what are its results? If the papers here are at all indicative, the regional perspective on economic systems provides answers to these questions that differ significantly from individual market and community studies on the one hand and macroeconomic national studies on the other. Yet each approach is equally valid, depending upon the questions of concern; therefore, our goal is not to replace the narrower and broader studies but to supplement them. We also hope that combining the empirical approach of microeconomic studies and the systemic approach of macroeconomic studies will help bridge the gap between the two main camps of economic analysis, whose efforts should not be opposed to each other. In this respect, regional analysis has a most important contribution to make.

REFERENCES

Adams, Robert McC.
  1974   Anthropological perspectives on ancient trade. *Current Anthropology* **15**: 239–258.
Baran, Paul A.
  1957   *The political economy of growth.* New York: Monthly Review Press.
Berry, Brian J. L.
  1961   City size distribution and economic development. *Economic Development and Cultural Change* **9**: 573–588.
  1967   *Geography of market centers and retail distribution.* Englewood Cliffs, N.J.: Prentice-Hall.
  1971   City size and economic development: Conceptual synthesis and policy problems with special reference to South and Southeast Asia. In *Urbanization and national development,* edited by L. Jakobson and V. Prakash. Beverly Hills, Calif.: Sage Publications. Pp. 111–155.
Berry, Brian J. L., and William L. Garrison
  1958   Recent developments of central place theory. *Regional Science Association, Papers and Proceedings* **9**: 107–120.
Berry, Brian J. L., and Frank E. Horton
  1970   *Geographic perspectives on urban systems.* Englewood Cliffs, N.J.: Prentice-Hall.
Bohannan, Paul, and Laura Bohannan
  1968   *Tiv economy.* Evanston, Ill.: Northwestern Univ. Press.
Bohannan, Paul, and George Dalton
  1965   Introduction. In *Markets in Africa,* edited by Paul Bohannan and George Dalton. Garden City, N.Y.: Natural History Press. Pp. 1–32.
Bromley, R. D. F., and R. J. Bromley
  1975   The debate on Sunday markets in nineteenth century Ecuador. *Journal of Latin American Studies* **7**: 85–108.
Bromley, R. J.
  1974   *Periodic markets, daily markets, and fairs: A bibliography.* Monash Publications in Geography, No. 10. Melbourne: Department of Geography, Monash Univ.
Brookfield, H. C., with Doreen Hart
  1971   *Melanesia: A geographical interpretation of an island world.* London: Methuen.
Chisolm, Michael
  1962   *Rural settlement and land use.* London: Hutchinson.

Christaller, Walter
  1966 *Central places in southern Germany.* Translated by C. W. Baskin. Englewood Cliffs,
        N.J.: Prentice-Hall. (Originally published as *Die zentralen Orte in Süddeutschland,*
        1933.)
  1972 How I discovered the theory of central places. In *Man, space, and environment,*
        edited by P. W. English and R. C. Mayfield. London: Oxford Univ. Press. Pp. 601–
        610.
Cowgill, George L.
  1975 On causes and consequences of ancient and modern population changes. *American
        Anthropologist* **77:** 505–525.
Crissman, Lawrence W.
  1973 Town and country: Central-place theory and Chinese marketing systems.
        Unpublished Ph.D. dissertation, Cornell Univ.
Dos Santos, T.
  1973 The crisis of development theory and the problem of dependence in Latin America.
        In *Underdevelopment and development: The Third World today,* edited by H.
        Bernstein. Baltimore: Penguin. Pp. 57–80.
Dupre, Georges, and Pierre-Philippe Rey
  1973 Reflections on the pertinence of a theory of the history of exchange. *Economy and
        Society* **2:** 131–163.
Elvin, Mark
  1973 *The pattern of the Chinese past.* Stanford, Calif.: Stanford Univ. Press.
Flannery, Kent
  1972 The cultural evolution of civilizations. *Annual Review of Ecology and Systematics*
        3: 399–426.
Frank, Andre Gunter
  1967 *Capitalism and underdevelopment in Latin America.* New York: Monthly Review
        Press.
  1969 *Latin America: Underdevelopment or revolution?* New York: Monthly Review
        Press.
Furtado, Celso
  1964 *Development and underdevelopment.* Berkeley: Univ. of California Press.
Garner, B. J.
  1967 Models of urban geography and settlement location. In *Models in geography,* edited
        by R. J. Chorley and Peter Haggett. London: Methuen. Pp. 303–360.
Geertz, Clifford
  1963 *Agricultural involution.* Berkeley: Univ. of California Press.
Gerschenkron, Alexander
  1962 *Economic backwardness in historical perspective.* Cambridge, Mass.: Harvard
        Univ. Press.
Haggett, Peter
  1966 *Locational analysis in human geography.* New York: St. Martin's Press.
Henshall, Janet D.
  1967 Models of agricultural activity. In *Models in geography,* edited by R. J. Chorley and
        Peter Haggett. London: Methuen. Pp. 425–458.
Hill, Polly
  1963 Markets in Africa. *Journal of Modern African Studies* **1:** 441–453.
Hodder, B. W., and U. I. Ukwu
  1969 *Markets in West Africa.* Ibadan: Ibadan Univ. Press.
Hodder, Ian, and Mark Hassall
  1971 The non-random spacing of Romano-British walled towns. *Man* **6:** 391–407.

Isard, Walter
  1956 *Location and space-economy.* Cambridge, Mass.: MIT Press.
  1975 *Introduction to regional science.* Englewood Cliffs, N.J.: Prentice-Hall.
Johnson, E. A. J.
  1970 *The organization of space in developing countries.* Cambridge, Mass.: Harvard Univ. Press.
Johnson, Gregory A.
  1973 *Local exchange and early state development in southwestern Iran.* Ann Arbor: Univ. of Michigan Museum of Anthropology, Anthropological Papers, No. 51.
Johnston, Bruce F., and Peter Kilbey
  1972 *Agricultural strategies, rural-urban interactions, and the expansion of income opportunities.* Paris: OECD Development Center.
Jones, William O.
  1972 *Marketing staple food crops in tropical Africa.* Ithaca, N.Y.: Cornell Univ. Press.
Kaplan, David
  1965 The Mexican marketplace: Then and now. *Proceedings of the American Ethnological Society.* Seattle: Univ. of Washington Press. Pp. 80-94.
Kelley, A. C., J. G. Williamson, and R. J. Cheetham
  1972 *Dualistic economic development: Theory and history.* Chicago: Univ. of Chicago Press.
Levine, David P.
  1975 The theory of the growth of the capitalist economy. *Economic Development and Cultural Change* **24:** 47-74.
Lösch, August
  1954 *The economics of location.* Translated by W. F. Stolper. New Haven, Conn.: Yale Univ. Press. (Originally published as *Die raumlishe Ordnung der Wirtschaft,* 1940.)
Marshall, John U.
  1969 *The location of service towns: An approach to the analysis of central place systems.* Toronto: Univ. of Toronto Press.
Meillassoux, Claude
  1971 Introduction. In *The development of indigenous trade and markets in West Africa,* edited by Claude Meillassoux. London: Oxford Univ. Press. Pp. 49-86.
Mera, Koichi
  1973 On the urban agglomeration and economic efficiency. *Economic Development and Cultural Change* **21:** 309-324.
Mintz, Sidney
  1960 A tentative typology of eight Haitian marketplaces. *Revista de Ciencias Sociales* **4:** 15-58.
Myint, Hla
  1964 *The economics of the developing countries.* New York: Praeger.
Nash, Manning
  1966 *Primitive and peasant economic systems.* San Francisco: Chandler.
Owen, Carol, and R. A. Witton
  1973 National division and mobilization: A reinterpretation of primacy. *Economic Development and Cultural Change* **21:** 325-337.
Parr, John B., and Kenneth G. Denike
  1972 Theoretical problems in central place analysis. *Economic Geography* **46:** 568-586.
Polanyi, Karl
  1944 *The great transformation: The political and economic origins of our time.* New York: Holt.
Polanyi, Karl, C. M. Arensberg, and H. W. Pearson (Eds.)
  1957 *Trade and market in the early empires.* New York: Free Press.

Rozman, Gilbert
  1973 *Urban networks in Ch'ing China and Tokugawa Japan.* Princeton, N.J.: Princeton
        Univ. Press.
  1976 *Urban networks in Russia, 1750–1800, and premodern periodization.* Princeton,
        N.J.: Princeton Univ. Press.
Russell, Josiah C.
  1972 *Medieval regions and their cities.* Bloomington: Indiana Univ. Press.
Sabloff, J. A., and C. C. Lamberg-Karlovsky (Eds.)
  1975 *Ancient civilization and trade.* Albuquerque: Univ. of New Mexico Press.
Simon, Herbert A.
  1973 The sizes of things. In *Statistics: A guide to the unknown,* edited by J. M. Tanur.
        San Francisco: Holden-Day. Pp. 197–202.
Skinner, G. William
  1964 Marketing and social structure in rural China: Part I. *Journal of Asian Studies* **24:**
        3–43.
  1965 Marketing and social structure in rural China: Part II. *Journal of Asian Studies* **24:**
        195–228.
  1971 Chinese peasants and the closed community: An open and shut case. *Comparative
        Studies in Society and History* **13:** 270–281.
  1976a Regional urbanization in 19th century China. In *The city in late Imperial China,*
        edited by G. William Skinner. Stanford, Calif.: Stanford Univ. Press.
  1976b Urban development in Imperial China. In *The city in late Imperial China,* edited by
        G. William Skinner. Stanford, Calif.: Stanford Univ. Press.
Smith, Carol A.
  1972 The domestic marketing system in western Guatemala: An economic, locational, and
        cultural analysis. Unpublished Ph.D. dissertation, Stanford Univ.
  1974 Economics of marketing systems: Models from economic geography. *Annual Review
        of Anthropology* **3:** 167–201.
  1975a Examining stratification systems through peasant marketing arrangements. *Man* **10:**
        95–122.
  1975b Production in western Guatemala: A test of Boserup and von Thünen. In *Formal
        methods in economic anthropology,* edited by Stuart M. Plattner. Washington, D.C.:
        American Anthropological Association. Pp. 5–37.
Smith, Thomas C.
  1973 Pre-modern economic growth: Japan and the West. *Past and Present* **60:** 127–160.
Stine, James H.
  1962 Temporal aspects of tertiary production elements in Korea. In *Urban systems and
        economic development,* edited by F. R. Pitts. Eugene: Univ. of Oregon Press. Pp.
        68–88.
Tax, Sol
  1953 *Penny capitalism: A Guatemalan Indian economy.* Washington, D.C.: Smithsonian
        Social Anthropology Publications, No. 16.
Thünen, Johann Heinrich von
  1966 *Von Thünen's isolated state,* edited by P. Hall. Translated by C. M. Wartenberg.
        Oxford: Pergamon Press. (Originally published as *Der isolierte Staat,* 1826.)
Uberoi, J. P. Singh
  1962 *Politics of the* kula *ring.* Manchester: Manchester Univ. Press.
Vance, James E.
  1970 *The merchant's world.* Englewood Cliffs, N.J.: Prentice-Hall.
Wallerstein, Immanuel
  1974 *The modern world-system.* New York: Academic Press.

Webber, M. J.
  1971 Empirical verifiability of classical central place theory. *Geographical Analysis* **3:**
        15–28.
Webber, M. J., and R. Symanski
  1973 Periodic markets: An economic location analysis. *Economic Geography* **49:** 213–
        227.
Wharton, Clifton (Ed.)
  1969 *Subsistence agriculture and economic development.* Chicago: Aldine.
Wolf, Eric R.
  1966 *Peasants.* Englewood Cliffs, N.J.: Prentice-Hall.
Wright, Henry T., and Gregory A. Johnson
  1975 Population, exchange, and early state formation in southwestern Iran. *American
        Anthropologist* **77:** 267–289.
Zipf, G. K.
  1949 *Human behavior and the principle of least effort.* Cambridge, Mass.: Harvard Univ.
        Press.

Section B

TRADE, MARKETS, AND URBAN CENTERS IN DEVELOPING REGIONS

In their treatment of market and economic system development, Plattner, Bromley, Schwimmer, and Appleby make considerable headway on some old and important problems. All describe regions where a rural marketing system has developed de novo or has shown considerable intensification in recent years, and all either present or test theories of market evolution. Since this is a problem with rather sweeping implications for economic theory, I have dealt with it and the contributions made by these authors at length in Chapter 1. But other topics and issues are broached here as well, which I will briefly summarize in this introduction.

Stuart M. Plattner is concerned with the necessary and sufficient conditions for itinerant firms—mobile traders or peddlers—throughout the world, especially those who work in rural areas. Since rural peddlers are typically displaced by periodic peasant markets, Plattner must consider them within the context of market evolution. He finds that peddlers who are located in an urban center and who exchange urban goods for rural goods in marketless areas play an important role in rural market development by stimulating demand, providing a market for increased and specialized production, and communicating general economic information. Successful peddlers, in fact, create the conditions whereby nonspecialized peasants in rural areas will become market dependent enough to institute their own market centers, thereby obviating the need for peddlers. Plattner supports his argument with data from highland Chiapas, Mexico, where he conducted an intensive study of peddlers. From these data he also shows how demand density and distance affect the trip frequency of peddlers, information that should be of considerable interest to geographers engaged in the market periodicity–firm mobility controversy.

Raymond J. Bromley, interested in the necessary and sufficient conditions for periodic markets, shows with data from highland Ecuador that the sufficient conditions are much broader than previously supposed. He provides an admirably complete and well-analyzed set of data on markets throughout highland Ecuador, divided into regional subsets, which he uses for intrasocietal and cross-societal comparisons. Bromley finds both the market hierarchy and the temporal integration of periodic markets to be quite immature throughout highland Ecuador, although regional variation is pronounced and the situation is steadily improving. On this basis he presents very briefly a theory of market evolution, one that gives added support to those developed more fully by Plattner, Schwimmer, and Appleby. Bromley's main contribution, however, consists of measurement techniques for assessing both the amount of hierarchical development and the degree of temporal integration in a central-place system; these techniques will almost certainly become important tools for future students of periodic markets.

Brian Schwimmer describes the evolution of an urban system and a regular central-place hierarchy in a region of southern Ghana. Because this system developed from scratch in a newly settled area recently, Schwimmer has relatively complete documentation on its growth, which he uses to test two theories of market evolution. These theories propose not only different kinds of initiating conditions for market growth but also different growth patterns in the organization and location of market centers. Schwimmer finds both theories to be correct in some particulars, but neither to be adequate predictors of the actual transformations in the system. What Schwimmer does find should be important information for any future students of market system growth, inasmuch as complete information about market and central-place changes is coupled with full documentation on changing economic conditions in the region. Schwimmer also reports and analyzes changes in social organization that accompanied the development and intensification of the marketing system, some of which had not been predicted by students of economic development.

Gordon Appleby finds two types of systems in Puno, Peru, one in the high *altiplano,* which supports only a herding economy, and one in the lakeside area, which supports intensive agriculture. One expects the ecology of a region to affect marketing patterns, but Appleby shows that the differences in the two marketing systems in Puno are determined by economic forces only indirectly related to the environment. Historically, the two zones supported similar central-place hierarchies, which diverged only with the development of trucking and urban demand. Had export centers and trade routes been located elsewhere, a distinct possibility, the regional system would have developed in an altogether different fashion. As Schwimmer does, Appleby tests several competing theories of market development, none of which seems to apply fully to Puno, and then presents his own explanation to account for the patterns he finds—the growth of a regular central-place system in one zone and the growth of a dendritic system in the other. Along the way he accounts for changes in periodic market schedules, traditional nonmarket exchange systems, and urban–ethnic populations. He also shows that the growth of rural markets in Puno was intimately associated with the development of a distinctive trader class.

Chapter 2

Periodic Trade in Developing Areas without Markets

Stuart M. Plattner
University of Missouri—St. Louis

INTRODUCTION

The theory of periodic trade in peasant regions was significantly advanced in 1962 with the appearance of a seminal paper by Stine. He discussed mobile retailing in the same terms as fixed store retailing, using concepts drawn from central-place theory (Stine 1962). [Central-place theory derives from Christaller (1966) and Lösch (1954).] Some recent papers have extended and criticized Stine's formulation (Hay 1971; Webber and Symanski 1973); in addition, Skinner's notable analysis of the prerevolutionary Chinese marketing system (1964, 1965), Smith's extensive study of the marketing system of highland Guatemala (1972a, 1972b) and Crissman's detailed investigation of the marketing system in Taiwan (1973) have provided excellent empirical studies using the same basic theoretical framework. This paper is intended to clarify and supplement some of the conceptual issues raised by previous authors with respect to mobile retailers, by more firmly embedding the model of periodic trade in the general sociopolitical development of the region. I will first discuss the general conditions for mobility in retailing, then describe three basic stages in the development of periodic trading systems, and finally present a more detailed model of the demand for and the supply of one type of mobile retailer, the long-distance peddler, in an early stage of regional development.[1]

CONDITIONS FOR MOBILE RETAILING

In this section I will summarize in some detail the factors influencing mobility in retailing, as these concepts will form the basis of a model of itinerancy in retail transactions. I will use the term "mobile vendor" to denote many types of sellers, including relatively heavily capitalized itinerant marketers who trade out from a central place to various market-places and set up fixed stalls in each place; long-distance itinerant ped-dlers who go out from central places to sell door to door among dispersed rural homesteads without marketplaces; itinerant street peddlers with fixed routes in urban neighborhoods relatively distant from fixed sources of similar goods; and street peddlers with minimal stocks who may sell in the marketplace itself—that is, adjacent to fixed sources of similar goods—as well as in the surrounding streets. Implicit in the list just presented is a ranking in amount of capitalization, as the long-distance market traders usually have many times the stock of the street peddlers. Goods involved range from dry goods and hardware for long-distance ped-dlers to prepared food, tobacco, and notions for the street and market peddlers.

THE COST OF A GOOD

I begin with the abstract notion that a consumer will purchase goods from the vendor who offers them at the least cost. The empirical value of such a statement will rest on the definition of least cost, which is com-monly taken to have three components: the price of goods at the place of the vendor's stock, the cost of transporting the goods from the vendor's stock to the consumer's home, and the cost of transporting the consumer from his home to the vendor's place and back again (Webber and Symanski 1973). Consumer transport includes the direct cost of the price of the trip and the indirect cost of the value of the activities foregone at

---

[1] My own empirical familiarity with periodic trading systems is based on 20 months of field work with a community of itinerant cloth peddlers from a small central town in southeastern Mexico and on some less intensive observations of the periodic marketing systems of the Oaxaca valley in Mexico (for 2 months) and midwestern highland Guatemala (for 10 months). This paper supplements previous articles in which I interpreted a particular sample of peddlers' economic behavior (Plattner 1975a) and described a computer simulation game of itinerant peddling (Plattner 1975b). My thoughts on these subjects have benefited greatly from conversations and communications with Carol Smith.

home while on the purchasing trip. Examples of the latter that are easy to measure because they are monetary are wages to field hands for farmers who leave the farm and wages to baby-sitters for mothers who leave the home. Examples of costs that are difficult to measure because they are nonmonetary are the loss in satisfaction of not doing a piece of work in the style or time one prefers because of an interruption for a shopping trip and the risk of unpleasant things happening if one crosses an ethnic boundary while on the trip. For example, an Indian farmer in Mesoamerica who goes to a mestizo town or an Indian or a black ghetto dweller in the United States who goes to a white shopping center risks potential harassment from all sorts of people, including the police. Note that these latter sorts of costs can be equated with sums of money in an imprecise and variable way, although it would be a mistake to presume that the cost is consciously thought of as monetary. Thus, while one may not walk through a hostile neighborhood in order to buy a $30 commodity for $30, one may decide to run the risk of harassment if the good is obtainable for $5.

Implicit in the notion of costs is that the cost of any trip can be shared among various goods. For the consumer, the more goods one buys per trip, the cheaper the total real cost of each item. However, this is true only up to a point, after which costs will rise again as special fees and trouble arise due to the large quantities. For the seller, economies of scale may permit prices at the consumer's door to be lower than those obtainable by the consumer himself. Trade discounts or lower unit transport costs due to larger bulk would permit such economies. The higher the consumer's opportunity costs for time at home or the larger the differential between transport costs for the trader and the consumer, the larger the probability that the trader's goods will have a lower final cost.

THE ATTRACTIVENESS OF A GOOD

The consumability of a good offered for sale by a retailer is not simply a function of its physical characteristics but must include its environment as well. A good is more attractive if it is made available at the precise place and time it is needed by a consumer. In addition, the conditions of payment are an intrinsic part of all transactions of goods. In many cases the merchandise is not purchasable if particular selling arrangements, especially credit, are not available.

Just as the physical characteristics of a good are not completely sufficient to ensure its sale, the actual need on the part of the consumer for a good is not in itself sufficient to ensure a purchase. Consumers obviously need the cash or the means of payment, which is not merely a function of present wealth and income but also a function of an estimate of future income. In addition, I assume that people have a notion of an "acceptable price" for things, which is continually undergoing reevaluation in response to changing market conditions. My point in introducing all these details is that a consumer's notion of the acceptable price for a commodity is tied to a particular place, time, and condition of payment. Any commodity can be a "good deal" at very different retail prices if each price is in the context of a different bundle of consumability attributes. I will argue later that it is the fact that more than one price is acceptable for different bundles of retail services that allows itinerant vendors to operate in the context of fixed stores.

A MODEL OF MOBILE RETAILING

The concepts just put forward can be combined to form a model of mobile retailing that will be consistent with previous efforts but will specifically include mention of town peddlers and long-distance, marketless, itinerant peddlers. The basic element is the maximum range of the consumers' demand for a good, which refers to the longest distance a consumer will travel to obtain a unit of the merchandise from a vendor. This range is constructed from the model of demand given in Figure 1. Assume that all consumers have identical demand curves and that their consumption of the good is purely a function of its price. The real price of a good to a consumer, however, is a function of its price at the center and

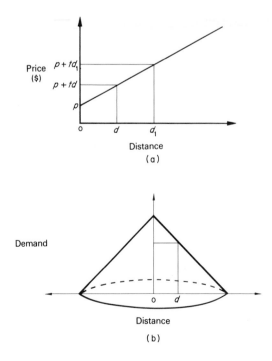

Figure 1. Price, demand, and distance from a central point. a. Price as a function of distance (t = transport rate). b. Demand as a function of distance: the spatial demand cone. [Based on Brian J. L. Berry, *Geography of Market Centers and Retail Distribution*, © 1967, pp. 60–61. Redrawn by permission of Prentice-Hall, Inc., Englewood Cliffs, New Jersey.]

the cost of transporting it from the center to the consumer's home (Figure 1, part a). An item that costs p at the center costs $p + td$ at a distance d from the center, where t is the transport rate. Thus, consumers with identical potential demands and opportunity costs purchase decreasing amounts of the same merchandise with increasing distance from the central point of offer, until sales (observed demand) drop to zero at some distance from the center. Since population density is related in a determinate way to distance from the center, the total quantity demanded can be expressed in units of distance from the central point of supply, holding price at the center constant. Figure 1, part b shows this relation rotated around the center to form the spatial demand cone (Berry 1967: Chapter 3).

Given the spatial demand cone, another important concept can be defined: the minimum threshold range of the trading firm. This refers to the volume of sales, corresponding to a definite spatial area, that creates the minimum income necessary for the firm selling a particular good to come into full-time existence. The size of the threshold range is determined by the opportunity cost of the trader's time and money as well as by the demand density in the area. Thus, the threshold range and the maximum demand range are both expressable in terms of area and are directly comparable. As is common in all such discussions, time is held constant.

Stine's important contribution was to point out that the relationship between the maximum and the minimum range establishes the necessary conditions for periodism. If the maximum demand range is smaller than the minimum threshold range, then the firm cannot be fixed, full-time, and survive. But if the firm becomes mobile, it increases its consumer population by relocating the point at which it offers goods, which in effect increases the maximum range of the goods it offers. With respect to Figure 2, in condition A the firm must visit seven demand areas to survive, while in condition B the firm must relocate only three times, and in C the firm is able to remain fixed. Note that the consumer's willingness to travel has not changed—the radius of each local demand area can remain the same. But the families in each place may buy more goods in each successive condition; more families may settle in each place; the trading firm's costs may decline; or its notion of an acceptable minimum income may decrease— any of these changes can influence the mobility of firms. Thus, Stine's model describes the conditions for the existence of trading firms that are able to stay in business full-time by offering part-time services to more than one local demand area.

PERIODICITY OF DEMAND

Mobility is related to the periodicity of demand for merchandise. The need for different goods varies with time: The demand cycle for food is

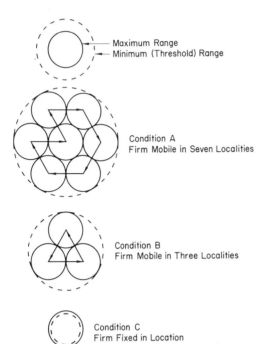

Maximum Range
Minimum (Threshold) Range

Condition A
Firm Mobile in Seven Localities

Condition B
Firm Mobile in Three Localities

Condition C
Firm Fixed in Location

Figure 2. Maximum and minimum ranges and mobility of a firm. [Based on Stine (1962). Redrawn by permission of the University of Oregon Bureau of Business Research.]

short, either daily or weekly; that for clothing is seasonal; and that for durables, such as tools and utensils, is annual or longer. In all cases, since fixed stores are usually open for most of the time (usually closing only overnight), little constraint is placed on the consumer's purchasing schedule. In periodic marketing, goods are *not* available in a place for a good part of the time, causing the demand to be "saved up" during periods when the vendors are absent. This retaining and condensing of the ongoing process of economic demand into a periodic process of need satisfaction is referred to by Stine in the statement "The consumer, by submitting to the discipline of time, is able to escape the discipline of space [1962:70]." From the point of view of the vendor, it is his relative monopoly that allows him to enforce this discipline and so achieve a high sales income per day. The potential demand for goods per time unit (defined as the quantity of goods that would be bought if they were offered continuously) is condensed into an actual sales period of a fraction of the time. This allows the seller to do something else—either travel to another selling area or go into another occupation in the remaining time.

Thus, both part-time and full-time periodic trading is explainable as an attempt to keep income above a threshold per time unit. Revenue is increased by the condensation of economic exchange into shorter time periods. The ability to condense sales is usually due to monopolistic competition, while the impetus for periodism is a function of low demand densities, as will be shown.

MOBILE RETAILING IN THE DEMAND
AREA OF FIXED STORES

There are various conditions under which mobile retailers can coexist with fixed stores. These can be summarized as conditions of different goods and different demands.

Different goods. If the mobile retailer offers services that fixed stores do not offer, he is in effect changing the nature of the goods he is selling. It is common in cities for peddlers to go door to door in ghetto areas and offer things for sale that are commonly offered in stores within commuting distance (see Caplovitz 1967). The difference is that the peddlers offer credit to people to whom the stores deny it. Such credit costs extra, since the default rate is presumably higher, and thus the final price is frequently higher from peddlers than from fixed stores. In addition, peddlers can personalize the goods by preselecting them to match the already known tastes of the consumer. Here the higher price is due to the increased labor per unit of the commodity instead of to a higher credit risk. This latter sort of peddler is commonly found in wealthy neighborhoods that are adjacent to very poor ones, where the poor neighborhoods define the very low opportunity cost of labor necessary to ensure a supply of urban peddlers.

Different demands. Some consumers will always be found in special demand circumstances, in which their schedule of wants is changed from its normal condition. For example, in times of sickness in the family, the opportunity cost of time spent away from the household (that is, away from the patient) rises above the normal opportunity cost of such time. What this does is revise one's expectations of the value of goods to where the convenience of having goods delivered to the house (that is, the saving in time spent away from the house) outweighs the additional monetary cost of such deliveries. In addition, the normal distribution of buying practices ensures that some households will exist in a neighborhood whose members will value the delivery to the house of goods more than the additional price and will therefore buy from peddlers. In modern societies this function is taken over by catalog selling, and the cost is not so much an increased price as a delay in the time between the purchase decision and the delivery of the goods and a loss in the precision of choice, since decisions must be made from printed descriptions of goods rather than from actual observation. Still, the niche exists in modern cities for itinerant peddlers, since retail vegetable trucks are observable from time to time.

In summary, periodic retailing is a viable economic response to varying conditions of demand and opportunity costs. Hay rightfully cautions, however, that "the existence of periodic marketing is a necessary, but not sufficient, condition for the existence of *periodic markets* . . . it is one step further still to *periodic market systems* [1971:401]." The concepts I have mentioned do not explicitly explain the grouping of traders in market-places, although Stine mistakenly claimed they do. Webber and Symanski give some of the logical conditions for agglomeration, but their treatment suffers from ignoring the evolution of economic functions in a region.

In the next section I will discuss periodic retailing in the context of the economic development of an area to illustrate its importance in a middle stage of the development of market systems. After that I describe a less abstract model of the demand for goods and the supply of traders in such a stage of regional development.

STAGES IN THE DEVELOPMENT OF PERIODIC TRADING SYSTEMS

It is important to distinguish three periods in the development of regional systems of exchange: (1) an uncentralized stage, (2) a centralized stage without rural marketplaces, and (3) a centralized stage with rural marketplaces. The lack of attention paid to these distinctions in previous discussions of the topic has weakened the empirical validity of their findings. For example, Stine formulated a model of trading applicable to independent mobile trading firms, but he mistakenly claimed that it describes firms grouped in periodic marketplaces. Webber and Symanski theorized about firms agglomerating in periodic marketplaces in a rural hinterland, but they completely neglected to consider the effects of the prior existence of a central town in such a region.

I should note that the evolutionary sequence implied by the stages is neither ubiquitous nor unidirectional, as the stages are conceived of as functional rather than genetic relationships. Thus, while the usual sequence in general economic history is that itinerancy precedes fixed establishments, the reverse sequence may be observed under the proper conditions. Benedict (1972), for example, describes fixed specialists in some Turkish towns reverting to itinerancy as demand for their services decreased because of the vigorous development of competing market centers in the region. Benedict is noteworthy precisely because he presents the exception that proves the rule, however.

The first stage is of multiple communities in dyadic, or reciprocal, exchange. It would be most typical of tribal societies and is represented by Malinowski's ethnography of the *kula* ring and its allied exchange systems (1922) or the highland New Guinea salt trade as described by Godelier (1971). A limited intercommunity exchange is certainly important in such societies, and some individuals may spend so much time at it that they merit the description of (part-time) specialists, but the relative absence of economic and political differentiation between communities and the extreme costliness (including the potential loss of life) of transport limits the scope for exchange.

The second stage exists when the region develops a central place that serves and controls certain economic and political functions. The stage is defined by the existence of two types of economic community: rural farm villages and a central manufacturing–distributing town. The town is the source, through manufacture or import, of nonfarm goods that are considered essential by the farm population. The region itself is not isolated but is an appendage of a larger system. This stage is descriptive of regions in present-day underdeveloped societies. The town also consumes a significant quantity of farm goods, and it provides the location and skilled services necessary for arbitraging differences in farm production. Therefore, a true functional integration exists in the region. Intercommunity exchange (between farming villages) occurs within the town and also in the far hinterlands through the services of traveling specialists based in the center, since the costs of transportation for farmers are too high and the demand density in the far areas too low to support fixed suppliers or even periodic marketplaces. This is a key stage in the development of the region because the traders are capable of stimulating farm demand for untraditional goods as well as the farm supply of consumables for the town.

The third stage evolves out of the second when some of the rural villages become the sites of periodic markets. This occurs as a consequence of increases in demand intensity and decreases in the costs of transportation for farmers relative to the opportunity costs of farm work not done while they are traveling.

There seem to have been two main lines of development for such multilevel systems of central places. One type is described in Skinner's study of the Chinese rural marketing system (1964, 1965). Here periodic markets form the structure of an integrated system of differentiated central places that serve to redistribute goods produced in specialist areas to one another. Goods produced in local areas are redistributed throughout the system, passing to and through higher-level markets (in larger communities) and having the capability of eventually reaching final consumption in other local farming communities. This sort of system integrates the region by facilitating the development of economic specialization, with the attendant increases in productivity that specialization implies. The key elements are that the incomes deriving from the central places' advantageous positions with respect to the flow of goods are reinvested in the same political–economic system they are derived from and that goods are exchanged horizontally (between communities of similar functional level in the hierarchy) through vertical flows (passing through higher-level markets). Thus, a small farming village can feel free to specialize in tomatoes because it will obtain its staple grain from another small agricultural village. This allows each village to increase its production through specialization, while the systematic reinvestment of profits allows increased production through economic development; that is, the investment of profits in communications systems or in the construction of differently scaled economic activities, such as manufacture, facilitates political integration in the region, which then increases the investments, all in a complex feedback system. This seems to have been the pattern of development in the industrial countries (see Berry 1967).

The second line of development consists of the same multileveled hierarchical structure and differentiation of economic function as the first, but with vastly different consequences for the development of the region. Here the central places serve as conduits for the upward flow of farm goods and the downward flow of manufactured and imported goods, but not for the *downward* flow of farm goods. It is in this sense that a local market for horizontal exchange of farm goods will be an isolated system. Thus, villages cannot specialize too heavily in any nonsubsistence commodity, since the farm goods that they do not produce will not be forthcoming from the market system. In addition, the entire regional system is an appendage to a larger national or international system. The key element here is that the lack of independence allows the investment of profits from trade in other national or international systems. This alienation of wealth impedes the development of subsidiary support systems of education, communications, and transportation that would facilitate economic development in the original region. In addition, the dominance of import–export channels permits the introduction of manufactured items from more developed places that are cheaper and better than locally manufactured products. This could, of course, be a description of a beneficial sort of economic differentiation of function if the benefits of investment returned to the originating system. But, for example, when part of the profits from trade in India were invested in the British educational system, the resulting increase in the productivity of British workingmen served only to develop further the British economy and make British goods even more competitive. The continued introduction of these goods into India then served only to squelch further any local development. This sort of market structure has been termed dendritic by Johnson (1970) and is well described for Guatemala by Smith (1972a, 1972b).

In the following discussion I am concerned with the second stage of development, in which the rural communities are serviced by traveling traders from a central place instead of local periodic markets. It can be understood as a miniature version of the dendritic type of system, since the central town is usually a hinterland outpost of the national economic system. This stage is the least described in the literature, is best fitted by Stine's sort of formulation, and is the one I am most familiar with. It is

crucial to the future development of the region, since the itinerant peddlers facilitate the continued advancement of the frontier. [See Neumark
(1957), for example, for a description of the pivotal role of peddlers along
the South African frontier.]

When economic differentiation develops to the point where a central
place exists, any discussion of commercial trade must take the effects of
the central town into account. The main effect is that a "halo" of
monopolization of sales by the town's grouped traders exists, based on the
attractiveness of the agglomeration of sellers noted by Webber and
Symanski (1973:221–225) and the decrease in demand that occurs with
the increase in distance from the center. Thus, the maximum range for
goods is stretched close to the center by the association of that good with
other attractions that the center possesses; or the cost of transporting the
good to the buyer's home can be seen as being spread across many goods
on a multiple-objective trip, thus making the real cost of the good at any
distance cheaper than if the good were purchased alone (see also Parr and
Denike 1970:577).

This sort of centralized region can be visualized as a series of concentric
demand zones surrounding the central town, as shown in Figure 3. Here
the central zone (A) possesses the largest demand density due to the posi-

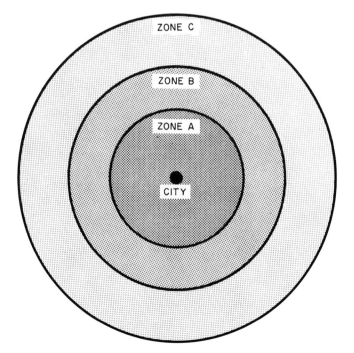

Figure 3. Zones of demand density in an underdeveloped region. Shading indicates density
of population and degree of commercialization. [Reproduced from Plattner (1975a).]

tive association of population density and commercialization with close-
ness to the center as well as the association of transport efficiency with
centrality. Since the sellers located in the city offer, in effect, all of the
services of the town in addition to their own wares, the population of this
zone will buy and sell only at the center. The ideal minimum range of a
lightly capitalized trading firm is relatively small due to the dense
demand, while the maximum range coincides with the size of the zone
itself by definition, since all or most purchases occur in the center. Here
the competition from heavily capitalized fixed stores increases the firm's
real minimum range to the point where it is not possible to trade in this
zone at all.

The second zone (B) is defined by the interaction of several parameters:
population density and commercialization, which decrease, and transport
costs, which increase as distance from the center increases; the degree of
monopolization of supply that the mobile firm possesses at any distance;
and its threshold income. Population density, commercialization, and
transport costs can be combined into a parameter of economic demand per
unit area (Figure 4). This falls with distance from the center, meaning that
the minimum range of a trading firm increases while the maximum range
decreases. The traveling seller's increased monopolization of supply can
also serve to increase the maximum range and decrease his minimum
range. All of these factors interact to produce a daily income, which is the
significant variable from the peddler's point of view. Zone B, the zone of
viable commerce for periodic traders, is defined as the distance from the
center where the daily income is above the threshold. Zone C is a hinterland where demand is too weak and transport too difficult to support even
itinerants. Historically the zones expand outward from the center, radiating across the landscape as the region develops economically, although, as
noted by Benedict (1972), this trend can be complicated by the development of competing centers.

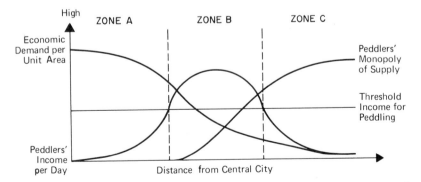

Figure 4. Income of itinerant peddlers and distance from a central town. [Reproduced
from Plattner (1975a).]

Itinerant peddlers are thus interstitial operators, coordinating and uniting center with hinterland. As the region develops, commercialization, density, and transport advance outward from the center, and the middle zone of viable long-distance peddling radiates across the landscape. The appearance of the new role of market trade allows the itinerants the choice of settling down as fixed storekeepers in an old selling location, converting to periodic marketers in the old areas, or continuing as itinerant peddlers in the new frontier zone. Thus, the success of the frontier operators in joining new areas to an old society brings changed conditions under which they must mutate or migrate.

It is interesting to note that some frontier itinerants may continue peddling on the borders of developed local systems. Here the costs will be highest for border consumers, and the same factors that make town peddling viable can operate to make rural peddling possible. Peddlers who buy farm goods as well as sell urban goods can even integrate disparate local systems. They may be thought of as heavy grease that allows ill-meshed local-system gears to interact smoothly. Thus, such peddlers can again be seen as facilitating the eventual development of an integrated system that inexorably eliminates their economic niche.

Given this basic characterization of the region, the determinants of the demand for goods and of the supply of goods (or "supply of suppliers") can be investigated.

THE DEMAND FOR GOODS

Commercialization of the rural families varies inversely with distance from the center. Those families close to the town consume relatively little of their own production and produce relatively little of their total consumption. At the other extreme, families in the most distant zones are almost completely subsistence oriented and have little use or demand for a wide range of purchased goods. In the middle, in the zone of viable periodic trading, are families who produce their basic subsistence food and some additional farm goods for sale (either animals, such as poultry or pigs, or specialty crops, such as coffee or tobacco) but who purchase items like cloth, clothing, hardware, pots and pans, and other manufactured goods of obvious utility. In the early temporal stages of the establishment of this sort of economic zone in an area, the list of items demanded by farm households would be small; however, the progression from subsistence–independence to market dependence seems to have been ubiquitous and inexorable (reversed only in times of disaster when the market structure breaks down).

The total demand for manufactured goods is thus linked to the degree of dependence on the market of the consuming family and its wealth. As

Stine pointed out, inelastic demand would tend to create larger maximum ranges and elastic demand smaller ones. But the demand for the sorts of goods the periodic trader would supply in this type of environment has, I believe, some special characteristics.

Demand is almost certainly income-elastic, both seasonally and in the long run. The hungry, preharvest season is usually a time of minimal purchases, limited to goods of absolute necessity. The postharvest season is then the time of expanded demand for goods. The quantity of goods sold per week or month is not constant throughout the year but is a function of the agricultural cycle. Over the long run, with increasing transport efficiency and commercialization of the region, money incomes will rise as will the total quantity of goods purchased per unit area.[2]

While the *income* elasticity of demand is elastic over annual and longer periods, the *price* elasticity of demand probably varies as the real income of the consumers changes. For poor consumers, there is reason to believe that their demand for clothing and hardware would be price-inelastic. Consider a family that has a small quantity of income to dispose of in each time period but a large number of needs—a poor family. Each expenditure must be allocated to the need that is most pressing at that time, so the household juggles[3] its purchases, spending capital on items only when their possession is absolutely necessary and ignoring other needs that, while real, are not as vitally important at that time. Thus, if the household has to choose among buying shoes for one member, a shirt for another, and food for supper, assuming equal costs for each, the item most cognitively pressing will be bought and the others put off until another time. If the person lacking a shirt must present himself in a situation requiring the dignity of proper clothing, his need may outweigh the family's need for supper that day. If this model is true, then the actual price at the time of purchase would count for relatively less than the absolute need for the object. The family is a prisoner of its own poverty, paradoxically paying more for goods because of its inability to delay purchases until more favorable terms are available. This condition has been described for the urban poor in a book titled *The Poor Pay More* (Caplovitz 1967) and seems likely to exist for poor rural peasantry as well.

The demand for goods by farm families is related in a dependent way to the long-run economic development of the area and to the annual agri-

---

[2] Note that this says nothing about real income, wealth, or satisfaction. My impression for the area of Mexico that I have studied is that the quality of life deteriorated for some groups and probably became better for others as they became more tied into the complex national social structure. The difference is in the particular niche each community is able to exploit in the expanded economy. Those who can capture some sort of trade or who exploit new opportunities for obtaining farmland can do well. Cancian (1972) gives a good example of agricultural innovation in this area.

[3] This idea is drawn from a model of the behavior of municipal governments formulated by Dr. Sherif El-Hakim (n.d.).

cultural cycle and in a circular way to the periodicity with which goods are offered for sale. Assume that the economic demand at any time is a function of the household's real need for goods and its possession of disposable income (since the lack of cash savings is customary among peasants). Assume also that the real need for goods is relatively constant throughout the year but that income is tied to the agricultural cycle. (In actuality the demand for some goods, such as clothing, is a function of the ceremonial cycle, which in turn is dependent on the agricultural cycle.) For simplicity, assume that income is derived from one basic crop harvested once a year. Then the economic demand, or quantity of goods that would be bought if they were offered for sale, can be diagramed as in Figure 5. There are three curves there: disposable income (the dotted line), real needs (the dashed line), and economic demand (the solid line). Note that purchases in excess of need exist in times of higher income to make up for purchases below need in bad times. Thus, demand is high in the good, postharvest seasons and low in the bad, preharvest seasons.

If goods are offered discontinuously on some regular schedule, then the sales that would occur if satisfactory goods were offered are charted by the continuous line and shaded areas in Figure 6, where they are distinguished from potential sales (demand), which are shown by a dotted line. At t_1, the trading firm has completed a period of selling, and actual and potential sales are near zero. In the period between t_1 and t_2, demand (potential sales) increases steadily, rising above the level of sales that would occur if goods were offered continuously, to make up for the period when goods will not be offered (just as the potential sales rise above real need to make

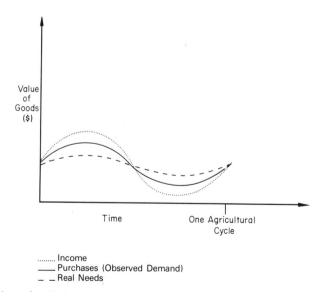

Figure 5. Annual variation in income, needs, and purchases in an agricultural village.

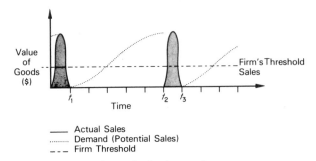

Figure 6. Demand for goods and actual sales in one place.

up for the time when lack of income prevents them from reaching that level). In between t_1 and t_2, the firm enters and leaves several other villages and returns home in order to replenish supplies and rest. At t_2 the trading firm locates in the village again and offers merchandise for sale. Actual sales may be less than the maximum in the first few days because the farm households are not constantly in possession of cash. They must activate exchanges, call in debts, and do the things necessary to obtain the cash when the trader arrives on the scene. The trader himself is not in a position to sell efficiently in the first few days because he must unpack, set up in the new place, and care for his animals. But in a short time, sales reach the potential level, assuming the stock presented is acceptable in quality and quantity (which may not be the case near the end of the trip), and then rapidly decline. It is clear here how the periodicity of supply increases the sales per day by concentrating a longer time span of real demand into a short time span of actual purchases. This is an inconvenience for consumers, who must save and plan ahead or delay a purchase in response to the vendor's periodism. The only way the seller can enforce this "discipline" (see Stine 1962) is through possession of a relative monopoly on sales. Consumers wait for him to arrive because he is the only one who will arrive.[4]

The basic determinant of an itinerant vendor's trip length is a complex function of the time it takes to travel from the central town to the rural selling area, the time it takes to exhaust demand in the average consuming community, the time it takes to travel between independent consumer settlements, and the period beyond which the vendor will not want to remain away from his customers (because of the danger of competing traders entering the route and establishing a niche for themselves). Travel difficulties that are seasonal in areas of dirt trails and wet–dry climates can

[4] Or he may be the only one who will sell on credit or provide special services, such as consignment buying, carrying items into the town for repair, and the like.

shorten or prolong a standard trip length. In southern Mexico, for example, traders report traveling in mud so deep that it reaches their horses' bellies. In these situations the difficulty of doing any normally simple task, such as cooking meals or catching animals that have been pastured for the night, is magnified immensely, so that trips are longer and fewer trips are taken. The relation between the sizes of the maximum and minimum ranges can also affect the duration of the trip. Similar ranges make for fewer moves between periods of selling and thus shorter trips, since fewer days are spent in travel. The degree of monopolization of supply that the firm has in each location is important as a determinant of the real maximum range for that firm's goods in that location (as distinct from the hypothetical maximum range at that point that would obtain if the goods were so perfect as to satisfy all demand completely). The more a firm can monopolize sales in a village, the more sales it achieves there and the fewer villages it must visit to achieve its desired income. The cost of traveling affects the decision as to the duration of the trip, when compared with the income attainable 'at any place. Increased sales income or decreased costs allow the firm to decrease the average trip length while keeping total income constant.

The mobile firm will try to manipulate its trip length so as to achieve high daily sales on each trip. This assumes that increases in capitalization are not too limiting a factor, so that the length of the trip is a strategic economic variable. [For itinerant peddlers in areas without motor roads, the main item of invested capital is the pack animal, since most goods can be obtained on credit (Plattner 1975a).] The firm will prefer to visit rural villages as infrequently as possible, other things being equal, so that the sales that occur represent the longest possible period of demand. Two factors militate against infrequent visits, however: (1) The existence of competing sellers in the region implies that the longer a village is left in a state of high demand, the greater is the likelihood that another seller will visit there and establish an economic niche. Peddlers' routes are highly personalized because of the large amount of specific knowledge required to trade in a peasant area, but the possibility exists that competing traders will visit new villages along their traditional routes. (2) In the stage of regional economic development we are considering, the potential demand for nonfarm goods by hinterland peasants is low and weak—implying that if it is not stimulated by periodic sales it will not remain asymptotic at a high level but will actually decline with time. Thus, if a family consumes 100 units of goods from a peddler who visits eight times a year, it might consume only 70 units if he were to visit twice a year. Increases in daily sales attributable to the collapsing of longer periods of demand into shorter periods of sales must be traded off against decreases in the total quantity of goods sold per year at that place.

THE SUPPLY OF TRADERS

In the previous section the focus was on the demand for goods. This section deals with the determinants of the minimum ranges of itinerant trading firms. I assume that central location gives an overwhelming advantage to town-based mobile traders over rural-based traders, since the wholesale supply points are all in the town (see Plattner 1975a; Smith 1972a). Thus, the socioeconomic structure of the town defines the alternative opportunities open to trading firms and, ultimately, the size of their minimum acceptable incomes. Traditional towns in peasant regions have special characteristics in their occupational structures connected with recruitment of labor into specialized trades (Sjoberg 1955). In general, there are four methods of training personnel: (1) The family can educate its children (or other kinsmen) in its specialization. Thus, children rarely confront the decision of which occupation to enter, since one is learned through the natural process of family socialization. (2) Individual specialists can contract independently for apprentices, whom they frequently take into their households as quasi-adopted children. (3) Specialized schools can provide the training. And (4) the occupations themselves can train people as adults while providing an income (this is similar to an apprenticeship program but is for independently housed adults). The last two methods are used in more developed countries, the first is generally used in tribal communities, and the second is mainly associated with peasant societies.

The distinction I want to draw is between the household-centered and the extrahousehold-centered modes of training (that is, between the first two and the last two types). Household-based training procedures impede the flow of labor between occupations, in effect demanding that only those who begin training as juveniles can learn enough to be adult practitioners. Since special skills and knowledge are needed in most occupations that yield more than subsistence incomes, those without training and without capital must work at extremely low-paid unskilled jobs, such as servant, field hand, or construction laborer. This means that the person who is unable to practice the occupation that he specializes in, usually because of a loss of working capital, will be forced to work at an unskilled job that pays far less than he is capable of earning. In technical terms, the market for labor is not finely arbitraged, and there is much disguised unemployment, people working at low-paying unskilled jobs who are capable of working at high-paying skilled occupations (see Robinson 1936).

In addition, the investment of capital in an occupation is frequently tied to the investment of labor. Since banks, post office savings programs, and so forth do not provide a widely available range of services in peasant societies, the opportunities to invest capital (independently of one's labor) are limited. Money lending, at high rates of interest, is always available, but in the absence of a developed and available system of courts and legal services, the potential lender must rely upon his personal qualities or personal relationship with the debtor to recover the debt. But not everyone has the prestige, political power, or imposing physique to ensure payment. Thus, money lending is not a universally available means of investing capital. In fact, the most usual means of capital investment is in land or in one's occupation.

In sum, the attractions of any particular occupation are that (1) the alternatives are usually extremely low paid and (2) the occupation offers a means to achieve a return on one's own capital. With respect to trade, it means that traders will work for seemingly low incomes because they are not qualified for skilled alternatives and because the unskilled ones are even lower paid. These factors combine to decrease minimum ranges, which serves to increase the extent of the ring of viable periodic trading territory surrounding the town. Thus, it is interesting to note that the occupational structure of the town creates conditions that increase the town's sphere of hegemony over the region—although at first the two variables may seem unrelated.

CONCLUSION

A model of itinerant retailing in an underdeveloped region without rural periodic markets has been presented. This stage of regional development is important because it sets the background for the future development of complex periodic market systems. Stine's concepts of maximum and minimum ranges are used, but the model is placed firmly in a description of the level of regional economic development. Hay's suggestion of the importance of temporal periodicity and Webber and Symanski's demonstration of the economic power of agglomerated sellers are developed in this context. Economic development is seen as radiating from a central trading–manufacturing–importing–exporting town, and itinerant peddlers are described as functioning in a middle zone of development in the region—far enough from the town so that consumers prefer to deal with itinerants rather than traveling to the center themselves, but not so far that consumers are extremely subsistence oriented and do not demand their goods.

The essential features of the demand and supply of such peddlers' services are that:

1. Demand is near zero close to the center, due to competition from already established, heavily capitalized, fixed stores. Demand rises in a zone far enough from the center such that transport costs deter farmers from making the trip. Beyond this zone, demand may fall below the firm's threshold if the region extends to a hinterland of low enough density of demand and high enough costs of transport.

2. Within the zone of viable trading activity, Stine's central-place ideas about maximum and minimum ranges are applicable.

3. The juggling of household resources by poor people serves to extend the maximum range of goods.

4. The occupational structure of preindustrial towns serves to keep the minimum range of the firm relatively small.

5. Periodic trading is best analyzed as an attempt to convert a monopolistic hold over supply into a concentration of the periodism of demand, which is equivalent to the supply firm to an increase in the density of demand.

REFERENCES

Benedict, Peter
    1972 Itinerant marketing: An alternative strategy. In *Social exchange and interaction,* edited by E. N. Wilmsen. Ann Arbor: Univ. of Michigan Museum of Anthropology, Anthropological Papers, No. 46. Pp. 81–93.
Berry, Brian J. L.
    1967 *Geography of market centers and retail distribution.* Englewood Cliffs, N.J.: Prentice-Hall.
Cancian, Frank
    1972 *Change and uncertainty in a peasant economy.* Stanford, Calif.: Stanford Univ. Press.
Caplovitz, David
    1967 *The poor pay more.* New York: Free Press.
Crissman, Lawrence
    1973 Town and country: Central-place theory and Chinese marketing systems, with particular reference to southwestern Changhua Hsien, Taiwan. Ph.D. dissertation, Cornell Univ.
Christaller, Walter
    1966 *Central places in southern Germany.* Englewood Cliffs, N.J.: Prentice-Hall.
El-Hakim, Sherif
    n.d. Garbage accumulation as a sociopolitical process. Unpublished manuscript obtainable from the Center for Community and Metropolitan Affairs, the University of Missouri—St. Louis.
Godelier, Maurice
    1971 Salt currency and the circulation of commodities among the Baruya of New Guinea. In *Studies in economic anthropology,* edited by G. Dalton. Washington, D.C.: American Anthropological Association. Pp. 52–73.
Hay, Alan
    1971 Notes on the economic basis for periodic marketing in developing countries. *Geographical Analysis* **3**: 393–401.
Johnson, E. A. J.
    1970 *The organization of space in developing countries.* Cambridge, Mass.: Harvard Univ. Press.
Losch, August
    1954 *The economics of location.* Translated by William Woglom and Wolfgang Stolper. New Haven: Yale Univ. Press.
Malinowski, Bronislau
    1922 *Argonauts of the western Pacific.* London: Routledge.

Neumark, S. D.

1957 *Economic influences on the South African frontier, 1652–1836.* Stanford, Calif.: Stanford Univ. Food Research Institute Miscellaneous Publication No. 12.

Parr, J., and K. Denike

1970 Theoretical problems in central place analysis. *Economic Geography* **46**: 568–586.

Plattner, Stuart

1975a The economics of peddling. *Formal methods in economic anthropology,* edited by Stuart Plattner. Washington, D.C.: American Anthropological Association. Pp. 55–76.

1975b Pedlar: A computer game in economic anthropology. In *Formal methods in economic anthropology,* edited by Stuart Plattner. Washington, D.C.: American Anthropological Association. Pp. 197–215.

Robinson, Joan

1936 Disguised unemployment. *Economic Journal* **46**: 225–237.

Sjoberg, G.

1955 The preindustrial city. *American Journal of Sociology* **60**: 438–445.

Skinner, G. W.

1964 Marketing and social structure in rural China: Part I. *Journal of Asian Studies* **24**: 3–43.

1965 Marketing and social structure in rural China: Part II. *Journal of Asian Studies* **24**: 195–228.

Smith, Carol

1972a The domestic marketing system in western Guatemala. Unpublished Ph.D. dissertation, Stanford Univ.

1972b Market articulation and economic stratification in western Guatemala. *Food Research Institute Studies* **11**: 203–233.

Stine, James

1962 Temporal aspects of tertiary production elements in Korea. In *Urban systems and economic development,* edited by F. Pitts. Eugene: Univ. of Oregon School of Business Administration.

Webber, M. J., and Richard Symanski

1973 Periodic markets: An economic location analysis. *Economic Geography* **3**: 213–227.

Chapter 3

Contemporary Market Periodicity in Highland Ecuador

Raymond J. Bromley
University College of Swansea, Wales

In recent years, periodic market systems[1] have attracted considerable academic attention because of their complex spatiotemporal configurations (e.g., Symanski and Webber 1974, Tinkler 1973; Ullman 1974). Particular attention has been given to the analysis of spatial patterns of market centers and market days (e.g., R. H. T. Smith 1971b) and to the comparison of periodic market systems in different parts of the world (e.g., Silverman 1959, C. A. Smith 1974; R. H. T. Smith 1972). In this article the spatiotemporal patterns of market activity in highland Ecuador are examined in order to test models and analytical techniques developed in other parts of the world and to establish the factors influencing the nature and evolution of market periodicity.

In highland Ecuador, as in most of Latin America, periodic markets are generally held in nucleated settlements one, two, or three times each 7-day week. Settlements with one or more markets are known as market centers, and markets usually coexist with other commercial institutions such as shops and warehouses. The temporal variations in commercial activity in shops and other commercial institutions outside the marketplace often

[1] Periodic market systems are central-place systems in which the principal commercial activity takes place in periodic markets. Periodic markets are authorized gatherings of buyers and sellers of commodities meeting at an appointed place at least once a month, but not as frequently as daily.

parallel those of neighboring periodic markets. Particularly for the larger market centers, there is a strong correlation between the population of the centers and the levels of market activity (R. J. Bromley 1975:158).

The market week can probably best be illustrated by arranging the days in a continuous circle (Figure 1). Using this arrangement, it is relatively easy to visualize a temporal form of distance (spacing) expressed as the minimum number of days separating any 2 days of the week measuring backward or forward. For the 7-day week, for example, Saturday and Sunday are only 1 day apart, while Wednesday and Sunday are 3 days apart. The temporal distance between any two markets with a 7-day week can range from zero if the markets occur on the same day to three if they are as widely separated as possible. Market cycles can be understood only in terms of market locations in both space and time. The spatial location of a market relative to its neighbors is concerned with geographical distance, measured in miles, kilometers, or other standard distance units, or with economic distance, measured in terms of travel cost or travel time. The temporal location of a market relative to its neighbors is concerned with the temporal distance separating their respective market days.

When a new market is founded in an area that already has periodic markets, two contrasting approaches can be adopted in the choice of market day for the new market. These can be described as the conflictive approach and the integrative approach. By adopting a conflictive approach, the organizers of a new market deliberately choose its market day to clash with some or all of the neighboring markets. Thus, proximity in space is inversely related to proximity in time. For any area, therefore, it is possible to assess the degree of spatial and temporal synchronization or integration of periodic markets. Highly integrated groups have an inverse relationship between spatial and temporal proximity, while poorly integrated groups have a direct relationship between the two.

R. H. T. Smith and various other authors following his lead have attempted to unravel the complexities of the relationships between the

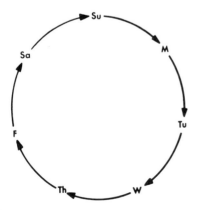

Figure 1. The 7-day market week. Su = Sunday, M = Monday, Tu = Tuesday, W = Wednesday, Th = Thursday, F = Friday, and Sa = Saturday.

spatial location and temporal periodicity of markets by analyzing available maps of market locations as point patterns in space and time (Fagerlund and Smith 1970; Good 1972; Hill and Smith 1972; R. H. T. Smith 1970, 1971a, 1971b, 1972, 1974; Wood 1972; Yeung 1974). In order to test the hypothesis that spatial proximity is inversely related to temporal proximity, they compare the spatial distances between neighboring periodic markets with the number of days by which their occurrences are separated. R. H. T. Smith (1972) has tested these relationships in 25 areas in Europe, Asia, Africa, and Latin America, and all but one of these areas give at least partial confirmation to the hypothesis. In addition, the hypothesis that spatial patterns of markets are essentially uniform (evenly spaced) has been tested using nearest-neighbor analysis, examining the patterns of all markets and of the markets taking place on each day of the week. These patterns have been examined in various areas of West Africa, and although a number of inconsistencies occur, there are indications that uniform patterns are the norm (see R. H. T. Smith 1971b:338–340).

HIGHLAND ECUADOR

In highland Ecuador, as in almost all of Hispanic America, the 7-day market week and the style of market administration are derived from colonial Spanish models established in the sixteenth and seventeenth centuries. Although some pre-Columbian features of market organization, such as barter trading and the giving of bonus quantities (*yapa*), still survive, colonial and postcolonial commercial organization is predominant (R. J. Bromley and Symanski 1974:8–11). Highland Ecuador is defined as the area of Ecuador above an altitude of 1500 meters and forms a continuous mountains belt stretching about 620 kilometers from the Colombian frontier in the north to the Peruvian frontier in the south. It has an area of about 77,000 square kilometers and averages about 120 kilometers in width. Altitudes range from 1500 meters to over 6000 meters, and substantial uninhabited areas are found above the altitudinal limit of agriculture at about 3500 meters. Settlement is concentrated at altitudes between 2000 and 3000 meters in various basins and valleys that are separated by uninhabited or sparsely populated mountain areas. In 1972 the population of the region was estimated to be 3.0 million, about 33 percent of whom lived in urban areas with over 5000 inhabitants. In 1972 the average population density of the region was about 39 persons per square kilometer. Highland Ecuador can be divided into three main subregions: the northern highlands, the central highlands, and the southern highlands. The four largest urban centers are Quito (1974 population 597,000), in the northern highlands; Cuenca (1974 population 105,000), in the southern highlands; and Ambato (1974 population 77,000) and Riobamba (1974 population 58,000), in the central highlands (Oficina de los Censos Nacionales 1974:7–15).

The data presented on contemporary market centers in highland Ecuador were collected in 1970 and 1971 as part of a broader study on periodic and daily markets in the region (R. J. Bromley 1975). As no major listing of market centers existed at the time of the field work, markets were located and studied by direct observation and extensive use of informants in all populated areas of the highlands. In total, 164 market centers were located,[2] and 139 were visited. Counts of market activity on one or more days of the week were made in 115 centers, and estimates were made for the remaining days and centers on the basis of information from local informants. In general, counts were made in all of the larger centers on all days of the week and in the medium-sized centers on all periodic market days. Coverage of the smaller centers was less complete because of their very limited importance. Livestock markets are not considered here, attention being focused on market-place trade in foodstuffs, consumer durables, and services.

In order to define the markets in highland Ecuador and to quantify their levels of activity, it was necessary to define the individual stalls and to assess their levels of turnover. The term "stall" is used to refer to all independent retailing, wholesaling, and service enterprises on public land,[3] whether fixed or mobile in location. The person in charge of that stall may work alone or may have one or more assistants at the same spot. The stall holder may display his merchandise on the ground, on his person, on benches or tables, in a booth or stand, or even in a motor vehicle or pushcart. All stalls are classified into two size groups: large, with a daily turnover of over 250 sucres;[4] and small, with a daily turnover of under 250 sucres. Detailed informal interviews and prolonged observation of individual traders showed that the average large stall has a mean daily turnover by value about four times as great as the average small stall. On the basis of these data, it was decided to create a measure of daily turnover called the trading unit. Each small stall working for 1 day is considered to be equivalent to 1 trading unit, and each large stall working for 1 day to 4 trading units. A market is then defined as any agglomeration of traders on public land having more than 10 trading units and occurring regularly on 1 or more days of the week. The number of trading units in a market on each day of the week gives a more accurate impression of the total activity and importance of the market than the number of stalls.

[2] It is unlikely that over eight market centers were missed during the research for this article. Those that were missed were almost certainly very small centers.

[3] In some parts of the world, markets are held on private land, although they are, of course, open to the public. In highland Ecuador, however, no markets are known to be held on private land, and the distinction between private and public land is a useful part of the distinction between nonmarket and market activity.

[4] In 1971, 25 sucres were equivalent to $1 (U.S.).

Market centers were initially classified on a logarithmic scale that was applied to the weekly total of trading units—that is, the sum of the totals for each of the 7 days of the week. The logarithmic scale was chosen because of the great variations in the weekly totals of market activity in the different market centers of highland Ecuador. Throughout this article the size of a market center is measured in terms of the amount of weekly market activity in that center. The average first-order market center is one-tenth the size of the average second-order market center, one-hundredth the size of the average third-order market center, and one-thousandth the size of the average fourth-order market center. (See Table 1.)

From Table 2, a number of important differences between the three subregions of highland Ecuador can be discerned. The northern and central highlands are almost twice as densely populated as the southern highlands. The northern highlands are about three and a half times as urbanized as the central and southern highlands because of the concentration of almost 600,000 people in the city of Quito. Over three-quarters of the total market trading units in the northern highlands are concentrated in Quito, so that the northern highlands have only about half the number of market centers per capita as the central or southern highlands. The density of market centers is notably higher in the central highlands than in the northern or southern highlands. (See Map 1.)

TABLE 1
The System Used to Classify Market Centers According to the Weekly Totals of Trading Units

Order		Logarithmic Number of Trading Units	Class Limits in Trading Units	
1	1b	$10^{1.01}$ to $10^{1.50}$	11 to	31
	1a	$10^{1.51}$ to $10^{2.00}$	32 to	100
2	2b	$10^{2.01}$ to $10^{2.50}$	101 to	316
	2a	$10^{2.51}$ to $10^{3.00}$	317 to	1,000
3	3b	$10^{3.01}$ to $10^{3.50}$	1,001 to	3,162
	3a	$10^{3.51}$ to $10^{4.00}$	3,163 to	10,000
4	4b	$10^{4.01}$ to $10^{4.50}$	10,001 to	31,623
	4a	$10^{4.51}$ to $10^{5.00}$	31,624 to	100,000

TABLE 2
*Principal Characteristics of the Three Subregions of Highland
Ecuador*

| Characteristics | Location[a] | | | Total |
	A	B	C	
Number of 1st-order market centers	25	39	31	95
Number of 2nd-order market centers	10	23	14	47
Number of 3rd-order market centers	6	10	2	18
Number of 4th-order market centers	1	2	1	4
1972 population (thousands)	1,195	1,048	757	3,000
1972 population density in persons per square kilometer	48	48	25	39
1972 percentage of population living in urban centers with over 5,000 inhabitants	57	17	17	33
Number of persons per market center (thousands) in 1972	28	14	16	18

a. *A = northern highlands; B = central highlands; C =
southern highlands. Total = highland Ecuador.*

DAY-TO-DAY VARIATIONS IN
MARKET ACTIVITY[5]

Aggregate Variations

Aggregating the 164 market centers of highland Ecuador together and
examining the totals of trading units for each day of the week (Table 3), it
is clear that weekly market activity is concentrated on Saturday and Sun-

[5] Throughout this article, Quito is treated as being similar in character to the other large
market centers of highland Ecuador. The fact that it is the only market center with separate
intraurban periodic markets meeting on different days of the week, and with mobile traders
following cyclical itineraries within the urban area, is ignored. Instead, the city is simply
considered in terms of the aggregate totals of market activity for each day of the week and for
the week as a whole. A detailed consideration of the intraurban markets of Quito is available
in R. J. Bromley (1974).

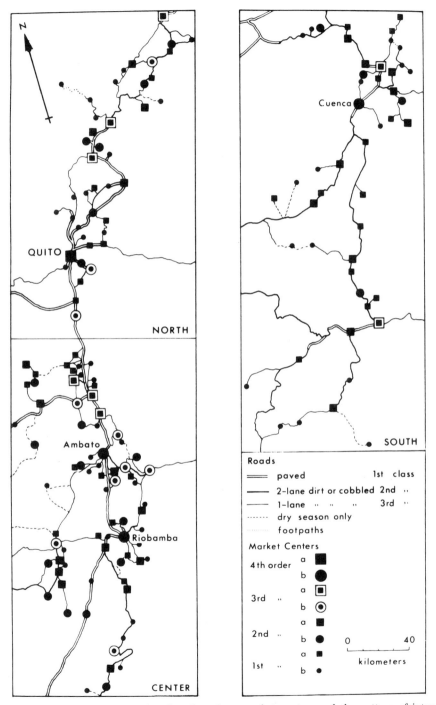

Map 1. The distribution and order of produce market centers and the pattern of inter-market road communications in highland Ecuador in 1971.

TABLE 3
Day-to-Day Variations in the Numbers of Trading Units in the Market Centers of Highland Ecuador,
According to the Order of the Market Centers

Market Centers		Su	M	Tu	W	Th	F	Sa	Total for Whole Week
4th order	N	17,731	23,952	17,978	17,774	16,929	16,653	26,356	137,373
	%	12.9	17.5	13.1	12.9	12.3	12.1	19.2	100.0
3rd order	N	13,911	2,809	4,711	3,496	10,841	3,952	17,799	57,519
	%	24.2	4.9	8.2	6.1	18.8	6.9	30.9	100.0
2nd order	N	10,529	427	311	360	1,821	1,704	1,914	17,066
	%	61.7	2.5	1.8	2.1	10.7	10.0	11.2	100.0
1st order	N	2,484	26	26	69	243	378	266	3,492
	%	71.2	0.7	0.7	2.0	7.0	10.8	7.6	100.0
All orders	N	44,655	27,214	23,026	21,699	29,834	22,687	46,335	215,450
	%	20.7	12.6	10.7	10.1	13.9	10.5	21.5	100.0

day, the 2 days of the weekend. If market activity were evenly spread over all 7 days of the week, each day would have about 14.3 percent of the weekly total. In reality, however, Saturday has 21.5 percent of the total weekly trading activity, and Sunday has a further 20.7 percent, while each of the remaining 5 days of the week has only between 10.1 and 13.9 percent. Thus, the average weekday has a little over half the market activity of either of the weekend days. Of the weekdays, Thursday and Monday are the most important, these 2 having significantly more market activity than the other 3 weekdays.

By examining the average number of trading units for each day of the week in relation to the size of the market centers, it is easy to discern that there are significant differences in periodicity between the different orders of market centers. Market activity in first-order market centers is heavily concentrated on Sundays (71.2 percent of the weekly total of trading units), with Thursday, Friday, and Saturday having small amounts of activity and Monday, Tuesday, and Wednesday almost no activity. This pattern is similar in second-order market centers, although Sunday's importance is less pronounced (61.7 percent). In contrast, third-order market centers show a concentration of market activity on Saturday (30.9 percent), Sunday (24.2 percent), and Thursday (18.8 percent), with only between 4.9 and 8.2 percent of the weekly market activity on each of the other four days. The fourth-order market centers have a concentration of activity on Saturday (19.2 percent), the most active market day in Quito and Riobamba, and on Monday (17.5 percent), the most active market day in Ambato. All of the remaining 5 days have been 12.1 and 13.1 percent of total weekly market activity in the fourth-order centers.

The simplest available measure of the amount of variation in the market activity on the different days of the week is the statistical measure known as the coefficient of variation (V), defined as the standard deviation of the daily totals divided by the mean daily total for the seven days.[6] For a 7-day week, V can range from 0, if all the days are exactly equal, to 2.65, if all market activity is concentrated on 1 day of the week. The coefficient of variation for all 164 market centers in highland Ecuador together is only .34, indicating a relatively even spread of market activity. This apparently even spread is a result of the low coefficient of variation for the fourth-order market centers $(V = .20)$, which make up 64 percent of total market activity, and the relatively low coefficient for the third-order market centers $(V = .73)$, which make up a further 27 percent of the highland Ecuadorian total of market activity. For the first- and second-order

[6] In calculating the coefficient of variation, the sample standard deviation is used for two reasons: first, because the counts of marketplace activity were not necessarily taken on consecutive dates, so that they cannot be considered as a "whole population" of a single week; and, second, because the 7 days considered are effectively 7 sample days from the year 1971.

market centers, however, coefficients of variation are much higher ($V = 1.78$ and $V = 1.49$), reflecting the overwhelming concentration of market activity on Sundays in these centers.

Day-to-Day Variations in Individual Market Centers

If the 164 market centers are examined individually, considerably more variation is apparent than is evident from simply comparing the totals for the different orders of market center. Of the 164 market centers, 23 have at least a single moderate daily market, with more than 10 trading units on every day of the week. With the notable exception of Empalme Aloag, a first-order market center that has a stable daily market and no periodic market day, daily markets are mainly concentrated in the higher-order market centers (Table 4).

If a periodic market day in any given market center is defined as a day with over 10 trading units and with over 25 percent more trading units than the least active day of the week, then, with the exception of Empalme Aloag, all of the market centers of highland Ecuador have between 1 and 4 periodic market days each week. On the whole, the larger a market center is, the greater the number of periodic market days it has each week (Table 5). Those market centers that have a daily market tend to have a greater

TABLE 4

The Size Distribution of Market Centers with and without Daily Markets in Highland Ecuador in 1971[a]

	Market Centers			
	With Daily Markets[b]		Without Daily Markets	
Order	N	% of total	N	% of total
4	4	100.0	0	0.0
3	13	72.2	5	27.8
2	5	10.6	42	89.4
1	1	1.1	94	98.9
All market centers	23	14.0	141	86.0

a. Aggregating 3rd and 4th orders to give a 3x2 matrix, $x^2 = 86.3$ with 2 degrees of freedom ($p < .001$).
b. Over 10 trading units on every day of the week.

TABLE 5
*The Number of Periodic Market Days Each Week in the Market
Centers of Highland Ecuador in 1971 in Relation to the Order
of the Market Centers[a]*

| Order | Number of Periodic Market Days Each Week | | | | | Total |
	0	1	2	3	4	
4	0	0	2	1	1	4
3	0	3	12	2	1	18
2	0	37	8	2	0	47
1	1	91	3	0	0	95
All market centers together	1	131	25	5	2	164

   a.   *Aggregating 3rd with 4th orders of market centers, 0
with 1 periodic market day, and 3 with 4 periodic market days
to give a 3x3 matrix, $X^2 = 78.7$, with 4 degrees of freedom
(p < .001).*

number of periodic market days than those that do not have a daily
market (Table 6), indicating a general tendency for the larger market
centers to have their market activity spread over more days in the week
than the smaller market centers.

   In any given market center with more than 1 periodic market day, the
largest periodic market day can be called the major market day, and the
remaining periodic market day(s) can be called the secondary market
day(s). Of the 163 market centers with periodic market days, 32, or
approximately one-fifth, have both a major market day and 1 or more
secondary market days. The remaining 131 centers have only 1 periodic
market day per week, which, to make them comparable with the centers
with more than 1 periodic market day, can be described as the major
market day. In the market centers with 2 or more periodic market days
each week, the ratio between the number of trading units on the major
market day and the number of trading units on the most important of the
secondary market days provides a useful indication of the relative
importance of different types of periodic market days. This ratio varies
from as much as 211:1 to as little as 1.03:1. Taking the 32 market centers
with 2 or more periodic market days each week, there is no statistically
significant relationship between the ratio of the major market day to the
largest, or only, secondary market day and the population of the market

TABLE 6
*The Number of Periodic Market Days Each Week in the Market
Centers of Highland Ecuador in 1971 in Relation to the Presence
or Absence of Daily Markets[a]*

Market Centers	Number of Periodic Market Days Each Week					Total
	0	1	2	3	4	
With a daily market	1	6	12	2	2	23
Without a daily market	0	125	13	3	0	141
All market centers together	1	131	25	5	2	164

a. *Aggregating 0 with 1 periodic market day, and 3 with
4 periodic market days, to give a 2x3 matrix, $X^2 = 40.6$, with
2 degrees of freedom (p < .001).*

centers ($r = -.07$). Similarly, there is no significant relationship between
this ratio and the size of the market centers measured in terms of the total
weekly number of trading units in their produce markets ($r = -.06$).
These noncorrelations are an indication of the importance of peculiar local
circumstances, and particularly of historical legacies, in the choice of
market days. The cases of low ratios between major market day and
largest secondary market day can usually be attributed to an incomplete
change of market day from the one day to the other, as in the cases of
Píllaro, Salcedo, and Patate (R. D. F. Bromley and R. J. Bromley
1975:105–106), or to the existence of a substantial daily market spreading
market activity more smoothly over the whole week, as in the cases of
Cuenca and Quito.

If the choice of major market days in the 163 market centers with
periodic market days is examined, there is a great concentration of
periodic markets on Sunday in the first- and second-order market centers,
a concentration on Sunday and Saturday in the third-order market
centers, and a concentration on Saturday in the fourth-order market
centers (Table 7). Of the market centers, 69.3 percent have Sunday as
their major market day, and a further 12.3 percent have Saturday, giving
a total of 81.6 percent of major market days on weekends and only 18.4
percent on the 5 weekdays together. The 2 most popular weekdays for
major market days are Friday, which is used mainly by first- and second-
order market centers, and Thursday, which is used by all orders of market
centers. Only two market centers use Monday, only one uses Wednesday,

and none uses Tuesday for a major market day. This distribution reflects a number of significant factors:

1. the preference of customers and market administrators for weekend market days, when commerce does not seriously conflict with primary and secondary production
2. the tradition of Sunday markets, which is still maintained in most of the smaller market centers
3. the official attempts to move large markets from Sundays to Saturdays or weekdays in the large market centers (see R. D. F. Bromley and R. J. Bromley 1975)
4. the tendency for some smaller periodic markets to be arranged on the days immediately preceding larger periodic markets (that is, on Friday and Saturday, before larger markets on Saturday and Sunday), so that traders and customers can move on from the smaller markets to the larger ones and so that goods bought by collecting wholesalers in the smaller markets can subsequently be sold in the larger markets on the next day
5. the tendency for some traders and market administrators to attempt

TABLE 7

The Distribution of Major Market Days amongst the 163 Produce Market Centers in Highland Ecuador with Periodic Market Days in 1971 by Order of Market Centers

Order		Su	M	Tu	W	Th	F	Sa	Total
					Major Market Days				
4	N	0	1	0	0	1	0	2	4
	%	0.0	25.0	0.0	0.0	25.0	0.0	50.0	100.0
3	N	8	0	0	0	3	0	7	18
	%	44.4	0.0	0.0	0.0	16.7	0.0	38.9	100.0
2	N	31	1	0	0	4	6	5	47
	%	66.0	2.1	0.0	0.0	8.5	12.8	10.6	100.0
1	N	74	0	0	1	3	10	6	94
	%	78.7	0.0	0.0	1.1	3.2	10.6	6.4	100.0
Total		113	2	0	1	11	16	20	163
	%	69.3	1.2	0.0	0.6	6.8	9.8	12.3	100.0

to "forestall" weekend market purchases by trying to persuade
people to buy a day earlier (Saturday forestalling Sunday, and Friday forestalling Saturday)

6. the traditional recognition of Thursday as the day with maximum
   temporal separation from Sunday markets and hence a logical day
   for midweek markets. Wednesday would be equally suitable, but the
   only example is Simiatug, a small and little-known first-order market
   in Bolívar Province. When asked why Wednesday was not chosen as
   a market day, local officials and traders often stress the "no
   precedent" argument, just as this argument was used against the
   choice of Monday as the major market day for Ambato in 1870 (R.
   D. F. Bromley and R. J. Bromley 1975:104–105).

Secondary Market Days

The distribution of secondary market days over the week is rather different from that of major market days because, of course, the definition of
major and secondary periodic market days precludes them from both
occurring in the same market center on the same day. Thus, secondary
market days are not so heavily concentrated on the weekend and have a
more even spread over the week as a whole (Table 8).

While the coefficient of variation for the number of major market days
on the different days of the week is relatively high at 1.73, reflecting the
high concentration of major market days on Sundays, the coefficient of
variation for the number of secondary periodic market days on the different days of the week is only .64. The most common secondary market
days are Sunday, Wednesday, and Friday, and the least common are Mon-

TABLE 8
*The Distribution of Secondary Market Days amongst the 32 Market
Centers in Highland Ecuador with More Than One Periodic Market
Day Each Week in 1971 by Order of Market Center*

	Secondary Market Days							
Order	Su	M	Tu	W	Th	F	Sa	Total
4	1	1	1	2	0	2	0	7
3	5	0	3	3	4	4	0	19
2	4	0	1	2	2	2	1	12
1	1	0	0	1	1	0	0	3
Total	11	1	5	8	7	8	1	41
%	26.9	2.4	12.2	19.5	17.1	19.5	2.4	100.0

day and Saturday. The importance of Sunday as a secondary market day is a reflection of the fact that a high proportion of the market centers that have a day other than Sunday as their major market day have Sunday as a secondary market day. This is presumably either a historical legacy from the days when their major market day was Sunday or a strategy of traders or local officials to capture the custom of the rural population attending Mass on Sunday.

In those market centers with 2, 3, or 4 periodic market days each week, there are, of course, various alternative spacings of the market days, ranging from a minimum spacing when all market days are adjacent (for example, with 2 periodic market days each week, the 2 days being Saturday and Sunday) to maximum temporal spacing when the market days are as far apart as possible (for example, periodic market days each week, the 2 days being Sunday and Thursday).[7]

Almost 70 percent of the 32 market centers with more than 1 periodic market day each week have maximum temporal spacing of their market days, indicating a strong tendency of market organizers to try to space the market days in their market center as widely as possible (Table 9). Minimum temporal spacing is rather more popular than medium spacing, indicating some tendency for an alternative polarization in a few market centers. The predominance of maximum temporal spacing in the market centers of highland Ecuador is paralleled by similar spacing in most other parts of the world (e.g., Hodder 1971:348–349; Skinner 1964:14, Wood 1973:68).

The 32 market centers with 1 or more periodic market days each week provide an opportunity to test Symanski's (1973) hypotheses on market day spacing in market centers with more than 1 market day per week. The high proportion of market centers with maximum temporal spacing is an indication that Symanski's minor market day hypothesis is correct—that

[7] Spacing scores are as follows:

> With 2 market days per week: max. 6, med. 4, min. 2.
> With 3 market days per week: max. 6, med. 5 or 4, min. 3.
> With 4 market days per week: max. 6, med. 5, min. 4.

These are calculated by taking each market day in turn, figuring the minimum temporal distance from that market day to the nearest market day, in days, and adding together the scores for the different periodic market days to give a total for the market centers. Temporal distances are measured backward or forward in the week, whichever is shorter. Thus, for example, Quito has 2 periodic market days each week, Saturday and Tuesday. These 2 days are temporally 3 days apart. Thus, the total temporal spacing score for Quito is 3 + 3, or 6, the maximum possible. Similarly, Zumbahua, a second-order market center in Cotopaxi Province, has 3 periodic market days each week, Friday, Saturday, and Sunday, the 3 days being adjacent. Thus, for each of the days, the minimum temporal spacing to another periodic market day is 1 day. As a result, the total temporal spacing score for Zumbahua is 1 + 1 + 1, or 3, the minimum possible with 3 periodic market days per week.

Raymond J. Bromley

TABLE 9
Temporal Spacing of Periodic Market Days in the 32 Produce
Market Centers in Highland Ecuador with More Than One Periodic
Market Day Each Week in 1971

Spacing of the Market Days	Number of Periodic Market Days per Week			Total	
	2	*3*	*4*	*N*	*%*
Maximum	18	3	1	22	68.8
Medium	3	1	0	4	12.5
Minimum	4	1	1	6	18.7
Total	25	5	2	32	100.0

"the most important minor market day occurs approximately midway between the occurrence of major market days [1973:264]."

Symanski's wholesale market day hypothesis is more difficult to verify because relatively few market centers have more than 2 periodic market days each week, and those with 2 generally have a minor market day rather than a wholesale market day. Of the 7 market centers that have 3 or 4 periodic market days each week, 4 have a periodic market day on the day immediately preceding the major market day. A build-up of wholesale trading, and sometimes of retailing, on the day immediately preceding the major market day is visible in many of the larger market centers of highland Ecuador. The existence or nonexistence of a wholesale market day can be tested by comparing the level of trading activity on the day immediately preceding the major market day with the level on the penultimate day before the major market day. Of the 22 third- and fourth-order market centers, 10 have a significant difference in trading activity between the day before the major market day and the penultimate day before the major market day. Of these 10 market centers, 8 have more trading activity on the day before the major market day than on the penultimate day (that is, they accord with Symanski's wholesale market day hypothesis), and 2 have the opposite condition (that is, they do not accord with the hypothesis). The wholesale market day hypothesis can therefore be tentatively accepted, but the wholesale market day must be considered rarer and less important than the minor market day(s).

Symanski's minimal market day hypothesis, that the day immediately following the major market day has the lowest level of trading activity of any day in the week, can be tested for the 42 market centers with a major market day and with a least one trading unit on 6 or 7 days each week. Of these 42, 38 have the day immediately following the major market day having the lowest, or equal to the lowest, total of trading units in the week. Hence, 38 out of the 42 show agreement with the minimal market day hypothesis, although it should be noted that, in most of these cases, the "minimal" market day is equal to, rather than smaller than, some other days of the week with low levels of trading activity. Like the wholesale market day hypothesis, therefore, the minimal market day hypothesis can be tentatively accepted as correct, although there are a few exceptional cases. It is clear that large Ecuadorian market centers generally exhibit a form of "temporal forestalling," with increased trading activity preceding the major market day and with decreased trading activity following it. (See Figure 2.)

Particularly in the smaller market centers of highland Ecuador, there is a high degree of day-to-day variation in market activity. Of these, 68 percent have coefficients of day-to-day variation of over 2.5 (Table 10), indicating a virtually total concentration of market activity on 1 day of the week in each of these centers. Less than 4 percent have coefficients of variation of under .5, which indicates a fairly even spread of market activity over the whole week. The remaining 28 percent of the centers have coefficients of variation of between .5 and 2.5, indicating a considerable degree of concentration of market activity on 1, 2, or 3 days each week in these centers. Not surprisingly, the larger market centers tend to have low coefficients of variation, because most of them have daily markets and more than one periodic market day each week. The smaller market centers tend to have high, and usually the maximum possible, coefficients of variation, indicating the absence of daily markets and the existence of only 1 periodic market day each week. The coefficient of variation is negatively correlated with average total weekly trading activity in the market centers ($r = -.45$; statistically significant at the .01 level) and with the population of the market centers ($r = -.39$; statistically significant at the .01 level).

Day-to-Day Variations: Summary Comments

The principal conclusions of this section can be summarized as five major points:

1. Market activity is concentrated at weekends, mainly on Sundays in the smaller market centers and mainly on Saturdays in the larger market centers. Taking all market centers, Sunday is by far the most common major market day in highland Ecuador. In terms of total volume of trading activity, however, Saturday is slightly more important because of its predominance in many of the largest market centers.

Raymond J. Bromley

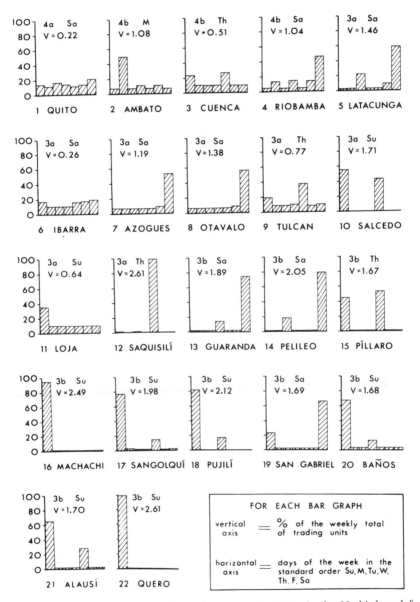

Figure 2. Day-to-day variations in produce market activity in the 22 third- and fourth-order produce market centers in highland Ecuador in 1971. At the top of each bar graph, the order of the market center, the major market day, and the coefficient of variation (V) are listed. At the bottom of each bar graph, the name and size ranking of the market center are given.

TABLE 10
Coefficients of Day-to-Day Variation in Produce Market Activity in Relation to Order of the Market Center, for All Highland Ecuadorian Produce Market Centers in 1971[a]

	Coefficients of Variation						
Order	0.00 to 0.49	0.50 to 0.99	1.00 to 1.49	1.50 to 1.99	2.00 to 2.49	2.50 to 2.65	Total
4	1	1	2	0	0	0	4
3	1	2	3	7	3	2	18
2	3	0	0	5	14	25	47
1	1	1	1	3	4	85	95
Total N	6	4	6	15	21	112	164
%	3.7	2.4	3.7	9.1	12.8	68.3	100.0

a. *Amalgamating 3rd with 4th orders, columns 1, 2, and 3 together, and columns 4 and 5 together, to give a 3x3 matrix, $X^2 = 73.6$, with 4 degrees of freedom (p < .001).*

2. The great majority of market centers in highland Ecuador have periodic markets as the dominant form of market activity. Daily markets are much less important than periodic markets and are mainly located in the larger urban centers. This is in accordance with the hypothesis that the development of daily markets is usually associated with urban growth (see Hodder 1971). Daily markets depend on a large and relatively stable daily demand for produce, and this is most frequently found in densely populated urban areas. Such a stable demand also occasionally occurs in smaller market centers where markets cater to regular passing traffic.
3. Most market centers have only 1 periodic market day each week, but some centers, particularly the larger ones, have 2, 3, or occasionally 4 periodic market days each week.
4. Secondary market days tend to be temporally separated from major periodic market days so as to minimize competition between the market gatherings occurring on different days of the week in any given market center. Thus, there is strong confirmatory evidence to prove Symanski's minor market day hypothesis.
5. There is a tendency in some of the larger market centers for market activity to increase on the day before the major market day and to decline to its weekly minimum on the day after the major market

day. Thus, there is at least a moderate agreement with Symanski's wholesale market day and minimal market day hypotheses.

When asked to explain these phenomena, market organizers and traders tend to lay emphasis on tradition, and particularly on the customary division of the week into working days (weekdays) and days for rest, recreation, religion, and commerce (weekends). Thus, the predominance of Sunday markets is explained by the traditional importance of Sunday markets (R. D. F. Bromley and R. J. Bromley 1975), the need to keep the weekdays free for primary and secondary production, and the opportunity Sunday affords to sell goods to the rural population attending Mass in the market centers. The avoidance of certain market days, for example, Monday and Tuesday, which are very unpopular for major or secondary periodic market gatherings, is usually explained by citing the preference for a weekend market day or by saying that there is no precedent for markets on those days. Most local officials seem to have a general understanding of the temporal spacing of market days, both within and between market centers. Thus, maximum temporal spacing between different periodic market days in the same market center is explained not only by tradition but, more importantly, by the logic of spacing the market days as widely as possible to reduce competition and to improve service to the consumer.

Although the generalizations cited for highland Ecuadorian market centers all apply to the majority of the centers, there are, in all cases, some notable exceptions. These exceptions are usually explicable in terms of unusual local circumstances, and particularly in terms of historical legacies and human idiosyncracies. Just as there are no "perfect" settlement and central-place patterns in highland Ecuador explicable solely in terms of present-day economic locational forces, there are no "perfect" patterns of temporal organization of market activity explicable solely in terms of optimum economically based spatiotemporal organization.

SPATIOTEMPORAL ASPECTS OF MARKET PERIODICITY

From Figure 3 it is clear that the spatial pattern of market activity in central highland Ecuador is markedly different on each day of the week and that anyone wishing to visit a market must know both when and where markets take place. Similar day-to-day variations in spatial patterns of periodic market activity are found in the northern and southern highlands. Knowledge of day-to-day variations in market activity in the nearest and/or most frequently patronized market center is almost universal in highland Ecuador. Most consumers are also familiar with the

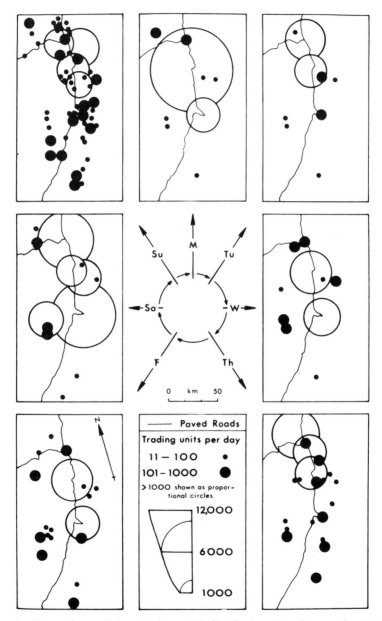

Figure 3. Day-to-day variations in the spatial distribution of produce market activity in central highland Ecuador in 1971.

weekly regime of market activity in anything from 1 to 10 nearby market
centers, and the market days of the main market centers in the highlands
are widely known throughout Ecuador. Many market traders have a
remarkably detailed knowledge of market sizes, days, and specializations
for a substantial section, or even for the majority, of the highlands. Such
knowledge of spatiotemporal patterns is particularly notable among the
Otavaleño Indian textile traders and among the larger-scale "white"
traders dealing in durable goods and livestock. To such traders, and also to
some transporters, a knowledge of when and where particular products
can be bought or sold in the marketplace may mean the difference
between prosperity and economic ruin. Details of times and amounts of
market activity are passed on by word of mouth between traders in the
same way as price and quality information. Surprisingly, no printed guide
to markets, such as the British *Markets Year Book* (World's Fair, Ltd.
1974) or the Nigerian market almanacs (e.g., Midwest State of Nigeria
1969) has ever been produced in Ecuador.

Tests Using R. H. T. Smith's Method of Analyzing Spatiotemporal Integration

An initial test of the degree of spatiotemporal integration of the periodic
markets in highland Ecuador can be conducted by using a slightly
modified version of R. H. T. Smith's method. Smith's method implicitly
assumes that all market centers have only 1 periodic market day per week
and that all periodic markets are equal in importance. In order to give
greater precision, results have been calculated separately for each of the
major subregions of highland Ecuador (north, center, and south), as well
as for the highlands as a whole. Results have also been calculated for
second-, third-, and fourth-order market centers together and for all
market centers together. Spatial distance between market centers is the
over-the-route distance in kilometers multiplied by an index of between
1.0 and 5.0 to take account of the varying friction of distance resulting
from different types of routes. The resulting spatial distance is given in
"distance units."[8] Temporal distance between periodic markets is
measured in days, using a terminology distinct from Smith's although
following the same method.

In a well-integrated system of periodic markets, one would expect an
inverse relationship between temporal distance and spatial distance,

[8] The numbers of distance units equivalent to 1 kilometer of over-the-route distance are as
follows: first class road (tarmac surface, two lanes, all weather), 1.0; second-class road (gravel
or well-maintained cobble or dirt surface, two lanes, all weather), 1.2; third-class road
(gravel, cobble, or dirt surface, one lane with passing places, all weather), 1.6; dry season
road, 2.4, and footpath (passable only for pedestrians and animals), 5.0.

because neighboring market centers tend to maximize the temporal spacing between their market days so as to minimize competition. In a poorly integrated or unintegrated system, one would expect a direct relationship between temporal distance and spatial distance, because neighboring markets tend to meet on the same day or on adjacent days, so maximizing competition. In order to measure the level of integration using Smith's method, the spatial distances between each market center and the nearest market centers with periodic markets occurring 3, 2, 1, and 0 days away are measured. These distances are tabulated for all market centers in the region or group under study, and the average distance is calculated for spacings of 3, 2, 1, and 0 days. The average distances are listed in Table 11, and they appear in graph form in Figure 4. The analysis is based on a population of 163 market centers, each having 1 major periodic market day per week.

TABLE 11

Average Distances between Market Centers and the Nearest Market Centers with Market Days 3, 2, 1, and 0 Days Away, by Region and Size of Market Center, Using R. H. T. Smith's Method[a]

Order	Sub-region	N^b	Temporal Separation in Days				r^c
			3	2	1	0	
2nd,	North	17	241.2	112.9	24.7	82.7	0.80
3rd,	Center	35	150.1	67.5	49.1	75.2	0.71
and	South	17	190.1	192.9	57.9	71.2	0.86
4th							
Total		69	182.4	109.6	45.3	76.1	0.84
	North	41	142.4	72.9	38.7	35.8	0.92
All	Center	74	75.4	44.7	32.4	51.1	0.61
	South	48	233.8	203.8	76.4	41.0	0.97
Total		163	138.9	98.6	46.9	44.3	0.96

  a. *Distances are calculated in distance units. The product-moment correlation coefficient (r) is between X (distance in hundreds of distance units) and Y (temporal separation in days). A strong positive correlation indicates a direct relationship between temporal and spatial separation (an unintegrated system), whilst a strong negative correlation indicates an inverse relationship between temporal and spatial separation (a well-integrated system).*
  b. *Number of market centers under study.*
  c. *Correlation coefficient between spatial and temporal distances.*

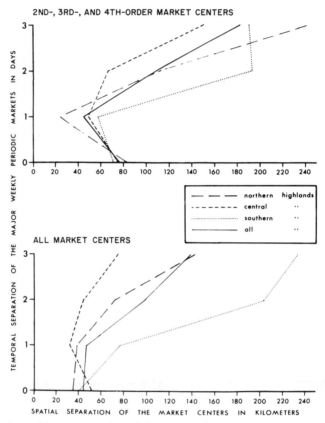

Figure 4. A graphic representation of the average distances between market centers and the nearest market centers with market days 3, 2, 1, and 0 days away, by region and size of market center, using R. H. T. Smith's method.

The analysis based on R. H. T. Smith's method[9] shows that spatiotemporal patterns of market activity are very poorly integrated in highland Ecuador as a whole and in each of the three major subregions when these are considered separately. In general, levels of integration are slightly higher in the central highlands than in the northern or southern highlands, and the highest levels of integration are shown when second-, third-, and

[9] With R. H. T. Smith's method of analyzing spatio temporal integration, a practical problem occurs when there is no market center in the whole highlands with a market day temporally separated by a given number of days from a particular market center. Thus, when only second-, third-, and fourth-order market centers are considered, there is no market center in the whole highlands with a major market day that has 3 days of temporal separation from a market occurring on Saturday; that is, there is no second-, third-, or fourth-order market center in the highlands with a major market day on Tuesday or Wednesday. This problem occurs for 14 market centers with major market days on Saturday. Rather than

fourth-order market centers are taken together, excluding first-order market centers. These results reflect the high concentration of major market days on Saturdays and Sundays and the particularly high proportion of Sunday markets in the first-order market centers. Distances tend to be low from most market centers to the nearest market centers with markets on the same day or with 1 day's separation and high to market centers with market days with 2 or 3 days' separation. Thus, for most of the market centers of highland Ecuador, their major market days are the same as or only 1 day apart from those of the nearest neighboring market centers.

The distances between market centers with different temporal spacings vary considerably according to the size of the market centers and the section of the highlands for which the analysis is being made. Naturally enough, distances tend to be high between higher-order market centers because these are relatively few in number and are spaced over the whole highlands. Distances tend to be lower when all orders of market centers are taken into account because the number and density of market centers are much greater. Both for higher-order market centers and for all market centers, intermarket distances tend to be lowest in the central highlands, where the density of market centers is greatest. Intermarket distances are highest in the northern and southern highlands, where the density of market centers is much lower, particularly in the southernmost province of Loja. The slightly greater levels of integration in the central highlands than in the northern or southern highlands indicate that the spatiotemporal integration of market days may well be largely a result of competition between neighboring market centers in close proximity. This conclusion is confirmed when the internal variations in levels of integration within the subregions are examined. In most cases the areas with relatively high densities of market centers have more integrated spatiotemporal patterns of major periodic market days than those areas where the density of market centers is lower.

Tests Using a New Method of Analyzing Spatiotemporal Integration

The implicit assumptions of Smith's method on the equality of market centers and the existence of 1 periodic market per market center per week

---

abandon the whole analysis or record a distance of "infinity," it was decided to record the same distance as the greatest distance on the whole matrix of calculated distances (518.4 distance units) for each of the problem cases. A similar problem occurred for the one first-order Wednesday market in the analysis of all market centers together. No other market center in the whole highlands had a major market day on Wednesday, so, again, the greatest distance on the whole matrix (746.4 distance units) was recorded for the temporal spacing of 0 days. This problem is eliminated in the new method described shortly because of the inclusion of midweek secondary periodic market days in the analysis.

are obviously unrealistic and distort the results of the analysis of spatiotemporal integration. Further distortions may result from the varying density of market centers in different parts of the highlands. Because of these distortions, a method has been devised that takes account of secondary market days and of the unequal importance of the market centers and that eliminates any anomalous effects resulting from the fact that the densities of market centers vary between the different zones of the highlands. Historical evidence (R. J. Bromley 1976) shows that larger market centers are usually older than smaller ones. The organizers of new, small markets generally choose their market days with full knowledge of the timing of nearby larger markets. While market organizers and traders in the smaller or incipient market centers tend to fear the competition of larger market centers, the market organizers and traders in larger market centers tend to ignore the competition of smaller market centers. In the new method, therefore, distances are measured from each periodic market to the nearest periodic market that is the same size or larger.[10] Distances to any smaller periodic markets are ignored. Secondary periodic markets are included in the analysis, and the spatial distances of these markets from larger periodic markets in the same market center are recorded as 0. Thus, for the purposes of this analysis, a market center with 2 or more separate periodic market days each week is considered as two or more separate periodic markets meeting at the same place on different days of the week. Days with fewer than 11 trading units are ignored, as are the days of lowest market activity in market centers with more than 11 trading units on every day of the week. These days of lowest market activity simply fill the interstices between the major market day and the secondary market days. Thus, no positive decision is made on their temporal location; there is just a negative decision not to locate the more important periodic markets on those days.

Distorted results due to variations in the density of market centers can be eliminated once the distances from each market to the nearest markets spaced 3, 2, 1, and 0 days away are calculated. For each periodic market, these four distances are averaged, and each distance is divided by the average distance, so as to give an index of distance relative to the average distance. Thus, if the distances are 0, 4.0, 8.0, and 12.0, the average is 6.0, and the indices are respectively 0, .67, 1.33, and 2.00. At the end of the analysis for all periodic markets, the indices for each temporal separation are averaged to give four key figures, the average indices for temporal separations of 3, 2, 1, and 0 days.

[10] Because all measurements are made from smaller periodic markets to periodic markets that are the same size or larger, no distances can be calculated for the largest periodic market in highland Ecuador occurring on each day of the week. Thus, no distances can be calculated for seven periodic markets (one for each day of the week). These seven occur in Quito on Sunday, Tuesday, Wednesday, Thursday, Friday, and Saturday, and in Ambato on Monday.

With this new method, spatial distance indices have been calculated for the periodic markets of northern, central, and southern highland Ecuador, for the whole highlands, and for periodic markets with over 100 and over 10 trading units on market day. These results are presented in Table 12 and in Figure 5. The results show that there is a moderate degree of spatiotemporal integration among the periodic markets of highland Ecuador and that this integration is most notable in the central highlands. The prime reason for the contrast between the results of this analysis and those of R. H. T. Smith's method is the inclusion of secondary periodic market days, which are predominantly located in midweek and which balance some of the high concentration of major market days at weekends. A further important factor in the contrast is the change to the measurement of distances to markets that are the same size or larger rather than to any markets. This means that a greater proportion of distances is measured to the third- and fourth-order market centers that have a better spread of market days through the week than the smaller market centers, whose market days are overwhelmingly concentrated on Sundays.

With the exception of the southern highlands, the highest distance indices are recorded for a temporal separation of 0 days. This is to be expected in a 7-day week because, for any given day, there is only 1 day

TABLE 12

Average Distance Indices between Periodic Markets and the Nearest Periodic Markets That Are the Same Size or Larger, by Region and Size of Market, Using the New Method for Analyzing Spatiotemporal Integration

Trading Units in Each Periodic Market	Sub-region	N^a	Temporal Separation in Days				r^b
			3	2	1	0	
Over 100	North	23	0.99	0.88	0.70	1.43	-0.47
	Center	48	0.79	0.83	0.96	1.42	-0.90
	South	18	1.09	1.02	0.89	1.00	0.62
Total		89	0.90	0.88	0.88	1.34	-0.75
Over 10	North	52	1.07	0.95	0.87	1.11	-0.04
	Center	99	0.83	0.90	1.04	1.23	-0.98
	South	55	1.17	1.01	0.97	0.85	0.97
Total		206	0.99	0.94	0.98	1.09	-0.68

a. *Number of periodic market days under study.*
   b. *Correlation coefficient between spatial and temporal distances.*

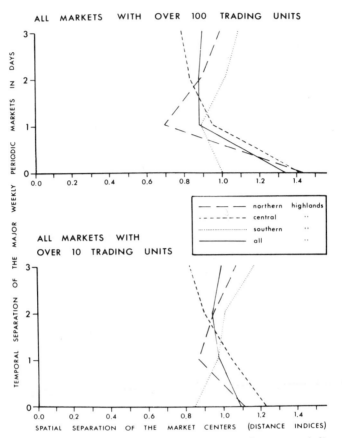

Figure 5. A graphic representation of the average distances between periodic markets and the nearest periodic markets that are the same size or larger, by region and size of market, using the new method for analyzing spatiotemporal integration.

each week with a temporal separation of 0 days, while there are 2 days each with temporal separations of 1, 2, and 3 days. This high index for a temporal separation of 0 days is normal in all but the most unintegrated market systems where periodic markets are overwhelmingly concentrated on 1 day of the week.

In a market system where there is a perfect inverse relationship between temporal distance and spatial distance, the lowest distance index must occur on the maximum temporal spacing—in this case, the spacing of 3 days. In reality, this occurs only in the relatively well-integrated central highlands. In the northern and southern highlands, the lowest indices are recorded for the temporal spacing of 1 day, reflecting the strong tendency for neighboring markets to occur on adjacent days. This allows a concentration of markets on Fridays, Saturdays, and Sundays and an easy movement of traders and commodities from one neighboring periodic market to another. For the highlands as a whole, the conflicting tendencies of the central highlands and the northern and southern highlands effectively balance one another, and the lowest index is for a temporal spacing of 2 days.

CONCLUSIONS

Highland Ecuador has a moderately integrated spatiotemporal pattern of periodic markets, with the central highlands being considerably more integrated than the northern or southern highlands. In general, the areas of highland Ecuador with a high density of market centers have better integrated market systems than the areas with lower densities of market centers. A study of historical evidence (R. D. F. Bromley and R. J. Bromley 1975) indicates that integrative changes of market day and integrative choices of new market days tend to occur as neighboring market centers come into greater contact and competition with one another. The poor levels of integration of the market systems in most of highland Ecuador can therefore be attributed to the strong preference for weekend, particularly Sunday, markets and to the relatively low density of market centers and limited competition between neighboring centers. It appears that levels of integration are gradually increasing through time as the density of market centers increases, the total volume of market activity grows, the communications system improves, and the old tradition of weekend markets gradually breaks down. It is unlikely, however, that highland Ecuador will ever have a perfectly integrated spatiotemporal system of periodic markets. Such a system would presuppose perfect knowledge of market location and periodicity patterns among market organizers and a universal tendency to choose integrative solutions to actual or potential clashes between periodic markets occurring on the same days. In reality, of course, information is never perfect, and conflictive choices of market days still occur, and are likely to continue occurring, because of the rivalry of many neighboring settlements.

In most parts of the highlands, levels of integration tend to be highest when the smallest periodic markets, which are overwhelmingly concentrated on Sundays, are excluded from the analysis. Thus, integration is greater between the larger market centers than between the smaller market centers. Any analysis considering only the major market day in each market center shows a lower level of integration than an analysis that includes both major and secondary market days. This is because secondary market days are less concentrated at weekends than major market days and because, within any market center with more than 1 periodic market day each week, the secondary market days are temporally separated from the major market days, and this temporal separation is usually the maximum possible. In seeking a nonconflictive market day, market organizers generally choose a day that does not clash with neighboring larger periodic markets. They tend to ignore potential or actual competition with smaller periodic markets. Thus, integrative choices of market day are essentially a response to competition from above in the hierarchy of market centers rather than to competition from below. Very frequently, a day adjacent to the major market day of a neighboring larger market center is chosen rather than a day that maximizes temporal separation from the major market day of the larger market center. This allows a moderate degree of temporal integration together with a clustering of market days on or around the weekends.

The historical development of periodic markets in highland Ecuador since the sixteenth century shows a slow but significant tendency toward the proliferation of new market centers (R. J. Bromley 1976) and the spread of market activity from Sundays to the rest of the week (R. D. F. Bromley and R. J. Bromley 1975). Up to the mid-nineteenth century, such developments were very slow, but, since then, there has been a marked acceleration of change in the market systems of highland Ecuador in association with population growth, urbanization, transport improvement, growing regional interaction, increasing consumer demand, and the replacement of subsistence by cash production. Evolutionary change in highland Ecuadorian market systems is continuing to accelerate, and contemporary patterns may be viewed as immature. Systemic evolution is leading to increased spatiotemporal integration, to a growing concentration of market activity in higher-order centers, and to the gradual replacement of periodic markets by daily markets and other commercial institutions such as supermarkets and wholesale warehouses. The disappearance of periodic markets, however, is much slower than one would expect from the models of economic location theory (Alao 1972; Stine 1962; Hay 1971; Webber and Symanski 1973). Lack of information, social resistance, and institutional inertia tend to slow the adaption of the existing periodic market systems to contemporary conditions (see R. J. Bromley et al. in press), perpetuating the concentration of periodic market activity at weekends and the moderate levels of spatiotemporal integration that are prevalent over much of highland Ecuador.

REFERENCES

Alao, N. A.
   1972 Theoretical issues in the geographical dimensions of market periodicity. *Nigerian Geographical Journal* **15**: 97–105.
Bromley, Raymond J.
   1974 The organization of Quito's urban markets: Towards a reinterpretation of periodic central places. *Transactions of the Institute of British Geographers* **62**: 45–70.
   1975 Periodic and daily markets in highland Ecuador. Unpublished Ph.D. dissertation, Univ. of Cambridge.

1976   Traditional and modern change in the growth of systems of market centres in high-land Ecuador. In *Internal exchange systems in Africa, Asia and Latin America*, edited by R. H. T. Smith. Melbourne: Sorrett Publishing Co.

Bromley, Raymond J., and Richard Symanski
1974   Marketplace trade in Latin America. *Latin American Research Review* **9**: 3-38.

Bromley, Raymond J., Richard Symanski, and Charles M. Good
in press   The rationale of periodic markets. *Annals of the Association of American Geographers* **65.**

Bromley, Rosemary D. F., and Raymond J. Bromley
1975   The debate on Sunday markets in nineteenth century Ecuador. *Journal of Latin American Studies* **7**: 85-108.

Fagerlund, Vernon G., and R. H. T. Smith
1970   A preliminary map of market periodicities in Ghana. *Journal of Developing Areas* **4**: 338-348.

Good, Charles M.
1972   Periodic markets: A problem in locational analysis. *Professional Geographer* **24**: 210-216.

Hay, Alan M.
1971   Notes on the economic basis for periodic marketing in developing countries. *Geographical Analysis* **3**: 393-401.

Hill, Polly, and R. H. T. Smith
1972   The spatial and temporal synchronization of periodic markets: The evidence from four emirates in northern Nigeria. *Economic Geography* **48**: 345-355.

Hodder, B. W.
1971   Periodic and daily markets in West Africa. In *The Development of indigenous trade and markets in West Africa*, edited by Claude Meillassoux. London: Oxford Univ. Press. Pp. 347-358.

Midwest State of Nigeria
1969   *Market calendar.* Benin City: Statistics Department, Ministry of Finance and Economic Development.

Oficina de los Censos Nacionales, Ecuador
1974   *Tercer censo de población, segundo censo de vivienda: Resultos provisionales.* Quito: Oficina de los Censos Nacionales.

Silverman, Sydel F.
1959   Some cultural correlates of the cyclical market. In *Intermediate societies, social mobility and communication*, edited by Verne F. Ray. Seattle: Univ. of Washington Press. Pp. 31-36.

Skinner, G. William
1964   Marketing and social structure in rural China: Part I. *Journal of Asian Studies* **24**:3-43.

Smith, Carol A.
1974   Economics of marketing systems: Models from economic geography. *Annual Review of Anthropology* **3**: 167-201.

Smith, R. H. T.
1970   A note on periodic markets in West Africa. *African Urban Notes* **5**:29-37.
1971a   The theory of periodic markets: Consumer and trader behavior. In *Preconference Publication of Papers, Annual Meeting of the Canadian Association of Geographers, Waterloo.* Pp. 183-189.
1971b   West African market places: Temporal periodicity and locational spacing. In *The development of indigenous trade and markets in West Africa*, edited by Claude Meillassoux. London: Oxford Univ. Press. Pp. 319-346.
1972   The synchronization of periodic markets. In *International geography,* edited by W. P. Adams and F. M. Helleiner. Toronto: Univ. of Toronto Press. Pp. 591-593.

1974   Periodic markets and travelling traders. Unpublished manuscript. Clayton, Australia: Monash Univ., Dept. of Geography.

Stine, James H.
1962   Temporal aspects of tertiary production elements in Korea. In *Urban systems and economic development,* edited by F. R. Pitts. Eugene: Univ. of Oregon, School of Business Administration. Pp. 68–88.

Symanski, Richard
1973   God, food and consumers in periodic market systems. *Proceedings of the Association of American Geographers* **5:** 262–266.

Symanski, Richard, and M. J. Webber
1974   Complex periodic market cycles. *Annals of the Association of American Geographers* **64:** 203–213.

Tinkler, Keith
1973   The topology of rural periodic market systems. *Geografiska Annaler* **55B:** 121–133.

Ullman, Edward A.
1974   Space and/or time: Opportunity for substitution and prediction. *Transactions of the Institute of British Geographers* **63:** 125–139.

Webber, M. J., and Richard Symanski
1973   Periodic markets: An economic location analysis. *Economic Geography* **49:** 213–227.

Wood, L. J.
1972   Rural market patterns in Kenya. *Area* **4:** 267–268.
1973   The temporal efficiency of the rural market system in Kenya. *East African Geographical Review* **11:** 65–69.

World's Fair, Ltd.
1974   *Markets Year Book.* (14th. ed.) Oldham, Lancashire: World's Fair, Ltd.

Yeung, Yue-man
1974   Periodic markets: Comments on spatio-temporal relationships. *Professional Geographer* **16:** 147–151.

Chapter 4

Periodic Markets and Urban Development in Southern Ghana

Brian Schwimmer
University of Manitoba

The study of peasant marketing is becoming an important tool for the anthropology of complex societies. It provides a method for delineating economic and social systems on a regional scale that allows us to approach structure and change beyond the limitations of the community concept. However, the substitution of market and other extralocal systems as units of study has introduced problems of defining geographical and institutional forms, which had been of only minor importance in community studies. What are the primary processes involved in the evolution of the market system? What are the resulting institutional and spatial structures? How is market system development interrelated with the emergence of overall regional patterns, which may be influenced by complementary or competing exchange systems, by administrative hierarchies, and by multifunctional urban centers?

There are currently two bodies of theory that deal with these issues. One conceives of marketing systems as emerging from the internal dynamics of the peasant economy and integrating peasant communities into the regional economy. It is formally expressed by central-place theory, which assumes internal intensification of marketing as the basis of an evolution of hierarchies, in relation to which overall regional systems emerge or become articulated. The other model derives from a critique of assumptions of endogenous evolution and concentrates upon the dynamics of externally oriented trade. Local systems devolve from urban centers that emerge as foci of long-distance exchange.

In this paper I will investigate the implications of these models for the integration of regional and local exchange systems and examine their applicability to the emergence of settlements in a recently inhabited area of southern Ghana. I will concentrate upon three major formative influences—a peasant marketing system, a colonial commercial system, and a local administrative system—in terms of the individual development of each and the interrelationships among them.

CENTRAL-PLACE AND
MERCANTILE MODELS

The dynamics of the central-place model have been most intensively developed by Skinner to describe market evolution in rural China (Skinner 1964, 1965). He assumes an initially isolated area in which limited specialization and exchange have emerged. Intensification results from an enlargement of the marketing area due to increase and expansion of the population or of the domestic exchange sector. Previously isolated areas thereby come into contact with adjacent ones. If homogeneous distribution of production and consumption units and minimization of transport cost differentials among customers can be assumed, a pattern of hexagonally shaped, contiguous service areas can be predicted. Centers will become interconnected by transport routes radiating from individual centers along six lines (see Figure 1). Levels of trade may be fairly low, but the demand

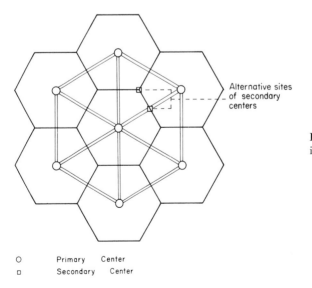

Alternative sites of secondary centers

Figure 1. Expansion of isolated market areas.

O   Primary   Center
□   Secondary Center

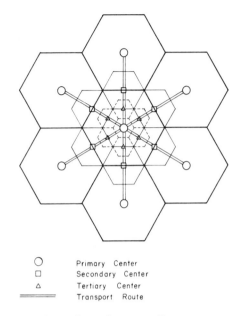

Figure 2.   Intensification cycles.

O   Primary   Center
□   Secondary   Center
△   Tertiary   Center
═══   Transport   Route

area can be increased by temporal staggering of markets to allow mobile firms to operate.

The second stage of development involves further intensification that encourages the growth of new centers. Optimally, they will be located at points equidistant from existing centers, relative to either triads of centers, at vertices of hexagons, or to pairs, at midpoints of their sides. (The latter pattern involves the location of centers along transport routes and occurs where additional route construction is expensive.) As secondary centers emerge, original centers assume additional functions. Continuation of the intensification process yields a hierarchy of at least three levels of centers. Central markets at the highest level provide higher-order goods and services and perform wholesale functions. On the basis of internal intensification, wholesaling should involve redistribution of local specializations, but Skinner also mentions the central market's role in articulating import–export trade.

Service areas will become hierarchically arranged in a parallel fashion, so that hinterlands of lower-order centers are included as components of higher-order hinterlands. Overall patterning of hierarchy and inclusion is continuous rather than discrete insofar as lower-order centers are articulated to multiple higher-order centers and lower-order hinterlands are divided between those of subsequently higher levels. Transport routes align to connect centers in a lattice pattern (see Figures 2 and 3).

Skinner's evolutionary model does not involve stages beyond internally oriented market intensification. He does not explicitly deal with import–export linkages, although he includes them among the functions of central

Brian Schwimmer

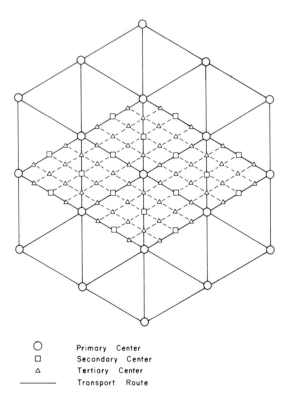

Figure 3. Lattice route and center articulation.

○	Primary Center
□	Secondary Center
△	Tertiary Center
——	Transport Route

markets. He does not define interrelationships between marketing and administrative or overall urban development. Yet he does indicate that urban functions become expressed at the higher levels of the central-place system. Increasingly higher-order centers have larger populations, are serviced by larger firms, maintain permanent rather than mobile establishments, and have a greater proportion of nonagricultural workers (Skinner 1964:9–10, 30). He also indicates that market systems are integrated into a more inclusive hierarchy of local and regional cities, serving administrative functions, but he does not discuss whether these functions emerge from the marketing structure or are imposed upon it.

Relationships between cities and markets are treated as aspects of "modern" change (Skinner 1965:212). This occurs with the development of mechanized transportation, which brings the city in more direct contact with central market systems and lowers costs of urban goods, such as long-distance imports or urban manufactures. Cheaper urban goods and improvement of transport facilities draw business away from the lower levels of the system toward the intermediate and central markets, which in turn become transformed into modern trading towns. Skinner does not proceed beyond his treatment of lower levels to discuss the effects that modernization might have on the structure at upper levels of articulation.

The alternative model, expressed most rigorously in Vance's mercantile model (1970), assumes a reversed order of causation. Vance assumes that local-level trade is too limited to generate a sufficiently large supply or demand to justify the emergence of wholesalers or wholesaling locations. Exchange systems emerge from linkages between regions, generated by long-distance traders seeking new markets and new sources of supply. Traders must cover transport costs by the economies of scale accruing to large turnovers and must therefore operate on a wholesale basis. Initial centers serve as wholesaling, import–export markets, optimally located between regions convenient to wholesalers rather than to ultimate suppliers and customers. Local systems devolve from the stimulation of the economies affected by wholesaling activities.

Intensification will not initially result in the location of new centers, as firms prefer to remain in intermediate locations between supply and demand areas and may continue to cover costs of servicing increasingly larger trading areas because of longer returns to scale. Expansion of trade eventually proceeds along single avenues from port locations. Subcenters may emerge by a process of penetration, in which supply and demand stimulated by the firms become large enough to encourage their relocation. Penetration will result in a line-and-branch pattern of transport and center articulation, issuing from the initial port location. Center size and function will decrease with distance from the port. Because of the tendency for growth to be confined to initial centers, there will be a pattern of primacy in which centers serving intermediary functions are not well developed and lower-level retail centers are articulated to single wholesale centers. Hierarchy and inclusion are discrete rather than continuous (see Figure 4).

Vance does not discuss the interrelationship between wholesale locations and overall urban development. However, he indicates that wholesale loca-

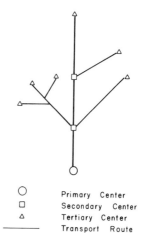

Figure 4. Dendritic route and center articulation.

○	Primary Center
□	Secondary Center
△	Tertiary Center
——	Transport Route

tions assume additional urban functions, which would be expected from
the restriction of business development to initial centers, the resulting
increase in population, and the development of infrastructure to service
both firms and population. Alternatively, existing cities—for example,
administrative centers—would be attractive locations for wholesale firms,
whose scale of operation would make them more dependent upon urban
services than upon transport costs or customer location.

A similar model has been suggested to explain commercial and administrative development in colonial situations. A developed economy expands
into a new area and initiates import–export trade between colony and
metropole. Centers are located along the boundary and maintain their
orientation toward the metropole. Urban growth is dependent upon the
interconnected activities of import–export firms and colonial administra-
tions. Extension of transport routes and dependent centers follows the
penetration pattern, and a line-and-branch or dendritic articulation results
(Johnson 1970:83–92).

Although Johnson's colonial model follows Vance's model in many
respects, there are some important differences. Johnson posits the
dendritic system as a special case in which normal central-place processes
are disturbed. Colonial dominance and commercial oligopoly result in
discrete articulation of localities through noncompetitive colonial centers
instead of the normal continuous articulation through competing central
markets. Local systems remain unarticulated, and a dual system develops
in which local systems stagnate and import–export systems expand under
colonial encouragement.

Vance's model, on the other hand, is applied to all systems of trade,
which are most usually instituted on a long-distance wholesale basis. Competition among firms emerges, but it does so *within* centers where
exchange concentrates rather than *among* centers where it proliferates.
Local systems do develop and interarticulate because of the commercialization of localities stimulated by external penetration. Under these
conditions, specialization and exchange develop on a more localized level,
and a system assuming a central-place ordering may emerge. The result is
an integrated system of local and import–export trade, expressing central-
place formation at the lower levels and mercantile formation at the upper
levels.

The contrasting features of Skinner's central-place model and Vance's
mercantile model may now be summarized. In the central-place model,
exchange systems are generated by a process of internal intensification.
Customers and suppliers are located in the same area, and centers proliferate evenly over the landscape to service them. Marketing is organized
through small, mobile firms. Transport routes develop to connect scattered
centers in a lattice pattern. Further intensification leads to the emergence
of larger centers, providing higher-order functions and expressing more

urban features. Firms become larger, assume wholesale functions, and develop permanent locations. The mercantile model assumes penetration of a system into a new area. Producers and consumers are located great distances apart, so firms must be large enough to assume import–export, wholesaling functions. Centers become located along regional boundaries convenient to wholesalers and increase in scale rather than in number. Access is oriented in a line-and-branch pattern. Later stages lead to the downward penetration of services, the stimulation of local specialization and exchange, and modification toward a central-place pattern.

On another level of analysis, there is a degree of similarity between the models. Whereas the colonial model and other positions similar to it (Hill 1966; Hodder and Ukwu 1969, on West African marketing systems) assume unintegrated, dual or multiple systems, both Skinner and Vance suggest interrelationships between internally and externally oriented exchange systems and between exchange and administrative systems. Skinner concentrates on lower levels and on the importance of internal evolution but makes allowance for a process in which modernization proceeds from urban centers. Vance concentrates on the upper levels and on the importance of exogenous influences but must invoke central-place theory to account for lower-level in-filling. As such, we might conclude that exchange systems exhibit two levels of organization and that locational patterning in any specific situation will express both central-place and mercantile ordering in varying degrees.

This comparison suggests relevant areas for investigating settlement growth in the Ghanaian case in question: (1) the initial exchange stimuli relative to local and external economic patterns, (2) the spread and articulation of exchange centers and transport routes, and (3) the integration of marketing with other regionally organized systems. I will show that in accordance with both models, the emergence of the market system in one region of Ghana was integrally related to the growth of complementary systems of import–export trade and local administration. In relation to each model, the overall settlement system assumes two patterns, one based on local intensification expressed in central-place ordering, the other on external penetration expressed in mercantile ordering.

EMERGENCE OF THE MARKETING SYSTEM

The area in question occupies approximately 200 square miles in the forest region of southeastern Ghana. In 1970 it had a rural population of 60,000; an additional 12,500 people lived in Suhum, the main commercial and administrative center. The area was formerly an unoccupied forest reserve owned by the Akim-Abuakwa kingdom, whose capital, Kibi, and main towns lie to the north. In the beginning of the century, cocoa farmers from more densely populated and economically active areas to the east and south migrated into the area to purchase land. The indigenous Akim took little part in the expansion and by 1920 had sold all their southern lands to the immigrants. Subsequent migration and diffusion extended throughout the forest region of what was then the British colony of the Gold Coast (Hill 1961).

Unlike many colonial areas, where export production was carried out on a plantation basis, cocoa farming was integrated into the agricultural system of small-scale farming households. Farmers owned their own land and could increase export production by limited use of hired labor. Production and consumption were organized through two separate systems. Cocoa exports and European manufactures were handled through European firms initially located in the colonial urban centers, external to the area. Export production was supplemented by starchy staple and vegetable cultivation for both subsistence and sale in local marketplaces that were established in the course of settlement. Markets also served domestic consumption based upon indigenous food and craft products.[1]

Import-export activities depended upon colonial government and foreign import-export firms, initially concentrated in Accra, the major port and center of administrative and commercial control. Between 1910 and 1920, a rail line was constructed along the eastern boundary of the Suhum area to connect Accra to Kumase, the main interior colonial center. Commercial and administrative subcenters were located in a series of towns along the rail line at Nsawam, Mangoase, and Koforidua. Sites occurred at indigenous marketing and political centers in a process of interaction between native and colonial systems that developments in Suhum recapitulate (Gould 1960).

Import-export transactions were carried out in Accra and eventually in centers along the rail line. European firms initially avoided establishing additional branches because of high costs of heating new establishments and because of their dependence upon the colonial infrastructure. Suhum area farmers were able to undertake trips to these centers, located up to 20 or 30 miles away, because their transport costs could be reduced by the infrequency of their trips and the high values of sales and purchases.[2]

[1] According to a current survey of Ghana's Eastern Region (Dutta-Roy 1969), the average rural household produces 60 percent of its goods for sale. My own data indicate that 60 percent of the cash income comes from cocoa sales and 40 percent from local market food sales. Although cocoa provides a greater income, the actual bulk of foodstuff sales is three times that of cocoa. This is important in considering the reasons for local route construction. On the consumption side, 64 percent is based on cash purchase. Food accounts for 30 percent; fish is the most important food purchase. Clothing is the major manufacture purchased and accounts for over 30 percent of all cash expenditure.

[2] The data presented are from oral histories collected from traders and town elders during field work from 1970 to 1972.

Indigenous exchange was based upon two levels of specialized production. One was internal to the area and involved sale of starchy staples, garden vegetables, and craft products. The other was interregional and involved trade of staples for fish caught along the coast. Staples flows were further affected by the growth of urban demand in Accra, located centrally to the fishing area. Trade in these items differed from import–export trade in that the field of exchange was more localized; the items were less valuable relative to their bulk and were not storable and therefore required continuous bulking and retailing facilities. Exchange sites had to be located at fairly frequent intervals convenient to producers and consumers. As a result, the first set of centers that emerged within the Suhum area serviced the indigenous rather than the import–export system. They were initially established because of trade between the area and the coast rather than because of purely localized trade and were situated along the main line of access to Accra. Markets at Asuboi, Amanase, Suhum, and Odumase were established between 1914 and 1920 along a road between Kibi and Nsawam that predated the actual settlement of the area (see Map 1).

Interregional aspects of trade were organized through coastal traders who purchased fish for distribution in a circuit of markets in the forest zone that included those of the Suhum alignment. They both retailed themselves and sold some of their goods through local retailers. For the return trip they collected local staples for distribution in Accra and other coastal markets. Local retailers acted as limited outlets for coastal traders and as agents for exchange between local specialists.

Roadside markets attracted an increasing level of business; the related increases of road use led to paving of the road between Nsawam and Kibi between 1924 and 1927. Resulting reductions of transport costs stimulated use of roadside centers and extended their hinterlands. A two-level growth pattern emerged whereby interior villages emerged as collection and outlet points, and roadside markets assumed more definite wholesale functions. By 1925 Suhum, the most central of the roadside locations, emerged as the superordinate market. Concurrently, dependent markets grew up at Akorabo, Nankese, Asafo, and Mfranor,[3] whose locations at points between Suhum and a set of similarly emerging central markets suggest a relationship of retail to multiple wholesale markets (see Map 2).

The growth of wholesale operations centering on Suhum involved the development of larger, more permanent firms. Accra-based traders began to specialize in either fish or staples. Fish traders began to locate permanently in Suhum and to organize supply lines through relatives on the

---

[3] The development of retail centers along this route has a complex history. Mfranor was the initial market but was superceded by Anum-Apapem. Kuano grew up as a retail market almost equivalent to Anum-Apapem in importance because it had road access for a longer period. Thus, there were two retail centers instead of the expected single one.

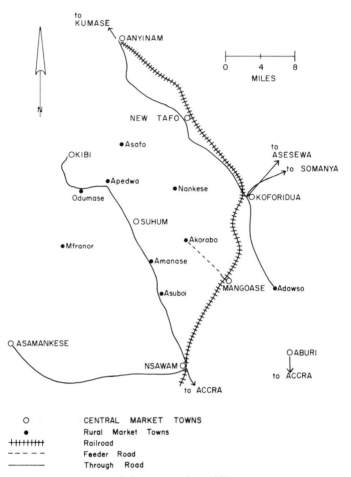

Map 1. Town development in the Suhum area, circa 1925.

coast. Business volume expanded through sales to retailers operating in the new secondary centers. Staple traders expanded their businesses on the basis of the growing market in Accra and on the emergence of Suhum-based bulking agents, who could collect a larger level of supplies in the circuit of secondary markets.

The final stages of development involved the growth of an internal transport network and the proliferation of a new set of centers. Efforts were undertaken to connect secondary markets to primary centers. Their orientation to pairs of primary centers involved the extension of roads in two directions and ultimately affected linkages among primary centers. A tertiary level of centers developed along the new roads and at scattered points within walking distance of either Suhum or the roadside locations.

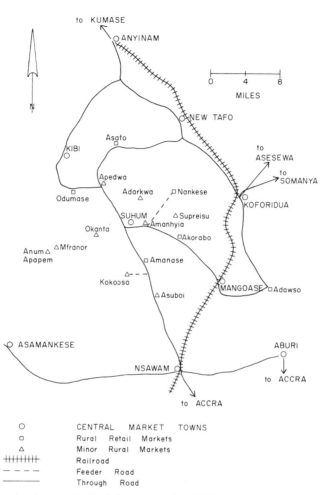

Map 2.   Town development in the Suhum area, circa 1940.

A new set of feeder roads was constructed to link tertiary centers to the emerging system. (See Maps 3 and 4.)

The processes of development reflect tendencies suggested by both mercantile and central-place models. Initial centers were established as indigenous markets rather than as outlets for import–export trade. However, stimulus to trade was not based purely upon localized differentiation but upon interregional exchange and urban demand. Thus, the initial orientation of routes and centers was influenced by features of the import–export and colonial systems. Alignment was dendritic, focusing upon Accra from Suhum and similarly oriented primary centers in neighboring areas. The trading firms that organized marketing in this period are

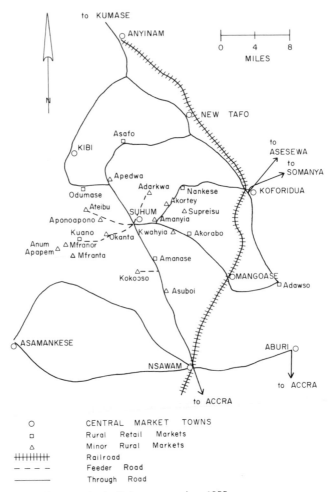

Map 3. Town development in the Suhum area, circa 1955.

not classifiable as definitely wholesale or retail in function. Differentiation seems to have been a function of increased scale that came with intensification of the system.

Later stages of development reflect the intensification pattern. Supply and demand structure of rural households affected the proliferation of conveniently located centers and roads. New markets emerged in the interstices between primary centers and influenced hierarchical ordering, in which the latter assumed more explicit wholesaling functions. Routes were constructed through secondary centers to link primary sites and were realigned from a dendritic toward a lattice pattern. Subsequently, a new series of tertiary centers developed in the interstices of the primary and secondary network.

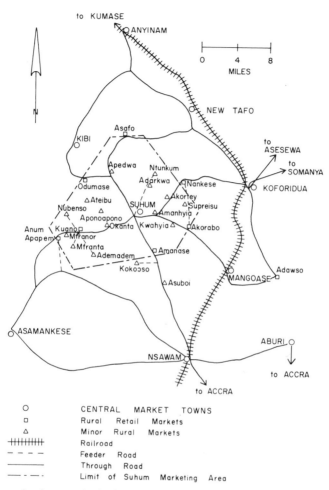

Map 4.   Town development in the Suhum area, circa 1970.

CONTEMPORARY SPATIAL AND
FUNCTIONAL SYSTEMS

Currently, the local system comprises a single central market hinterland organized through three levels of centers. At the highest level is Suhum, the central market that is the functional and spatial focus of the local system. It is surrounded by six equivalent-order centers of adjacent systems to which it is connected by roads. The Suhum market performs functions at three levels, including retailing and assembling, which are also performed by successively lower order centers of the system. At the highest level it serves wholesaling and higher-order retailing functions. Wholesaling includes internal redistribution of goods between local specialists and assembling and breaking bulk for goods exchanged with other areas. Temporal periodicity differs according to function. The market meets daily for lower-order services and once every third day as a wholesale market. During wholesale sessions, up to 1000 traders may attend.

Retail markets, occupying the intermediate level, are located at the midpoints of the six routes connecting Suhum to adjacent central markets. They provide functions at two levels: assembling, which is also characteristic of lowest-order centers; and retailing produce received locally or from central markets. Meetings occur every third day and are adjusted to the Suhum wholesale cycle, so that no market, except Kuano, meets on a Suhum wholesaling day. Approximately 200 traders attend each meeting.

Two sets of assembly markets occupy the lowest level. One occupies the midpoints of roads connecting Suhum to its retail markets; a second falls off the main routes and is articulated to Suhum or to secondary markets by feeders. They serve mainly as bulking points for sale of foodstuffs to a small group of wholesale buyers. They meet according to the 3-day cycle, usually on the same day as the retail markets that service their users.

The current functional differentiation and spatial articulation of the system approximates the form of the central-place model. (Compare Figure 5 and Map 5.) Centers are discretely divided into functional levels; higher-order functions are added to lower-order functions in successive levels of the hierarchy. Locations approximate the vertices of a lattice that covers the area; higher-order sites occur at less frequent but evenly spaced points. As such, the processes of proliferation and hierarchical development, due to internal intensification, have generated the predicted pattern. However, analysis of flow patterns indicates basic distortions more representative of the mercantile than the central-place model.

There is little interaction between assembly and retail points. There is no downward flow to the lowest level, and goods assembled there are not usually reassembled in retail markets. They are either shipped to Suhum for local retailing or for resale to traders from coastal markets or they may even by-pass Suhum and travel directly to the coast. Thus, intermediary bulking between ultimate producing and consuming points is quite limited. Skinner's theory accounts for this situation as "modernization," a process in which mechanized transport influences the disappearance of lower-level markets. In the present case, motorized transport seems to have drawn retailing toward the intermediate-level centers but to have suppressed their functions as actual intermediaries. Vance accounts for the stituation in terms of an absence of intermediary centers between basic retail and wholesale centers, because of the primacy of wholesale centers (Vance 1970:83–85).

A second distortion is reflected in interrelationships between retail and central markets. According to central-place theory, lower-order markets

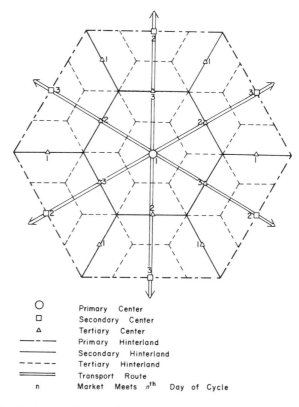

Figure 5. Ideal arrangement of a three-level periodic market system according to central-place theory.

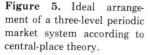

○	Primary Center
□	Secondary Center
△	Tertiary Center
—·—	Primary Hinterland
——	Secondary Hinterland
– – –	Tertiary Hinterland
═══	Transport Route
n	Market Meets n^{th} Day of Cycle

should trade with multiple higher-order markets. This does occur to some extent, especially for goods assembled in retail centers for sale in central markets. However, Suhum is the dominant wholesale supplier of goods trucked in from other regions for many of the retail markets of its system. This is attributable to the importance of external rather than internal supply of most consumption items. In having a direction, external products are more cheaply available in sources nearest to the supply area, and Suhum achieves an advantage over central markets located to the north and west.

On the central market level, flows again diverge from the predictions of central-place theory. Suhum does not exchange goods with neighboring central markets within an intraregional system of specialization but with the more distant centers within different ecological zones to the east and south. Thus, although central-place theory accurately predicts spatial patterning, spatial expression does not fully account for the flow pattern. In assuming external orientation and the resulting directionality of trade, the mercantile model can better account for the overall flow and its effects: the reduction of intermediary functions and partial discreteness of system boundaries.

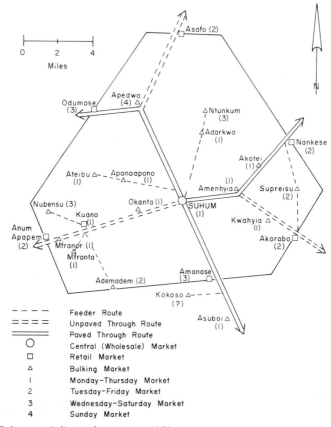

Map 5. Suhum periodic market system, 1970.

EMERGENCE OF THE URBAN SYSTEM

The evolution of the marketing system described initially assumed a separate pattern from the articulation of the import–export system. Market development involved the emergence of a hierarchy of centers and a central market internal to the area; growth of the import–export system led to the emergence of colonial urban centers on a rail line along its boundaries. As such, the import–export system represents the classical colonial model, and, from Johnson's point of view at least, little articulation with the peasant system should be expected. However, a number of modes of articulation did develop, resulting from the pattern of transportation routes, the structure of the domestic economy, and the growth of import retailing.

One force for articulation involved the dependence of both systems upon motor transport, so that the flow of goods in each form of trade followed the same route patterns. Thus, the initial alignment of route to service the import–export trade and articulate colonial centers became lines of development for periodic marketplaces. Alternatively, the elaboration of routes in response to the proliferation of local marketplaces channeled the flow of cocoa and manufactured imports between the area and the import–export centers. A second force resulted from the common locus of production and consumption for both indigenous and import–export exchange within the rural household. Supply and demand were distributed over the same area for both spheres, a situation that created opportunities for import retailing and resulted in the relocation of import–export firms.

Local retailing of imports first emerged within the market system itself. Markets acted as outlets for the distribution of some manufactures that were subject to fairly continuous demand and that could be bulk broken into small quantities by traders operating on low capital. Beyond the market outlets, a number of small shops run by Ghanaian owners developed as more stationary and continuous outlets for imports. They retailed the more expensive items and wholesaled less valuable items retailed in the market. Such firms evolved within the central market town during and subsequent to its elaboration as a wholesale center for indigenous goods.

Thus, Suhum in the late 1920s had become an important commercial center with a large marketplace, composed of wholesalers of local products and retailers of many manufactured items, and with a central business district composed of 30 to 40 small shops. The processes of transport and communications improvement, demand concentration and growth, and retail firm evolution focusing on Suhum soon influenced the location of branch offices of European firms, both as competitors and suppliers of local shopkeepers and as cocoa-buying stations. By 1930 Suhum had been transformed from an indigenous market to an important commercial town with an increasingly urban character.

The Suhum case represents a process of growth and elaboration of both local and colonial commercial systems that led to their spatial convergence in a single center. Suhum emerged as the highest level of one system and the lowest level of the other, and it thereby served an intermediary and a unifying function. The unitary system involved the addition of import–export bulking and distribution services to Suhum's functions and the addition of two levels above the three-level central-place system already described. The regional city, presently Koforidua, acts as a wholesale outlet for imported manufactures; the national city, Accra, acts as the export center for cocoa bulked in Suhum and as the import center for European goods (see Table 1).

ADMINISTRATIVE PARALLELS

While the main pattern of center location was established by commercial forces, community development as such involved political

TABLE 1
Commercial and Administrative Functions of Central-Place Levels in Ghana

Levels	Functions		
	Market	Import-Export	Administrative
Village: Population 1,000 or less	Foodstuff bulking		Village administration Elementary school
Town: Population 1,000–2,000	Retailing	Market outlets	Post office agency Agriculture office branch
City: Population 5,000–20,000	Wholesaling	Permanent shops Cocoa buying	Secondary school Main post office Main agriculture office Hospital Local council center
Regional City: Population 50,000		Wholesale outlet	Ministerial branch offices Regional administrative center
National City: Population 100,000 or more		Import-export centers	University Ministerial offices Administrative head- quarters

processes that led to local town development along multifunctional lines. As in the case of the commercial system, administrative growth proceeded in two directions due to the intensification of a locally organized system and a dissemination of higher-order services from the national system.

The initial pressure for the establishment of centers derived from the need for bulking and retailing points within the internal marketing system. However, market formation depended upon conditions that local farmers, only loosely organized as land-purchasing groups,[4] could not provide. Land and labor were needed for market construction and maintenance; a system of tolls had to be devised; participants had to agree to use one of a number of competing market sites; disputes had to be settled. Under the conditions of settlement, no traditional coordination and control mechanisms were available.

The basic pattern of organization that evolved was an association in which a number of settler groups met to establish a common market and a common administration. Each group was given a particular office on a town council. Usually the post of *odikro* (pl. *adikrofo*), or headman, was given to the group that had the status of first occupancy, but this depended upon its willingness to donate land for the market. An alternative arrangement was based on each group's contributing to a common fund for the purchase of the necessary land. Town positions were rotated among the component groups.

Although the market was the main force behind the formation of these associations, other functions of the associations emerged, encouraging the development of general settlements around the market site. The original grant as such was not merely related to the market but was an agreement that placed land, labor, and a certain amount of capital at the disposal of the association. Of the land given, a certain amount was set aside for the development of a town center in which members of participating companies could build houses and in which public buildings, most frequently schools, could be constructed. Beyond this, the association had control of labor through the authority of each official within his own group. Labor was used in the construction of the market and school and sometimes of a feeder road if the level of market trade was promising. The association also had control of capital composed of market tolls.

There was no initial overriding organization of *adikrofo* within the area. Each headman and each association were subordinate to the traditional

---

[4] In traditional systems, migration to a new area was a political process and involved the acquisition of land rights through political relationships. This was not the case in Suhum, where land was acquired through purchase. Purchases were made in groups or "companies" usually composed of men from the same town. Company members settled in the same area and maintained a loose form of organization, but the company as such had no claim on property purchased, which was considered the personal possession of individual company members (Hill 1961; Hunter 1963).

chiefs who had originally sold the land and who retained rights of political control under the British policy of indirect rule. Local associations and their leaders maintained informal control over specific spheres of activity but were not formally invested with general political authority. The cohesiveness and importance of these towns rose and fell with the fortunes of their markets.

Yet the articulation and hierarchy of markets provided the base from which an areal structure was to emerge. Suhum, as the main commercial center, provided its administration with the resources and the field of relationships to cultivate political development. Suhum initially emerged as an informal appeal court for disputing *adikrofo* of its hinterland. Later its administration developed an alliance of Suhum area leaders to exert pressure on the newly independent government in Accra to establish the Suhum area as an autonomous local authority. The pressure was effective, and a Local Council Area, with headquarters at Suhum, was established.[5]

Local administrative growth followed the commercial pattern. Intensification of settlement and activity led to the emergence of a hierarchy based on the location of higher-level functions in the central market town. (It forms a parallel although not an isomorphic structure, since administrative hierarchy assumes only two levels, its hinterland is more discretely bounded, and not all dependent commercial centers are involved.) Local elaboration provided a structure along whose lines penetration of national institutions could develop. Thus, along with its local political evolution, Suhum became the center for agricultural branches, post offices, and other facilities administering to commercial needs. At later stages it became a location for national investment in a secondary school, a hospital, pipeborne water, and electrification. Subsequent growth involved the penetration of some of these institutions into secondary centers (see Table 1).

CONCLUSIONS

The history of functional systems in the Suhum area substantiates the hypothesis of integrated institutional development. Peasant marketing, import–export trade, and administrative systems have reinforced one another and have led to the growth of a set of local centers that perform multiple functions and articulate the local, regional, and national systems.

The initial emergence of centers is attributable to the development of a system of marketplaces in which a coordinating, central market town emerged. Import–export nodes were initially located outside the area, in

[5] Ghana achieved partial independence in 1951. The new government changed the policy of indirect rule and instituted elected local councils as instruments of local government. Some positions on the council were reserved for traditional officials, in this case the Suhum *odikro*.

centers and along transport lines developed by colonial authorities. Local demand and infrastructure, and the growth of a higher-order node within the local marketing system, influenced the relocation of import–export firms. Marketing and import–export trade systems became articulated within an emerging intermediate town, and urban services penetrated further to lower levels of the hierarchy. Settlement and administration paralleled commercial development. Market centers acted as foci for the growth of political institutions and related nucleation of population. Marketing areas influenced the definition of administrative units. Thus the market hierarchy influenced the emergence of a dominant center which provided a point of articulation between intensification of a local urban system and penetration of a national system.

The Suhum example demonstrates the importance of local evolution in the development of regional systems. It therefore precludes application of Johnson's version of the dendritic system as a force for inhibiting local growth and for dualization of economy or society. Yet it does not suggest any definite choice between Vance's version of the mercantile model or Skinner's application of central-place theory. Both suggest processes of regional system articulation, and both explain some aspects of local structure and fail to explain others.

Relevant mercantile processes include the penetration of a developed system that both maintains its external orientation and stimulates internal supply and demand. They are reflected in the Suhum case in: (1) an indigenous trading pattern based on specialization and exchange between ecologically differentiated regions rather than within the region; (2) reinforcement of that pattern by colonial urban centers, which create an external demand for rural staple products; and (3) an initial pattern of linearly articulated transport routes and urban centers. These factors affected the direction of development of initial centers and routes, the continued external orientation of trade, and a degree of primacy of higher-order centers relative to development of intermediary levels. They also resulted in the continued primacy of colonial urban centers and in the linear orientation of major rail patterns.

Relevant central-place processes included the intensification of local marketing, which influenced the proliferation of centers relative to customer convenience, and the emergence of a hierarchy. They are reflected in: (1) the uniform and extensive integration of all households into a single marketing system (2) the centralization of local-level commercial and political functions in a single node of the system, and (3) the radiation of transport patterns away from lineal dominance toward a lattice that covers the whole area. These factors have affected further development in providing a system with the inclusiveness, complexity, and infrastructure to influence the relocation of national institutions from higher-order urban centers to the central market town. Subsequent penetration of institutional services to lower levels has followed the initial pattern. Thus, local organization tends to deflect the linearity and primacy of the national pattern.

The overall settlement pattern shows the interaction between the two levels of growth. One emanates from the dynamics of the domestic unit and indigenous trading firms; through a process of intensification, it leads to the evolution of a system assuming a central-place form. The other emanates from the intrusion of a developed commercial system; through processes of stimulation and penetration, it leads to the evolution of a system assuming the form of the mercantile model. It may be suggested that both sets of forces are generally active in the emergence of particular settlement systems but that there is always a variation in their relative importance. In the Suhum case, both sets of forces appear equally present. The Chinese case, on which Skinner's model is based, exhibits a much longer and more extensive history of peasant market development. As a result, central-place forces are more clearly expressed and more dominant in patterning subsequent political and commercial developments. The American case, from which most of Vance's examples are taken, represents a more intrusive settlement of groups articulated to externally organized trading systems. Forces for central-place patterning did not emerge until rural populations had grown to the point at which internal intensification could develop.

Two factors have been especially important for the balanced expression of forces and for the growth of a viable local system around Suhum in a situation in which colonial influences have been of such apparent importance:

1. Unlike many other colonial areas where commercialization of agriculture took place within a plantation system, cocoa farming in Ghana involved the integration of the major export crop into the system of peasant production. The rural economy became uniformly commercialized, and no dualization of production or consumption patterns among rural areas or between rural and urban economies developed (compare to Smith 1972, Chapter 8 of this volume). Consequently, scattered farm households could generate enough demand to maintain a relatively sophisticated local marketing system.

2. The area was settled for primarily commercial reasons. Thus, the settlement structure reflected economic influences and requirements and was relatively unaffected by deviations introduced by political considerations. Political institutions as such emerged late, and their location, growth, and articulation were more dependent upon the commercial system already established than upon traditional or colonial authorities.

REFERENCES

Dutta-Roy, D. K.
1969   *The eastern region household budget survey.* Accra: Ghana Univ. Press.
Gould, Peter
1960   *The development of the transportation pattern in Ghana.* Evanston, Ill.: Northwestern Univ. Studies in Geography, No. 5.
Hill, Polly
1961   The migrant cocoa farmers of southern Ghana. *Africa* **31:** 209–230.
1966   Notes on traditional market authority and market periodicity in West Africa. *Journal of African History* **7:** 295.
Hodder, B.·W., and U. I. Ukwu
1969   *Markets in West Africa.* Ibadan: Ibadan Univ. Press.
Hunter, John M.
1963   Cocoa migration and patterns of land ownership in the Densu Valley near Suhum, Ghana. *Transactions of the Institute of British Geographers* **33:** 61–87.
Johnson, E. A. J.
1970   *The organization of space in developing countries.* Cambridge, Mass.: Harvard Univ. Press.
Skinner, G. W.
1964   Marketing and social structure in rural China: Part I. *Journal of Asian Studies* **24:** 3–43.
1965   Marketing and social structure in rural China: Part II. *Journal of Asian Studies* **24:** 195–228.
Smith, Carol A.
1972   Market articulation and economic stratification in western Guatemala. *Food Research Institute Studies* **11:** 203–233.
Vance, C.
1970   *The merchant's world.* Englewood Cliffs, N.J.: Prentice-Hall.

Chapter 5

The Role of Urban Food Needs
in Regional Development, Puno, Peru[1]

Gordon Appleby
Stanford University

Two formal models of distribution systems have been devised to depict actual patterns of market exchange. Each model treats one form of market distribution, which gives rise to a particular spatial network and a distinctive economic operation. Central-place theory posits an interlocking hierarchy of market centers through which traders and consumers may sell or buy goods. Here economic operations are governed by considerations of retail trade. The dendritic–solar[2] model depicts a tree system of market centers oriented to funneling produce out of an area. Here economic operations are channeled in lines conducive to wholesale trade.

Each model also embodies certain ideas about the evolution and intensification of the marketing system. Central-place theory locates the impetus for economic development in village economics. Skinner (1965) proposes that as a sparsely populated plain fills in, new markets will be sited equidistant from two or three earlier centers, so that when the plain

[1] The research reported here was funded by a NIMH predoctoral fellowship.

[2] The dendritic–solar pattern of marketing may develop where extraction for export occurs in an area of small producers rather than point extraction of a mineral. Such cases constitute instances of the enclave model of economic development, although capital requirements may be less and feedback effects greater. [My use of "solar" in this case rests on Smith's (1974) classification of solar systems with other irregular peasant marketing systems.]

is fully populated, markets will be articulated by ever greater consumer movement for ever more specialized goods. Previously independent local markets become interlinked through the internal dynamic of population growth, and the road network is improved in rough proportion to increasing demand. The dendritic–solar model, by contrast, posits greater outside penetration of a region as the stimulus to market development. Either increased demand for the local primary staples stems from outside or increased local demand is stimulated and met with goods from outside. In either case, the same linear spatial ordering between centers occurs because goods are flowing out of or into the region, not among centers of the same region. Growth extends roads further into the countryside, creating a new frontier. In this view, circumstances external to a region create and intensify a dendritic pattern of market centers.

Neither dynamic adequately explains what triggers market development. The central-place mechanism of increased densities does not specify how quantitative increases will lead to qualitative change. Moreover, many marketing systems have developed in already fully populated areas, which underwent no increase in commercialization, so that greater demand densties cannot be the fundamental dynamic. The mechanism contained in the dendritic model evades the question by locating the impetus outside of the region where economic conditions are already qualitatively different. Also, a regional economy based upon international export need not spark a retail marketing system. In short, neither critical density in traditional societies nor external impetus in contemporary societies need lead to the development of a central-place marketing system.

A dynamic for the rise of central-place marketing systems does lie within the realm of central-place theory. Christaller (1966) recognized the characteristic difference in occupation between urban and rural areas. Indeed, he made urban–rural exchange a fundament of his theory. Occupation, however, can create more than a production basis for exchange. It can entail income level and class differences that pattern in space. People of all classes live in the larger or more central places, but most of the upper classes concentrate there, while the lower class scatters between both town and country. The aggregation of the upper classes into the more central places concentrates demand there not because the upper classes are rich but because the lower class is very poor.[3] Since some of this urban population does not produce its own food, cities are, in Eighmy's phrase, "intense food deficit areas [1972:299]." When transportation is difficult, cities necessarily depend upon their local area for food. This dependence may stimulate markets. When transportation improves, cities can extend

---

[3] A conquest situation like that of Spanish America emphasizes the class difference between town and country by adding the factor of ethnicity. The minority of upper classes are also the town-based controlling ethnic group.

their hinterlands, share hinterlands through trader and consumer movement, and thus constitute the backbone of a regional central-place system.

This same rationale applies to the beginnings to interregional trade. Once a region can produce and bulk foodstuffs for its cities, the same foodstuffs can be shipped to cities in other regions when there is a surplus. These places will in return send their surfeit commodities to the elite in the first exporting area. In this manner, urban demand for food, conditioned by the class composition of the cities, provides a mechanism for central-place development at levels intermediate between the local marketing system and the international market. As Smith notes, "marketing systems occur only in stratified societies with a distinct class of nonfood producers . . . through 'top-down' penetration rather than 'bottom-up' intensification." Markets evolve from top-down within regions of agrarian societies for the simple reason that stratified societies, by definition, contain "an elite class that requires regular and efficient food provisioning [1974:193]."

Three characteristics make the Department of Puno an ideal site to investigate these ideas about the role of urban food demand in market development. First, the department boasted markets long before it possessed a marketing system. Second, the Department of Puno comprises both an agricultural zone and a pastoral zone, so that production constraints that impinge on the rural population may be evaluated. Whether an area produces food or wool for trade determines the nature of market linkage between the supply of the rural producers and the demand of the immediate consumers. Where a subsistence-oriented rural population produces food, supply determines price because urban demand remains constant while yearly harvests vary. Here, central-place development will occur. Where the rural population produces wool for export, external demand determines price because the producers' need to sell remains constant despite the volatility of the international wool market. Under these conditions a dendritic–solar pattern with many fewer markets will arise. Third, the department, despite outrageous odds and conventional wisdom, is largely self-sufficient in basic regional staples. Thus, the history of market exchange, the spatial patterning of production, and an autonomy in basic foodstuffs make Puno an ideal site for testing the proposition that urban food needs spark the development of a central-place marketing system.

THE REGION

The Department of Puno encompasses 27,940 square miles, of which 4920 square miles are classified as tropical jungle (*selva*) and another 1952 square miles are covered by Lake Titicaca. The remaining land surface, known as the *altiplano*, is a very high plain covered by stiff pasture grass. Agriculture is viable only along the lakeshore where soils are more fertile and the otherwise severe climate is moderated by the lake. With distance from the lake, agriculture gives way to a variously mixed farming and herding economy. At the foot of the Andes, which rim the *altiplano* to the east and west, only herding is possible. Population densities naturally vary according to this economic base. Along the agricultural lakeshore, densities reach 250 people per square mile, while in the herding areas they dip to 10 or fewer per square mile. The absolute population of the department has been variously estimated at 1 million to 1.5 million, of whom only 70,000 live in the jungle (Dew 1969:41; provisional results of the 1972 national census enumerated 779,594 people in the department). In relation to the resource base, the *altiplano* is everywhere heavily populated. The rural population lives from "subsistence agriculture" and migrant wage work. The urban population is occupied chiefly in government and commerce. There is almost no industry in the department, and large estates, or *latifundia*, predominate in the herding areas whereas small-hold *minifundia* are characteristic of the more densely populated agricultural area.

The contemporary marketing system in the Department of Puno constitutes a natural unit of study. Physical and political obstacles impede communications beyond the Peruvian *altiplano*. The western branch of the Andes, which here runs northwesterly, sharply restricts commerce with the two coastal Departments of Moquegua and Tacna; the parallel eastern branch similarly precludes much communication with the tropical jungle. The juncture of the two branches on the northwest boundary between Cuzco and Puno Departments reduces local traffic there. To the southwest, high, unpopulated desert separates Puno from Arequipa. On the eastern boundary of the department, the international border with Bolivia truncates trade relations. These obstacles weaken marketplace relations in southern Peru. Although marketplace systems exist in Arequipa, Cuzco, and Tacna, neither trader nor consumer movement links these marketing systems to that of Puno. Arequipa merchants sell in the markets of southern Cuzco now that a new road has been built between the two departments, but neither of these systems relates to Puno. The recent development of a marketing system in Tacna remains focused on the mines and the capital city there. As yet, no marketing system has arisen in Moquegua. Finally, though many goods pass from Puno markets to Bolivia, this is a wholesale–contraband trade that affects certain border markets but has not determined the shape of the Puno marketing system. Thus, the Department of Puno constitutes a bounded unit of study for both geopolitical and marketing reasons. (See Map 1.)

From rather inauspicious beginnings, marketing in Puno has continually increased, so that 27 markets in 1900 have grown to 118 today, and the number keeps growing (Table 1). The increase has not come evenly through time. It took 50 years for the number of markets to double and

Map 1. Department of Puno: agricultural and pastoral zones.

then only 25 years for it to double again. Neither is the increase in markets even across space. Political capitals were heavily favored as the sites of early markets, and markets appeared earlier and in greater numbers in agricultural areas than in herding areas. In fact, almost all political capitals in the agricultural zone of the department have had markets since at least the beginning of this century. Similarly, no country market has

TABLE 1
Number of District Capitals, District-Capital Markets, and Rural Markets in Puno by Decade[a]

Decade	District Capitals			District Capitals with Markets			Rural Markets			Total Number of Markets
	Agri.	Past.	Total	Agri.	Past.	Total	Agri.	Past.	Total	
to 1901	21	39	60	16	11[b]	27	0	0	0	27
to 1911	21	43	64	16	11	27	0	0	0	27
to 1921	21	43	64	16	11 [i]	27	3[e]	1[g]	4	31
to 1931	22	43	65	19	13	32	8[f]	2	10	42
to 1941	22	46	68	20	15	35	12	5	17	52
to 1951	22	46	68	21	18	39	13	10	23	62
to 1961	23	49	72	21	24[c]	45	17	11	28	73
to 1971	25	50	75	23	35[d]	58	25	30[h]	55	110
1972 –	25	50	75	23	33	56	32	30	62	118

a. Markets shown by political level and production zone.
b. One of these early markets died in 1954.
c. One of the markets, founded in the 1950s, died in 1969.
d. One of the markets, founded in the 1960s, died in 1968.
e. One rural community was raised to district capital in 1964.
f. One rural community was raised to district capital in 1961.
g. One of the markets, founded in the 1920s, died in 1968.
h. One of the markets, founded in the 1960s, died within the decade.

Agri.:   Agricultural zone.
Past.:   Pastoral zone.

been founded in a district where the political capital had not already established a market. The increase in the number of marketplaces thus resolves into a series of particular questions: Why have capital towns always been favored over rural places? Why were capital towns in the agricultural zone favored over those in the herding zone? Why did market foundation begin at once in rural places in both the agricultural and the herding zones? Why has market foundation in rural communities recently proceeded apace in both zones? Will the herding area ultimately, if belatedly, develop a marketing pattern similar to that of the agricultural areas?

SUPPLY, DEMAND, AND EARLY MARKET FOUNDATION

Market foundation is most often related to population density as a shortcut measure for demand. Hodder (Hodder and Ukwa 1969:61) concurs with Skinner's finding (1964:33) that areas with fewer than 50 people per square mile seldom support marketplaces. Only 14 districts in Puno, according to the 1940 census, had densities of even that level. Several of these more densely populated districts did not then host a weekly market, whereas some of the more sparsely populated districts did. McKim (1972:337), however, found market development in the Yendi area of northeastern Ghana despite densities as low as 30 people per square mile. While most markets in Puno before 1940 met this lower critical density, several districts with markets were extraordinarily thinly populated—10 and even 3.5 people per square mile.

McKim (1972:337–338) proposes three additional factors to account for the existence of markets in the low-density Yendi area: the nature of the population distribution and a nucleated settlement pattern, the well-developed transportation system and low transport rates, and the thin market periodicity in the region. The conjunction of these factors may account for the Yendi case, but they patently fail in Puno. Population within a district is everywhere scattered across the countryside except for the one nucleated political capital. Roads, even today, remain miserable at best and impassable at worst. Already high transport costs rise with isolation. And all pre-1940 markets in Puno met weekly, on Sunday. In short, the complex of economic factors usually considered within central-place theory to explain marketplace existence does not adequately account for the situation in Puno before 1940.

Insofar as these strictly economic factors affect demand densities, they do influence market evolution. Population density, for example, structures the general pattern of marketing. Before World War II those districts in Puno with densities greater than 10 people per square kilometer were

TABLE 2
Markets by Population Density: Puno Region[a]

Population Density	Pre-1940 Market[b]	
	Market	No Market
Less than 10/km^2	9	23
More than 10/km^2	25	9

a. *Pre-1940 markets in district capitals.*
b. $x^2 = 13.59$ *(p < .0001).*

much more likely to hold a Sunday market than those with fewer than 10 people per square kilometer (Table 2). Nonetheless, this overall result masks the failure of population density to predict markets in each production zone (Table 3). In the more densely populated agricultural zone, almost all political capitals hosted a weekly market regardless of population density. In the herding area, although the proportion of thinly populated districts with markets was low, the proportion was only 50 percent in the more densely populated districts. Thus population density does not predict the existence of marketplaces in either production zone.

Productivity and political level of a district better predict the existence of local markets in each production zone before World War II. In the lower, more fertile agricultural areas of the department, namely the apron of land skirting Lake Titicaca, regional staples yield more. These yields

TABLE 3
Markets by Population Density: By Production Zone[a]

Population Density	Agricultural Zone[b]		Pastoral Zone[c]	
	Market	No Market	Market	No Market
Less than 10/km^2	2	0	7	23
More than 10/km^2	18	2	7	7

a. *Pre-1940 markets in district capitals.*
b. $x^2 = .24$ *(not significant).*
c. $x^2 = 3.14$ *(not significant).*

TABLE 4
Markets by Absolute White Population of Districts: Puno Region[a]

Absolute White Population	Pre-1940 Market[b]	
	Market	No Market
Less than 200	6	23
More than 200	28	9

a. *Pre-1940 markets in district capitals.*
b. $x^2 = 19.67$ *(p < .001).*

support denser rural populations, as well as more towns with more "white" townsmen, than those in the relatively barren areas of the *altiplano* where herding constitutes the major economic activity. Were urbanization a function solely of agricultural productivity, early markets in Puno might have occurred only in the circumlacustrine area. However, other endeavors support town growth. In the herding zone administrative offices and mines often attracted white populations. These populations required foodstuffs despite the evident difficulty of local agriculture.

The importance of an elite class (arbitrarily fixed at 40 white[4] families of five members) for the existence of a market before 1940 is clear (Table 4). Those districts capitals with fewer than 200 white residents were less likely market sites and, conversely, those districts capitals with more than 200 white residents were more likely market sites before World War II. When production is controlled, this finding is upheld for both the herding zone, and the agricultural zone (Table 5).[5] Significantly, the three markets in agricultural districts with fewer than 200 whites were sited in district

[4] These racial categories derive from the 1940 census, which classifies people as white and mestizo (*blanca y mestiza*), Indian (*india*), black (*negra*), yellow (*amarilla*), and unknown (*no declarada*). In these terms, the 1940 population of the Department of Puno was approximately 10 percent white and mestizo and 90 percent Indian.

[5] Examination of the remaining unpredicted cases underscores the importance of a dynamic analysis of class composition and size. Three markets (Table 5, footnote *f*) portend changes in marketing that had just begun by 1940. Another eight "errors" arise from coding decisions (Table 5, footnotes *e* and *g*). Three districts simply never had a white population as large as that enumerated in the 1940 census, and five districts without a market had only slightly more than the operational 40 white families. Thus, only two districts supported sizable white populations without a market. Both of these towns are on the rail line, and both depended completely upon the wool trade with centers outside the Department of Puno. Both are sited in the highest parts of the department, which produce fine wool but no agriculture. People there had to buy everything in stores, which again demonstrates the interaction between rural production and urban consumption.

TABLE 5
Markets by Absolute White Population of Districts: By Production Zone[a]

Absolute White Population	Agricultural Zone[b]		Pastoral Zone[c]	
	Market	No Market	Market	No Market
Less than 200	3[d]	2[e]	3[f]	21
More than 200	17	0	11	9[g]

   a. *Pre-1940 markets in district capitals.*
   b. $x^2 = 4.47$ *(p < .05).*
   c. $x^2 = 9.10$ *(p < .01).*
   d. *Some markets provided opportunities for horizontal exchange among peasant producers. These are they: Huata, Coata, Chupa.*
   e. *One town, Paucarcolla, has an extraordinarily large white population of 721 for a small district capital. The enumerated white population is a function of census definitions, not reality. Paucarcolla is a town near the department capital of Puno and was specialized in various branches of commerce like the cattle trading even before 1940, for which reason the census takers enumerated the inhabitants as "white." While people from Paucarcolla are not simple subsistence farmers, they are not white in any political or dietary sense.*
   f. *The market in the district capital of Calapuja was founded in reaction to the Adventist movement in a rural community of that district; one market, Huacullani, represents the then beginning new order in the Ilave'area, as does the last, Atuncolla, near Puno City.*
   g. *Five of these districts without markets had less than 235 whites: Achaya, 203; Pizacoma, 203; Caraacota, 207; Mazo Cruz, 232; and Orurillo, 234. Since any cutoff point is more or less arbitrary, these might not be considered real exceptions. Two towns, Nuñoa and Santiago de Pupuja, like Paucarcolla, never had the white population enumerated by the census of 1940. Two other towns, Santa Lucia and Santa Rosa, grew as points on the rail line, which also provisioned them. For one reason or another, none of these nine is a true exception to the theoretical expectation that districts with more than 200 whites will have a market before 1940.*

capitals. These markets presumably occasioned more horizontal exchange among country producers than vertical exchange between classes. Nonetheless, that they were sited in the capital town rather than the countryside signals the mutual advantages to both groups. The towns offered goods and services not available elsewhere in the countryside, and the countrymen willingly went to town to obtain them. Such interaction characterizes all markets, but elsewhere it appears that the size and class composition of capital towns provided a wider basis for urban–rural exchange. For this reason, the numbers of the upper classes significantly predicts the occurrence of markets in the department as well as in both production zones.

This situation arose from the socioeconomic context of the period. Towns depended on local agriculture for supplies because each town maintained a topological monopoly over the production in its hinterland. But agriculture is very risky in the pastoral area and it is often not possible to produce all or even many of the desired foodstuffs. Nonetheless, even under these adverse conditions, rural populations planted some hardy crops for market sale when sufficient urban demand existed. In short, urban demand called forth rural production which was exchanged in the town marketplace although, store purchases of wheat, flour, sugar, rice, and corn might provide much of the urban diet because these commodities are nowhere grown locally. The closed, local economic context had created the two conditions for market development in pre-World War II Puno: the size of the consuming population and the local production in an area.

The explanation for markets in the Department of Puno before 1940 is relatively simple: Social demography called forth markets where local agricultural production matched urban taste. Almost all political capitals sited in the agricultural zone of the *altiplano* had markets whereas only half those in the herding zone had markets. Market development in this era had little to do with peasant convenience or with international export interests. It was very simply a local response to urban food needs. The locus for market development was the town, and its occurrence was regional. Yet there was no regional system. Markets were small, isolated, local happenings in each place.

THE PRE-1940 MARKETING PATTERN

The general basis of marketing activity in Puno before 1940 resembles that described in other undeveloped regions (Sayres 1956; Siverts 1969). Countrymen came into town on Sunday to transact their business. They brought with them small quantities of staples to sell in the marketplaces so that they might purchase some few small things in the town stores to take back to their community for redistribution. Market abuses were unfortunately common. Local police collected the municipal market tax. Political authorities might confiscate a chicken or a sack of potatoes for their personal use. Townspeople could force the final sale price on vendors because they had the political clout. To cite an extreme case, a country vendor who refused to sell his grains for less than half his asking price was accused of being a member of an Indian rebellion and jailed for 2 years before the charges were dropped.[6]

Such behavior by townsmen would dampen the interest of any countryman in market selling. It is unnecessary to call upon a value of "rural mutual assistance" that may limit the amount of produce that rural producers bring to market (as posited, for example, by Ortiz 1967:401). The country producer is generally a community member enmeshed in very local systems of rural social security. But he is also a free agent, willing to sell some of his produce in town in exchange for other commodities. Market abuses made countrymen reluctant to sell their produce in town. This reluctance reinforces the townsmen's coercive behavior. Since the amount of produce that might come in on any Sunday could never be predicted, the only certainty was that there might not be enough for everyone. Townsmen then had to meet the incoming countrymen in order to assure themselves a purchase.[7] Market abuse and forestalling thus become artifacts of an economic situation in which independent small producers create weekly shortfalls in a static, local economy.

The self-limiting nature of this type of market operation should be clear. The small quantities usually available in even the most productive areas militated against the rise of wholesale buyers of staples anywhere. Each town had the same problem, and no town really had more foodstuffs brought to town than any other place, regardless of productivity. There was little reason for traders to look to the marketplace for possible wholesale sources. Had traders attempted to do so, the relationship between the local political authorities and the town shopkeepers would have thwarted them. Because the local shopkeepers enjoyed the security of a local areal monopoly, they pressured the local authorities into imposing greater and more frequent fines on any intruding vendor, who understandably would be less likely to return. As long as the markets remained local, they were plagued by the problem of insufficient supply, ultimately of their own making. The pre-1940 markets of Puno were an operable, though self-defeating, means of provisioning towns, completely embedded in the complex of social relations of that era.

The first rural markets in the department were established after 1915 in reaction to market abuses, but they only extended this closed, local system. In the first quarter of this century, North American Adventist missionaries arrived in Puno and converted several groups of families in rural communities to the south of Puno City. Whenever Adventist countrymen went to market, they were quickly singled out for extraor-

---

[6] This case was kindly provided by Laura Maltby, who found it in the judicial archive of Lampa, Department of Puno. The case began in 1920.

[7] Although the national government penalized this business of forestalling in 1929, the legislation never had any effect in Puno (see Davies 1970:183).

dinary official and extralegal treatment.[8] Adventists often suffered special fines, confiscation of their produce, physical abuse, and judicial action; for example, one local Adventist leader who donned jacket and trousers to attend the market in his district capital was spat upon, stripped, dunked in the town fountain, and charged with disorderly conduct (Chambi 1961:5). The Adventists quickly realized that their only remedy was refuge. Between 1915 and 1935, Adventists founded a series of rural markets in order to emancipate themselves from dependence on the district capitals. Even this reaction was not easy. Heretofore the town authorities had maintained their areal monopoly by sanctioning no rural marketplace anywhere in their district.[9] The Adventist reaction was economic heresy, and it literally required forceful action by the North American leader of this sect to assure that these rural markets could continue.

The founding of markets under Adventist auspices in no way signaled the beginning of a marketing system. Where the Adventist religious movement met success, they founded markets, in the herding areas as well as along the lake. Each Adventist-sponsored market met in front of the church school on Sunday, and people from the surrounding countryside came to exchange produce or purchase some staples brought in by Adventist merchants. There reportedly was no price benefit, the only advantage being personal safety. With all Adventist markets meeting on the same day and offering the same goods as the district capital markets, there could be no vendor or consumer articulation. In short, while the Adventists' addition to the marketing landscape was revolutionary in that it broke the town monopolies, it did not change the nature of marketing in the department. Socioeconomic control remained with the townspeople.

A new economic force had been added to Puno with the construction of a railroad into the department in the 1860s. The railroad facilitated the export of wool from the *altiplano* and attracted new settlers to the area. According to Quiroga (cited in Romero 1928:426), the number of haciendas in the *altiplano* increased from 705 in 1876 to 3219 in 1915. These haciendas sold their wool to commercial houses based outside the Puno region. Only the very few larger producers of finer wools shipped to the commercial houses directly. Most haciendas dealt with agents of the

[8] Although many of the actions taken against the Adventists were illegal, so was the practice of Adventism itself. Peru recognized freedom of worship only in 1915 (Pike 1967:115).

[9] Catholic countrymen in the rural communities of Choko (District of Chupa, Province of Azangaro) and Huancho (District of Huancane, Province of Huancane) also founded local markets in this era. Residents of these rural communities mention abuses suffered in the market of the provincial capital of Huancane as the motive for establishing their own market. Dan C. Hazen (1974) adds that the townsmen in the provincial capital of Huancane forbade access to their market by countrymen from this area because it was then in revolt.

commercial houses who were based in *altiplano* towns on the rail line, where wool was processed for transshipment outside the region. These agents also distributed goods imported to the region by the railroad. The system of bulking and distribution supported warehousing, accounting, and similar services in the towns on the rail line, and it created a classic dendritic structure in the department.[10] Each rail town effectively controlled the commerce away from the rail line because local transportation in the off-line areas remained primitive. Boat service to lakeside towns extended this pattern to areas not directly served by the railroad.

The growth of the international wool trade during the second half of the nineteenth century profoundly affected the mass of small rural producers. The indigenous rural population has always controlled production of the highly esteemed alpaca wool. Any single producer, however, had only a limited quantity in any year, often not enough to warrant the long journey to the major buying town in his area. In order to obtain this wool, the buying agents retained "collectors," who made the rounds in the distant countryside, bulking wool and selling merchandise. From these beginnings a new distinction arose within the rural lower class—that between country producer and country buyer. The two groups not only played different roles but also underwent different fates.

The country buyer could profit whether the price of wool was high or low. As a middleman, his concern was whether the market was rising or falling. The country producer, however, was very much concerned with price per se. As long as the price was high, the capital invested in his herd was productive without any rise in productivity. Were it to fall, his family firm might no longer be viable. At the end of World War II, this structural situation created a large number of unlanded countrymen and a much smaller number of their wealthier confreres. The first group, stemming from the rural producers, went to town in search of a livelihood; the smaller group, made up of wool buyers, went to town in search of new investment opportunities. Wool export thus supported the peculiar phenomenon in the rural lower class of surplus labor and surplus capital. Regional towns provided an outlet for both.

Together these children of agriculturists who live in town are known as *cholos*,[11] and collectively they constitute a new social class, albeit divided, which transformed the social and economic character of the department through urban migration. This process overloaded the traditional

---

[10] The Navajo situation delineated by Klara Kelley in Chapter 7 of this volume well describes a comparable case of production type and marketing system development that applies to the earlier era of Puno economic history.

[11] *Cholo* can be a word of vile connotations, although it is an old and respectable word. It is used here only to denote the new class of people who left the country to find work in the cities as their major source of income. Bourricaud (1964) describes this process in Puno during the early 1950s.

mechanism of provisioning the towns with food. Around the lake, towns-women began making forays to rural communities and to the few rural markets then in existence in order to exchange small urban goods like dried chilies (*ajis*) and bread for agricultural staples they needed in their homes. In time, these occasional forays were regularized and eventually institutionalized as a major bulking mechanism for agricultural staples sold in the cities of the department. Meanwhile, in the herding zone, inde-pendent agents who resold wool to export firms outside the region began looking for new and reliable sources of wool. After 1950, these men founded markets in political capitals to tap supply. Thus, the department underwent an increase in marketing with the growth of towns, although the basis for this expansion differed in the two zones. Urban food demand extended marketing into the rural agricultural areas, while international wool demand supported market development in the capital towns of the herding areas. It was in response to these forces that a regional marketing system was emerging.

Whichever the reason for a thickening market system, it posed a new problem for traders. Until the post–World War II era, trade was centered in the major towns, and markets met only on Sunday. As traders began bulking staples and selling goods in more outlying places they agitated to have town schedules changed from Sunday in order to deal in more than one market per week. Several of the provincial capitals did change their market days: Juliaca to Monday, Ayaviri to Wednesday, and Puno to Saturday. Once the new scheduling of provincial markets was set in the early 1950s, lower-level markets changed their schedules through local experimentation or trader initiative. In either case the success of a local market depended upon its ability to attract traders who resided in the pro-vincial capital, for which reason articulation came from above. While many of the earlier district capital markets have continued to meet on Sunday, most of the newer markets are held on weekdays. Today almost three-quarters of the markets in the department occur on weekdays.

Rural market foundation in the past decades has fleshed out the present marketing landscape in accordance with the expectations of central-place theory. These markets depend upon improvement in transportation because trader participation is crucial. Local authorities always select a market day other than that of their provincial market, which also promises least competition from similar lower-level markets. This consideration stems from a self-conscious concern with the participation of outside vendors. Without them, local authorities will say, a market would be *triste* ("sad" or, more meaningfully, "slow"). This local recognition of the role of town-based traders in marketing development reflects the top-to-bottom filling out of the marketing space in the Department of Puno, even though the initiative may now be strictly local.

CONTEMPORARY PATTERNS—
A MARKET HIERARCHY

Unlike the markets before 1940, contemporary markets in the Department of Puno constitute a multilevel system articulated by the movement of goods, vendors, and consumers. Remnants of the old situation—Sunday markets in many capital towns—persist, but the quantitative increase in the number of markets has been accompanied by a qualitative change in the nature of marketing. Today, despite one or two country markets of strictly local significance, markets mesh with the cities and with one another. Indicative of the new order is the behavior within contemporary markets. The larger towns collect municipal taxes, but officials no longer abuse their authority. Townspeople, rather than complain to authorities about prices above those set officially, quietly pay, thankful to have been able to buy. Traders circulate freely among markets. And, where forestallers still purchase, they do so from friends and relatives because forestaller buying price continues to be slightly lower than that offered by city buyers.[12] In part, these changes reflect the greater experience and better education of the countrymen. But they also reflect the changed nature of marketing on the *altiplano*.

Market size before 1940 was related directly to the white and rural population resident in a district and to the productivity of an area. These markets generally preferred the same array of goods. In contrast, the contemporary market hierarchy, revealed through the types of goods that each market displays, presumes nonlocal hinterlands. To analyze the changed nature of marketing through hierarchical articulation, an index of goods that could rank markets was constructed. All commodities were classed into one of nine categories defined by function[13], level of demand for a good—that is, elasticity—and whether the item sold is produced by

[12] In some instances a forestaller may sit on the road to town, perhaps a mile or more from the market. More commonly, forestallers locate much nearer to the market. In the town of Taraco, for example, local forestallers sit along the roads leading directly into the market in the lower square. This square was traditionally the "Indian" market and even today displays a characteristically more "Indian" array of goods. Buyers of eggs, cheese, and tubers from the nearby major center of Juliaca locate in the upper square, which is only a block away and was customarily the white or mestizo market. These buyers pay a bit more per egg or cheese, yet countrywomen continue to sell to local forestallers because these buyers are relatives or friends. Forestallers who depend upon their personal network of acquaintances to buy are bulking for their domestic use and for sale to buyers in the upper square later in the day. Thus, while not all aspects of marketing have changed in the past 30 years, the situation and operation today are quite different.

[13] Generally, three things happen in a market: Goods are sold, services are performed, and produce is bulked. Since the performance of services directly parallels the sale of goods, no service was specifically included in the index; goods of a particular category may be understood to represent such services. (Barbering, for example, occurs where clothes are sold, and games of chance appear in markets where radios are sold.)

the vendor. Then one commodity was selected from each category. Each of these commodities is typical of all others in its category, so that together the nine selected commodities capture all that may occur in a market. Table 6 presents the index goods categorized by function, demand level, and origin.

The selection criteria themselves order the index goods. Level of demand structures the index generally. Low-level goods (those with inelastic demand) are more widely sold than medium-level goods, which, in

TABLE 6

Index Goods, According to Market Function, Origin, and Level of Demand

	Market Function		
	Selling (Services)		Bulking
	Imported	Seller-Produced	
High	Imported food staples (sugar, flour, noodles)	Regional food staples[a] (barley, chuno, potatoes)	Produce buying[b]
Medium	Clothing	Onions[c]	
Low	Plastic and aluminum utensils ----------------- Bicycle parts ----------------- Radios	Clay pots	

a. In the agricultural zone, regional food staples are sold in miniscule amounts by a multitude of buyers; on the altiplano, resellers usually vend these products.

b. In the agricultural zone, produce buyers bulk regional food staples like barley and potatoes for the cities in the department; on the altiplano, produce buyers bulk wool for international export.

c. Onions are imported from the Departments of Arequipa, Tacna, and Cuzco for sale in the Department of Puno. The distribution of these onions parallels that of imported dry food staples and they are available in almost any market from a seller of dry food staples. The distribution of seller-produced onions, however, is distinctive. Several areas of onion production in the Department of Puno each supply a part of the department. Seller-produced onions for the Ilave subregion (Province of Chucuito) come mainly from the community of Ichu outside Puno City (Province of Puno).

turn, are more widely sold than specialized, high-level goods. Moreover, within each level of demand, goods imported into the department are more widely sold than craft goods produced within the department. Apart from this ordering of retail goods, produce bulking is taken as a fundamental function of markets because at the same time that merchandise is retailed to country consumers, rural foodstaples are wholesaled for urban distribution.

Since the goods are ordered from the least common (highest-level) good to the most common (lowest-level) good, the presence of the highest-level good in any market implies the presence of all lower-level goods. This ordering permits a theoretical classification of markets with nine categories, each less inclusive of index goods than the one before. However, the number of theoretical classes of markets may be realistically reduced from nine to six by collapsing the distinction between imported and regional goods at each demand level (Table 7).

This classification of markets has been tested with data from the area

TABLE 7

Theoretical Classification of Markets Based upon the Ordered Index of Goods

Level of Markets	Presence of Ordered Goods 1–9[a]									Description of Market
	1	2	3	4	5	6	7	8	9	
I	X	X	X	X	X	X	X	X	X	All goods available
II	X	X	X	X	X	X	X	X		All but most specialized goods available
III	X	X	X	X	X	X	X			Food and consumer goods, both imported and regional; some low-demand goods
IV	X	X	X	X	X					Food and medium-demand consumer goods available; imported and regional
V	X	X	X							Food markets; outside buyers and sellers
VI	X									Store-like markets; imported dry food staples only; no outside buyers or sellers

   a. *Ordered goods 1–9 are as follows: 1 = imported food staples; 2 = produce bulking; 3 = regional staples; 4 = clothing; 5 = onions; 6 = plastic or aluminum utensils; 7 = clay pots; 8 = bicycle parts; 9 = radios.*

centering on the market town of Ilave in the southern sector of the department. Although this subregion is hardly typical of any other, all the processes that occur in Ilave may also occur elsewhere. Since it is the combination of processes that makes each area unique, the Ilave area constitutes a microcosm wherein the processes may be more carefully detailed. These data were collected during censuses of each market in the Department of Puno. The censuses were done systematically by area during the calendar year 1973. In each market, information was collected from every vendor concerning his place of residence and the goods offered for sale.[14]

Testing the index and its derived market levels against market composition in the Ilave subregion demonstrates that the index scales markets with relatively few errors and that all six theoretical market levels exist.[15] (See Table 8.) As for scaling errors, Zepita boasts a bicycle repairman who sells parts from his shop in the market, although it fails to attract producer–sellers of onions because of its small size and inconvenient scheduling. Zepita, a Sunday market, suffers much competition, with many of its rural residents going elsewhere to market. The *altiplano* district capital of Pizacoma and the two rural *altiplano* markets of Patalaca and Pasto Grande lack regional staple sellers because they are so far from the distribution center of Ilave. In this zone there is no agriculture that would allow local producers to go to market with small quantities of staples from their larders. Local people do take wool, but this is for sale to produce buyers. Along the lake, two markets, Suancata and Isani, attract local people with their tubers and grains, while two other markets, Marquesquena and Culta, predictably attract produce buyers but no local sellers of produce. Since these are incomplete local markets without outside sellers, they are classified together as nonstandard markets. In brief, six scaling errors occur among nine items for 36 markets; but each error is conditioned by factors not included in the ordering criteria for reasons of generality.

Although the theoretical classification of markets (Table 9) generally depicts commercial movement in this subregion, it more accurately reflects the composition of urban markets than of rural markets. The artisanal item of a demand level invariably does not appear in rural markets when its imported counterpart does. That is, in rural markets, clothing will appear without producer-sold onions; plastic and aluminum

---

[14] Data from the Ilave subregion are presented here because information from other areas has not been completely analyzed. Preliminary analysis of these other data confirm the interpretations made here. For fuller treatment see Appleby (1976).

[15] The simple number of vendors in a market, however, does not index level. Level II markets attract 200 to 600 vendors in the agricultural zone but only 100 to 150 in the herding zone. This difference relates to production. Markets around the lake typically attract between 50 and 500 producer–sellers; in the herding area, where agriculture is not widely practiced, this form of "horizontal exchange" cannot exist.

TABLE 8
Market Hierarchy of Ilave Determined by Index of Goods

Market	Number of Sellers	1	2	3	4	5	6	7	8	9
Urban--Agricultural Zone										
Ilave	1,066	X	X	X	X	X	X	X	X	X
Yunguyo	1,239	X	X	X	X	X	X	X	X	X
Desaguadero	1,143	X	X	X	X	X	X	X	X	X
Acora	558	X	X	X	X	X	X	X	X	
Pilcuyo	244	X	X	X	X	X	X	X	X	
Pomata	113	X	X	X	X	X				
Juli	103	X	X	X	X	X				
Zepita	45	X	X	X	X					X
Urban--Pastoral Zone										
Pizacoma	107	X	X		X	X	X	X[b]	X	
Mazo Cruz	136	X	X	X	X	X	X	X		
Huacullani	7	X	X							
Rural--Agricultural Zone										
Tinancachi[c]	69	X		X	X		X		X	
Chipana	90	X	X	X	X	X[d]	X			
Jayujayu	118	X	X	X	X	X				
Chakachaka	210	X	X	X	X					
Huallata	73	X	X	X	X					
Socca	53	X	X	X	X					
Copana	79	X	X	X						
Sulkacultura	21	X	X	X						
Cachi	26	X	X	X						
Suancata	34	X		X						
Marquesquena	49	X	X							
Culta	21	X	X							
Isani	24	X		X						
Santa Rosa	22	X								

　　a. *See Table 6 for a list of the index goods.*
　　b. *Clay pots are not available in the Pizacoma market, which is actually sited in a rural community on the international border with Bolivia. Clay pots are available, however, in the market on the Bolivian side which occurs simultaneously with the Ventilla-Pizacoma market. Since there is free movement between the two markets, clay pots are coded as available in Pizacoma.*

(continued on next page)

TABLE 8 (continued)

Market	Number of Sellers	1	2	3	4	5	6	7	8	9

Market	Number of Sellers	Index of Goods 1-9[a]								
		1	2	3	4	5	6	7	8	9
Rural--Pastoral Zone										
Lopis	119	X	X	X	X	X	X	X[e]	X	
Totorani	140	X	X	X	X					
Condoreri	57	X	X	X	X					
Santa Rosa de Juli	46	X	X	X	X					
Pasto Grande	33	X	X	[f]	X					
Patalaca	22	X	X	[f]	X					
Quillahuyu	31	X	[g]	X	X					
Tuturumi	11	X	X	X						
Huapaca	42	X	X							
Capazo	23	X	X							
Ancomarca	14	X	X							
Chika[h]	6	X								

c. *Tinancachi, in the District of Yunguyu, is sited near the international border with Bolivia and most goods sold here are destined for resale in La Paz. Because there are no seller-produced goods of any demand level, this market is excluded from the analysis of the Puno marketing system.*

d. *Chipana, in the District of Pilcuyo, was censused twice but only once were there producers selling onions. Whether or not producers go to Chipana to sell their onions depends upon the availability of transportation. Therefore, onions are coded as available in the Chipana market.*

e. *One or two sellers of clay pots go to the Lopis market about every other week, so clay pots are coded as available.*

f. *Resellers of regional staples bulked in the agricultural lakeside zone do not go to the markets of Pasto Grande and Patalaca because of the great distance from their residence in Ilave. Clothing sellers, in contrast, live in Mazo Cruz. These two markets, therefore, might be considered in Class III--Rural Pastoral Zone--along with Tuturumi, Huapaca, Capazo, and Ancomarca. They are included in Class II because clothing sellers do attend them.*

g. *Produce buyers do attend the Quillahuyu market during the dry season, when trucks can enter. The dry season coincides with shearing time. Since produce buying is everywhere seasonal, this should not be considered a scaling error.*

h. *Chika is in competition with Lopis and losing.*

TABLE 9
Levels of Markets by Site and Production Type in the Ilave Subregion

Market Class	Goods Expected	Urban		Rural	
		Agricultural	Pastoral	Agricultural[b]	Pastoral
I	1-5	1-9 (3)			1-8 (1)
II	1-8	1-8 (2)	1-8 (1)		
III	1-7		1-7 (1)	1-6 (1)	
IV	1-5	1-5 (3)		1-4 (4)	1-4 (6)
V	1-3		1-2[a] (1)	1-3 (3)	1-2 (4)
VI	1			1&3 (5)	1 (1)
				1-2	
				1	

a. Without any regional staple production on the altiplano, there can be no local producer-sellers. These are, therefore, not considered incomplete markets.
b. One market, Tinancachi, has been excluded from this analysis. See footnote c of Table 8.

168

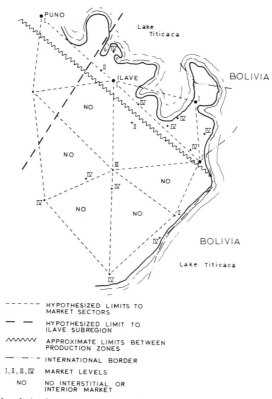

------- HYPOTHESIZED LIMITS TO MARKET SECTORS

— — HYPOTHESIZED LIMIT TO ILAVE SUBREGION

мммм APPROXIMATE LIMITS BETWEEN PRODUCTION ZONES

—··—··— INTERNATIONAL BORDER

I, II, III, IV   MARKET LEVELS

NO   NO INTERSTITIAL OR INTERIOR MARKET

Map 2. Market levels in the Ilave subregion, Chucuito Province, Puno.

utensils will appear without clay pots. This consistent "failure" of locally produced goods in rural markets, like the belated appearance of country markets, underscores the weakness of local artisans and supports the proposition that rural markets arose through exogenous stimulus in the Department of Puno.[16]

Map 2 depicts the market orders in space. The two lower orders, Levels

[16] Another way of stressing the top-down development of marketing in Puno is to examine the numerical ratios between market levels. If the Ilave subregion is structured in a central-place manner, one would expect either a $K = 3$ marketing ratio between centers (of $1:2:6:18:54:162$) or a $K = 4$ transport ratio (of $1:3:12:48:192$). (See Marshall 1969:20, 31.) The geographical configuration of this area, an agricultural strip of land along the lake whence penetration roads take off across the *altiplano*, should favor the transport ratio. The actual ordering in Puno $(3:3:2:13:8:6)$ may be considered closer $(1:3:4:13:14)$ to that predicted if the two Level I markets on the international border are reduced to Level III on the grounds that international wholesale trade supports the specialized commerce that occurs there and if Levels V and VI are combined into one category of local markets. In either case, the point of note is the precipitous drop-off in the numbers of lower-level markets in the Ilave area. This drop-off in the numbers of marketplaces accords with a process of market founda-tion that has proceeded from top-down, as it has in Puno, rather than from bottom-up, as is predicted in theory.

V and VI, have been dropped from this analysis on the grounds that any market without clothing cannot, in Puno, constitute a standard market in Christallerian terms. Higher-level markets define regular hexagonal patterns around the major lakeside center of Ilave and around the major *altiplano* center of Mazo Cruz. Theoretically, Level II markets should occur within each triangular sector. Level II markets, however, occur interstitially in only 3 of the 10 sectors, and these interstitial markets are sited exclusively in the agricultural zone. (In a minor deviation from this pattern, the development of the two southernmost Level I markets depends upon contraband trade across the international border, with a consequent lowering of market levels in that sector.) Although market levels on the pastoral *altiplano* are expectedly lower than along the agricultural apron because demand densities are lower, the herding areas show no interstitial or interior placement of orders. Markets here are sited along major routes to the coast with little penetration to areas between routes. The basis for this consistent irregularity in the herding zone when a normal central-place pattern has developed in the agricultural zone lies in the nature of marketing in Puno, particularly in urban food needs.

EFFECTS OF MARKET EVOLUTION IN
ONE SUBREGION

The process of market foundation in the Ilave area confirms the importance of towns and urban food needs in the top-down thickening of marketing in the Department of Puno. The two political capitals in the agricultural zone that lacked weekly markets at the turn of the century, Zepita and Desaguadero, founded markets once the circumlacustrine road was extended to the international border. Meanwhile, the Adventists were busily establishing refuge markets in the rural areas of Ilave and Acora. Neither phenomenon portended any change in the nature of marketing. The foundation between 1939 and 1950 of the first markets in the pastoral areas, by contrast, signaled a significant change reflecting the growth of towns, the construction of more and better roads, the advent of truck transport, and the development of trader specialists. Because roads pushed out across the *altiplano* from the lakeside agricultural corridor, the first markets in the herding area were sited near the ecological divide and thus also near the commercial centers where trade was increasing. Although traders from the agricultural area did not found these markets, they did staff them. It is unlikely that these markets could have been sustained without the presence of full-time traders from the agricultural zone, who bulked wool and retailed merchandise.

The Ilave area, like the department itself, has undergone a veritable explosion of markets since the 1950s. The pattern of expansion in each zone was distinct. In the agricultural zone rural residents have initiated the markets, and as a result interior areas are more completely filled, regardless of the existing road net. In some cases the rural people have even built roads themselves and, with support from the traders, petitioned the government for aid with bridges in order to sustain their markets. In the pastoral area, markets continue to be sited near the major roads which cross the altiplano. Here countrymen still travel long distances on foot to attend their local market, while vendors arrive in trucks. This disjunction in transport availability allows traders to reach relatively isolated sites on the road to which people come from afar, thereby creating the linear pattern of markets along penetration roads of the *altiplano*. Eight-hour walks to market, two or three times a month, are common in the pastoral zone but no longer in the agricultural zone. Beyond the spatial patterning of markets and the servicing of local populations, articulation among markets appears to vary by zone. In the agricultural area a hierarchy of competing centers services many small markets. Trade in the herding area, by contrast, continues to be controlled by traders who reside in the higher-level lakeside capitals and, only recently, by traders from district capitals in the pastoral area itself. In sum, marketing in the two zones has developed differently, although they constitute one system.

The demise of a dendritic structure in the agricultural area and its development in the pastoral area relate to the different growth rates of towns in each zone. In the Province of Chucuito, lakeside towns, especially the commercial center of Ilave, grew rapidly. District capitals in the herding area of the province have grown less rapidly during the past 30 years, and town demand there has remained low. Also, the extremely thin population density in this zone supports fewer traders of specialized goods. Merchants from the agricultural area bring medium- and low-demand consumer goods to markets in the pastoral area. These merchants tap their home area and the larger, more accessible markets in the pastoral zone. Thus, the pastoral zone of the province is served by markets dominated by vendors of higher-order goods from the lake area. The dendritic structure which earlier channeled commodites throughout the department is now limited to the herding area, where it is appended to the central-place structure that has arisen around the lake.

Although market development in the pastoral zone has lagged behind that in the agricultural zone, it is not assured that the pastoral zone will ultimately evolve a more typical central-place system. Insofar as this lag occurred because of thinner population densities in the pastoral areas the area should develop a more typical spatial pattern. But the spatial patterning and operation of markets depend on the relationship between towns and the production of an area. It appears that the factors of urbanization and production, which called forth markets in the agricultural area, will strictly limit the extension of marketing in the herding area.

The major "export" product of a zone affects the needs for marketing in that area. Traders bulk food staples in the lakeside zone for the regional urban food market. These staples are siphoned out of family larders. In years of bad harvest, prices rise dramatically because urban demand is inelastic. If prices did not rise, producers would consume more of their harvest, and the city stores would be quickly depleted.

In the pastoral area where traders bulk wool for export, small producers depend on the sale of wool to itinerant collectors or in the marketplace precisely because they cannot eat it.[17] Unlike the demand for food staples, the international demand for wool is highly volatile, so that the means of bulking the product vary. In low-price years, countrymen will not want to market their wool, though some nonetheless must; in high-price years, many small producers will sell almost all of their product at market. Efficient wool bulking under either condition, however, does not require many small markets because local agents can go from house to house in order to fulfill contracts should the supply offered by small producers not satisfy the orders placed by the commercial houses. But windfall orders simply cannot support a system of markets. Also, it is inherently advantageous for the producer to sell as far up the transshipment line as possible because the basic price for wool is set ouside the region and transport charges consume more value at the lowest levels. Because of these two factors, relatively few markets exist in the great expanses of the pastoral zone. Thus, the difference in the thickness and patterning of markets between the agricultural and pastoral zones relates systematically to differences in the locus of demand, the price-setting mechanism, and producer interest in sale.

The importance for marketing development of the relationship between export staples and urban food needs may be illustrated by the positive example of produce bulking along the lake and by the negative example of the lack of food bulking in the *altiplano,* where some foodstuffs are in fact produced. Agricultural produce in Puno and especially in the Ilave area is bulked through outright purchase of pound lots and through the tedious piling together of handfuls of staples obtained from countrywomen in exchange for such petty household needs as dried chilies bread, oranges, bananas, candy, and plastic bags. This form of bulking, known as *chala* locally, is widespread in the agricultural areas, where it is associated with urban items of consumption needed daily in rural homes, and with a scarcity of disposable ready cash among countrymen. It is eminently rational in that the countrywoman receives in her rural market the urban market value of her staples. Although *chala* involves purchase-with-com-

---

[17] For example, traders bought barley at a base rate of $.70 (U.S.) for 25 pounds of barley during the harvest of 1973 and at $1.40 (U.S.) during the harvest of 1974, when rains, hail, and frost characteristically combined to destroy much of the crop. The prices of other regional food staples rose comparably. That of wool, however, did not.

modities, it is definitely not barter. Price very precisely underlies the exchange: Each urban product has a known sale price, and each handful of staple is valued at 10 Peruvian cents (1 real is equivalent to about $.002 U.S.). In fact, this form of *chala* arose in connection with the marketing system and is spreading as the latter expands; it is a new form of exchange that occurs only in markets.[18]

While commodity exchange among rural producers has a long history in the department, purchase and *chala* are more recent. They have competed successfully with the older forms of rural provisioning. Traditional barter for small items, such as dried chilies and oranges, which countrymen obtained during long treks to the warm producing areas, has disappeared. Barter is now limited to large goods of elastic demand, such as ponchos and grinding stones. This constriction in the scope of barter has freed larger amounts of staples for "vertical" exchange with the cities.

Spatial and temporal factors influence the relative importance of cash purchase and *chala* in any market. Spatially, both forms of bulking occur in all agricultural markets, but bulkers who buy with cash are concentrated in the larger rural and urban markets (Levels I, II, III, and IV). Those who buy with urban commodities are concentrated in the smaller rural markets (Levels V and VI), later selling to bulk buyers in the larger rural markets. During a "normal" year, *chala* now equals purchase in both volume and value as the bulking mechanism for agricultural produce. But in years of harvest failure, small producers prefer *chala* to sale in order to meet their own needs, thereby directly assuring the supply to regional towns and, indirectly, the continued existence of their local markets. In sum, in the agricultural zone the mechanisms that provision towns developed within the context of rural needs. The consequence is a thick development of markets that serves local populations more efficiently.

The situation in the pastoral zone illustrates the converse case, in which the weakness of urban food demand limits the extension of a marketing system and permits "traditional" exchange mechanisms to persist. Wool and meat (from llama, alpaca, and sheep) here constitute the major salable products. Most wholesalers bulk wool for export through commercial houses outside the department. Very few specialize in fresh mutton for the lakeside capitals. None deals in alpaca and llama meat, which has no urban market in the region. Nonetheless, pastoralists do have a market for jerky (*charqui*) on the Tacna coast, where it is exchanged with the rural population there for fruit. In the district of Mazo Cruz, Province of Chucuito, for example, each of the 300 families sends an adult man to one of the approximately 30 valley areas on the coast. Each man goes alone

[18] In some parts of the department, *chala* is the word for barter (Romero 1928:496), but the distinction between customary barter and market bulking is clearly understood throughout the department.

once a year to just one area, usually during the coastal harvest season (March–April) which mercifully follows the season of torrential rains in the *altiplano*. Individual routes and schedules vary yearly according to the produce desired by the man's family.[19] Each trip takes about 2 weeks, so that in theory a man could make two trips a season where there is jerky enough. No one does make two trips because these treks must be coordinated with the seasonal low of coastal harvest season prices. Thus, even this customary barter responds to the market values of the commodities.

Altiplano pastoralists acknowledge that they would sell more jerky in local markets if there were buyers, but there are not. Rural demand in the Department of Puno is very limited and urban taste does not prize this foodstuff. Traders are therefore not interested in penetrating to the interiors of the highland area. As they say, there are few people to whom they might sell and nothing that they might bulk. That there is nothing to buy is an overstatement wholly conditioned by what can be sold to the upper classes in the urban centers where the traders reside. Without reason to seek out market sources in the interior of the *altiplano,* traders are content to attend markets of easier access established along the major routes. This development leaves much of the pastoral area poorly served by markets. Paradoxically, consumption data indicate that it is precisely in this region, which is least well served by markets, that people are most market dependent. Previously, pastoralists wove their own clothing and obtained food staples and various artisanal goods directly from lakeside production centers. (This trade involved wool because the agriculturalists were not "accustomed" to eating jerky.) Today imported clothing is less expensive than homespun woolens. Food, including regional staples, is distributed through the marketing system and local stores. And manufactured products have displaced the less expensive and less durable artisanal goods like pottery. While the regions still complement each other, organized trade through the marketing system has displaced much of the customary horizontal rural–rural exchange that by-passed urban centers.

In sum, the regional structure of markets has newly joined urbanites and countrymen in both the agricultural and pastoral zones. The marketing structure in the herding area lags behind the lake area because it is

---

[19] Edward Tuddenham kindly provided much of the ethnographic detail about trading trips in the Mazo Cruz area. [See also Flores (1968:107–138) for an example from another area of the Department of Puno.] Mr. Tuddenham argues that long-distance trade may disappear because government policy favors the formation of cooperatives that buy all local production. In his view, people on the coast now have less to exchange with their highland brethren. However, this long-distance rural trade may disappear for another reason: The recent rise of a marketing system in the Tacna Department may organize this trade. A very few Puno traders have recently begun to bulk jerky for distribution through the Tacna markets. Whether jerky distribution becomes organized through the marketing system will probably depend upon demand at the coastal mines rather than upon dispersed rural demand. But whatever actually happens, long-distance rural trade is doomed.

derivative, a consumer market based on neighboring development. That it remains a dendritic or linear system results not from its thinner population densities, which is compensated in part by greater market dependence, but from the lack of exportable products for the regional urban food market. The belated parallel growth of marketing in the pastoral zone, therefore, holds no further promise. Local consumption markets analogous to stores may flourish, but the basic pattern is fixed. Markets here will be sited along the major roads like beads on a string because traders who might regularly penetrate the interior to buy have no reason to do so. And the belated, development of marketing has hindered the growth of the few traders on the *altiplano* who specialize in expensive low-demand arrays, giving further advantage to the initially favored traders from the lakeside area. The interplay of these factors means that pastoral populations in the department are less well served by markets. Local people have no choice but to continue their annual treks to the coast in order to trade their jerky. This barter trade is definitely part of the present economic system of the department, conditioned by the marketing system yet apart from it. This trade continues outside the market system because markets exist largely to bulk produce for urban people and because the pastoral areas of the department produce no desirable foodstuff.

SUMMARY AND CONCLUSION

Christaller based central-place theory on the exchange that arises from production differences between city and countryside. The occupational differentiation that underlies these production differences is, of course, patterned in space. There is a strong tendency for the upper classes to live in the cities. Although urban residents of whatever class position do not usually produce their own food, upper-class urban residents have the wherewithal to purchase a greater variety of foodstuffs. Nonetheless all urban residents must deal with the agricultural countryside. Since transport costs consume too much value for bulky food staples to come from afar, urban food needs determine the composition and operation of markets because only what the city classes eat will be brought in for sale.

When this argument is applied to Puno, this century must be divided into two eras: the years before 1940, when there were markets but no system; and the years after 1940, when a marketing system had arisen. Similarly, the territory of the department must be divided into two ecological zones: an agricultural zone and a pastoral zone. Only the lakeside agricultural zone, it was assumed, could respond to urban food demand. The higher-altitude herding areas, which produce wool, would presumably not be directly affected by regional food needs. These distinctions of urban demand and rural supply underlie the analysis of marketing in Puno.

In the earlier era, markets were small, isolated, local happenings. Markets barely provisioned the upper classes in each district when each capital depended upon the production of its administrative hinterland. Although population density generally predicted the presence of markets in this period, consideration of the class composition of capitals and the production type in districts clarified the dynamics of marketing in the Department of Puno before 1940. Areas of heavy rural densities, which are limited to the agricultural zone in the department, had significantly greater probability of markets. But more significantly, the larger the absolute size of a town's upper classes, the more likely it was to expect a market. The relationship between simple density and the class composition of a district is readily explained by the ability of the more densely populated agricultural areas to support larger classes not directly involved in agriculture. Nonetheless, political administration required nonagricultural populations resident in various towns sited in the pastoral area, and here too markets arose.

This system of town provisioning could continue only as long as the urban population remained small. Once natural population increase and the unnatural expansion of the hacienda squeezed countrymen out of rural areas and into urban places, the static mechanism for local food provisioning became insufficient. A more flexible mechanism, a central-place system, staffed by the very people who broke the old situation, arose.

To document the existence of a central-place system, markets were classed into levels based on whether or not they offered certain index goods. Index goods were selected according to the criteria of demand level, origin, and function. It was assumed that level of demand would structure the index generally and that a theoretical classification of markets could therefore be constructed. The theoretical market levels were then compared with systematic data collected in market censuses conducted in the subregion centering on the town of Ilave (Province of Chucuito). The analysis revealed the weakness of artisanry as a basis for marketing in the Department of Puno, an ordering of markets in central-place fashion, and a distinct spatial patterning in each production zone.

The difference in the evolution of marketing structures within parts of the same system relates directly to the commodities exported. The evolution of special forms of bulking and the increasing presence of outside vendors have supported the veritable explosion of locally established markets in the agricultural zone because these markets are providing appreciable quantities of food for the regional towns. Market foundation in the pastoral area, by contrast, remains tied to major routes. This limitation exists because the major product, wool, is exported from the department and is not responsive to supply. The major foodstuff produced in this zone, jerky,

not heretofore been fully appreciated—they do not just reflect economic conditions but actually structure them. Since I find that indicators of imperfect competition are associated with the different central-place types, I suggest that this factor "causes" both variable and irregular central-place patterns and economic growth patterns.

Chapter 6

Specific Central-Place Models for an Evolving System of Market Towns on the Changhua Plain, Taiwan[1]

Lawrence W. Crissman
University of Illinois at Urbana–Champaign

INTRODUCTION

This paper describes the emergence and development of a system of market towns on the Changhua Plain, Taiwan. The hierarchy of central places existing in the late 1960s was investigated in the field; and enough information was obtained on the development of Changhua under the Nationalists and the Japanese to allow for reasonably accurate historical reconstructions of the marketing system back to the first decade of this century.

Explanation, as opposed to description, of what has occurred on the Changhua Plain depends upon some sort of theoretical model unless the explanation is to be purely historical. In this case, extensively modified elaborations of G. William Skinner's models for Chinese marketing systems, themselves outgrowths of Walter Christaller's formulations, are employed. While the alternative general models presented here are entirely satisfactory in terms of their logic, their geometry, and the extent to which they capture certain important aspects of real Chinese marketing systems, they cannot directly inform the situation on the Changhua Plain.

[1] I am indebted to the London-Cornell Project for East and Southeast Asian Societies, Cornell University, for supporting my field research.

The reason they cannot is that being wholly general (in the Chinese context), there is no way they can reflect the topographical and historical realities of the evolution of any real system of central places. However, it is possible to derive from them vastly weakened versions specific to Changhua at various points in time. The specific models are created by modifying the general models to represent only those central places and transport routes that actually existed at given time periods. Despite the incorporation of such empirical facts induced from reality, the specific central-place models are essentially deductive in that the location and spacing of the towns represented are derived from the assumptions and principles incorporated into their more powerful and general precursors.

Such formal, yet specific, central-place models make it possible to ascertain the extent to which the principles that motivate general central-place theory and derivative models are manifested in particular real-world cases. As such, they can provide scientific explanations for some aspects of the empirical reality of rural marketing systems. Such specific models also provide a satisfactory formal means of comparing different real systems— either various temporal stages in the development of rural marketing in one locality or systems of market towns in different localities. Perhaps most important, such specific models can identify those features of real systems that require their own unique (historical) explanations. In fact, there is no rigorous method for segregating general from specific causes without some such means of formally relating actual arrangements of towns and cities to powerful theoretical models such as Christaller's, Skinner's, or the alternatives to theirs that have been developed.

THE PRESENT

Changhua Hsien (or County) lies midway between the northern and southern extremities of the island of Taiwan and encompasses the northernmost part of the populous western coastal plain. The county has an area of 1000 square kilometers, and in 1967, when the field research reported in this paper was conducted, it had a population of almost 1 million. Except for a low range of hills that marks most of its eastern boundary and one township that lies to the east of their northern promontory, Changhua is unusually low and level, and the land is all under cultivation. The east-central portion of the plain produces Taiwan's greatest yields of rice, but the soil diminishes in quality and water becomes much more of a problem as the coast is approached. The southwestern third of the plain, where the field work was concentrated, is much less prosperous and densely populated than other regions, having only 565 persons per square kilometer (1580 per square mile). (See Map 1.)

The Changhua Plain is a remarkably well-bounded region. The hills to

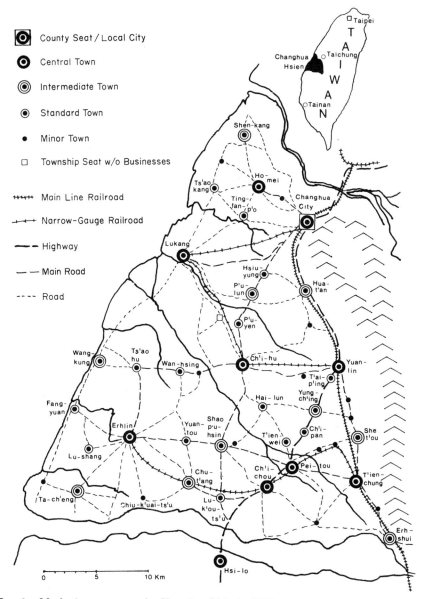

Map 1.   Marketing centers on the Changhua Plain in 1967.

the east are traversed only by one infrequently used gravel road, and sizable rivers form both the northern and the southern boundaries. All traffic of any kind from the north and east must pass through Changhua City. In the south there are only two bridges across the Ch'o-shui River; one bridge is for road traffic (in about the middle north of Hsi-lo in Yun-lin County) while one is for the railroad (at the eastern extremity near Erh-shui, where there is also a road leading up into the mountains to Sun–Moon Lake). The discreteness of the plain is one of the major reasons that Changhua was selected as a field site, since it was assumed that as a result there would be no great problems in demarcating the limits of the total system of central places to be studied.

Headquarters for the field work was the large town of Erhlin. Its hinterland and those of the surrounding smaller towns (comprising the five townships of Erhlin, Fang-yuan, Ta-ch'eng, Chu-t'ang, and P'i-t'ou) were studied intensively in order to ascertain the marketing preferences and habits of the rural population. The towns themselves were, of course, the major foci of the study. Very soon after work began, a business census was conducted in every settlement in the field area that had anything other than normal village-level businesses, such as general stores, rice mills, and barber shops. In addition, frequency counts of kinds of business activities as well as enumerations of the total number of businesses were made in the towns of Lukang, Ch'i-hu, Pei-tou, Ch'i-chou, and T'ien-chung. These towns lie outside the field area to the north and east and are of the same order of complexity as Erhlin. Three places with 15 to 35 businesses in the southeastern part of the plain were also included because the field area is deficient in such small centers. A survey of rural marketing habits, which was conducted in every village with more than 10 households in the field area, also determined the number and kind of businesses found in each one.

The central goods available in the 207 sample settlements were used to construct a giant Guttman Scalogram which has very high reproducibility. It ranked them all along a single dimension of commercial complexity defined by the 156 items that occurred in 3 or more. The scale contains nine major steps, those at the lower (less complex) end being defined by 1 to 4 items and containing numerous cases, while those at the upper end are marked by dozens of items and contain only a handful of cases each. The top three steps contain all the indisputable towns and define the contemporary Taiwanese equivalent of the three-level hierarchy of rural marketing towns that Skinner (1964) describes for traditional mainland China. Following his lead, the central places on the Changhua Plain are called standard, intermediate, and central towns in order of increasing complexity. A reasonably complete description of the central-place hierarchy and associated marketing behavior in the field area can be found in Crissman (1972 or 1973).

Erhlin, the only central town in the field area, is fairly representative of other towns of that rank in Changhua, although their idiosyncratic histories and distinctive circumstances make it impossible to generalize about all seven or eight of them. In any event, Erhlin has a population of close to 10,000 persons[2] and has 850 businesses of just under 150 different kinds. They include market stalls and regular street peddlers in addition to fixed business establishments ranging from retail stores of all varieties to craft shops, notaries' offices, and hospitals. Although Ch'i-hu has 12,000 people and 1000 businesses and T'ien-chung has 9300 inhabitants and only 725 businesses, they are both very close to Erhlin in having 150 and 141 different kinds of businesses, respectively. Lukang, which during the early nineteenth century was the most important junk port on the central coast, has a population of 28,000 but only 1075 businesses (144 kinds), while Pei-tou, also an important place early on, has a population of 12,000 and 725 businesses (138 kinds). Ch'i-chou, with a population of only 7000, is a mere 2.5 kilometers from Pei-tou along the main north–south highway and is the headquarters for the Taiwan Sugar Corporation, a government monopoly. It can be considered a "twin town" with Pei-tou, or it can be considered a central town in its own right on the basis of the Guttman scale (it has 119 different kinds of businesses even though there are only 400 of them). Ho-mei, a textile center northwest of Changhua City, is also smaller than the other central towns, at least in terms of its number of nontextile-oriented businesses. Yuan-lin, on the other hand, is twice as large, having over 4000 licensed commercial enterprises.[3] Yuan-lin is, nonetheless, clearly less complex than Changhua City, which has twice again that number of businesses and a population of well over 100,000. Changhua deserves to be ranked as a local city, while Yuan-lin is just a very large central town.

The field area contains four intermediate towns, Ta-ch'eng, Chu-t'ang, Shao-p'u-hsin, and Wang-kung. They have from 65 to 90 different kinds of businesses each, the totals ranging from 165 to 240. Their populations are highly variable, however, ranging from a low of 1700 (Chu-t'ang, the most complex) to a high of 8800 (Wang-kung, the least complex). Similar differences in population size are also found with respect to the standard towns in the field area (Fang-yuan, Lu-k'ou-ts'u, Wan-hsing, Ts'ao-hu, Lu-shang, and Yuan-tou, listed in order of decreasing complexity). The two

---

[2] All of the population figures given in this paper refer to the late 1960s, and come from government censuses, which are taken on a monthly basis from the Household Registration records. Some districts contain villages as well as portions of towns, so that estimates by local officials of the proportion who actually reside in the towns were sometimes used to arrive at total figures.

[3] The number of businesses in Yuan-lin and Changhua City were not actually counted, the figures presented here having been taken from business license records. While correspondence between existing licenses and ongoing businesses is not exact, the error involved was determined to be insignificant in comparison with the enormity of taking actual censuses in those large places.

smallest have 2000 residents, while the two largest have 6000 and 6500. The most complex standard town (Fang-yuan, which is also a township seat) has 110 businesses of 56 distinct kinds, while the least developed has only 60 businesses of 30 kinds. Minor towns, which are in one way or another all nascent or aborted standard towns, have 15–35 businesses of 10–20 varieties. Their populations vary throughout approximately the same large range.

The fact that the size of a town's population is not at all an accurate predictor of its placement in the local central-place hierarchy is understandable. With only a few exceptions (and those are the places with low populations but large numbers of businesses), intermediate and standard towns in Changhua are simply agricultural villages that have acquired commercial functions, and the bulk of their population is not dependent upon business for a living. Only Ch-t'ang, which was founded as an administrative center by the Japanese, is totally commercial, having a ratio of 1 business to every 7 residents, or about one per family. The next most completely commercial places are the central towns of Erhlin and Ch'i-hu, which have 1 business to every 12 people. Each supports a number of bureaucrats, clerks, and wage laborers, but there are also a few hundred ordinary peasant farmers among their residents. Business-to-population ratios of from 1:50 to 1:75 are the norm for standard towns in the field area, while ratios of nearly 1:200 are not uncommon for minor towns. (See Crissman 1972 or 1973 for particulars.)

It can be expected that the poor correspondence between population size and commercial complexity would obtain for similar reasons in any traditional agrarian society as it develops commercially. Any attempt to use census figures to distinguish villages from towns, or low-level towns from higher-level centers, must be greatly mistrusted, especially without field investigation of the units of census enumerations, which often include portions of towns' rural hinterlands. The number of central goods and services a town provides is of course the only true measure of its commercial complexity.

In the field area the total number of businesses correlates absolutely with rank on the Guttman scale defining the central-place hierarchy. This is to be expected (Marshall 1969) when an actual functioning *system* of central places is examined, as was the case with Erhlin and the surrounding lower-level centers. The very close similarities in numbers of businesses among all the central towns included in the business census add weight to the a priori contention that the Changhua Plain contains a single central-place system dependent upon the county capital. The number of businesses in a Taiwanese town can be ascertained with ease by simply counting market stalls and functioning shop–houses, but recording kinds of commercial activities is considerably more difficult. Therefore, the discrete ranges of numbers of businesses associated with intermediate, standard, and minor towns in the field area were used to assign rank in the hierarchy to towns throughout the plain. The only difficulties encountered were with respect to Yung-ch'ing and She-t'ou, which both have about the same number of businesses as Ch'i-chou, the anomalous twin of Pei-tou. Unlike Ch'i-chou (or Ho-mei, the textile center), however, they both gave the impression of being only intermediate in rank despite their size. They have been portrayed as such on Map 1. They both, along with Yuan-lin (the overlarge central town), lie on the periphery of the richest agricultural area of the plain, which has an extremely dense population (4500 per square mile). That fact could very easily account for their large size without causing them to be significantly more complex in terms of the central goods and services they offer.

THE PAST

During the period in which the field work was conducted, new buildings were continually going up in Erhlin and some of the other towns. New businesses were of course established in the new structures, and their appearance was a continual reminder that towns change and grow.

Investigation of the history of the towns on the Changhua Plain was an important aspect of the field research, but one that presented a great deal of difficulty. Available local histories[4] have some interesting and occasionally useful information about the circumstances and incidents of initial settlement and about driving out the aborigines. They also go into detail about changes in administrative organization in the earliest part of the Japanese period, but then invariably jump into a discussion of what occurred after retrocession of the island to the Republic of China, effectively excising the latter part of the Japanese colonial occupation. There are some statistical compilations dealing with the prewar period that occasionally mention numbers or even kinds of businesses, but they practically never go below the level of the townships and therefore do not discriminate between the multiple centers in some of them. Moreover, many are concerned only with specific kinds of businesses, and usually small factories at that. As a result, it is possible to find out how many fractional-horsepower motors there were in Erhlin in 1935, but not the number of cloth sellers or coffin makers.

No occasion was missed to ask people when particular towns began to develop and the sizes they had reached at various points in time, but it soon became apparent that the ethnographer and his assistant were the

[4] *Changhua Chan Wang* (publisher unknown, 1954); *Changhua Wen Hsian* (Changhua Hsien Wen-hsian-wei-yuan-huì Fan-hang, 1954); and *Taiwan Sheng Changhua Hsien Yi-hui-ti-erh-chieh-chi-nien-ts'e* (Changhua Hsien Yi-hui-pi-shu-shih Pien-yin, 1955).

TABLE 1
Guttman Scale of Commercial Complexity for 1952, Ranking Twenty Settlements That Had at Least Four Businesses at That Time

Step	Items	Percent of Sample	Number or Names of Cases	Higher-step Errors	Lower-step Errors
1	Village store	95	2	0	0
	Barber	85	3	0	0
	Rice mill	70	1	1	1
2	Western drugs	65	2	1	1
	Chinese drugs	55	1	1	2
	Fruit parlor	50	1	2	0
	Peanut oil mill	45	1	1	1
	Cotton bedding			1	1
	Agricultural implements	40	1	0	1
	Variety store			1	1
	Fertilizer			2	0
	Butcher			0	1
3	Bicycle repair and sales	35	Fang-yuan	0	0
	Baker			1	0
	Photographer			1	1
	Farm supplies	30	Lu-k'ou-ts'u	0	1
	Cloth			0	1
	Restaurant			0	0
	Dressmaker			0	2
	Noodle maker	25	Shao-p'u-hsin	1	0
	Hardware			1	0
	Blacksmith			1	0
	3 other items			6	0

TABLE 1 (continued)

Step	Items	Percent of Sample	Number or Names of Cases	Higher-step Errors.	Lower-step Errors
4	Household goods	20	Ta-ch'eng	0	0
	Hotels			0	0
	Furniture			0	1
	3 other items			2	1
	Spirit money maker	15	Chu-t'ang	0	1
	Laundry			1	0
	Wine house			0	0
	3 other items			0	1
5	Seeds	10	Erhlin	0	1
	Electric appliances			0	0
	Shoes			0	0
	Tailor			0	1
	Tombstone carver			0	0
	9 other items			4	6
	Goldsmith	5	Lukang	0	0
	Movie theater			0	0
	Spectacles			0	0
	Gas and oil			0	0
	18 other items			0	0

only ones who knew for certain how many businesses the towns had at the *present* time. People's memories of the Japanese period could not be trusted for specific kinds of information, although some useful generalities were obtained. For these reasons, it was not possible to reconstruct the prewar marketing system in any real detail. However, it was possible to define levels of commercial complexity for the field area (plus Lukang) in the early postwar period.

Licenses have been required for all businesses since 1951, and records of those granted (as kept by the county government) were obtained.[5] Table 1 is a Guttman scale constructed on the basis of business license records for 1951–1952, the years when they were inaugurated and for which they should be most accurate. Of the 80 recognizable or usable kinds of businesses recorded, 74 make up into a beautiful scale (coefficient of reproducibility = .965) that ranks the 20 places in the field area that had four or more businesses. Except for those places with only a few businesses, each has a scale step to itself. Since the 15 steps in the scale discriminate rather more than necessary for heuristic purposes, only 5 have been enumerated in Table 1, although the protocol for the display does allow the other steps to be discerned.

Table 1, like the Guttman scale discussed earlier, ranks its cases along a single dimension of commercial complexity. The 20 places in the sample were also among those considered before, and the ranks it assigns can therefore be compared directly with those for 1967. Before this is done, however, it will be necessary to determine which steps correspond to which levels in the hierarchy of market towns.

The places where prewar marketing was reported are all in steps 3, 4, and 5 in Table 1, except for Wang-kung, which is in step 2 and indisputably belongs there. The amount of marketing claimed for it in the early period is, however, small. So was that for Fang-yuan, but its position on the scale is higher and places it adjacent to the other towns that have the same marketing areas they now enjoy. Following the same reasoning that was employed earlier, places in step 3 can be equated with the standard towns of their day, and those in step 4 with intermediate towns. Erhlin was put in step 5 with Lukang (even though the latter was far more complex) because of its clear separation from the towns immediately below and because its official promotion to the status of "urban" township, which occurred in 1939. Both Erhlin and Lukang will be considered to have been

[5] There are a number of difficulties in working with the business license records. For instance, the kinds of operations for which licenses are issued are sometimes identified by such specifics as "buying and selling," which translates as "doing business." Also, the existence of a license by no means guarantees the existence of an establishment, and different townships vary considerably in the degree to which they bother to notify the county government of changes or closings. Use could be made of the records, nonetheless.

central towns. The places in step 2 will be considered minor towns, and those below simply villages.

Table 2 presents certain facts pertaining to 17 of the towns contained in Table 1. Ts'ao-hu, at the very bottom of the list, did not even have a village store in 1952 but did have a bicycle shop and a rice mill. (They are included in the errors in Table 1.) The association between level of commercial complexity for the two points in time is very strong. The only differences occur as a result of certain places having jumped a level or two. No place has gone down in rank, showing that while some towns may be deadly dull, none is actually dying.

Of the 17 places, 10 have the same status now as they did 15 years ago, 2 in each of the five levels. Two places with no development worth mentioning in 1952 are now standard towns. One of them is Lu-shang, which benefited tremendously from the extension of irrigation canals in the area after the war. The other is Ts'ao-hu. Some of the Taiwanese who replaced the Japanese colonists to the north of Ts'ao-hu report marketing there, but the principal reason for its growth is probably water. Deep wells and motor-powered pumps have increased prosperity considerably in the immediate vicinity. This factor has also influenced Wang-kung's remarkable growth.

Of the four places besides Wang-kung that are ranked as minor towns for 1952, two have developed into standard towns while two have not. The ones that grew are located on main highways. One of the others, Chiu-kuai-ts'u, is located in a relatively prosperous region far from any town. It would seem that there really ought to be a town right there, and the presence of a covered market and a short row of vintage 1930s shop-houses shows that an attempt was made to get one started; but it apparently just did not work out. Despite the prime location, the roads leading to it are neither very good nor very heavily traveled, and that appears to be the only factor militating against its growth. Nor is it an isolated case. Of all the possible influences for or against commercial development that have been examined (including distance from other towns, population size, and agricultural productivity), location on a good, well-traveled road running between large towns is far and away the single most important one ($Tau = .487$, significant at the .0001 level). Improved agricultural productivity, which can be achieved most dramatically in this rather dry area by increasing water available for irrigation, is also important in some cases, but each of those places also has good roads. Attention was also paid to the numerous towns and villages that have not grown commercially in proportion to other places with similar attributes, and over and over again the answer is the same: If towns, they are on minor roads; if villages, oxcart trails are their only links with the world. In Changhua, towns do not build roads; roads build towns.

TABLE 2
Comparison of Seventeen Places in 1952 and in 1967[a]

Town	Rank[b] in 1952	Change by 1967	Firms in 1952	Percent Change by 1967[c]	Size in 1952	Percent Change by 1967[d]
Lukang	5	0	350	200	25,000	12
Erhlin	5	0	175	400	7,000	30
Chu-t'ang	4	0	95	150	1,200	42
Ta-ch'eng	4	0	80	200	3,500	43
Shao-p'u-hsin	3	1	45	275	1,600*	40*
Lu-k'ou-ts'u	3	0	45	100	950*	42*
Fang-yuan	3	0	25	380	6,500	15
Wan-hsing	2	1	20	300	3,800	45
Wang-kung	2	2	15	1000	6,600	33
Yuan-tou	2	1	15	375	1,400	43
P'i-t'ou	2	0	15	200	4,800*	30*
Chiu-kuai-ts'u	2	0	15	85	2,500	14
T'an-ch'ien	1	1	5	250	2,000	30
Lu-shang	1	2	5	1800	4,800	30
Hsi-kang	1	1	5	450	3,200	25
Wai-chi	1	0	5	60	1,500	27
Ts'ao-hu	0	3	2	3000	-	-

a. *Estimates indicated by* *.
b. *Ranks are as follows:* 5 = central town; 4 = intermediate town; 3 = standard town; 2 = minor town; 1 = village with some businesses; 0 = villages with no businesses. *The ranks for 1952 are equivalent to the step numbers shown in Table 1.*
c. *Overall increase in the number of businesses for the period is 260%.*
d. *Overall increase in population size for the period is 36%.*

The relationship between number of shops and commercial complexity was as perfect in 1952 as it was for 1967. An inverse association between scale rank in 1952 and rate of growth since the early 1950s exists, but it is not particularly strong and cannot support sweeping conclusions, mainly because the sample is not large. Places that have grown less than the average can be found at all levels of complexity, but those that have grown very rapidly were mostly of low status in 1952. This is, of course, mainly a reflection of the fact that there were five more real towns in 1967 than there were just after the war. If numbers of new businesses are examined instead of growth rates, then the relationship reverses and becomes even better than the one between scale ranks for the two periods, to which it is clearly related very closely.

The association between population size and commercial complexity for 1952 is even worse than it is for 1967. The slight improvement in the relationship over the last 15 years is due to the fact that, given a period of rapid economic development such as Taiwan has experienced recently (and other things being equal), large places tend to get businesses before smaller ones do. Once a place has developed, however, the degree of its development has no influence on subsequent population growth. This is demonstrated by the total lack of association between scale rank in 1952 and percentage increase in population over the following 15 years, which can be observed in the last column in Table 2.

Practical considerations precluded obtaining business license records for all the townships on the Changhua Plain, and the entire central-place system cannot be definitively described for the early 1950s. However, on the basis of the foregoing knowledge of the hierarchy in the field area and other information concerning various towns, the general outlines of the system as it probably existed then can be traced. In addition to informants' memories and a few documentary sources, one very important basis for determining when towns developed was the architectural styles in which various of a town's buildings were constructed. Newly constructed shop–houses are distinctively different from those built in the decade after World War II, and there are a number of styles associated with the Japanese period that reflect prosperity as well as age. Careful attention to the style of buildings that predominates in various sections of all the towns (center versus periphery, and so on) allowed their history to be reconstructed with some accuracy, especially since detailed information from the field area could be used as a basis for analogy.

Map 2 depicts the towns on the Changhua Plain as they are thought to have been in about 1950. With the exception of Ch'i-chou (Pei-tou's twin), the central towns were the same as they were in 1967. There are far fewer intermediate towns, but again except for Ch'i-chou, all of those that existed in 1950 are still only intermediate towns, although they have of course

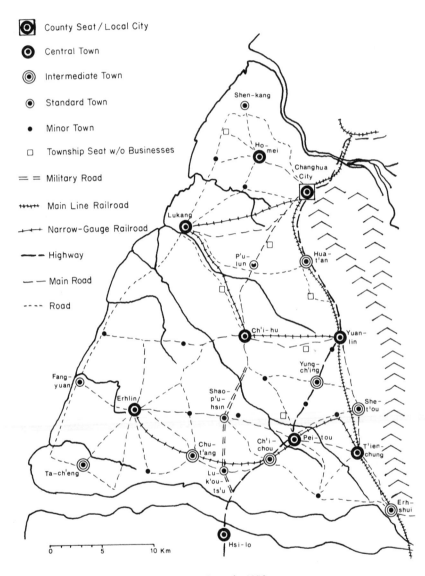

Map 2. The Changhua Plain as of approximately 1950.

grown considerably and now offer a variety of goods available nowhere in the area 20 years ago. Three of the five standard towns existing in 1950 had become intermediate towns by 1967, those that did not make it being Fang-yuan and Lu-k'ou-ts'u. Note the absence of any central places, apart from two minor towns, between Erhlin and Lukang, the poorest area of the plain.

The situation as it has been reconstructed for circa 1930 is shown in

Map 3. Assignments to levels in the central-place hierarchy are somewhat more conjectural than those preceding.[6] However, it is known that by 1930 all the rivers were under control, although there was no road bridge across the Ch'o-shui River. By that time the Japanese had established most of the present basic infra-structure of all-weather roads and narrow-gauge rail lines and had finalized the townships as the basic level of local administration with the same boundaries and seats that they have today. In addition to the county seat, which was by then a local city, and the old port of Lukang, which had already declined considerably in relative importance, there were only two central towns on the plain, Yuan-lin and Pei-tou, the latter also being an important nineteenth-century center. All of the intermediate towns are located at important transportation nodes (except Ho-mei, which had a developing textile industry). Their growing importance became manifest when they were all promoted in the late 1930s to the status of *gai* (meaning "street" and referring to an "urban" as opposed to "rural" township, being the equivalent of today's *chen*). Fang-yuan is the only standard town that did not reach intermediate status by 1950.

The Changhua Plain as it may have been in about 1910 is shown in Map 4. By then the Japanese had been on the island for 15 years and had been in full control for over 10. The roads depicted had all been improved somewhat over their earlier existence as muddy and often impassable trails. The railroad linking Taipei and Tainan had already been constructed, but the northern branch of the Ch'o-shui River had not yet been brought completely under control. With the cessation of the junk trade with Amoy, Lukang had begun to be surpassed in commercial importance by the county seat, through which the rail line was run. Pei-tou, long the most important central place in the southern portion of the plain, is depicted as a central town, while Yuan-lin and Erhlin are shown

---

[6] Because buildings constructed in the 1920s and 1930s are still extant, by noting their number and the affluence displayed in their construction it was possible to arrive at a fairly good idea of when some places enjoyed their greatest period of growth. T'ien-chung, located due east of Pei-tou on the railroad, is thought to have been only a minor town in 1910, but judging from its present number of prewar brick buildings, it had reached at least intermediate status by 1930. By that time it had certainly pulled well ahead of She-t'ou to the north and Erh-shui to the south. Yuan-lin was definitely a central town by that time, as was Hsi-lo, the site of the ferry across the river. Since Changhua City, Yuan-lin, and T'ien-chung were major stops on the main line railroad and the points where the sugar company's narrow-gauge rail lines branched off, it is assumed that the three standard towns on the main line had not achieved intermediate status by that time. Ho-mei, because of its textiles, and Ch'i-hu, because of its sugar refinery, are thought to have become intermediate towns by 1930 at least, bringing them up to the level of Erhlin. Ch'i-chou also had a refinery, but it was ranked as a mere standard town because it is thought that it could not at that time have begun to encroach on nearby Pei-tou. Although some minor towns had made their appearance, the only other new standard town was Chu-t'ang. Established de novo in the decade before 1910 as an administrative center for a prosperous area, its buildings show that it blossomed during the prewar years.

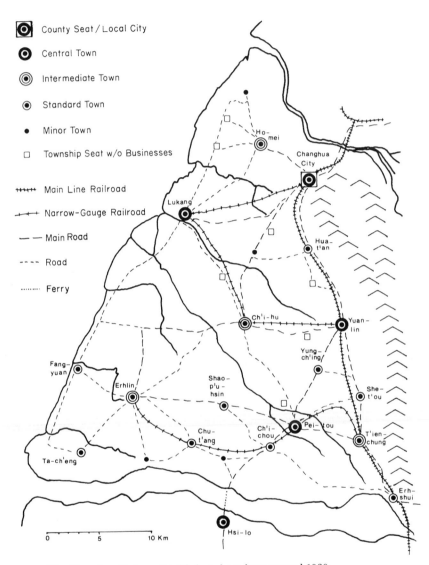

Map 3. The Changhua Plain as it is likely to have been around 1930.

as intermediate rather than standard towns primarily because the *Chang-hua County History* of 1831 indicates that they were apparently larger and more important than other low-level towns even at that early time. Fewer than half of the additional 11 towns listed in 1831 (Fang-yuan, Ta-ch'eng, Shao-p'u-hsin, Yung-ch'ing, and She-t'ou) made it into the twentieth century as functioning central places. Erhlin itself was virtually destroyed by intersurname rivalries and a disastrous fire in the late nineteenth

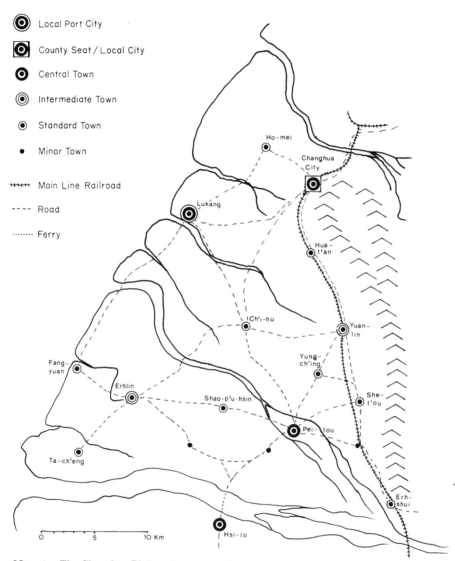

Map 4. The Changhua Plain as it may have been circa 1910.

century and may have only regained standard town status by 1910. Ch'i-hu had clearly begun to develop by that time in an area that supported three nearby towns in the early nineteenth century. Ho-mei, Hua-t'an, and Erh-shui may only have been minor towns in 1910 but for various reasons have been shown as standard towns. (There is a lack of any hard information on their circumstances or, for that matter, any way of actually defining levels of commercial complexity for that early period.)

EXPLANATIONS

Those are some of the facts of the situation, or as close to them as matters for present purposes. All of the foregoing descriptions of towns on the
Changhua Plain at various points in time constitute inductions from
reality in the sense that a large number of specific features have been
sorted and compared in order to produce certain generalizations. No two
towns at any time are exactly or, for that matter, even roughly alike: No
one finding himself anywhere in one of them with which he was at all
familiar would mistake it for another of them. Despite the infinitude of
ways in which they all differ one from another, it was possible to create
certain categories in which they could be grouped, the presumption being
that all those places labeled intermediate towns at any one time period are
more similar to one another in some significant and definable ways than
the towns classified differently.

The method employed in constructing the categories is explicit and as
nearly mechanical as possible. For instance, out of the enormous (and
literally infinite) diversity of facts that could have been observed about
any one of the towns, an infinitesimal fraction that concerned the variety
of goods and services available in each was recorded. (Even at that stage,
generalization was employed in the use of categories such as "grocery
stores," which obscure vast amounts of real differences between establishments so classified.) The lists of commercial functions found in the centers
were then manipulated according to the procedure devised by Louis Guttman (1950), and a scalogram that could be used to demarcate categorical
levels in a hierarchy of commercial complexity was created. The process
provides a means for distilling unmanageably detailed and copious
information down to simple categories such as "standard towns." Useful
as such labels are, a tremendous amount of information is clearly sub-
merged, or even lost, when they are employed.

The categories induced from information about the towns in the scale
for 1967 were used to classify other towns on the plain. This amounted to
assuming that if the other towns had been included in the original sample,
the resulting scale would have been similar enough so that the same categorical placements would have resulted. The bases for that presumption
were the perfect correlations among scale rank, number of commercial
functions, and total number of businesses. The basis for the similar extension of the 1952 scale is far less rigorous, since it does not involve an actual
count of businesses but uses impressions gained from talking with people
and noting architectural styles. Reconstructions for 1930 and, especially,
1910 admittedly involve guesswork, since there are not even any real
definitions of the central-place hierarchies for those times.

However, notwithstanding possible caveats concerning the portrayals of
the earlier periods, maps such as those displayed are extremely efficient
and useful devices. They display the gross geomorphic features that

demarcate and dissect the Changhua Plain and the spatial locations and hierarchical ranks of the towns, as well as routes between them differentiated as to type and condition. They are inductions from reality both in the sense that they are derived from measures of the real world in a direct or (ideally) mechanical fashion and in the sense that they represent only very limited aspects of that portion of the earth's surface. With regard to marketing activities alone, which are after all only a tiny fraction of the activities that take place on the plain and which could be portrayed, they are still highly selective. Not only do they ignore the myriad features unique to each town in favor of categorical levels, but they also fail to represent marketing areas, for instance. The marketing habits of the rural population are being ignored as extraneous in this context, although they are treated at some length elsewhere (Crissman 1972, 1973, Chapter 5 of Volume II). The point is that tremendous amounts of information have been cast aside in producing such abstract representations, or generalizations. Another crucial point is that, being inductive models, such maps cannot tell one anything that did not have to be known beforehand in order to create them. They may call attention to certain features or configurations, but they cannot *explain* anything.

And explanations, or understandings, are what one is ultimately after, not descriptions, however generalized. Valid explanations can be of two kinds, historic or scientific. A historical explanation accounts for some circumstance or event in terms of its unique antecedents and the causal connections thought to exist between them. Sometimes attempts are made to account for categories of situations in terms of what are held to be the same kinds of causal relations with what are assumed to be similar kinds of antecedents. However, the loss of information involved in inducing the multiple generalizations involved can make the historical value of such ventures highly problematical. In a sense, historical explanations are the only real explanations, but in the same sense they are very limited in scope and cannot produce understandings of any general value or utility. Scientific understandings, on the other hand, very often suffer from too much generality and are often difficult to apply to specific situations. They are essentially deductive in that a priori assumptions and postulates are employed to deduce abstract analogues of some set of real phenomena. To the extent that such models are judged to correspond to reality, it may be concluded that the principles and causations built into them may also be operative in the real world.

The advantage of scientific explanations is that they create information rather than submerging it, as do the "lowest common denominator" generalizations necessary in any attempt to apply the same historical explanation to more than one event. Juxtaposition of a real case with a valid and useful general deductive model, on the other hand, can serve to highlight the unique aspects of the case that require further, perhaps historical, explanations. If it appears that a class of cases departs in similar ways, then a new deductive formulation can be created by adjusting premises and constraints in order to produce a weaker and more specific formulation that will adequately capture the significant aspects of those particular cases.

There are possible historical explanations for what has occurred on the Changhua Plain during this century as it is depicted on the foregoing maps, but there are problems in adducing them. For instance, Fang-yuan is the only town portrayed as a standard town in 1910 that was still a standard town in 1967. Whatever challenges might be made to its placement in either period, it is clear that it did not grow nearly as much as other township seats before the war and has not grown nearly as much as Wang-kung since. Why? First of all, the fact that it is located on the relatively poor coast must be a factor, but then so is Wang-kung. In addition, Fang-yuan is only 6 kilometers from Erhlin, where 30 percent of its own population's retail custom goes, but Lu-shang is even closer to Erhlin and loses a greater portion of retail business to it, yet it has grown rapidly as a central place during the 1960s, even though it has not yet fully reached Fang-yuan's size or complexity. All roads leading into Fang-yuan (and the other two places mentioned) are in generally poor condition, and, more important, they do not go anywhere else. Fang-yuan is in fact located in a traffic backwater, but then so are the others.

All of the foregoing reasons are in the nature of historical generalizations, of course. The poverty of the surrounding population can only affect Fang-yuan's prosperity and growth when this poverty enters into thousands of daily individual decisions not to go to Fang-yuan and spend money. The same applies to Erhlin's proximity, since individual people have to decide to go there rather than to Fang-yuan for their own personal reasons. It might be contended that Fang-yuan has suffered from a dearth of entrepreneurial talent or capital for some reason—for instance, that Erhlin might have drawn them both away—but that too would ultimately get one down to the level of individual decisions once again. So, ultimately, do all the numerous factors that have in one way or another entered into Fang-yuan's retardation. So, ultimately, do all causes for the development of the system of central places on the Changhua Plain, and the task of identifying and tracing them all, and then determining which kind was most important in which cases, is literally beyond human capabilities. Even if it could in fact be done, it is doubtful if any useful generalizations could be drawn that would explicate the overall evolutionary patterns.

GENERAL CENTRAL-PLACE MODELS

The alternative to purely historical explanations for the evolutionary sequence depicted in Maps 4, 3, 2, and 1 is to apply a theory and create a model or models that will hopefully inform what is held to have occurred.

Central-place theory of some kind is clearly relevant and, as will be demonstrated, is in fact of great aid both in gaining a general understanding of what has occurred on the Changhua Plain in this century and in calling attention to significant departures from predicted situations that require their own special (historical) explanations.

G. William Skinner's monumental series of articles (1964, 1965a, 1965b) on marketing and social structure in rural China, which motivated the field research discussed herein, presented some formal models for the development of Chinese marketing systems. Skinner drew, at least implicitly, upon Christaller for his basic theoretical assumptions but modified two of Christaller's extremely general models in an attempt to capture certain features of specifically Chinese systems. Christaller's unbounded, isotropic transport surface was invoked, as is usual in order to create central-place models with any degree of generality.[7] In addition, again following Christaller, the friction of distance was held to be constant, and people were assumed to economize in space by always patronizing the closest market that could meet their needs. When, in conjunction with the foregoing assumptions, it was postulated that no one living on the boundary of a marketing area could be any more or less disadvantaged than any other in similar circumstances, a system of equidistantly located central places was engendered. An appeal to packing efficiency then produced a hexagonal rather than a triangular or square grid of marketing areas. Skinner's logic is not as rigorous or well motivated as Christaller's, but it purports to achieve similar results.

Where Skinner departs from Christaller is by inducing from his deep and scholarly knowledge of China the generalization that there were three levels of rural markets in China, held in what he has termed standard, intermediate, and central marketing towns,[8] and that, on the average,

---

[7] A large number of misdirected criticisms and objections to classical central-place theory have centered around these basic assumptions. As is argued briefly later, and at some length in Crissman (1973), no central-place model with any semblance of generality can incorporate the analogues of any real topographical features. It should be possible to devise a deductive model of any subset of marketing systems that display regular topographical as well as cultural features, such as location along a coast, in bounded valleys, or on river systems, and indeed there have been rather successful attempts along such lines (Dacey 1960; Johnson 1970; Leamer 1968). However, they are inevitably only weak versions of more general formulations that do not involve geographic features or bounds of any kind. A transport surface on which travel is possible from any point directly to any other point is the only one of the classical central-place spatial assumptions that can be relaxed while preserving complete generality, and it is in fact done away with in the alternative models for Chinese marketing systems presented herein and in much greater detail in Crissman (1973).

[8] Standard markets are held in all three levels of towns, while intermediate-level markets are held in both intermediate and central towns. Periodic marketing schedules segregated the three distinct levels of goods and services, but standard markets were held in intermediate and central towns for the same reasons that a Guttman scale is an appropriate device for defining commercial complexity—anything obtainable in a low-level center is also available in higher-level centers.

there were approximately 18 villages per standard marketing area. In order to model these peculiarly Chinese features, Skinner created a grid of equidistantly spaced villages and then superimposed a $K = 19$[9] grid of standard marketing areas on top of it, so that surrounding each town is an inner ring of 6 and an outer ring of 12 villages. He then induced, from maps of portions of the Szechuan landscape, the existence of both $K = 4$ and $K = 3$[10] relations between standard and higher-level centers, which he accounted for in terms of ease of transport and road building in different kinds of terrain. The $K = 4$ pattern, Skinner's Model A (which Christaller derived from the traffic principle), was attributed to rough and sparsely inhabited regions, while the $K = 3$ system, termed Model B (which Christaller created from the marketing principle), was said to be associated with level and densely settled areas. One cannot question the cogency of Skinner's observations concerning the general distributions of the two patterns on the Chinese landscape, but the causes he adduces for them are suspect insofar as they incorporate generalized historical explanations.

Skinner's great contribution to central-place theory, and it cannot be overestimated, is his realization that systems of central places can intensify over time. He also showed that models of central-place systems should be able to replicate themselves at intensified levels with the establishment of new settlements in between old ones, the emergence of new low-level towns, and the growth and maturation of old ones. His are the first relatively general central-place models to incorporate an explicit and well-defined temporal aspect that has marketing systems progress from one equilibrium stage to another as they intensify through time.[11]

Other extremely important aspects of his work involve crucial contributions to the understanding of the articulation of rural Chinese society. This is not the place to go into detail, but, to be as concise as possible, Skinner hypothesized that standard marketing communities (the social manifestations of standard marketing areas) defined the limits of peasant social horizons and constituted basic and very significant units of rural society. Not only did they set limits on peasant connubium[12] and otherwise serve as important economic, social, and cultural units but they also constituted

[9] K numbers were used by Christaller to characterize the relation between high- and low-level centers. They refer to the number of next-lower-level places (including the sum of fractions as well as the higher-level center itself) that are part of the regular hexagonal marketing areas of higher-level centers. Possible K numbers are 1, 3, 4, 7, 9, 13, 16, 19, 21, 23, 25, 28, 31, 37, 39, 43, 48, 49 (twice), 52, 57, 62, 76, 84, . . .

[10] In a $K = 4$ pattern, each lower-level center is located midway between two more complex centers, while in the $K = 3$ distribution each lower-level center is equidistant from three higher-order places.

[11] Stochastic growth models (Morrill 1962, 1963) and "learning monad" models (Dyreson 1973) have been devised but they are either specific to particular regions or are not yet of general value in modeling real central-place systems, respectively.

[12] See Chapter 5 of Volume II for some substantiation of this hypothesis.

the constituencies that the local gentry represented in their political dealings in higher-level marketing communities and with respect to the county magistrates, the lowest level of the imperial administration. It has long been realized that the Chinese Empire could not have been governed without the unofficial participation of local gentrymen, and it can now be understood how their activities must have been structured spatially and socially by marketing communities.

In addition, Skinner's models were able to inform some of the effects of the introduction of modernized transport (1965a). Mechanical conveyance had the initial effect of changing cost–distance equations and inducing greatly increased commercialization of production and consumption. This immediately resulted in "false modernization" as marketing activity increased greatly and new standard markets sprang into existence around larger centers served by the improved transport. However, as improvements spread into the hinterlands, peasants were themselves able to make use of mechanical conveyances to take advantage of attractive prices in larger centers. The result was that standard markets and the social communities they supported disappeared and were replaced by modernized trading areas centered on intermediate and central towns. Under such conditions of modern change, peasant social horizons and connubia expanded to the old intermediate marketing areas while their sense of community retracted to their villages. Certain important aspects of the history of social experiments by the People's Republic of China can also be explicated by Skinner's models, as he demonstrates in the third of his articles (1965b).

Despite the magnitude of his achievements, there are some critical flaws in Skinner's models, although they do not necessarily affect the uses to which he puts his formulations or the conclusions at which he arrives. They are nonetheless significant and worthy of correction, primarily because his contributions to the understanding of the articulation of Chinese society and some of the changes that have occurred in it derive from his geometrical models and cannot logically be supported without them. The first test to which any theoretical formulation, deductive or inductive, must be subjected is logical rigor. If a formulation does not follow from its stated premises and postulates, or otherwise contains fallacious logic, and if it does not in fact achieve what is claimed for it, then there can be no scientific or other valid purpose in pursuing its applications and ramifications. The reason is, of course, that the basic purpose in creating deductive analogues of real-world situations is to determine the extent to which the principles and relations built into a model are manifested in the real world, and that cannot be done in the absence of theoretical legitimacy and rigor. Skinner's errors are primarily in the realm of inadequate premises and faulty geometry and can be corrected while preserving his essential inductions and insights. His conclu-

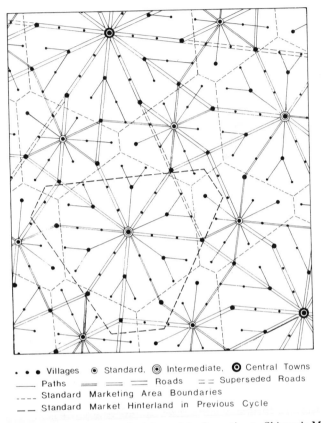

• • • Villages ◉ Standard, ◎ Intermediate, ◉ Central Towns
—— Paths ══ ══ ══ Roads ═ ═ Superseded Roads
- - - - Standard Marketing Area Boundaries
— — Standard Market Hinterland in Previous Cycle

Figure 1. The $K = 3$ marketing principle model, alternative to Skinner's Model B. Only standard marketing areas are indicated.

sions are modified only in certain details that at general levels of analysis may not have any overwhelming significance.

After expending considerable time and anguish, alternative models of Chinese marketing systems have been created. Not only do they satisfy tests for logical and geometrical rigor with regard to both derivation and intensification cycles but they also make explicit certain ramifications of the marketing and traffic principles with regard to village-to-market and intertown routes. Perhaps most important, they also capture the empirical fact that marketing areas for low-level goods centered on higher-level centers are significantly larger than those surrounding low-level centers. This was an indisputable finding of the field work in Changhua (Crissman 1972, 1973) and can be demonstrated for those mainland marketing systems for which adequate data are available (Crissman 1973). In fact, the phenomenon would appear to be quite general, since it has been an empirical finding whenever marketing behavior has been investigated in the field. It therefore needs to be incorporated into models as completely

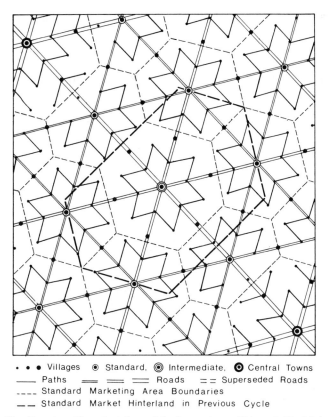

• • • Villages   ⊙ Standard, ◉ Intermediate, ◎ Central Towns
——— Paths   ═══ ═══ ═══ Roads   ═ ═ Superseded Roads
____ Standard Marketing Area Boundaries
— — Standard Market Hinterland in Previous Cycle

Figure 2.   The $K = 4$ traffic principle model, alternative to Skinner's Model A. Again, only standard marketing areas are shown.

general as Christaller's as well as into those specific to any particular society.

The complete motivation and derivation of the alternative models for Chinese marketing systems is to be found in Crissman (1973). As concisely as possible, the spatial assumptions and behavioral postulates employed in creating them are as follows: An unbounded surface without natural features but containing the analogues of uniformly distributed human settlements was assumed. A three-level hierarchy of rural market towns distributed according to either $K = 3$ or $K = 4$ patterns was then postulated, the ratio of villages to towns having been induced (by Skinner 1964) to be in the neighborhood of 17–20: 1 on the average. It was then required that roads exist between all adjacent towns and that paths lead from every village to a town or to an intertown road. Marketing areas for the various levels of goods were required to vary in size depending on the hierarchical level of the town on which they were centered. The actual amount of variation involved was determined by constraints on changes in boundaries as the systems intensify and existing lower-level central places are promoted as new ones come into existence in preexisting villages.

In the case of the model governed by the traffic principle, new central places are located on preexisting intertown roads. That constraint produces a $K = 4$ pattern associated with the traffic principle emphasis on intertown travel. In addition, the traffic principle requires that routes between towns be direct and village-to-town routes detour in order to reach an intertown road as directly as possible, provided that paths intersect roads only in other villages. On the other hand, the marketing principle ($K = 3$) locates new towns most advantageously for a dispersed rural population. It is therefore necessary for village-to-market paths to be as direct as possible, while all intertown routes detour, within limits, in order to pass through as many villages and smaller towns as possible, and are even rerouted during intensification cycles in order to pass through new low-level centers. It was discovered that a $K = 21$ relation between the locations of towns and villages allowed all of the foregoing conditions to be met for the marketing principle (the $K = 3$ alternative to Skinner's Model B). A $K = 16$ distribution satisfied the requirements of the traffic principle (and produced a $K = 4$ replacement for Skinner's Model A). The resulting models, which represent equilibrium stages between intensification cycles, are shown in Figures 1 and 2.

SPECIFIC CENTRAL-PLACE MODELS
FOR CHANGHUA

Formal deductive models such as Figure 1 or Figure 2 can be used to make defined and controlled comparisons among inductive models such as Maps 1–4. The enormous and unmanageable number of differences between maps of any two areas can be reduced and controlled by juxtaposing each to a formal model and then comparing the ways in which each differs from the "ideal." Valid comparison is not the only reason to juxtapose an inductive map with a deductive model, however. Valuable information can be created by discovering the precise ways in which a particular map departs from a specific formal model of its significant features.

But how does one go about comparing things as disparate as, for instance, Map 1 and Figure 2? They are, after all, just as utterly different as any two inductive maps. However, since one is a deductive model, the conditions that it satisfies are precisely known. Like all general central-place models, Figure 2 has been constructed on an isotropic surface, and the central places it contains are all located equidistantly from one another on a triangular grid. Despite the fact that central-place models have come under a vast amount of misguided criticism precisely because of those features, it *should* be obvious that no general central-place model can be constructed without them. The essential object of central-place theory is to generate coherent hierarchical patterns, and topographical variance disturbs regular patterns while locational vagary obscures them. It comes down to the fact that every segment of the earth's surface is so massively different from every other that the only way to control for all possible geographic factors is simply to deny all topographical features whatever. Equidistant location of central places is related to isotropy and has been partially derived from it. But equidistant location of centers is independently motivated for general central-place models because the causes of the precise locations of real towns must ultimately be traced to individual human decisions, and they can only be accurately accounted for, at the present state of the art anyway, by historical explanations that are incompatible with powerful deductive models. Certainly, central-place models could be created that involve regular distortions of isotropy and comcomitant regular variation in the location of hypothetical central places, but they would, logically, be weaker versions of general models that began with isotropy and equidistant location.

Since Figure 2 controls topography and location in order to create a coherent and repetitive pattern and since topography and location are perhaps the most noticeably unique features of Maps 1–4, direct comparison is difficult. But if the maps were to be distorted by ignoring topography and by somehow regularizing the locations of towns, then the pattern of central places on the Changhua Plain could be compared precisely with the model for Chinese marketing systems governed by the traffic principle as depicted in Figure 2. (It need not be compared with the alternative model governed by the marketing principle, since the basic pattern appears, by inspection, to be basically $K = 4$.) This is what Skinner did by making "abstractions" from portions of the Szechuan landscape in his Figures 2 and 3 (1964). A better way to create a theoretical model representing exactly those towns existing on some real portion of the earth's surface is to read actual features of a landscape (such as the presence of real towns, their level of complexity, and the existence of roads between them) into a general model. This will produce a vastly weaker version specific to that precise locality only. Such a specific model is both deductive and, in a sense, inductive. Being derived by weakening a general model, it lends itself to direct comparison both with more powerful versions of the same model and with other weak versions for other regions or other times. These are clear advantages over the sort of Skinnerian map "abstractions" that abound in the literature.

Figures 3–6 are such weak central-place models. They were created from Figure 2 by the addition of information concerning the real features of the Changhua Plain as portrayed on Maps 4–1. The procedure was as follows: Figure 2 represents equilibrium stages in an ongoing process of intensifica-

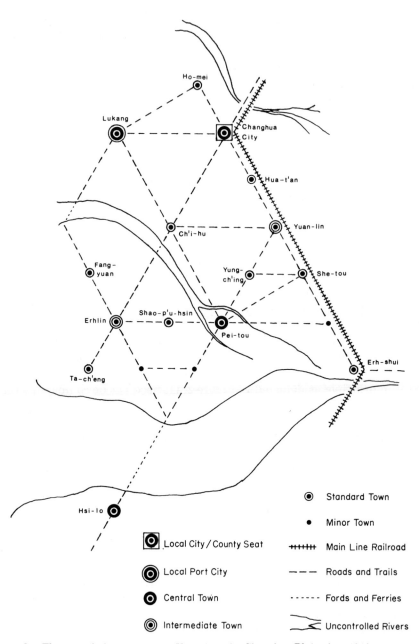

Figure 3. The central-place structure ($K = 4$) on the Changhua Plain circa 1910.

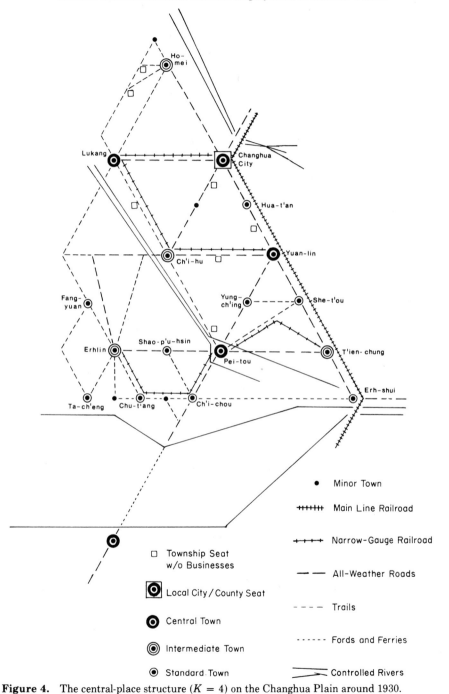

Figure 4. The central-place structure ($K = 4$) on the Changhua Plain around 1930.

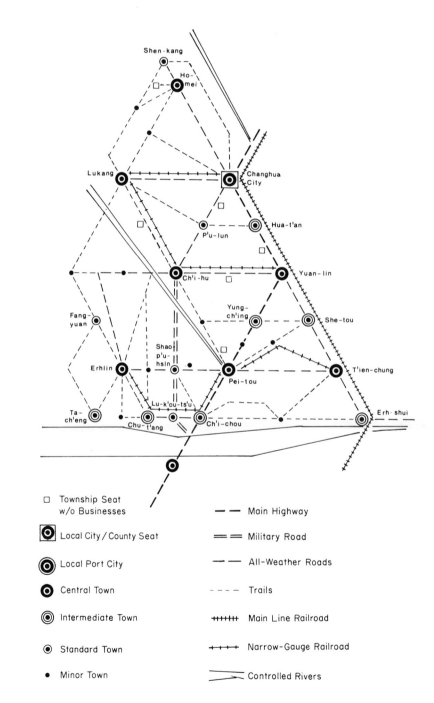

Figure 5. The central-place structure ($K = 4$) on the Changhua Plain as of 1950.

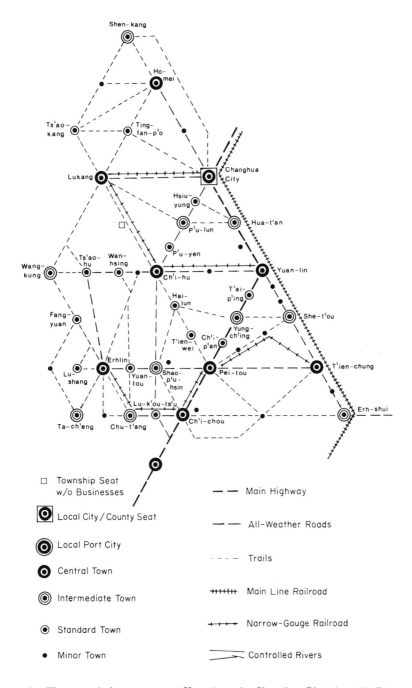

Figure 6. The central-place structure ($K = 4$) on the Changhua Plain in 1967. Rivers are omitted for clarity.

tion of a marketing system in which existing central places rise in level of complexity as new lower-level places come into existence in relation to them. Therefore, the central towns on Maps 4–1 were first arrayed equidistantly from one another on a grid of equilateral triangles, the basic patterns being readily discernible on the maps. If any intermediate towns existed between central towns, they were placed midway along the roads. Standard towns were located in relation to both central and intermediate towns. If two of them occurred between higher-level centers, they split the distance between them. Minor towns were located according to the same logic, but with reference to all other central places. Towns such as Ta-ch'eng, which are not located between higher-level towns, were placed at appropriate distances in the appropriate directions. It was occasionally necessary for reasons of parsimony to place towns as if they occupied higher or lower hierarchical levels, as has been done with T'ien-chung in 1910 and Yuan-lin in 1930, for instance. The implication is that such places were out of phase with regard to the normal stage of intensification.

The only portion of the plain that consistently caused any major difficulty was the west-central region, which consists of sand dunes laid down along the southern bank of the old channel of the northern branch of the Ch'o-shui River. For 1967, it was decided that the best compromise solution was to allow Wang-kung to occupy the position of a central town. Its location therefore becomes a part of the basic structure with regard to locating roads and other towns in Figure 6. Roads between Erhlin and Wang-kung and Erhlin and Ch'i-hu were then placed in relation to the central places through which they actually pass.

The changing positions of towns and roads from one time period to another depicted in Figures 3–6 is of course possible in a series of such abstract deductive models, since they portray structures, not actual locations. However disturbing such rearrangements might appear to be at first glance, there is nonetheless a one-to-one relation between the features of Maps 4–1 and Figures 3–6, respectively. Despite differences in the arrangement of central places on succeeding figures, the adjacency relations on the maps are all retained in the respective figures. It is as if the general model (Figure 2) had been used to transform the maps, the results sacrificing locations, distances, and even sometimes directions in return for regularities in structure. In fact, however, quite the opposite logical procedure was employed, since the existence of actual towns and roads were used as weakening conditions on Figure 2 in order to produce Figures 3–6, which therefore retain their essentially deductive nature. They clearly portray the structural evolution of the central-place system on the Changhua Plain during this century.

Although the traffic principle clearly applies, it has not applied uniformly. New towns have emerged and flourished on the railroad lines and on some roads, but not on all roads. The establishment and growth of towns since 1950 has been particularly closely tied to roads rather than rail lines, but again some roads between higher-level centers contain no lower-level centers. Nor do all possible roads between towns actually exist. The result is a very spotty $K = 4$ pattern of central places that has large gaps in its structure where no towns occur at predicted locations.

The alternative traffic model describes equilibrium conditions, and there is no reason to suppose that the arbitrary times for which the specific models for Changhua have been constructed are anything like equilibrium stages. In fact, the system has grown continuously during this century, although its growth has accelerated during the last 20 years. There is clear evidence that no real central-place equilibrium stages have existed in Changhua at least since the Japanese began their occupation. As a result, different sectors of the plain, and even specific towns, are out of phase with one another. This causes further departures from the traffic model predictions.

Explanations for the ways the existing system departs from a complete $K = 4$ pattern are not easy to adduce, although it is easy enough to describe what has occurred. Before the Pacific war, most central-place development occurred along rail lines, including those parts of the narrow-gauge network of sugar company tracks that provide public transport. Since the war, new standard towns have emerged on certain heavily traveled roads. Foremost among these roads is the major north–south highway linking Taichung to the southern half of the island, which runs through Changhua City to Yuan-lin, on to Pei-tou and Ch'i-chou, and then crosses the Ch'o-shui River at Hsi-lo. Why there has been no intensification between Changhua and Yuan-lin, but considerable growth of towns between Yuan-lin and Hsi-lo, is not known. The road leading southwest from Changhua City to Erhlin via Ch'i-hu and, to a lesser extent, the road between Erhlin and Pei-tou have also been the loci of intensification. They are indeed heavily traveled, but no more so than the one between Changhua and Lukang. Although almost all other roads between higher-level centers give the impression of carrying a far lower traffic load than those just mentioned, it is clear that traffic patterns alone cannot provide a full explanation for why there has been central-place intensification on some routes but not others.

The field area has enjoyed a disproportionate amount of growth since the war in comparison with the remainder of the plain. It has less than one-fifth of the total population, yet it has experienced approximately two-fifths of the total growth in central places as measured by jumps in status. Factors that have induced local growth in central places may include the reversion of some sugar company lands to private tillage under the land reform program, the increased use of wells for irrigation, and the introduction of new cash crops such as asparagus and mushrooms. The northern portion of the plain has intensified similarly, but it is not known whether or not the same causes are involved. In any event, it can be noted that the greatest number of new lower-level central places has emerged in relatively sparsely inhabited regions where high-level centers are far apart. Such factors, as well as differences in increased local prosperity from one cause or another, may have acted in conjunction with traffic flow to cause the unique patterns of central-place intensification that have occurred on the Changhua Plain.

In summary, explanations for the specific ways in which Figures 3–6 differ from Figure 2—for example, the reason that a full $K = 4$ pattern of towns exists along one particular road but not on another—would perforce have to be historical. The amount and nature of traffic along different roads vary immensely and can in some instances be rather directly related to the existence and function of individual towns. Differential productivity and rate of development in different areas of the plain, as well as the actual distance between towns, also play a large part. The level of detail invoked in such historical causes can of course vary without altering their nature, and ultimately one could again get down to the level of myriads of individual human decisions. No such explanations are provided by models such as Figures 1–6, and must come from other knowledge of real antecedents and impinging circumstances. The important thing to note in this context is that Figures 3–6 *do* provide a rigorous basis for determining what it is about Maps 1–4 that needs explaining in terms of deviations from a complete traffic principle system. In addition, some basis is provided for evaluating the relevance of alternative causations.

To repeat, since the recognition of facts and notions about their causes all depends on theory of one sort or another, any attempt to do science requires that the theories used to inform a domain be formal ones. Explanations can then be either scientific or historical, as when additional facts about the Changhua Plain are adduced in order to account for why Figures 3–6 depart in particular ways from Figure 2. No scientific (that is, deductive) explanations can be provided for such occurrences, nor are any particularly needed, since the historical ones not only suffice but are far more parsimonious and cogent. Just as it is often best to induce a map, so it is often best to explain things in terms of their own unique history. If, however, a number of weak versions of Figure 2 that are specific to real marketing systems were to reveal apparent regularities, then it would of course be useful to attempt to come up with a scientific account of the similarities.

CONCLUSION

The method developed for constructing the specific central-place models for the Changhua Plain at various periods in its development can be used to weaken other general central-place models to fit other real marketing systems about which the necessary facts are known. In order to produce informative deductive analogues for some kinds of central-place systems, it may be necessary to construct new general models that reflect relevant aspects of particular cultural or geographical features and depart from patterns created by Christaller's marketing, traffic, or administrative principles. For example, in addition to the aforementioned necessity of incorporating different-sized marketing areas for goods at the same level depending on the hierarchical level of the place where they are offered (which needs to be incorporated into all marketing and traffic principle models), the general models presented herein represent an accommodation to the average ratio of villages to towns in traditional rural China (following Skinner). An example of special geographical features that might have to be incorporated would be the dendritic pattern of the river bottomlands that apparently structured the Upper-Mississippian-Period Cahokian Empire. It should be possible to create general central-place models on the basis of as yet undiscovered or undefined principles.

Two of the advantages of specifically weak versions of valid general deductive models were demonstrated: (1) They allow for formally controlled comparisons between different real systems or among the same real system at different points in time, and (2) they identify departures from patterns created by general principles that require their own, uniquely historical, explanations. However, their principal value was perhaps too quickly passed over and therefore needs to be emphasized in this conclusion. The identification of anomalies is, of course, only a corollary to the portrayal of the manifestation of the basic principle used in creating a general model. The specific models for Changhua at any of the time periods clearly display structural features that can be accounted for by the traffic principle.

That statement means that the infinitude of individual decisions affecting retail purchases, entrepreneurial ventures, administrative structures, and bureaucratic programs on the Changhua Plain during the twentieth century have created a system of central places that is in some ways optimally located with respect to the rural population, given the constraint that new centers arise only on established transport routes between older higher-level towns. In other words, the traffic principle to some extent describes, in aggregate, the nontopographical and nonhistorical parameters of choices with regard to marketing behavior that have created the towns on the Changhua Plain. It can therefore serve as a scientific explanation for some of the causes of the evolution of the system of marketing centers there.

REFERENCES

Crissman, Lawrence W.
   1972   Marketing on the Changhua Plain, Taiwan. In *Economic organization in Chinese society,* edited by W. E. Willmott. Stanford, Calif.: Stanford Univ. Press.
   1973   Town and country: Central place theory and Chinese marketing systems with

particular reference to southwestern Changhua Hsien, Taiwan. Unpublished Ph.D. dissertation, Cornell Univ.

Dacey, Michael F.
   1960   The spacing of river towns. *Annals of the Association of American Geographers* **50:** 59–61.

Dyreson, Del
   1973   Conceptualizing settlement systems as sets of learning monads. Paper presented at the Conference on Formal Methods in Regional Analysis, Santa Fe, N.M., October 1973.

Guttman, Louis
   1950   The basis for scalogram analysis. In *Measurement and prediction,* edited by S. A. Stouffer, L. Guttman, E. A. Suchman, P. F. Lazarfeld, S. A. Star, and J. A. Clausen, Princeton, N.J.: Princeton Univ. Press.

Johnson, E. A. J.
   1970   *The organization of space in developing countries.* Cambridge, Mass.: Harvard Univ. Press.

Leamer, Edward E.
   1968   Location equilibria. *Journal of Regional Science* **8:** 229–242.

Marshall, John U.
   1969   *The location of service towns in southern Ontario.* Toronto: Univ. of Toronto Press.

Morrill, Richard L.
   1962   Simulation of central place patterns through time. Lund Studies in Geography, Series B, *Human Geography* **24:** 109–120.

Morrill, Richard L.
   1963   The development of spacial distributions of towns in Sweden: An historical–predictive approach. *Annals of the Association of American Geographers* **53:** 1–14.

Skinner, G. William
   1964   Marketing and social structure in rural China: Part I. *Journal of Asian Studies* **24:** 3–43.
   1965a Marketing and social structure in rural China: Part II. *Journal of Asian Studies* **24:** 195–228.
   1965b Marketing and social structure in rural China: Part III. *Journal of Asian Studies* **24:** 363–399.

Chapter 7

Dendritic Central-Place Systems and the Regional Organization of Navajo Trading Posts

Klara Bonsack Kelley
University of New Mexico

It seems often to be the case that in the poor regions of the world, one or a few large towns dominate a landscape full of small and poor settlements. This type of settlement system has been called "dendritic" (Johnson 1970:85) because flows of goods, information, and the like branch outward from a large center to progressively smaller and more distant settlements. In these systems, long-distance trade is generally important and the same large town is at once the destination of most goods bulked in the region and the source of most goods retailed in the region. Economic and political functions are commonly centralized in the one large town, and economic development takes place there at the expense of its hinterland.

The notion of different levels of development within the same region is at variance with the implications of the central-place model of settlement distribution (Christaller 1966). This model has been found to fit some but not all empirical settlement systems in various parts of the world (Berry 1967; Marshall 1969; Skinner 1964, 1965a, 1965b. The central-place model, I should emphasize, applies specifically to settlements with retail commercial functions. In this model, settlements are spaced uniformly over a flat, unbounded plain [or, in Berry's (1961) modification, uniformly with respect to the distribution of purchasing power]. A hierarchy of retailing exists, and a high-level settlement will also have all the retailing func-

tions found in settlements below it. The central-place model also predicts a
certain kind of pattern in which lower-level settlements are distributed
relative to higher-level settlements: Each settlement of a given level is at
equal distance from two or three settlements of the next-higher level. The
resulting pattern is one in which lower-level centers are located in the
interstices between higher-level centers (see Figure 1).

There are probably few regions in the world, however, in which goods
flow through the simple retailing system postulated by the central-place
model. In those cases in which wholesaling is absent (by definition),
retailers must also be producers and consumers, bringing their products to
market to exchange for the products of other producer–consumers. One
might also expect to find small-scale wholesaling in which goods are
transported by middlemen through the same network in which producer–
consumers move. If the goods were bulked in small scale, were diverse,
and were for local exchange, such wholesaling would amount to a situation
in which a small-scale wholesaler acquires products in a market center
from a small number of producers (or from other small-scale wholesalers)
and then "stands in for" these producers at any one of the three different
markets in the next-higher level. Or it would amount to the situation in
which the small-scale wholesaler buys from another small-scale wholesaler
in a high-level market center and takes the products to the neighboring
low-level markets (Skinner 1964, 1965a, 1965b; Smith 1972).

Economic development in such a system presumably is uniform: All
consumers are uniformly advantaged because there is no unmet demand
for any level good, and retail prices for a given good are uniform
throughout the area. More important, perhaps, is the fact that each low-
level retailing area is split between two or three high-level retailing centers,
so that people who patronize the same low-level retailing center may
choose between different high-level centers. This allows economic information to be dispersed widely through the system, which in turn promotes
rational allocation of goods, labor, and capital, with no long-run local surpluses in search of an outlet, or deficiencies crying to be met.

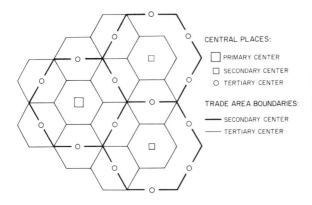

CENTRAL PLACES:

☐ PRIMARY CENTER
☐ SECONDARY CENTER
○ TERTIARY CENTER

TRADE AREA BOUNDARIES:

—— SECONDARY CENTER
—— TERTIARY CENTER

Figure 1. A Christallerian
hierarchy of central places:
retailing areas for second-
level and third-level centers.

However, the marketing system just described would be fairly unusual, for a number of reasons. In the first place, certain important resources are often plentiful in some regions and scarce in others, leading to long-distance trade between regions. Second, different kinds of production specialization often occur in different regions, partly as a result of the variable resource distribution and the resulting trade. Such production specialization intensifies interregional trade (Vance 1970:14). For whatever reasons, wholesaling seems to be important in most empirical marketing systems. Therefore, we need a model for central-place systems in which wholesaling affects central-place locations and functions. The dendritic system model outlined here considers the effect of wholesaling activities on a central-place system.

THE DENDRITIC SYSTEM MODEL: AN ALTERNATIVE TO CENTRAL-PLACE THEORY

In contrast to the central-place model and the empirical systems cited earlier that conform to this model is a rather large set of empirical cases (Johnson 1970; Mintz 1960; Ortiz 1967; Smith 1972, 1975; Vance 1970) that seem to have the following features: (1) a hierarchy of commercial centers lacking interstitial placement of levels, often showing instead descending level with increasing distance from the highest-level center; (2) more low-level centers than predicted by the central-place model; (3) orientation of each lower-level center to only one center in the next level rather than to two or three, as in the central-place model; (4) a draining of hinterland population, income, or resources by the highest-level center; and (5) concentration of a political elite in a single high-level center, which is also the most important economic center.

I would like to suggest that two characteristics—the convergence of regional economic networks (bulking, redistribution, and retailing) on a single high-level center[1] and the dominance of long-distance wholesaling—are, taken together, the most important causes of the other features. Regions in which either long-distance trade or convergence of economic

[1] I consider the redistribution and retailing systems to differ as follows. The redistribution system for a given good is composed of a set of centers and the network of links between centers through which the good flows. The movement of goods is such that successively smaller volumes of the good fan out from its point of maximum bulked volume to successively larger numbers of redistribution centers, ending with the retailers who sell the good (a bulking system, of course, is the reverse of this). The retailing system is composed of a set of centers containing retailers of different goods and the network of consumer movements connecting these settlements. In the network of consumer movements, the same consumers go to different centers for different goods. In other words, the retailing network connects the end points of many different redistribution networks.

networks is present may not have all the other dendritic system features. However, a region with both of these features is very likely to have the other dendritic system features as well. In what follows I suggest the relevance of network convergence and long-distance wholesaling for each of the other dendritic system features. I emphasize that the dendritic system model agrees with the central-place model in postulating threshold and range as forces behind central-place distributions.[2]

A Hierarchy of Commercial Centers
Lacking Interstitial Placement of Levels

Figures 2a and 2b show two central-place systems, one with centers at different levels interstitially placed and one without. In both bulking and redistribution hierarchies, we may assign a commercial center to a particular level by knowing the hierarchical level of the center from which it gets goods (for redistribution) or to which it sends goods (for bulking). In other words, the hierarchical level of a given wholesaling center reflects the number of points at which goods change hands between that center itself and the network's highest-level center.[3] The diagrams show that the smallest centers (retailers or bulking centers at the lowest level) are interstitially placed in both cases. Successive levels of centers continue to be interstitially placed in the retailing system (Figure 2a). However, above the lowest level of centers in the wholesaling system (Figure 2b), one finds a hierarchical chain of links between progressively larger centers that is spatially different from such a chain in the retailing system. In the wholesaling system each bulking center sends goods to one higher-level bulking center closer than itself to the region's primary bulking center; each redistribution center receives goods from one center nearer than itself to the region's primary redistribution center.

This feature of descending central-place levels is caused by the wholesaler's attempt to minimize the cost of transport. Since the ultimate destination of the goods bulked within the region is (by definition) the region's highest level of bulking center, then a low-level bulking firm can only minimize its transport costs by sending its goods to a center nearer

---

[2] The threshold of a good is the minimum volume of a good, given its price, that must be sold to keep its retailer in business. Since the consumers who will buy this good are dispersed spatially (at least to some degree), the notion of threshold can be put in spatial terms. Threshold is then the area from which consumers demanding the minimum volume of the good (given price) must be drawn. The farther a consumer lives from the retailer, the greater his travel expense to get the good, and therefore the higher the ultimate price of the good to him. The farther a consumer lives from the retailer, the lower will be his demand for the good. At some distance, therefore, demand will fall off to nothing. The total area within which there is some demand for the good is the maximum range of that good.

[3] A retailing center, of course, is assigned to a level in the retailing hierarchy according to the highest-level good it offers.

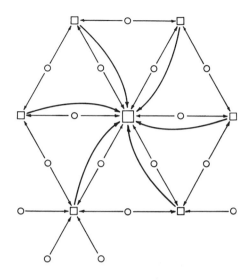

Figure 2a. A settlement hierarchy showing consumer movement between interstitially placed centers.

than itself to the primary bulking center. Similarly, a low-level redistribution firm can only minimize its transport costs by receiving goods from a center nearer than itself to the region's primary redistribution center. Therefore, the shorter the distance between a given center and the highest-level center in the relevant network, the higher the level of that center. This pattern will show clearly when the highest-level bulking and redistribution firms are in the same center—thus when bulking and redistribution networks converge on the same center.

Now consider a set of commercial centers interrelated at once by bulking, redistribution, *and retailing* networks. This set would also lack interstitial placement of high-level centers if the impact of wholesaling flows on settlements were much greater than the impact of *retailing* flows—that is, if the wholesaling systems were much more hierarchically elaborated than

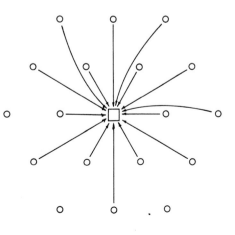

Figure 2b. A settlement hierarchy showing flows between bulking centers not interstitially placed.

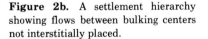

the retailing systems. A poorly elaborated retailing system (one with perhaps two levels, or even one) might occur when consumers are very limited in their traveling range (even for the highest-level goods) as compared with firms that transport goods in the wholesaling networks. This sort of difference could occur when modes of transportation available to consumers and to wholesaling firms differ and when goods in the wholesaling networks ultimately must be transported over large distances. Then, if all these networks have the same settlement as their highest-level center, the settlement hierarchy defined by all systems combined will also lack interstitial placement of centers.

Furthermore, if the retailing system later on develops a more elaborate hierarchy, the existing wholesaling systems may affect the locations of particular types of retailing firms. This would happen if these new, high-level retailing firms wanted to capture items already flowing through the wholesaling networks (for example, if retailing firms wanted to capture, as consumers, producers bringing their goods to low-level bulking merchants in a wholesaling network). Therefore, new, high-level retailing firms may often locate in settlements that already have wholesaling functions. The highest-level center of the retailing system would then commonly be the same as the highest-level wholesaling center. In this case, development of the retailing system in a region where a well-developed wholesaling system already exists might reinforce, rather than undermine, the highest-level center's dominance over the region.

An example of a system in which interstitial placement of centers is absent (for the three highest levels of centers) appears in western Guatemala as described by Smith (1972, 1975). In the Ladino market town (LMT) system, long-distance wholesaling is important, and these wholesaling networks all converge on a single high-level center, Quezaltenango. Low-level centers funnel trade goods upward to Quezaltenango and in turn receive from Quezaltenango goods produced outside the region. Levels as defined by function are as follows. The highest-level center, Quezaltenango, is the region's largest commercial and administrative center and also imports goods produced outside the region and exports goods produced within the region. At the next level are 6 intermediate centers, commercial–administrative centers smaller than Quezaltenango. Finally, at the lowest level are 12 minor centers, which have lesser commercial functions and no administrative functions. This system shows central-place level *descending* with distance from Quezaltenango. In other words, Quezaltenango is surrounded by two concentric rings of settlements, an inner ring of the 6 *intermediate* centers and an outer ring of the 12 *minor* centers. All 19 centers also serve as retailing centers but in this regard can be considered functionally equivalent. Smith (1975) argues that what differentiates the 19 centers into three separate hierarchical levels, and can account for the spatial distribution of levels, is not *retail-*

ing function but rather administrative and import–export wholesaling functions.

More Low-Level Centers Than Predicted by the Central-Place Model

In many wholesaling systems, wholesaling firms at a given level have a very large threshold as compared with the threshold of firms at the next level below. To put it another way, central-place theory predicts that the minimum volume of trade necessary to support a firm in a given level (the threshold of that firm) will normally be one-third or one-fourth the volume required to support a firm in the next (higher) level. This results in a ratio of three or four low-level firms for each high-level firm. However, in some wholesaling systems the threshold of a firm in a given level may be much less than even one-fourth of the threshold of a firm in the next level. Under these conditions one would expect more low-level centers for each high-level center than the three of four predicted by the central-place model.[4] A large difference in thresholds between firms on two different levels of a wholesaling hierarchy could result from a number of factors, including large differences in the distance over which firms would have to pay transport costs.

The convergence of wholesaling networks on a single center may or may not, by itself, result in a larger than expected ratio of low-level to high-level centers. To see why, consider four possible ways for a region's commercial centers to be interrelated by a wholesaling and a retailing network: (1) Both can converge on the same high-level center and also share the same low-level centers; (2) both can converge on the same high-level center and have different low-level centers; (3) both can have different high-level centers and the same low-level centers; and (4) both can have different high-level centers and different low-level centers. Figure 3 illustrates these possibilities. The second possibility will always give the highest ratio of low-level to high-level centers, and the third possibility will give the lowest ratio.[5] However, the first and fourth possibilities will give the same ratio, even though one involves the convergence on a single center and one does not. Therefore, the convergence of wholesaling networks on a single center and an unelaborated retailing system may be insufficient to cause a larger than expected number of low-level centers.

Ortiz (1967) describes a feature of Colombian market systems that sug-

---

[4] This should be true unless the tendency of small firms to agglomerate in single settlements is sufficiently greater than such a tendency among the next level of firms, so as to reduce the central-place ratios to those predicted by the central-place model.

[5] The number of low-level centers per high-level center can be very large. Johnson notes a range of between 4 and 635· villages per central place of over 2500 inhabitants in the Middle East (1970:175).

226   Klara Bonsack Kelley

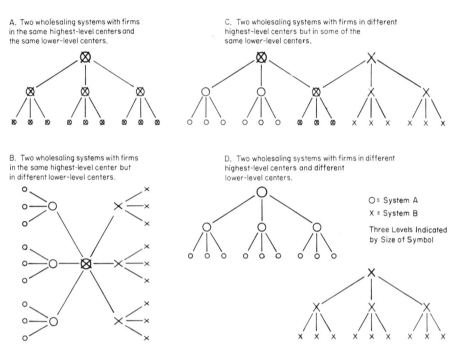

A. Two wholesaling systems with firms in the same highest-level centers and the same lower-level centers.

C. Two wholesaling systems with firms in different highest-level centers but in some of the same lower-level centers.

B. Two wholesaling systems with firms in the same highest-level center but in different lower-level centers.

D. Two wholesaling systems with firms in different highest-level centers and different lower-level centers.

O = System A
X = System B

Three Levels Indicated by Size of Symbol

Settlement ratios for levels I: 2:3 = I:3:9 in all cases for each system separately. But for both systems combined, they differ: A = 2:6:18; B = I:6:18; C = 2:5:15; D = 2:6:18.

Figure 3. Wholesaling hierarchies with and without convergence on the same high-level center.

gests the mechanism that produces a large ratio of low-level to high-level centers. Settlements in these Colombian systems are interrelated mostly by the flow of manufactured goods and certain staple foods *downward* from the highest-level commercial centers. The hierarchy of retailing centers seems to have four levels. Large commercial centers are in the highest level, each having permanent retailing establishments and import–export functions for its hinterland. In the next (lower) level are municipal markets, which are periodic and in which imported goods and staple foods, brought in by traders from a large commercial center, are sold. A still lower level includes the few small rural marketplaces (those not located in municipal towns). Finally, at the lowest level, are small trading stores, where imported goods are sold. Small centers or marketplaces usually trade with only one commercial center (Ortiz 1967:400). The wholesaling network through which cash crops (for example, coffee) move converges on these commercial centers, although cash crops do *not* move through the low-level marketplaces.

Ortiz does not give the ratios of settlements in these different levels, but she does say that the number of small trading stores tends to *proliferate* in relation to the number of municipal markets, because poor road quality and sparse population limit the number of consumers who can regularly attend a municipal marketplace (1967:405–406). The proliferation of trading stores also occurs because, beyond the municipal markets, road quality deteriorates to the point that these roads are often navigable only by pack animals and by people on foot. This makes areas outside the municipal marketplaces unattractive to a trader who realizes advantages of scale by using motor vehicles to transport his wares. If such a trader were to venture beyond the municipal marketplace, he would have to change his mode of transportation and would not be able to carry the full volume of his wares. Thus, he would be forced to sell at least part of his stock in the municipal marketplace. In fact, it seems he would want to sell all of it there, since itinerant trading beyond the trade area of a municipal marketplace in itself would probably require the trader's full-time attention if he were to get normal profits. In other words, due to poor roads, ranges of consumers, who travel on foot, are small relative to the threshold of traders, who use motorized transport. Therefore, the thresholds of retailing establishments serving consumers beyond the retail reach of the municipal marketplace must be equally small. But the traders can also operate at their much larger thresholds because the better road quality in the area *near* the municipal marketplace allows them to attract sufficient business—and also, presumably, because they sell at wholesale to people who run the small trading stores.

Thus, it seems that large threshold differences between the firms at different levels in the hierarchy are necessary to produce a larger than expected number of low- to high-level centers. The contrast between *wholesaling* transportation over long distances, on the one hand, and low *producer–consumer* mobility, on the other, are likely to create this threshold difference.

Orientation of All Low-Level Centers to a Single High-Level Center

In a region in which all networks converge on a single high-level center, each center in the *next* level obviously would be oriented only to the one center. In regions where long-distance wholesaling networks determine the interrelations between commercial centers, the following would apply to the lower-level centers. A center whose hierarchical level n is determined by the level of its wholesaling firms would be oriented primarily to one higher-level center m if the firms in the n-level center shipped or received all products from a firm in the m-level center. This apparent short-run dependence on one place would be emphasized in a bulking network if production were seasonal and shipments were therefore widely spaced in time. Furthermore, wholesaling ties between firms are likely to be contractual, to involve the promise of shipments or orders of at least a stated minimum-volume, and to involve price advantages given to large-volume orders or shipments. Unit transport costs also will be lower if all units are shipped to or from one place. All of these factors encourage a firm to deal with only one wholesaler of a given type of good. This feature of dendritic systems contrasts with the central-place model, in which each low-level center is oriented to two or three high-level centers.

Vance's (1970:80–128) description of the evolution of settlement systems in the frontier United States, especially his notion of the "unraveling point of trade," provides an example of this feature. The unraveling point of trade is the center in a wholesaling (redistribution) network at which the bulk of imported goods is broken. From this point smaller lots are sent on to many smaller centers, all dependent on the one unraveling point. At each lower-level center, in turn, bulk is further broken, and so on until it reaches the ultimate consumer. Each center at successively lower levels in this redistributive chain gets a given type of good from only one high-level center. In the frontier United States the redistributive wholesaling network was for general merchandise, so that lower-level centers received not just one type of good, but all types of goods, from one high-level settlement. Dependence of each small center on one entrepôt city at the unraveling point of trade was due to the periodic and contractual nature of wholesale trade, as well as to very high transport costs, which put extreme pressure on firms in small frontier centers to minimize transport costs. This could be accomplished by getting all goods from only one high-level center. Transport costs were very high for frontier firms because population was sparse, so that settlements were also sparse, with hinterlands extending very far from the entrepôt city. They were also high because transport systems beyond the entrepôt city were primitive and because frontier firms, trading with small, sparse, and often poor populations, ordered in small bulk.

Drain of Hinterland Income, Population, and/or Resources by a High-Level Center

If profits made on the purchase of producers' goods, or the sale of consumer goods, in the hinterland are invested *outside* the hinterland (either in the highest-level center or outside the region completely), then the hinterland loses income. Profits made by the major firms in particular regions need not, of course, be reinvested in the hinterland from which consumers and goods bulked for export are drawn, or to which goods are redistributed for retail. The greater the number and magnitude of wholesaling and retailing networks that converge on a single center, the larger and more populous that center will be, and the greater the likelihood of attractive investment opportunities in that center. Also, the region's major center may be part of one or several economic networks extending *outside* the region. The larger the number and more diverse the type of such networks to which the region's major center belongs, the greater the *information* on investment possibilities outside the region, and the greater the likelihood of actual investment outside the region. Taxes, too, may serve to drain income from the hinterland. As with private investment, the region's major center may be an attractive place for the government to invest tax moneys—it being most likely to have adequate infrastructure and external economies. Furthermore, if the major center is also the region's political hub, tax moneys allocated to government officials and functions will be spent there.

Smith (1975) suggests that such an investment mechanism may be operating to drain hinterland income in western Guatemala. Of all commercial establishments in the region, 70 percent are located in 7 towns (out of some 250), and in view of the economic functions of these towns, it seems likely that profits invested in these commercial establishments come from sales of import goods *to* hinterland people or purchases and export of trade goods *from* the hinterland. Johnson (1970:158) mentions that in many underdeveloped countries, government expenditures (at least some of which are financed by taxes) intended to promote industrial expansion are often concentrated around the largest city because of its well-developed infrastructure. Mintz (1960:44–45) points out that in Haiti, the government, which is centralized in Port-au-Prince, collects taxes on commercial transactions in hinterland marketplaces. However, these taxes are *not* reinvested in the marketplaces where they are collected.

The population drain may occur in the following way. In any bulking system, all other things being equal, the producer farthest from the center to which his produce is ultimately sent receives the lowest price. One reason for this is that the cost of shipping his produce increases with the distance from its destination. For a similar reason, in the redistribution system for any particular good, the consumer farthest from the center from which that good is ultimately sent pays the highest price. When all bulking and redistribution networks in a region converge on the same center, the prices of the bulked and redistributed goods at varying distances from that center should be negatively correlated (all other things being equal). Therefore, since the region's producers are also consumers, people in the region are doubly penalized by distance. When the bulking and redistribution networks converge on a single center, the stress on hinterland producer–consumers will be more intense than when they do not. If these networks were to converge on *different* centers, prices on producer and consumer goods at varying distances from the respective high-level centers for these goods would not necessarily be negatively correlated. For the resulting price variations caused by distance from the relevant major center will not penalize the hinterland people *doubly.*

Since information flows through these economic networks, people are likely to know how their standard of living compares with standards of people elsewhere in the region. Therefore, poor people far from the region's major center will want to move nearer that center and/or find another way to make a living. If wage work is a feasible alternative, the largest center in the region will probably be the most attractive place to look for wage work. The greater the number and magnitude of economic networks feeding into it, the larger and more attractive it will be. Poor people in the periphery of a region would not necessarily turn toward the major center in their own region. Presumably, however, in regions where all retailing and wholesaling networks converge on a single center, the flow of information about economic opportunities *outside* the region would be lower than in regions where economic networks do not converge.

A drain on resources would eventually occur in any system when these resources are not renewable. A drain on renewable resources (for example, land productivity) might occur if the hinterland producers using such a resource could not find feasible alternative sources of income (at least in the short run). In such a situation, producers would continue production or starve. Population, and therefore competing producers, might increase faster than the resource could be renewed. If so, then, at a given level of demand, the prices paid for the output would tend to fall (unless overridden by external factors), putting additional stress on the producers. These producers, unable to turn to another significant source of income, could only try to intensify production and produce more, again lowering prices.[6]

---

[6] This point may remind the reader of Johnson (1970), so I will try to specify the areas of difference. As I understand Johnson, he considers the basic problem with dendritic systems to be that prices fail to equilibrate supply and demand. This failure occurs because long-distance trade, on which such systems are based, allows trader monopolies, which distort prices. It is also due to the failure of producers to respond rationally even to undistorted prices because they mistrust the whole system and because their production is earmarked for debt payment. Such earmarking keeps them from withholding production from the market if prices are too low. I think that producers *do* know about prices within their system. Furthermore, traders need not have effective monopolies over output and therefore may be to some degree competitive. For instance, if traders both buy producer goods and sell consumer goods and if the product is seasonal and can be transported in bulk, one trip at high bulk reduces the unit transport cost to the producer and extends his range as a producer beyond his range as a consumer. Therefore, if traders are located to satisfy consumer demand, they will compete for producer goods. Furthermore, I think that producers can withhold production in the face of low prices, even if in debt to the trader, if they can substitute a different medium of payment for the withheld production. The problem, as I see it, is not that the producer's ignorance of prices within the region causes imperfect response to changes in demand levels. Rather, a producer's knowledge of alternative income opportunities outside the region is poor due to network convergence on a single center (which may diminish the flow of information from outside the region), or opportunities that producers could feasibly take advantage of do not in fact exist, either inside or outside the region.

Concentration of a Political Elite in the Highest-Level Center

Since the degree of control over the regional economic system available to people in a particular place is influenced by the position of that place in the various economic networks, one would expect elite political groups to be located in centers in which such control can be maximized. The single point from which the greatest political control can be exercised over a single network is the major center in that network. Particularly if the centers of several networks coincide in the same place, the political officials in that single place could exert the greatest control. Therefore, in regions in which economic networks converge on the same major center, one would expect the region's political elite to be concentrated in that center. In systems lacking this convergence, by contrast, one might expect elite groups to be located in several high-level economic centers, dispersing their control and their *access* to people in the region.

The preceding discussion implies that the centralization of a political elite *is caused by* the convergence of all economic networks on the same highest-level settlement. However, it also seems possible for the centralization of a political elite to *cause* the convergence of economic networks. The latter might occur if a spatially aggregated elite could force hinterland firms to allocate goods through a network that would have as its major center the town occupied by the region's elite. Therefore, it would appear that a positive feedback relationship exists between the convergence of regional economic networks and the centralization of a political elite. Once an elite has forced networks to converge on its capital, this convergence enhances the power of the elite. Or, once the power of an elite is established by its position at the point of convergence of regional economic networks, the elite can use that power to promote further convergence.

Haiti, as described by Mintz (1960), is an example of an economic system in which the political elite is concentrated in one town, which is also the major center for the region-wide economic networks, including the import and export wholesaling networks. Traders can move their goods over much better roads if they go through the major political center, Port-au-Prince. Since these better quality roads are maintained by the government, it is clear that the political elite can influence the flow of trade into its capital by investing public moneys in and around the capital.[7]

For a case in which the convergence of large-scale economic networks *causes* political centralization, we have Vance's description of the develop-

---

[7] Smith (1972, 1973) suggests a similar pattern for western Guatemala. She sees the initial location of the Spanish conquerors in Quezaltenango, today the major town in western Guatemala, as pushing the development of the regional economic system toward the dendritic pattern.

ment of the settlement system in the frontier United States (1970:85). Denver, Colorado, is an example of a major regional political and economic center (entrepôt city, in Vance's terms) that started out with only economic functions (as a mining town and later an unraveling point of trade), later assuming political ones (as the territorial capital).

The dendritic system model I have described applies not only to regions in which all economic networks converge on one highest-level center and in which wholesaling networks are the most important networks (important in the sense of handling the largest volume of goods or generating the largest proportion of regional income). It also applies to any region in which either of the following conditions holds.

Under the first condition wholesaling networks that converge on one major center are sufficiently important to influence the locations of other firms, whether or not their economic links converge on the major wholesaling center. The influence of wholesaling will cause other firms to locate in the same centers used by the wholesaling firms, such as retailers who locate in wholesaling centers in order to capture the patronage of people who work in the centers' wholesaling and transport sectors.

Under the second condition the wholesaling networks that converge on one major center are the *only region-wide* networks in the region. Other economic networks may exist, of only local extent. The locations of the centers linked through such local networks may be *totally uninfluenced* by the locations of the centers linked through the region-wide networks. However, the latter centers may actually influence the locations of the points of exchange in these local exchange networks because the same people may produce, transport, and consume goods allocated through both local and long-distance wholesaling networks. As Ortiz has pointed out (1967), such local exchange networks may operate *because of* regional wholesaling networks, since they buffer local producers and consumers against fluctuations of the price and quantity (supplied or bought) of wholesale goods (especially of locally produced cash crops for export).

DENDRITIC SYSTEM TYPES

The reader who is familiar with the cases I have offered as examples of dendritic systems will realize that many system differences are obscured by the label "dendritic." There appear to be two main differences among these systems. One is in the presence or absence of clear *functional stratification* of centers. In some systems—western Guatemala, region-wide (Smith 1972, 1975), Haiti (Mintz 1960), and Colombia (Ortiz 1967)—commercial centers fall into clear levels, and each level includes all functions appearing in all the lower levels, plus a new set of functions not present in any of the lower levels. In these systems one can place a particular center in its proper level simply by knowing which types of retailing and wholesaling functions (as well as social and political functions) it offers and which types it does not. On the other hand, in some systems—frontier United States (Vance 1970) and the northern periphery of western Guatemala (Smith 1975)—settlements have primarily wholesaling functions, all participate in the bulking or redistribution of the same types of goods, and one cannot easily classify settlement levels by knowing which functions are present and which are not. The first type of system I will call mature, while the second type I will call immature.

Immature systems often seem to have only two types of centers: many very small centers and one much larger center. These larger centers often do not have special functions lacking in the small centers, but only *more* of the *same type* of functions. Furthermore, while the major center in an immature system is larger than the small centers in the system, it is proportionately much *smaller* than the largest center in a mature type of system. The size of a center in an immature system is correlated with the level in the wholesaling hierarchy to which it belongs. The level of a given center in a wholesaling hierarchy is determined by the number of places at which goods change hands between the beginning of the bulking or redistribution process and the time they reach that center. In other words, each center is in its proper hierarchical level when it is placed in the level *below* that of the center from which it gets goods (for redistribution) or to which it sends goods (for bulking).

There is a second important difference between mature and immature systems. In mature systems the primate centers, in addition to importing and exporting goods to and from the region, gather goods produced in some sections of their hinterlands and redistribute these goods to other sections of their hinterlands, while the major centers in immature systems do not. Major centers in immature systems gather goods produced in their hinterlands to *export* from the region altogether, and only redistribute goods that have been *imported* from outside the region.

Immature systems develop into maturity as follows. When long-distance wholesaling networks develop in a region (as they must if a wholesale-oriented dendritic system is to appear), centers linked through such networks are not likely to start out with functions other than wholesaling. Firms providing other (nonwholesaling) functions will appear in or around the wholesaling centers after the wholesaling network becomes established and starts generating income and demand for these other functions. Therefore, the growth of wholesaling also leads to the agglomeration of other political and economic functions in centers that began with only wholesaling functions. Ultimately, a functionally stratified hierarchy of settlements emerges. However, the levels assigned to these centers according to their retailing functions will descend with distance from the region's highest-level center, just as wholesaling levels do. This is because, in a wholesale-dominated system, the terms of trade for producer–consumers become worse with increasing distance from the highest-level center, and therefore purchasing power becomes more sparsely distributed.

The growth of wholesaling and the agglomeration of nonwholesaling functions in the original wholesaling centers will also eventually lead to the following kind of arbitrage of regional products (especially agricultural products). As population increases in the growing wholesaling towns, so does the demand for agricultural products. This demand stimulates rural production and wholesaling of these products to the towns. Once agricultural products from their hinterlands start moving to all the wholesaling towns, it is a short step to shipping these same products downward from the wholesaling town into *other* areas in its hinterland, or horizontally to other wholesaling towns, where there is demand for these products. Also, products shipped to the region's highest-level wholesaling center may be reallocated among the lower-level centers and their respective hinterlands. However, such region-wide arbitrage would occur only after hinterland products are drawn into individual lower-level wholesaling towns by the demand concentrated there. Only these towns would have adequate information on demand levels elsewhere in the region.

APPLYING THE DENDRITIC SYSTEM
MODEL TO THE NAVAJO REGION

To illustrate the workings of the dendritic system model just presented, I will apply it to the pre-1940 Navajo regional economy. The Navajo region is a contiguous area of around 30,000 square miles in northeastern Arizona and northwestern New Mexico. It is inhabited, outside the five major (border)[8] towns in the area, mostly by Navajo Indians. The area includes Navajo, Hopi, and Zuñi Indian Reservations as well as a large area east of the Navajo Reservation in New Mexico (see Map 1). It is a sparsely populated region, with a mean population density in 1940 of around two people per square mile. Livestock raising (mostly of sheep), both for direct household consumption and for trade, was the mainstay of the Navajo economy between the 1870s and 1940. The people augmented income from livestock with some subsistence agriculture, weaving, silversmithing, and wage work; today, of course, wages and public assistance make up the greater portion of Navajo income.

Both factors that I have postulated as creating dendritic central-place organization—dominance of long-distance trade and the convergence of

---

[8] I use the term "border town" for these towns because that is what people in the area call them. They are called border towns because they are all located near the border of the Navajo Reservation. All except Gallup are also located along the border of the region.

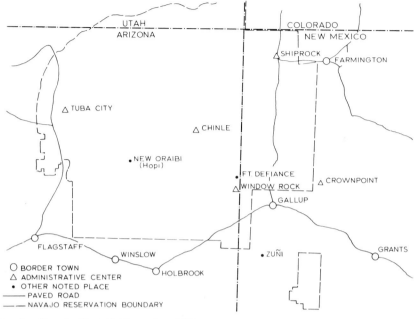

Map 1. Navajo Hopi Zuñi country, 1950.

networks on one major center—are present in the Navajo region. The Navajo regional economy before 1940 was based on long-distance wholesaling. Wool and lambs were bulked and sent out of the region, ultimately bound for the midwestern and eastern United States; and manufactured items (general merchandise) were brought in and redistributed, also from the Midwest and East. There were two functional levels of centers: trading posts (low level) and border towns (high level). Centers in these two levels were interrelated mostly by wholesaling ties, not by consumer movements between the retailers of high- and low-level goods. When Navajos wanted to buy general merchandise, the traders extended them credit, and the Navajos paid up their accounts in the spring with wool and in the fall with lambs. By the same token, wholesalers in four of the border towns supplied the traders with general merchandise on credit, and the traders paid up *their* accounts with the lambs and wool received from the Navajos. The wholesalers shipped wool and lambs out of the region by train, which also delivered, from points outside the region, their stock of wholesale general merchandise. Virtually all retailing to the Navajos occurred at the trading post level. Trading posts sold all levels of goods except automobiles (and sometimes even those, though never new ones). Before 1940, Navajos occasionally also bought things in the border towns (Adams 1963; Boyce 1974; Gillmor and Wetherill 1953; Hegemann 1963; Kennedy 1965; McNitt

1962; Newcomb 1966; Schmedding 1951; Utley 1961). However, most Navajos made most of their purchases at the trading posts.

The border towns were all much busier retailing centers than one would expect from their rather minimal Navajo patronage before 1940. However, all of these towns had such extraneous functions as that of railroad division point or service and residence center for nearby coal mines, oil and gas fields, and so on. Therefore, most of the retailing firms in these towns were probably "city serving" (serving the residents of the city) rather than "city forming" (serving people in the city's hinterland). Long-distance wholesaling was more important than retailing in linking low-level and high-level centers. This assertion is supported by a study of the relationship between the number of trading posts, the number of wholesalers, Navajo income from livestock, and Navajo income from all sources (including cash) for the period 1895 to the present (Kelley n. d.). The number of trading posts and real income from livestock were highly correlated ($r = .81$, $p < .01$), as were the number of wholesalers and income from livestock ($r = .82$, $p < .01$) and the number of trading posts and the number of wholesalers ($r = .92$, $p < .01$). The correlation between the number of trading posts and total Navajo income from livestock plus *cash* (wages and public assistance) was only .50 ($p < .05$),[9] indicating that cash income was less likely to be spent at the trading posts than was (future) income from lambs and wool.[10] The most likely places for cash income to be spent were the border towns. However, since cash income was low for most of the period before 1940, these correlations support the assertion that ties between the two levels of centers, trading posts and border towns, were based more on wholesaling than on retailing and that the trading post system was based on long-distance wholesaling.

Economic networks in the Navajo region also converged on single high-level centers. The Navajo region was, until 15 or 20 years ago, actually a "superregion" of four *nodal regions* under the four border towns in which wholesalers were located (see Map 2). In each of these nodal regions, bulking and redistribution networks not only converged on the same major

[9] In making these correlations, I used a sample of those trading posts for which I could find (or estimate) the dates between which they existed. This sample includes about 75 percent of all the trading posts ever referred to in the literature or mentioned by informants and is probably close to 75 percent of all the trading posts that ever existed. However, with continued research, the size of the trading post sample may increase, possibly causing slight changes in the correlation coefficients.

[10] This possible Navajo propensity to spend cash income in the border towns does not contradict my earlier statement that, before 1940, Navajos patronized border town retailers only rarely; for most of the time before 1940, cash was a rather small proportion of total income. Until 1920, real wages were less than 4 percent of total income (Kelley n.d.). Today, on the other hand, cash (wages and public assistance) is the largest source of income, while income from wool and lamb sales has declined absolutely.

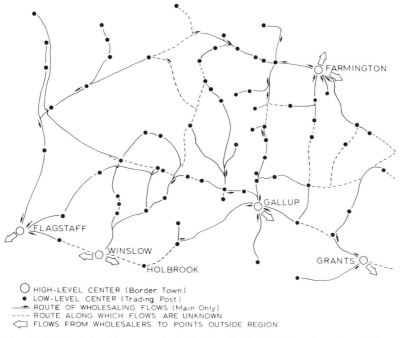

FARMINGTON

GALLUP

FLAGSTAFF

WINSLOW

HOLBROOK

GRANTS

○ HIGH-LEVEL CENTER (Border Town)
● LOW-LEVEL CENTER (Trading Post)
——▶ ROUTE OF WHOLESALING FLOWS (Main Only)
- - - - ROUTE ALONG WHICH FLOWS ARE UNKNOWN
◁ FLOWS FROM WHOLESALERS TO POINTS OUTSIDE REGION

Map 2.   Probable wholesaling networks in the Navajo–Hopi–Zuñi region, circa 1940.

center but also coincided in the lower-level centers. The reason is that wool and lambs were always traded for general merchandise, between traders and Navajos, and between wholesalers and traders, as described earlier. Thus, the same firms that bulked wool and lambs also redistributed general merchandise. These four nodal regions were not, however, all oriented to a single, still larger center. All the border towns were located on a railroad, and wholesale goods were shipped in and out of the border towns by way of the railroad to or from different centers far from the region.

The information just given suggests that the Navajo system before 1940 was immature. This is borne out by the absence of clear functional stratification between border towns and trading post centers. The border towns had many functions not present in the trading post centers (for example, florists, funeral parlors), but these functions were generally city serving (for example, the florist and the funeral parlor provided goods and services that the Navajos did not demand). City-forming functions tended to be retailing firms specializing in various types of goods also available in or through the trading posts and, more important, wholesale goods also handled by the trading posts (see Table 1). That the Navajo system was immature is also borne out by the fact that none of the wool or livestock

TABLE 1
Central-Place Functions in the Navajo-Hopi-Zuni Region, 1920-1940[a]

	Border Towns		
Year	City-Forming Functions	City-Serving Functions[b]	Trading Posts[c]
1920	General merchandise retailer Post office Auto repair shop Lumber retailer Auto retailer[d] General merchandise wholesaler	Personal services (barber, shoe repair) Amusements Physician Other professional services (dentist, lawyer, etc.) Undertaker Insurance agency Newspaper Bank	General merchandise retailer (food, dry goods, patent medicine, hardware, saddlery, pawn/jewelry; sometimes lumber, used cars) Post office
1930	Same as 1920, plus Specialized retailers (drugs, food, clothing) Jewelry/pawn shop Hospital Auto retailer	Same as 1920, plus Florist[d] Plumber[d]	Same as 1920
1940	Same as 1930	Same as 1930	Same as 1920

a. *Source: Gazetteer Publishing and Printing Co., 1921, 1931, 1941. Data available for Gallup and Farmington.*
b. *These are also central-place functions for Anglos in the towns' hinterlands.*
c. *Trading posts have only city-forming functions.*
d. *Present in Gallup only.*

drawn from a nodal region and bulked in its border town was then reallocated to areas within that nodal region (Adams 1963; McNitt 1962).

In the rest of this paper, I will try to show how the preeminence of wholesaling and the convergence of these bulking and redistribution networks on the same high-level centers created the five dendritic system features in the Navajo region.

Noninterstitial Placement of Settlement Levels

The absence of interstitial placement of settlement levels in the Navajo region is somewhat difficult to show because, like many immature regions, it lacks three clearly defined levels of centers. Before 1940 there were clearly two levels: major centers in four border towns, which had general merchandise wholesalers and large numbers of specialized retailers, including automobile dealers; and minor centers in about 140 centers containing trading posts. (Often a single trading post constituted the entire settlement.) The trader, as described earlier, was both a general merchandise retailer and a low-level bulking merchant of wool and livestock. He received his stock of general merchandise from a wholesaler in one of the border towns on credit and paid his bill with the lambs and wool received from his Navajo customers. Wholesalers in the regional border towns would send the livestock and wool to still higher-level centers outside the region, receiving general merchandise in return. If the three levels of centers, including the centers outside the region, are considered, settlement levels are not interstitially placed, because the border towns are nearer (in transport time and distance) to wholesalers outside the region than are the trading posts. (See Map 2.)

The reason that this pattern was not obscured by a retailing hierarchy (with interstitial placement of levels) is, as proposed by the dendritic system model, due to the difference in transport technology available to consumers and wholesalers. Navajo consumers had to rely on horses or on walking for transportation, so that consumer ranges were not large even for the highest-level goods. The range was lessened further because rather frequent trips to the store were necessary. Food was the most important item bought, and since many people lacked wagons, they were unable to transport staples in large bulk. Therefore, a retailing hierarchy in the period before 1940 was not well developed. On the other hand, while the traders also relied on horses for most of the period, they could transport in bulk (using large freight wagons) and could hire people to drive the teams and wagons for them. The traders usually had to transport goods from the wholesaler's border town warehouse, or at least from the nearest railroad stop. Therefore, traders' ranges were larger than consumers' ranges.

Wholesalers used the railroad for transport, thus having transportation means much superior to that available to both traders and consumers.[11]

Larger Than Expected Ratio of Low-Level Centers to High-Level Centers

The Navajo region before 1940 had a maximum of four high-level centers (with seven wholesalers) and about 140 low-level centers (with about 175 trading posts). This gives an average of 20 low-level centers per high-level center (or 25 trading posts per wholesaler). Looking at individual border towns, the number of low-level centers per border town depended on the number of *wholesaling firms* in the border town. Thus, Flagstaff, which never had more than one wholesaler, had between 12 and 22 dependent centers (between 13 and 24 dependent trading posts), while Gallup, with between one and four wholesalers, had between 32 and 60 dependent centers (between 40 and 72 dependent trading posts). The threshold number of trading posts seems to have been in the range of 12–16 (Kelley n. d.).

To contrast the Navajo wholesaling (dendritic) system and an empirical standard central-place (retailing) system, these ratios can be compared to the ratios of four levels of centers in two normal central-place systems in Ontario, Canada, studied by Marshall (1969), as follows. Marshall found a $1:2:8:52$ ratio for one system and a $1:6:12:60$ ratio for the other (Marshall 1969:142–143). In the Navajo system the smallest number of low-level centers for each major border town before 1940 is as follows: $1:32$ (Gallup); $1:12$ (Farmington); $1:12$ (Flagstaff); and $1:15$ (Winslow). Another interesting contrast between the two Ontario systems and the Navajo system is in the magnitude of population differences between different levels of centers. Marshall found four levels in each system, with the following ranges of population for each level. System I: level 1, 21,000; level 2, 2000–8000; level 3, 500–2000; and level 4, 100–600. System II: level 1, 17,000; level 2, 1000–3800; level 3, 350–500; and level 4, 65–200 (Marshall 1969:142–143). In contrast, the two levels of settlements in the Navajo region had the following ranges of population around 1940: level 1,

---

[11] Parenthetically, I note that in the period since 1940, retailing systems in the Navajo country have become more elaborate. The trading posts still function as low-level retailing firms, but the border towns have been transformed into a heavily used higher level of retailing centers. Navajos after 1940 visited these towns often, not only for high-level goods not available elsewhere (for example, new automobiles), but also for middle-level goods (clothes). While in town, they probably would stock up on groceries (low-level goods) as well. These two levels of retailing settlements correspond to the settlements in the wholesaling system before 1960 (after 1960, two of the border towns lost their wholesaling functions but retained their retailing functions). This two-level retailing hierarchy has probably developed, as noted earlier, because of large increases in Navajo cash income (from wages and public assistance) during the period, and also because of the government road-paving program during the 1950s.

2000–8000 (U.S. Bureau of the Census 1940); level 2, 1–500 (Gazetteer Publishing and Printing Co. 1941). The vast difference between levels in settlement population is a feature noted for immature systems in particular.

The reason proposed in the dendritic system model for an excessively large number of low-level centers was the presence of large differences in the thresholds of firms in centers of adjacent hierarchical levels. This notion is supported by the Navajo case. In the Navajo region, wholesalers used trains to ship goods over long distances, which forced them to bulk large volumes of goods in order to realize advantages of scale. This made wholesalers' thresholds much higher than the threshold of the average trader, who used horse and wagon, shipped over shorter distances, and had to keep his threshold within the range of the isolated and sparsely distributed Navajos with whom he traded.

Orientation of Each Lower-Level Center to Only One Center in the Next-Higher Level

In the Navajo country, traders infrequently dealt with different high-level bulking or redistribution firms (Adams 1963; Gillmor and Wetherill 1953; Hegemann 1963; Kennedy 1965; McNitt 1962; Newcomb 1966; Schmedding 1951). Often this was because a wholesaler owned sole or part interest in many of the trading posts in his area. While I lack detailed information on changes in trading post ownership through time, some information is available on trading posts ever owned by certain firms. Thus, the single Flagstaff wholesaler held at least part ownership, at one time or another, in at least 16 of the 40 stores ever in the estimated Flagstaff wholesaling area (Adams 1963:155–156; Hegemann 1963; McNitt 1962:263). [See Kelley (n. d.) for the wholesale-area estimating procedure.] Similarly, Lorenzo Hubbell, the famous trader at Ganado, Arizona, who established a wholesaling house in Winslow, at one time or another held at least part interest in at least 10 of the 24 stores ever in the estimated Winslow wholesaling area (McNitt 1962:205n, 275). Finally, of the 49 stores ever in the estimated Farmington wholesaling area, at least 14 stores were owned at least in part by the relatives of partners in a wholesaling firm near Farmington (McNitt 1962:300n).

Most traders, of course, were not *compelled* to trade with a single wholesaler in a single center by virtue of the fact that the latter was either the trader's boss, his partner, or his relative. However, trader dependence on the credit extended by the wholesaler did tend to tie many traders to one wholesaler. Also, as mentioned earlier, wholesalers usually did not deliver goods to or transport livestock and wool from the trading posts; the trader himself did so. Most traders had to travel long distances over roads

TABLE 2
Number of Trading Posts Tied to One Wholesaler and to More Than
One Wholesaler[a]

Time Period	One Wholesaler[b]			More Than One Wholesaler	Unknown[c]
	A	B	Total		
1890–1900	3	6	9	4	67
1900–1910	14	5	19	1	93
1910–1920	18	5	23	2	123
1920–1930	22	7	29	2	121
1930–1940	26	7	33	1	138

    a. Sources: Adams 1963; Gillmor and Wetherill 1953;
Hegemann 1963; Kennedy 1965; McNitt 1962; Schmedding 1951.
    b. A = owned or partnered by wholesaler or his relative;
B = tied to one wholesaler due to transport cost.
    c. Assuming that trading post sample used for each period
represents 75 percent of contemporary trading posts. "Unknown"
figures are inflated so that known plus unknown equals 100 percent estimated total number of trading posts.

that were often impassable, so that they were forced, by the high transport
costs (in time as well as money), to trade with the nearest wholesaler
(Adams 1963; Gillmor and Wetherill 1953; Hegemann 1963; Kennedy
1965; McNitt 1962; Schmedding 1951). (See Table 2.) Therefore, the
distance from the ultimate source or destination of goods, plus the
contractual relations inherent in wholesaling, as proposed in the dendritic
system model, seems to have caused each trading post in the Navajo
country to be linked mostly to one wholesaler, and therefore to only one
major wholesaling center.

Draining of Hinterland Income, Population, or Resources by the Highest-Level Center

The dendritic system model proposes that the failure of major firms to
reinvest their profits in the hinterland is a major cause of hinterland
income drain. While profit levels for border town firms are unknown, few
if any such firms seem to have invested in hinterland enterprises, judging
from records of the enterprises present in the hinterland during the period
(see Table 3). Wholesalers do not seem to have invested large amounts in
the trading posts. Furthermore, such investments did not provide the
hinterland population with sources of income alternative to livestock rais-

TABLE 3

Income-Generating Investments in the Navajo-Hopi-Zuni Region, 1940[a]

Type	By	Location[b] A	B	Total
Irrigation project	U.S. gov't.	27	0	27
Extractive enterprises (mines, oil companies, etc.)	Private and U.S. gov't.	10	6	16
Guest ranches	Private[c]	4	1	5
Large sheep herds (500-13,000 head)	Private	0	22	22
Ordnance depot	U.S. gov't.	0	1	1
Slaughter house or cannery	U.S. gov't.	1	0	1

a. *Sources: Van Valkenburgh 1941; Pearce 1964; Barnes 1935. Sample included all named places in the region.*
b. *A = on reservation; B = off reservation.*
c. *Individual trading post owners.*

ing. On the other hand, at least some of these firms made investments outside the Navajo region (see Table 4). Therefore, it seems likely that income (in the form of profits on purchases from and sales to hinterland producer–consumers) was drained from the hinterland.[12]

There seems to have been little out-migration from the region before 1940. This assertion is supported by annual net rates of increase for the Navajo population, which increased steadily from 2.02 percent in 1890 to

[12] This is not to say that no investments have been made in the hinterland that provide alternative sources of income for the people living there. However, it is the federal government that has made these investments (for instance, in irrigation project development). It may be argued that the relationship of the federal government to Indians (especially with regard to land) has discouraged private investment in the hinterland. Most land in the Navajo region is not a marketable commodity, being held in perpetuity by the Navajo (or Hopi or Zuñi) tribe and under the jurisdiction of the U.S. government. Therefore, an investor cannot own the land in which he invests but can only lease it from the tribe. Furthermore, investment in Indian lands under federal jurisdiction may be discouraged by various government policies regulating commercial, productive, extractive, and so on activities on lands under its jurisdiction. While these are sensible objections, I would call attention to the fact that much of the Navajo region, particularly the eastern portion, is *not* tribal territory and is *not* under special federal regulation; yet if there is a contrast between the economic development of off-reservation and on-reservation areas, it is the *on*-reservation areas that seem more developed (see Table 3).

TABLE 4
Income-Generating Investments (Other Than Trading Posts) by Wholesalers and Traders, 1940[a]

		Location[b]		
By	*Type*	A	B	C
Wholesalers:				
Flagstaff 1	Cattle ranches			X
	Specialized retailing firms		X	X
Gallup 1	Statewide enterprises of larger firm of which this wholesaler is a branch			X
Farmington 1	Same as Gallup 1			X
Farmington 2	Same as Gallup 1			X
Winslow 1	Freight line	X	X	
Grants 1	Oil distributing co.		X	
Traders:				
5 traders	Sheep herds (500–8000 head)	X		X
5 owners	Guest ranches	X		
1 trader and family	Specialized retailing firms		X	
	Contracting firm		X	

a. *Sources: Gazetteer Publishing and Printing Co. 1921, 1931, 1941; McNitt 1962:220, 269; U.S. Senate Committee on Indian Affairs 1937:17,754; Armitage 1959. This is a partial listing only.*
b. *A = hinterland; B = border town; C = outside region.*

2.84 percent in 1940 (Aberle 1966:362; James 1914:181; U.S. Senate Committee on Indian Affairs 1932; Young 1958:323). In the period before 1940, therefore, it seems doubtful that border towns were draining population from their hinterlands to any significant extent.

The reason proposed to account for this apparent anomaly is an effective lack of jobs for Indians, possibly created by the language barrier. While the proportion of the total Navajo population with some formal education has climbed steadily from a little over 1 percent in 1890, only about 31 percent of the total population in 1940 had been exposed to any formal schooling (Aberle 1966:367). Even in 1968, half of a sample of

Navajo children began school without sufficient control of English to do
first grade work in English, a phenomenon that reflects the language used
by their parents (Spolsky 1970). Another reason for a possible lack of jobs
for Indians is racial–ethnic prejudice. This was a luxury that border town
employers could afford because the populations of most border towns were
growing rapidly for most of the period, and this growth meant a plentiful
labor supply (see Table 5).

TABLE 5
*Border Town, Core Area, and Trade Area Population Growth Rates
in Percentages[a]*

	Gallup	Farmington	Holbrook	Winslow	Flagstaff
1890-1900:					
Town					32
Core Area[b]					
Trade Area[c]					
1900-1910:					
Town	-25	100			29
Core Area					29
Trade Area					
1910-1920:					
Town	78	-7	98	57	95
Core Area	43	-21	98	57	95
Trade Area	38	19	43	14	8
1920-1930:					
Town	53	85	-8	5	22
Core Area	46	66	-8	5	22
Trade Area	43	14	22	44	21
1930-1940:					
Town	18	60	6	17	31
Core Area	-2	38	6	17	31
Trade Area	18	31	25	3	38
Period of greatest core area growth	1910-30	1920-40	1910-20	1910-20	1910-20

a. *Sources: U.S. Bureau of the Census 1910, 1920, 1930,
1940; James 1914:181; U.S. Senate Committee on Indian Affairs
1932:8902, 8937, 9112, 9118, 9314, 9461, 9575, 9578, 9724.*
    b. *Town population plus the contiguous area of population
agglomeration adjacent to the town.*
    c. *Includes town itself and area for which town supplies
highest-level functions common to all 5 towns (livestock shipping and some specialized goods and services consumed by rural
Anglos).*

The likelihood that the lack of jobs for Indians in the border towns kept people from moving out of the hinterland makes intelligible the drain of resources occurring during the period before 1940. The important resource that could be "drained" from the Navajo hinterland (by intensified primary production) is the grazing capacity of the land. The grazing capacity of the land has probably been decreasing since around 1890 (Aberle 1966:30–33).[13] The decrease in the grazing capacity has been due to overgrazing, according to the U.S. government (Boyce 1974). The Navajos, as one would expect, seem not to have been unaware that the land was overstocked. Since stocking to carrying capacity or above would have filled up all the grazing areas, people presumably would have understood from their increasing difficulty in finding fresh pasturage that the land was filled up. Evidence that Navajo stock owners did respond to the shortage of grazing land by regulating herd size comes from Aberle's (1966:30–33) and Young's (1961:167) figures, which show that the combined population of sheep and goats increased explosively (at a rate of 27 percent per year) until around 1890, after which it fluctuated around (but often above) the total range carrying capacity. Since the Navajo population increased at an estimated rate of between 2.02 and 2.84 percent per year between 1890 and 1940 (Aberle 1966:363), livestock per capita declined during most of the 1890–1940 period. Perhaps it was the increasing difficulty for a family to subsist directly off its herds that made the Navajos willing to trade, first wool and later lambs, at the trading posts. One may wonder why, if the Navajos saw the need to regulate herd size, total stock population remained above the range carrying capacity. A possible reason is that the people could not support themselves on fewer stock, due to the lack of reasonable alternative sources of income.

The following are examples of income alternatives and their lack of feasibility. (1) The percentage of the total area of the Navajo country capable of producing a regular crop if water resources were developed in 1937 was .2 percent (U.S. Senate Committee on Indian Affairs 1937:17,976). (2) Wage work as seasonal agricultural labor would have required too costly travel over long distances (virtually no commercial crops requiring seasonal labor were grown in the area surrounding the Navajo–Hopi–Zuñi region before 1940). (3) There was very little demand for Navajo seasonal railroad labor until World War II (Adams 1963:51). (4) Various kinds of wage work in the border towns were probably limited due to the language

[13] Mindeleff (1898) notes, using data from the 1880s, that Navajo house types were changing from the old forked-stick hogan to the larger, more permanent polygonal hogan. He suggests that people were becoming less mobile and that, as a consequence, residence groups were becoming larger. This lends further, if indirect, support to the possibility that stock had increased to the region's carrying capacity by 1890, since the filling up of the grazing areas would constrain extended and nuclear family mobility.

barrier and discriminatory hiring practices, as discussed earlier. (5) Craft production required a large investment of time to gain the skill, faced a relatively low level of demand, and provided an extremely low return for labor. [An experiment within the last 20 years showed that, even if the weaver observed for the experiment had received the full retail price for her work, it would have come to less than 18 cents an hour (Maxwell 1963:19–20).]

The dendritic system model presented earlier suggests that, in the long run, low prices paid to producers call forth increased production in the absence of alternative income sources for producers. Furthermore, this increased production depletes resources and induces still greater production, which lowers prices further, the whole process constituting a deviation-amplifying feedback loop.

There is no information available on price variations within the region for any time during the period, so that the preceding hypothesis cannot be tested directly. However, to approximate a test, I correlated the Arizona wool price and the volume of Navajo wool sold at 5-year intervals from 1895 to 1930 (Kelley n. d.).[14] The correlation coefficient (r) obtained is only .65 ($p < .10$). On the other hand, the correlation between the number of sheep and the volume of wool marketed is .95 ($p < .01$). This suggests that variations in wool prices over time were less important in influencing Navajo decisions on how much wool to sell than was the potential amount of wool that they could clip. The positive (though insignificant) correlation between price and volume does not contradict the dendritic system model, which says that price and volume should be negatively correlated where a resource drain exists. For the model also suggests that, where factors other than the number of competing suppliers influence the price level, the predicted negative correlation may be overridden. The wool price used here is that for the state of Arizona, which is influenced by factors other than the number of Navajo producers—short-run fluctuations in worldwide demand. Therefore, one would expect the predicted negative correlation to be overridden in the Navajo case. Furthermore, a likely reason for the high correlation between the number of sheep and the volume of wool sold is that people sold all the wool they could spare. If this interpretation is correct, then the correlations tend to support the notion that range depletion was due to the fall in potential income (as measured in sheep per family) spurring production, although production-level increases were also constrained by the desire to minimize overgrazing.

[14] After 1930 the number of pounds of wool would have decreased, regardless of price, because the number of sheep decreased, due to the stock reduction program. The Arizona wool price was used because there are no price data for the Navajo country, and I assume that the Arizona price influenced prices in the Navajo region.

Concentration of a Political Elite in the
Region's Single Highest-Level Center

In the Navajo country the political situation is complicated by the fact
that Indian reservation lands are under federal jurisdiction rather than
under the jurisdiction of regional political institutions. Nevertheless,
before 1940, regional elites were concentrated in and around the border
towns. One indication of a center's political importance is its government
functions. Of the four border towns having general merchandise
wholesalers between 1895 and 1940, the three with the earliest and most
important wholesalers were (and are) county seats (Gallup and Flagstaff)
or are part of a core area containing the county seat (Farmington,
separated by only 14 densely populated miles from its county seat). Winslow, the fourth wholesaling town, is located in a county that also contains
the one border town that did *not* have a general merchandise wholesaler;
surprisingly, the *latter* is the county seat. I believe a possible explanation
for this apparent anomaly appears when the distribution of the political
elite is considered.

The proportion of a region's elite that is concentrated in a center is
another indication of the center's political importance. In the Navajo
region Anglos comprise the political elite. Table 6 shows, for each border
town trade area, the proportion of the total trade area population living in
a core area made up of the border town and contiguous adjacent settlements. It also shows the proportion of the trade area population composed
of Anglos living outside the core. (The trade areas here are for the highest-
level functions common to all the border towns, including Holbrook—
livestock shipping and certain specialized retailing and service functions.)
Border town populations are at present predominantly Anglo; in 1960 (the
earliest census giving ethnic breakdown), "others" (mostly Indians)
represented 15 percent of the population of Gallup, 2 percent of Farmington, and 4 percent of Flagstaff; Spanish-surnamed people were 31
percent of Gallup, 6 percent of Farmington, and 18 percent of Flagstaff
(U.S. Bureau of the Census 1960).[15] There is no reason to expect that the
situation before 1940 was any different. Therefore, we can assume that
core area populations are members of the political elite, just as the Anglos
outside the core are. Table 6 shows that in all but one of the trade areas,
for most of the 1910–1940 period, the core area population is close to or
exceeds the rural Anglo population as a proportion of the whole trade area.

The region's ethnic elite is thus concentrated in and around the border
towns, with one exception: Holbrook. The southern part of Holbrook's
trade area contained many small Mormon farming villages and also a

[15] Census enumeration districts are too large to allow an estimation of core area
populations.

TABLE 6

Border Town, Core Area, and Rural Anglo Populations as Proportions of Total Trade Areas[a]

Population	Gallup	Farmington	Holbrook	Winslow	Flagstaff
1910					
A. Town	2,204	785	609	2,381	1,633
B. Core Area[b]	5,483	3,492	609	2,381	1,633
C. Trade Area[c]	19,104	15,528	10,105	6,420	12,687
D. Rural Anglo[d]	536	2,059	4,789	1,149	3,254
B as % of C	29	23	6	37	13
D as % of C	3	13	47	18	26
1920					
A. Town	3,920	728	1,206	3,730	3,186
B. Core Area	7,843	2,766	1,206	3,730	3,186
C. Trade Area	26,365	18,463	14,400	7,312	13,732
D. Rural Anglo	1,471	2,901	8,001	1,601	3,546
B as % of C	30	15	8	51	23
D as % of C	6	16	56	22	26
1930					
A. Town	5,992	1,350	1,115	3,917	3,891
B. Core Area	11,460	4,592	1,115	3,917	3,891
C. Trade Area	37,649	21,056	17,514	10,553	16,588
D. Rural Anglo	4,823	2,493	12,857	3,809	5,661
B as % of C	30	22	6	37	24
D as % of C	13	12	73	36	34
1940					
A. Town	7,041	2,161	1,184	4,577	5,080
B. Core Area	11,206	6,430	1,184	4,577	5,080
C. Trade Area	44,240	27,594	21,855	10,914	22,836
D. Rural Anglo	5,395	2,407	>6,542[e]	?[e]	8,610
B as % of C	25	23	5	42	29
D as % of C	12	9	>30[e]	?[e]	38

a. See Table 5, footnote a.
b. See Table 5, footnote b.
c. See Table 5, footnote c.
d. Anglos living outside the core area.
e. New census enumeration districts include large sections of both reservation and off-reservation areas, without a separate designation for reservation population.

number of centers that may have offered middle-level central-place functions. In addition, it included the county seat of a neighboring county. The location of the county seat in Holbrook, rather than in Winslow, may be due to the fact that all these dispersed Anglo villages are closer to the former than to the latter.

There remains the question of why no general merchandise wholesaler ever appeared in Holbrook. Before 1940 there were not sufficient trading posts to support more than one wholesaler in the area between Gallup and Flagstaff (Kelley n.d.). Winslow may have been more attractive to a wholesaler supplying trading posts in the Navajo region because it was closer to two population agglomerations in that region: Hopi and the government settlement of Leupp. The example of Holbrook is interesting because this town, which lacks a concentrated political elite, also lacks at least one of the two causal dendritic system features: the dominance of long-distance trade in its hinterland. Many Anglos raised crops as well as livestock for a living, and they probably marketed much of their produce locally or directly to settlements outside Holbrook's trade area.

For most border towns, an early convergence of economic networks probably caused the concentration of an elite, rather than the other way around. Gallup began as a coal-mining center, a railroad division point (because of the coal), and a wholesaling center for the "Indian trade." All these developments occurred between 1890 and 1900, while the town's population did not begin to grow rapidly until 1910 (Gallup Chamber of Commerce n. d.). (See Table 5 for growth rates.) Flagstaff began as a lumbering, railroad, and ranching center around 1880, had a general merchandise wholesaler by 1890, and began its period of rapid growth only after 1900 (Barnes 1935; McNitt 1962:263). Winslow became a railroad division point and ranching center before 1900 (Barnes 1935), experiencing moderate growth after 1910. It did not have a wholesaler until 1920 because until that time its hinterland had too few trading posts to support a wholesaler (Kelley n. d.). All these towns were like many other small railroad, ranching, and mining towns in the region until they began to grow (Barnes 1935; Pearce 1964). Furthermore, since the immigrants seem to have been mostly non-Indians, rapid population growth from small beginnings may be taken as an indication of the concentration of the elite group.

The same process can be seen for Farmington, although growth occurred later. Farmington was founded around 1880 as one of several small farming communities along the San Juan River. By 1910 it was connected to Durango, Colorado, by a railroad spur and had a wholesaler in neighboring Fruitland (MacDonald and Arrington 1970; McNitt 1962:300). However, the railroad and wholesaling activities were not strong enough to pull in a concentration of Anglos; this occurred only after 1920, when oil and natural gas were discovered in the vicinity.

CONCLUDING REMARKS

In closing, I will deal with one last question that points out a direction for future research. Is the Navajo regional system today changing into a mature dendritic type? This question is important because it points up the need for research on the Navajo regional economy in the present and because it suggests the way in which the dendritic system model can be used to analyze the present-day system.

Since 1940 there have been at least three changes in the pre-1940 economic picture. One of these changes has occurred in the wholesaling sphere: Bulking of wool and livestock has become a relatively minor economic function and is no longer mediated exclusively by border town firms. The second major change has come about in the sphere of Navajo income: Wool and livestock have become a minor source of income, outweighed by wages and public assistance. Since most families have regular cash incomes rather than the seasonal income of the old stock-based economy, they are not nearly so dependent on the traders for credit. Furthermore, since trading posts are small-scale enterprises, their prices are higher than prices in the large border-town retailing establishments (which originally grew up to serve large resident populations and those Indian people who occasionally went to town to shop before 1940). This price difference, together with the comparative freedom from credit dependence, induces hinterland people to shop in the border towns. The road-paving program staged by the U.S. government between 1950 and 1960 also increased consumer mobility and therefore consumer ranges. The third major change is that a true hierarchy of retailing functions seems to be developing in the region. Increased consumer ranges and the greater volume of cash sales, as opposed to credit sales, have probably caused this development. Two border towns with both wholesaling and high-level retailing functions are emerging in a level above the other border towns, which have only high-level retailing functions. There is also, perhaps, the glimmer of another level in the retailing system, forming between the original border towns and the trading posts: government administrative towns in the hinterland.

In considering these three changes, one can see that one distinguishing feature of mature dendritic systems is emerging: clear functional stratification of settlement levels. It is difficult to see the other distinguishing feature, regional arbitrage. The only goods allocated by border towns to their hinterlands are still, as before 1940, general merchandise produced outside the region. On the other hand, it is possible that labor (at least for non-government jobs) is allocated within each nodal region by employment information networks centered on each border town (or at least on the two border towns with wholesaling functions). Further research is needed to see how far a clearly stratified functional hierarchy has developed and whether border towns conduct different kinds of arbitrage in their respective nodal regions. Such research is also needed to test the general dendritic system model more rigorously by gathering the appropriate present-day information.

ACKNOWLEDGMENTS

I am greatly indebted to the following people for help with this paper: Professor Carol A. Smith for help in refining the model and for editing; David M. Kelley for editing; Professors Harry W. Basehart and Henry Harpending for overall advice; and Dr. Robert Young and Professors William Y. Adams, Tom T. Sasaki, and Oswald Werner for help with the data. I am also indebted to the traders who were able to provide historical information, and to the Grants, Gallup, Holbrook, Winslow, and Flagstaff Chambers of Commerce.

REFERENCES

Aberle, David
  1966   *The peyote religion among the Navaho.* New York: Wenner-Gren Foundation for Anthropological Research.
Adams, William Y.
  1963   *Shonto: A study of the role of the trader in a modern Navaho community.* Bureau of American Ethnology Bulletin No. 188. Washington, D.C.: U.S. Government Printing Office.
Armitage, Merle
  1959   *Stella Dysart of Ambrosia Lake.* New York: Duell.
Barnes, Will C.
  1935   *Arizona place names.* Univ. of Arizona General Bulletin No. 2. Tucson: Univ. of Arizona Press.
Berry, Brian J. L.
  1961   City size distribution and economic development. *Economic Development and Cultural Change* **9:** 573–588.
  1967   *Geography of market centers and retail distribution.* Englewood Cliffs, N.J.: Prentice-Hall.
Boyce, George A.
  1974   *When the Navajos had too many sheep: The 1940's.* San Francisco: Indian Historian Press.
Christaller, Walter
  1966   *Central places in southern Germany.* Translated by C. W. Baskin. Englewood Cliffs, N.J.: Prentice-Hall.
Gallup, N.M., Chamber of Commerce
  n. d.   *Statistical information.* (Mimeograph.)
Gazetteer Publishing and Printing Co.
  1921   *New Mexico state business directory.* Denver: Gazetteer Publishing and Printing Co.
  1931   *New Mexico state business directory.* Denver: Gazetteer Publishing and Printing Co.
  1941   *New Mexico state business directory.* Denver: Gazetteer Publishing and Printing Co.
Gillmor, Francis, and Louisa Wade Wetherill
  1953   *Traders to the Navajos: The story of the Wetherills of Kayenta.* Albuquerque: Univ. of New Mexico Press.

James, George Wharton
   1914 *Indian blankets and their makers.* Chicago: McClurg.
Johnson, E. A. J.
   1970 *The organization of space in developing countries.* Cambridge, Mass.: Harvard Univ. Press.
Kelley, Klara B.
   n. d. Changes in the Navajo trading post system, 1870–1970. Unpublished manuscript, Univ. of New Mexico.
Kennedy, Mary
   1965 *Tales of a trader's wife.* Albuquerque: Valliant.
MacDonald, Eleanor D., and John B. Arrington
   1970 *The San Juan basin: My kingdom was a county.* Denver: Green Mountain Press.
Marshall, John Urquhart
   1969 *The location of service towns: An approach to the analysis of central place systems.* Toronto: Department of Geography, Univ. of Toronto.
Maxwell, Gilbert S.
   1963 *Navajo rugs: Past, present, and future.* Palm Desert, Calif.: Best West Publications.
McNitt, Frank
   1962 *The Indian traders.* Norman: Univ. of Oklahoma Press.
Mindeleff, Cosmos
   1898 Navajo houses. In *Bureau of American ethnology: Seventeenth annual report.* Washington, D.C.: U.S. Government Printing Office.
Mintz, Sidney
   1960 A tentative typology of eight Haitian marketplaces. *Revista de Ciencias Sociales* **4:** 15–58.
Newcomb, Franc Johnson
   1966 *Navajo neighbors.* Norman: Univ. of Oklahoma Press.
Ortiz, Sutti
   1967 Colombian rural market organization: An exploratory model. *Man* **2:** 393–414.
Pearce, T. M. (Ed.)
   1964 *New Mexico place names: A geographic dictionary.* Albuquerque: Univ. of New Mexico Press.
Schmedding, Joseph
   1951 *Cowboy and Indian trader.* Caldwell, Idaho: Caxton.
Skinner, G. William
   1964 Marketing and social structure in rural China: Part I. *Journal of Asian Studies* **24:** 3–43.
   1965a Marketing and social structure in rural China: Part II. *Journal of Asian Studies* **24:** 195–228.
   1965b Marketing and social structure in rural China: Part III. *Journal of Asian Studies* **24:** 363–399.
Smith, Carol A.
   1972 Market articulation and economic stratification in western Guatemala. *Food Research Institute Studies* **11:** 203–233.
   1973 The evolution of marketing systems in western Guatemala: A central place analysis. *Estudios Sociales* **10:** 38–71. (English version.)
   1975 Examining stratification systems through peasant marketing arrangements. *Man* **10:** 95–122.
Spolsky, Bernard
   1970 Language maintenance III: Accessibility of school and town as a factor in language shift. *Navajo Reading Study Progress Report No. 4.* Albuquerque: Univ. of New Mexico Press.

U.S. Bureau of the Census

1910 *Census of population.* Washington, D.C.: U.S. Government Printing Office.
1920 *Census of population.* Washington, D.C.: U.S. Government Printing Office.
1930 *Census of population.* Washington, D.C.: U.S. Government Printing Office.
1940 *Census of population.* Washington, D.C.: U.S. Government Printing Office.
1960 *Census of population.* Washington, D.C.: U.S. Government Printing Office.

U.S. Senate Committee on Indian Affairs

1932 *Survey of conditions of the Indians in the United States: Hearings before a subcommittee of the Committee on Indian Affairs: Part 18.* Washington, D.C.: U.S. Government Printing Office.
1937 *Survey of conditions of the Indians in the United States: Hearings before a subcommittee of the Committee on Indian Affairs: Part 34.* Washington, D.C.: U.S. Government Printing Office.

Utley, Robert M.

1961 The reservation trader in Navajo history. *El Palacio* **68**: 5–27.

Vance, James E., Jr.

1970 *The merchant's world: Geography of wholesaling.* Englewood Cliffs, N.J.: Prentice-Hall.

Van Valkenburgh, Richard F.

1941 *Dine bikeyah.* Window Rock, Ariz.: Navajo Agency. (Mimeograph.)

Young, Robert W.

1958 *The Navajo yearbook.* Window Rock, Ariz.: Navajo Agency.
1961 *The Navajo yearbook.* Window Rock, Ariz.: Navajo Agency.

Chapter 8

Causes and Consequences of Central-Place Types in Western Guatemala

Carol A. Smith
Duke University

THE PROBLEM

Within the conceptual framework of central-place theory, one can define an organizational system at any level as long as the area encompassed includes a major market center, smaller dependent centers, and a contiguous related rural hinterland. Depending on the extent and development of the area under consideration, one might have a "national" system, a "regional" system, a "local city" or "local marketing" system, or a small "market town" system. It is usually assumed that the conditions that give rise to a particular kind of central-place organization at a high level will lead to similar forms of organization in the encompassed lower levels. Most assume that the principles of integration—the particular manner in which a regular market hierarchy is formed[1]—will be uniform (Marshall 1969); others argue that several principles of organization will usually be

---

[1] The known principles of integration, developed by Christaller (1966), are the market principle ($K = 3$), the traffic principle ($K = 4$), and the administrative principle ($K = 7$). Other ways of relating centers to one another in a hierarchical pattern were developed by Lösch (1954), but their determinants are not well-known. These various principles describe the ways in which small and large centers are related within integrated marketing systems. For a review of these principles and the basic literature on central-place theory, see Chapter 1.

combined (Crissman 1973; Skinner 1964, n. d.). But no one has described a regular central-place system made up of smaller systems that are both different from one another and different from the high-level organization of the larger system. Western Guatemala provides just such a case.

Western Guatemala can be termed a region simply because it is large enough—its area includes about one-fourth of Guatemala—and because its social, economic, and organizational characteristics vis-à-vis the rest of the country are distinctive. It can be termed a regional system because a single major central place, Quezaltenango, serves to integrate a marketing system that is region-wide by means of its high-level and comprehensive market functions. From my previous analyses of the regional central-place system, it is clear that the major centers of western Guatemala are integrated and form a regular market hierarchy. These studies, however, dealt with only the higher-level market centers of the region.[2] Subsequent attempts to fit the smaller centers and local trade relationships into the larger regional pattern failed, leading to the present analysis. I have now found that the 12 local marketing systems that make up the regional system are patterned along three or four basically different lines and that irregularities in their organization lead to irregularities in the numbers and distribution of smaller centers.

The finding of local system diversity and irregularity within an integrated and regular regional system brings up four important questions: (1) What accounts for variability in central-place organization? (2) What are some of the economic consequences of different and sometimes irregular central-place systems? (3) How do different kinds of local systems with diverse economies and ecologies form regular and integrated regional systems? (4) What might one be able to predict about the organization and development of a region made up of diverse and irregular constituent elements? Each of these questions is addressed here, but primary focus is placed on developing and validating a model that can account for and predict economic characteristics in diverse types of central-place systems.

Model building and testing will proceed as follows. Several specific but "irregular" central-place types are proposed, based on the distinctive characteristics of the 12 local systems that form the region of western Guatemala. Then the actual functional types of central-place organization in the region are found through the use of formal grouping and scaling techniques and compared to the pyramidal central-place structures found in

[2] My previous analyses of the central-place organization in western Guatemala dealt only with the top three levels in a five-level hierarchy. At these levels a regular pattern of inter-relationship between centers was found. My dissertation (Smith 1972a) describes the methodology used for ascertaining the regional hierarchy; this analysis forms the basis of the assertions made here about the regional hierarchy. A brief description of the regional system can be found in Smith (1975).

each local system of the region. Central-place variations in these systems are explained with data on environment and control of resources, and the economic effects of central-place variation are described with data on economic alternatives or opportunities. The causal and consequential data are submitted to the same formal grouping techniques as the central-place data to see if the same groups of local systems emerge and if each functionally related group has similar central-place structure. Finally, a specifically Guatemalan model of the causes and consequences of central-place types is tested using regression and a type of path analysis.

While the immediate objective is to explain certain properties of the regional system of Guatemala, the more important objective is to relate central-place theory to regional systems analysis. I hope to show that disparate systems and variable forms of regional organization can be handled by the principles of a theory commonly thought to be inflexible and highly restricted in application. Thus, I will provide from the specifics of the study a number of general hypotheses about the causes and consequences of different types of central-place organization.

THE MODEL

Central-place theory is based on a number of quite rigid assumptions: an isotroic or featureless landscape, total dedication to profit maximization on the part of suppliers, complete rationality in the choice of market centers by consumers, and a differentiated and locally integrated marketing economy (these will be referred to as the first list of assumptions). It also assumes an unbounded marketing region saturated by suppliers, even distribution of or equal access to purchasing power for all parties in the system, and the unrestricted play of competition in the formation and maintenance of the central-place hierarchy (to be referred to as the second list of assumptions). Such conditions would rarely be met anywhere, so one would expect to find countless irregular or distorted marketing hierarchies in the real world.

Geographers seem to be concerned mainly with the problems presented by irregular landscapes, which invariably produce distortions in the even distribution of population (and consequently of centers) assumed by central-place theory. Berry and Garrison (1958) have shown this particular problem to be of little moment to the theory: A hierarchical system can be maintained in an irregular landscape; and with perfect knowledge of the irregularities, one could still predict the distribution and relationships between centers. (Of course, it is not easy to do.) More recently, some geographers have argued that the assumptions of profit maximization and complete rationality on the part of buyers and sellers make central-place theory a rather useless ideal model (Bromley 1971; Webber 1971; Webber and Symanski 1973). While the marketing idiosyncrasies of each one of us would appear to support their argument, most economists assume that such idiosyncrasies rarely have great effect on marketing systems. Thus, economists have been able to use the "perfect market model" in societies that irrationally eschew profit maximization 2 days out of the week. According to economists, the major deviations from any perfect market model usually stem from imperfect competition. This source of irregularity will be the primary concern here.

I can ignore irregularities that might stem from deviations from the first list of assumptions because these are as closely met in western Guatemala as anywhere. Market centers are distributed as evenly as any reported, despite the irregular and diverse landscape.[3] According to McBryde (1947) and Tax (1953), Guatemalan consumers and suppliers are as rational and profit conscious as any in the world. And my previous work showed the regional marketing economy to be well developed and relatively well integrated (Smith 1972a, 1972b). Thus, the models of irregular central-place hierarchies that I construct deal only with irregularities produced by deviations from the second list of assumptions, particularly the assumption of perfect competition.

Virtually all central-place hierarchies will have fewer high-order centers than low-order centers, simply because more people (demand) are required to support a large center than a small one. In addition, articulated central-place systems usually show a particular ratio of small and intermediate-level centers to large ones—a well-articulated hierarchy would not have a single center serving an extremely large number of small undifferentiated centers. A good index of central-place articulation is the number of developed intermediate-level centers in the system. The "classical" ratios of small and intermediate centers to high-order centers are the following: $1:2:6:18$ and $1:3:12:48$.[4] The irregular systems in western Guatemala can most easily be identified by their particular pyramidal patterns as follows.

1. *Primate systems.* These systems are characterized by a few poorly differentiated, small centers dominated by a single large center, usually one with more central functions than all of the other centers in its hinterland combined. Typical of the numbers of centers in the hierarchy are

---

[3] The distribution index for market centers in western Guatemala is 1.31, as determined by nearest-neighbor analysis. (With this measure, 1.0 indicates random distribution, and 2.15 indicates perfectly even distribution.) In a study of central-place distribution in the United States, King (1961) found that most centers were distributed randomly; the most even distribution found was for the state of Missouri, which had a distribution index of 1.38.

[4] The classical ratios are based on the known principles of integrating central-place hierarchies—$K = 3$ and $K = 4$. The market principle ($K = 3$), most efficient for servicing a rural hinterland, is the one with the largest proportion of intermediate centers. The traffic principle ($K = 4$), also shown here, sacrifices some rural servicing efficiency for transport efficiency between centers.

$0:1:0:18$. The gap between the first- and third-order centers indicates that no intermediate-level centers exist in the system, even though intermediate-level centers exist in the region. This gap is consistent with the primate character of the major center in the system.[5]

2. *Feeder systems.* These systems are characterized by a virtually flat hierarchy and no single major central place. Typical of the numbers of centers in the hierarchy are: $0:0:3:27$. Although the region and most of its component systems have centers that fill the first two positions, these particular systems do not. Moreover, there is a very large number of small, undifferentiated centers, marking a general lack of central-place articulation in feeder systems.

3. *Top-heavy systems.* In western Guatemala there is only one top-heavy system. It is characterized by many high-order centers and relatively few small centers. The number of centers in its hierarchy is $1:1:5:5$. The largest center in this system serves the entire region as a central place; the next center is the local high-order center. The smallest centers in this system are typically larger and more differentiated than the smallest centers in other systems, and the many intermediate-level centers have important market functions for the region as well as the local system. This system is not particularly pathological in and of itself, but its distinctive characteristics mark a general pathology in the regional marketing system, about which more will be said later.

In addition to these "irregular" systems, there are a number of systems in western Guatemala that display "regular" central-place pyramids.

It is my thesis that each of the irregular kinds of systems can be linked to a particular type of imperfect competition. Specific hypotheses about causality must await a description of the region, but the general models of causality for these irregular central-place systems are as follows.

Primate systems are created by a low level of production diversity coupled with highly concentrated ownership of the production resources and a nondomestic market orientation. The concentration of ownership in a few hands (and thus the concentration of wealth and purchasing power), together with external market orientation, leads to the development of a single large center that bulks and ships commodities produced locally to places outside the system. And the development of a single dominating center that looks for support outside instead of within the system leads to poor development and articulation of the small domestically oriented market centers. In consequence, the economic opportunities available in

[5] There is already some literature on primate systems, reviewed in Berry and Horton (1970). So far, however, the relation between primacy and the organization of small centers in a primate hinterland has been little treated. Most efforts have been directed toward understanding the causes and not the consequences of primate systems, and little has been done to relate the development of primacy to particular violations of the assumptions made by central-place theory. A notable exception is the discussion of primacy by Johnson (1970).

the system are unevenly distributed, such that the rural hinterland is both poorly serviced and underdeveloped. This simple verbal model can be summarized as follows: *Low production diversity, concentrated ownership of resources, and external market orientation lead to primate central-place systems (which reinforce the determining variables), and primate central-place systems in turn lead to few economic alternatives, poor rural development, and marked socioeconomic stratification in the primate marketing area (which reinforce the determining variables).* This is clearly a negative or deviation-amplifying feedback system, with all of the variables highly interdependent.

Feeder systems are created by little division of labor and undifferentiated production systems coupled with an outside source of income and of market provisioning. The undeveloped production systems lead to poorly developed domestic market centers, but the outside source of income and market provisioning lead to many small, undifferentiated retail centers. Dependence on external support systems is a critical feature of this kind of system—hence the term "feeder system" instead of "immature system." I am arguing that this kind of flat, undifferentiated hierarchy will not be found in immature developing systems—marketing systems probably always begin with a strong hierarchy and flesh out intermediate-level centers as a final rather than an early stage.[6] It is hypothesized that a flat, retail type of system is usually associated with dependence on the more developed areas of the regional or national economy and that they are most frequently found in the peripheral areas of the regional or national economy. In economies where capital is concentrated and does not flow freely, peripheral systems have little opportunity for development. This is particularly true where a "dependent" market structure has grown up. The dynamics of such systems can be summarized: *External market dependence, low division of labor, and poor economic infrastructure lead to feeder central-place systems (which reinforce the determining variables), and feeder central-place systems in turn lead to few economic alternatives, poor rural and urban development, intensification of production without growth, and/or migration in the feeder marketing area (which reinforce the determining variables).* Again, this is a negative feedback system, with all of the variables highly interdependent.

Top-heavy systems are created by monopoly opportunities in regions with poorly developed subsystems. Advantages of scale, lead time, developed capital and infrastructure, and frequently location give these systems opportunity to exploit areas of unsaturated demand that less developed systems cannot serve. In essence, these systems develop more of

---

[6] At this point the assumption that the kind of hierarchy described here is *not* immature must be considered part of the hypothesis. For a review of the various theories about immature market organization, see Chapter 1 and Smith (1974).

the important intermediate-level centers than they need, to serve areas that lack them. Because such centers allow traders in top-heavy systems to meet the needs of poorly developed systems in the same region with relative efficiency, they rob the surrounding areas of their own growth potential. While a relatively efficient region-wide marketing system can grow up with this kind of structure, such concentrated growth places disenfranchised areas at strong disadvantage in terms of production, specialization, and growth of local opportunities. It may be that all marketing systems develop from this stage or have this inherent tendency. But it is hypothesized here that a revolutionary kind of change is required to break the monopoly hold of top-heavy systems over undeveloped surrounding areas. Without a radical break, the whole tendency of the region-wide system is to feed back into the growth and economic power of the top-heavy system: The development of the one system is dependent on the underdevelopment of the region. Thus, top-heavy systems are dependent on the maintenance of underdeveloped systems as follows: *High production diversity and advantages of scale, capital, and infrastructure in a region that is partly underdeveloped lead to top-heavy central-place systems (which reinforce the determining variables), and top-heavy central-place systems in turn lead to concentrated growth, monopoly control, and internal stratification in the top-heavy marketing area (which reinforce the determining variables).*

It was stated that each of these irregular kinds of marketing systems was created by some form of imperfect competition. In the case of western Guatemala, the irregular marketing systems and the forms of imperfect competition are highly interrelated, such that feeder systems are dependent upon top-heavy systems (and vice versa), and both are directly related to primacy and the primate systems. The kinds of imperfect competition from which they all stem are these: (1) concentrated ownership of productive resources and income streams by a small elite, (2) regional dependence on very few export commodities for cash where small-scale producers have little opportunity to enter the market, and (3) political control of the development of economic and marketing infrastructure. All of these can be boiled down to certain kinds of monopoly. But to describe these features of the economy concretely, a brief description of the region is necessary.

It should first be made explicit that the models and hypotheses just mentioned are meant to be general. Even though my data allow me to discuss only the function and structure of marketing in western Guatemala, I would like to suggest that the models may be applied to other systems, regions, and nations. I do not expect that every primate system, for example, will be caused by a plantation-oriented economy, or to have precisely the same numbers and distributions of centers in each order that I have described. But I do expect that every primate system will have an easily identifiable form and that the cause of such systems will usually lie in low production diversity, highly concentrated control of production resources, and nondomestic market orientation.

Most people who have dealt with central-place theory have not thought it possible to predict function from structure, particularly when the structure was irregular. If these particular models do have general applicability, it will show that the logic of central-place theory helps explain many *irregular,* as well as regular, marketing systems commonly encountered in the real world.

THE REGION AND THE LOCAL SYSTEMS

The distinctive character of western Guatemala as a region stems from the fact that it was dominated by the Quichean civilization before the Spanish conquest (Carmack 1973) and was from that time forward a battleground in the struggle between indigenous and Spanish cultures. More recently, its regional integration stems from the fact that it is the maximal market hinterland of Quezaltenango, the second largest urban center in Guatemala. The region encompasses 10,000 square miles, 1.8 million people, nine administrative districts (*departamentos*), 174 townships (*municipios,* the smallest administrative divisions in Guatemala), and about 250 market centers. The region is a diverse one, and the following description will show some of the variability within it.

Two-thirds of the land mass is situated between 4500 and 9000 feet in altitude, divided from the lowlands to the south by a high volcanic mountain chain and from the lowlands to the north by rugged granitic outcroppings. In between, the country is mountainous, with little level land. One-third of the land mass is situated between sea level and 4500 feet in altitude, gently sloping southward to the Pacific Ocean and northward to the Carribean lowlands. The highland–lowland division at 4500 feet seems to be a basic one, since the former supports peasant agriculture, while the latter supports plantation agriculture. Map 1, which locates both Quezaltenango in the region (very near the significant highland–lowland division) and the region within the country, also shows the major agricultural and altitudinal zones. Quezaltenango is about 100 miles west of Guatemala City, the national capital and largest city of Guatemala.

The economy of western Guatemala can be characterized as agrarian, divided into a subsistence-oriented (peasant) sector and an export-oriented (plantation) sector. Manufacturing and industry play no significant role in the region. It is, however, a market economy, where most households are dependent on the marketplace for the provision of many basic goods. Virtually all exchanges that take place outside the household and extended family are market exchanges utilizing cash. Most peasant households sup-

0   50
Scale in miles

BRITISH
HONDURAS

M E X I C O

Quezaltenango

•Guatemala
City

HONDURAS

EL SALVADOR

Guatemala
Major Ecological Zones

Highlands (peasant farming)
Lowlands (main plantation area)
Lowlands (some plantation, some peasant farming)

Map 1. Major agricultural regions of western Guatemala.

plement their agricultural earnings with either craft production, market trade, or seasonal work on plantations. Much of the plantation labor force is made up of seasonal workers from the highlands; they work from 1 to 3 months each year as such. The plantations of the western region raise coffee, cotton, and sugar, primarily for export, and produce some 60 percent of the gross agricultural output (in market value) of the country (Fletcher *et al.* 1970). Most of the large plantations are in the southern lowlands of the region.

Fewer than 10 percent of the population of western Guatemala live in towns of more than 10,000 population, and the largest urban center, Quezaltenango, has a population of only about 40,000. Most of the people

live in dispersed rural farmsteads. Population tends to be somewhat
denser in the central highlands and to thin out at the peripheries both
north and south. Yet, given the very uneven topography of the region,
population and market centers are distributed fairly evenly. *Major* market
centers are not distributed evenly, however, being concentrated near the
central portion. The rural–urban index thus varies considerably from one
local system to another.

The population can be divided into two basic groups, Indians and
Ladinos. Indians are descendants of the Quichean and related civilizations. Most of them live in the highlands, maintain indigenous languages
and traditions, and are primarily rural peasant farmers. Ladinos, or His-
panicized mestizos, are most succinctly described, in both their terms and
ours, as non-Indians. They live mainly in the lowlands or in town centers.
Those who live in the lowlands (or the very few rural highland communities) are peasants or agricultural laborers; and those who live in town
centers (of either the lowlands or the highlands) are members of the
regional administrative–commercial elite. Throughout the region any
Ladino, regardless of class position, is considered of higher status than any
Indian. Because Ladinos live mainly in towns or the lowlands, they are not
uniformly distributed by local system.

As the economy and society of western Guatemala are dualized, so too is
the regional marketing system. There are basically two different kinds of
major central places, called here market towns and marketplaces. Market
towns are controlled, politically and economically, by Ladinos, who
usually make up the major share of their populations; hence, I call them
Ladino market towns (LMTs). Marketplaces outside the market towns are
utilized primarily by Indian peasants, are periodic, and are usually
located in very small "towns" of some 10 to 50 permanent shops, or even
in entirely rural areas. Since the primary function of these rural centers is
to bulk goods for distribution to the market towns, they are termed here
rural bulking centers (RBCs). Together, these two types of centers make
up the regional trade system of high-level centers. Map 2 shows the distribution of all the major market centers in the region—both the major
LMTs and the major RBCs.[7] These are, of course, only a few of the
market centers to be found in the region, consisting only of the three
highest orders.

The spatial pattern of the major central places in western Guatemala
(analyzed in detail in Smith 1972a, 1975) is quite regular. For those

[7] Many market centers have some of the characteristics described for the *major* LMTs and
the *major* RBCs. For instance, many marketplaces have bulking functions like the RBCs, but
only 19 bulking marketplaces also have high centrality indices and bulk goods for more than
a single township; these 19 centers are the RBCs shown on Map 2. Similarly, only some
Ladino market towns have sufficiently high centrality indices to be a part of the region-wide
system of *major* LMTs, shown on Map 2.

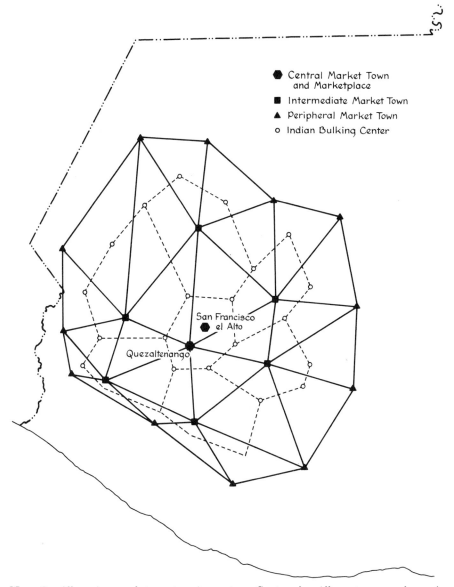

Map 2. All major market centers in western Guatemala. All centers are shown in approximately true relative locations; lines are used to indicate the regularity of the spatial pattern, not to show special trade ties. [Based on Smith (1972a, 1972b).]

acquainted with central-place theory, I can say that the following pertains:
(1) The distribution of the Ladino market towns generally conforms to a
$K = 4$ pattern (the traffic principle); (2) the distribution of the rural bulking centers in relation to the Ladino market towns generally conforms to
a $K = 3$ pattern (the marketing principle); and (3) the regional system
displays primate characteristics, conforming to a type that Johnson (1970)
has termed dendritic. (The last means that central-place orders fall off
with distance from the center and that overall there are many more lower-
order centers than one expects in a "normal" central-place hierarchy.) For
those unacquainted with central-place theory, I will only say that the distribution is regular, conforms to certain predictions of central-place
theory, but displays certain irregularities that one might expect to find in
"dualized" or "colonized" regions.

With respect to general trade articulation in the region, two important
characteristics should be mentioned. Rural bulking centers (RBCs) bulk
goods—mainly basic foodstuffs—that they send primarily to Ladino
market towns (LMTs). This RBC role is significant because the basis of
market articulation in the region is in the flow of foodstuffs. Hence, RBCs
are critical in regional arbitrage. But while RBCs see to the general market
articulation of the region, LMTs play no such role. Each of the LMTs is
by and large independent of others in domestic trade. Their links to one
another are mainly in import–export exchange, particularly in the trade
with Guatemala City, where regional domestic goods are exchanged for
manufactured imports. Because LMTs play no significant role in domestic
commodity redistribution, each tends to be the hub of a relatively independent local marketing system—a "solar" system. Of the 12 local marketing systems to be described here, all are in fact the hinterlands of
particular LMTs.

It should be noted that while there are 19 LMTs, there are only 12
locally integrated marketing subsystems in the region. This is because
many of the "peripheral" LMTs are as yet poorly developed; in consequence, several of the local marketing systems have two or three
peripheral LMTs in them, without any one of them yet dominant.

The 12 local systems were isolated in previous analyses of commodity
flow and consumer movement. In these analyses intrasystem trade relationships were established by drawing boundaries around market centers
that had frequent trade contact in basic commodities and by asking
consumers where they commonly shopped for goods not carried in their
local center.[8] At the level of local or domestic trade, little overlap between

---

[8] The analysis of commodity flow is found in Smith (1972a, 1972b). Data on consumer
movement were obtained in the field along with data on market functions; these data have
been partially analyzed for the purpose of showing marketing system boundaries but have
not yet been published. It should be noted that the local systems were defined in my dissertation before any thought had been given to the present kind of analysis. The local systems

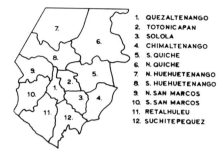

Map 3. Boundaries of the 12 local systems in western Guatemala.

1. QUEZALTENANGO
2. TOTONICAPAN
3. SOLOLA
4. CHIMALTENANGO
5. S. QUICHE
6. N. QUICHE
7. N. HUEHUETENANGO
8. S. HUEHUETENANGO
9. N. SAN MARCOS
10. S. SAN MARCOS
11. RETALHULEU
12. SUCHITEPEQUEZ

systems was found. Hence, it is possible to describe the regional system of western Guatemala as made up of 12 relatively independent local systems, integrated primarily through long-distance RBC trade and the central (regional) functions of Quezaltenango. Map 3 shows the limits of the 12 local systems. The 12 local systems do not vary greatly in either size or population. Average population is 150,614, with a standard deviation of 39,288; and average size is 190.8 square kilometers, with a standard deviation of 80.9.

GROUPING THE LOCAL SYSTEMS

One way of testing the relationship between central-place function and structure is to see if "functionally" related systems fall into the same groups as "structurally" related systems. This kind of grouping strategy will be followed here. The 12 local systems will be grouped into types along functional central-place dimensions (based on 20 central-place variables). In this grouping analysis no account of the distinctive pyramidal sequences found in the different local systems will be taken. A structural measure, however, can be derived directly from the pyramidal sequence characteristic of each local system and compared to the groupings derived from the analysis of functional marketing characteristics. If the groups derived from the two independent measures are essentially the same, we can expect market structure and function to be related.

For the functional measure, 20 central-place variables were selected that measure such characteristics as marketplace type and orientation, types of goods and types of traders found in marketplaces, town sizes, transport organization, and the amount of development found in both towns and marketplaces. (The 20 variables are listed and measures of them explained in the appendix.) Many variables were used in order to develop a relatively unbiased single measure of central-place organization for each

defined here are identical to the local systems defined in my dissertation except that the southern lowland area, excluded from the earlier analysis, is included here.

of the 12 local systems.[9] The particular variables chosen were dependent on the information collected on central places during field work, before this problem was conceptualized. However, each variable reflects some aspect of how the local system operates as a local system, so that the final summary measure developed from these variables is a reasonable "operational" measure of central-place organization. The summary measure will be a principal component taken from all 20 variables; I assume that it describes the *functional* characteristics of the local central-place systems.

It is expected that the functional central-place characteristics of the 12 local systems are directly determined by certain economic variables and that certain other aspects of the economy stem from the functional central-place characteristics of the 12 local systems. In the model proposed here, measures of imperfect competition are assumed to be *causes* of market organization. The five measures of imperfect competition that can be used here generally relate to ethnic (Ladino) control of wealth: (1) percentage of land in export-oriented plantations (by definition in Guatemala an ethnic and class monopoly); (2) percentage of land owned by Ladinos (by and large a measure of absentee ownership as well as minority ethnic control); (3) percentage of town businesses owned by Ladinos (by and large a measure of business monopoly by the ethnic minority); (4) land concentration (taken from the Lorenz curve of land distribution); and (5) percentage of Ladino population (a crude measure of external income streams, since Ladinos are the only people in the region with access to major outside sources of income, such as from national government positions or businesses in the import–export trade). (Further details on these and the following measures can be found in the appendix.) As can be seen from the list, the measures of imperfect competition are indirect, but interpretations made by other Guatemalan students (Adams 1970; Fletcher *et al.* 1970; Tax 1953) support the interpretation made here.[10]

The following five measures of economic alternatives in a local system are expected to be *consequences* of market organization: (1) wages paid to unskilled farm labor: (2) percentage of labor migration; (3) percentage of people in agricultural occupations; (4) amount of craft–trade specialization; and (5) amount of capital accumulation by Indian peasants (to be measured by number of trucks and permanent business establishments

---

[9] There is undoubtedly some redundancy in the variables used to determine central-place characteristics. But an attempt was made to select as many variables as possible that had no necessary relationship to one another and that would show the full diversity of central-place organization.

[10] Most Guatemalan experts would not quarrel with equating Ladino control of economic resources with imperfect competition because Ladinos in western Guatemala monopolize the major businesses wherever their numbers will permit and prevent "open" entry of all qualified people. I would have preferred measures that made fewer assumptions, but such were not available.

owned by them). Again the measures used here were constrained by information collected during field work. They can be interpreted as rough indicators of the options available to people within a local system—that is, measures of economic opportunity.

Another five basic measures of the economic structure or environment in the 12 local systems might be either causal or consequential: road condition, number of motor vehicles, percentage of urban population, population density, and average peasant farm size. No predictions are made about these variables, although most are indicators of economic development and may be intervening variables. In a later section, regression will be used to test the causal links suggested here. If the test shows a causal sequence that begins with indicators of imperfect competition to predict particular central-place structures and concludes with the predicted economic consequences, the particular central-place models proposed here will be validated for western Guatemala.

The following preliminary steps are taken in this section. First, the functionally related local system groups are isolated by several different grouping procedures. Then the functional groups are described in terms of pyramidal structure to see if central-place function and structure are related. The prediction is that there is a close relationship. The next step is to compare the groups isolated by central-place characteristics to groups isolated by general economic characteristics—both causal (one dimension of contrast) and consequential (another dimension of contrast). The prediction is that the groups of local systems obtained from general economic characteristics will conform to the groups obtained from central-place characteristics.[11]

Three different grouping procedures are used here: cluster analysis, principal component analysis, and multidimensional scaling. All of these methods are based on analalysis of variance and covariance, and all data methods are based on analysis of variance and covariance, and all data $[Z = (X - \bar{X})/S]$. Since none of the methods has a true significance test, I will derive groupings independently with each procedure, using a comparison of the results as a check on the degree to which the groups chosen are fairly robust. The groups obtained from the 20 central-place functional measures by the three different formal procedures are shown in Figures 1, 2, and 3.

The most easily graphed and intuitively simple method to interpret is the cluster analysis. This method calculates Euclidean distance measures between the cases based on the scores of the standardized variables, in this case the 20 central-place variables. I used Harpending's maximal linkage

[11] The grouping analysis was stimulated by Berry's work (1961, 1967). But it was Harpending who suggested that if the groups pulled out by the central-place variables were similar to those pulled out by the general economic variables, one would have reason to expect a causal relationship between the two sets of variables.

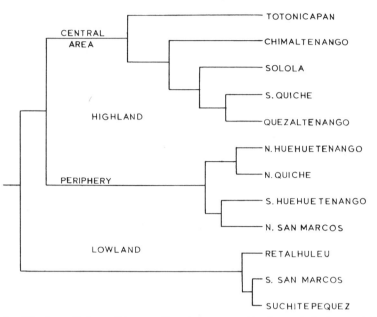

Figure 1.   Maximum linkage distances: 12 systems grouped by the central-place variables.

cluster program written for APL to derive the distance tree shown in Figure 1.[12] Three basic clusters emerge. The first division is between highland and lowland systems; almost as soon is the division between central area and peripheral area systems. There is least variation in the southern lowland grouping of three local systems (Suchitepequez, Retalhuleu, and southern San Macros) and most variation in the central area grouping (Quezaltenango, southern Quiche, Solola, Chimaltenango, and Totonicapan). The most distinctive local system is Totonicapan, linked but distantly to the other central area systems.

Principal component analysis, a form of factor analysis, is the next method used to group the local systems. This kind of analysis has the advantage of showing the grouping of cases along particular dimensions of the variables. Table 1 shows the first two principal components of the 20 variables—these two components take up 77.7 percent of the variance among the variables. The first component shows high loadings on variables related to central-place or market functions, so it will be termed the market function component. Positive loadings indicate high marketplace

---

[12] According to Harpending and Jenkins (1975), there are many computer routines that convert a table of distances into dendograms, or trees, and no explicit reason for preferring one technique over another. In this case both "maximal linkage" and "minimal linkage" techniques were used, and the results were not significantly different. The matrix of "distance" measures used here can be obtained from the author by writing, as can the measures for each variable in all the cases.

diversity and high bulking function; negative loadings indicate high retail or terminal functions and to some extent primacy in a single center.[13] The second component will be termed rural central-place development, for the variables that load highly on it are indicators of many large, viable marketplaces and towns as well as of transport development outside the major towns. Three variables are not closely related to the two principal components—major town size, average marketplace size, and average population per market center. This suggests that market development is not necessarily related to market size.

Since two components explain 77.7 percent of the variance, I was satis-

TABLE 1

Two Principal Components of Central-Place Variables Shown in Figures 2 and 3

	Central-Place Variables	$F-1^a$	$F-2^b$
1.	% bulking markets	.94	
2.	Other-system traders	-.93	
3.	% producer-sellers	.90	
4.	% terminal markets	-.84	
5.	% wholesale sellers	.83	
6.	Variety index	.83	
7.	Town-market correlation	-.81	
8.	% major sellers	-.77	
9.	Market primacy	-.66	
10.	Town primacy	-.57	
11.	Rural truck index		.92
12.	Average market days		.90
13.	Rural town development		.89
14.	Town establishment index		.78
15.	% major markets		.77
16.	Trader origin index		.74
17.	Viable markets		.67
18.	Major town size		
19.	Average market size		
20.	Average population/market center		

a. *F-1 = market function factor.*
b. *F-2 = rural central-place development factor.*

[13] Variables highly loaded on this component that are not directly related to market function are 2, 7, and 9: Many other-system traders (2) is related to terminal or retail market functions because nonlocals tend to do much of the retail trade in the region; the town–marketplace centrality correlation (7) tends to be high in retail-oriented markets because these markets support large towns with appropriately high centrality indices, whereas there is usually a poor correlation between market and town size where there are many large bulking markets that are usually found in rural areas; and market concentration (9) tends to be high in the high retail marketing areas because a few large towns have most of the market centrality (the opposite is true where there are many bulking markets).

fied with graphing local system relationships in two-dimensional space (Figure 2). This graph shows essentially the same local system groupings shown in Figure 1. The most closely related group (Suchitepequez, Retalhuleu, and southern San Marcos) are the southern lowland systems; then there is a cluster of the peripheral area systems (northern Quiche, northern Huehuetenango, southern Huehuetenango, and northern San Marcos); the central area systems are less clustered, with Totonicapan an outlyer. In this case Solola, which I expected to be anomalous (having some central area characteristics and some peripheral area characteristics), is more closely associated with the peripheral area grouping than with the central area grouping.

Finally, multidimensional scaling was done with the same variables. The results of the scaling analysis, shown in only two dimensions, which have been rotated to the principal component axes, are depicted by Figure 3. The program used was Harpending's APL program, following the algorithm of Kruskal (1964b). Nine iterations were made to arrive at the best solution, which was reached when the stress measure was .07. The Gower fit between the principal component analysis and the multidimensional scaling analysis is .348, which by rule of thumb is considered highly significant.[14] As can be seen, the principal component program and the scaling program give virtually identical results. (The only difference is that in the latter Solola is intermediate between the peripheral area and central area clusters.) These are also the groupings shown in Figure 1. From the three analyses, it is possible to conclude that three basic groups and one outlyer are distinctive with respect to central-place functions. Now we shall see if they are distinctive in central-place structure.

The most closely related group by the preceding analyses is the southern lowland group (Suchitepequez, Retalhuleu, and southern San Marcos). The central-place orders of these systems[15] are illustrated as:

Suchitepequez	0:1:0:18
Retalhuleu	0:1:0:13
Southern San Marcos	0:1:0:18

[14] The stress level is a measure of the departure of the rank orders of the fitted distances from the rank orders of the corresponding distances among the data points. The program follows Kruskal (1964a, 1964b), who suggests that a stress level of .07 is fair to good. There are no true significance tests for multidimensional scaling, but Gower (1971) suggests that a least-squares measure of association between two sets of coordinates may be used. With this measure, the lower the number, the better the fit.

[15] Certain differences from the central-place orders derived in Smith (1972a) can be observed, following these changes: (1) The fourth and fifth levels of the original orderings were joined into a single level here, since no functional difference obtained between the two lowest orders; (2) township centers that do not support a marketplace were placed in the local system hierarchy as low-level centers; and (3) some changes were made in the assignment of levels in the second and third orders, following the analysis put forth in Chapter 5 of Smith (1972a). These changes were made to give the fullest picture of central-place orders in the region, not to bolster the argument made here.

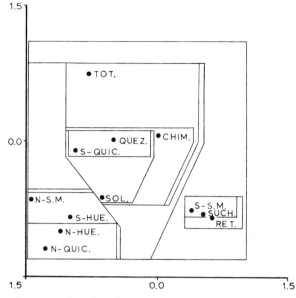

Figure 2.   The 12 systems plotted on the first two principal components of the central-place variables.

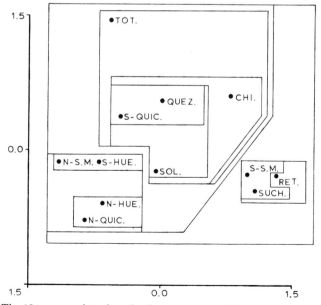

Figure 3.   The 12 systems plotted on the first two scales of the central-place variables. The two-dimensional scale is rotated to the axes of Figure 2.

These are clearly similar central-place structures, resembling the type termed primate system.

The next most closely related group according to the grouping analyses is the peripheral area group (northern Quiche, northern Huehuetenango, southern Huehuetenango, and northern San Marcos). The central-place orders of these systems are as follows:

Northern Quiche	$0:0:3:27$
Northern Huehuetenango	$0:0:3:28$
Northern San Marcos	$0:0:3:25$
Southern Huehuetenango	$0:1:3:39$

Again these are closely related central-place structures, except for the fact that southern Huehuetenango has a single large center. But all of these systems have the distinctive feature of very high numbers of the smallest-order centers. By and large, these systems resemble the type termed feeder system.

The most variable but clearly related group of systems in terms of the central-place function analyses is the central area group (Quezaltenango, Solola, southern Quiche, and Chimaltenango). Their central-place orders are also most variable, but clearly related:

Quezaltenango	$1^{16}:1:2:18$
Solola	$0:1:2:19$
Southern Quiche	$0:1:3:12$
Chimaltenango	$0:1:3:11$

While each of these systems has a relatively large number of centers in the smallest order, they most closely resemble a normal central-place hierarchy. Hence, these will be termed the regular central-place systems.

The most unusual central-place system, according to both analysis of central-place functions and central-place orders, is Totonicapan. Its pyramidal structure is the following:

Totonicapan $1^{17}:1:5:5$

This is the system I have termed top-heavy because the intermediate-level centers are as numerous as the small centers.

I consider this finding—that central-place functions are closely related to a determinate central-place structure (the pyramidal sequence of orders)—to be highly significant. But in order to see what these types of system, regular and irregular, portend for economic development, it is necessary to

---

[16] The highest-level center in the Quezaltenango system is of course Quezaltenango, the highest-level center in the region. Its importance derives from its regional rather than local system position.

[17] Again the major center here, San Francisco el Alto, is a regional rather than local center.

link the system types to economic variables, both dependent and independent.

The second part of the grouping analysis involves an examination of the economic variables by local system to see if they show the same general configuration or clusters. The same three grouping procedures are used: cluster analysis, principal component analysis, and multidimensional scaling. The 15 economic variables used in this analysis include the 5 "dependent" variables, the 5 "independent" variables, and the 5 "other" environmental variables that show other aspects of the economic environment. (All 15 variables are defined and described in the appendix to this chapter.) Although independent and dependent variables are grouped here, principal component analysis shows that the independent variables generally load highly on the first factor, while the dependent (economic alternatives) variables load highly on the second factor (see Table 2). The two principal components defined in Table 2 are the axes along which the local systems will be scaled. Results are shown in Figures 4, 5, and 6.

Figure 4 shows the results of the cluster analysis. This figure shows a slightly different configuration from that given by the cluster analysis of central-place variables (Figure 1). The southern lowland systems (Suchitepequez, Retalhuleu, and southern San Marcos) remain closely clustered and relatively independent of the others. But they are grouped at

TABLE 2
Two Principal Components of Economic Variables Shown in Figures 5 and 6

	Economic Variables	F_{-1}[a]	F_{-2}[b]
1.	Road condition	-.90	
2.	Plantation area	-.90	
3.	% Ladino land	-.87	
4.	% Ladino population	-.82	
5.	Ladino town control	-.80	
6.	Land concentration	-.80	
7.	Labor migration	.77	.52
8.	Motor vehicle index	-.75	
9.	% urban population	-.64	
10.	Wage		-.90
11.	Population density		-.87
12.	% agricultural occupations		.85
13.	Craft-trade specialization		-.82
14.	Indian capital ownership		-.75
15.	Indian farm size		.72

a. F_{-1} = ethnic group and plantation orientation factor.
b. F_{-2} = economic alternatives factor.

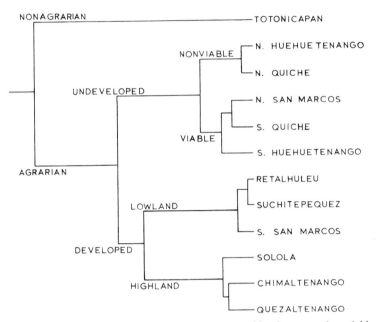

Figure 4. Maximum linkage distances: 12 systems grouped by the economic variables.

a higher level with three developed central-area systems (Quezaltenango, Solola, and Chimaltenango). As indicated in Figure 4, I believe this grouping involves a basic separation of the developed systems from the undeveloped systems (northern San Marcos, southern Huehuetenango, southern Quiche, northern Huehuetenango, and northern Quiche). The undeveloped systems divided into two groups, which I have termed subsistence oriented (the first three) and unviable (the second two).[18] Again Totonicapan is the most unique system, even more so than before.

The two other methods show essentially the same groupings. Figures 5 and 6 show the results, respectively, of the principal component analysis and the scaling analysis. Both methods give a virtually identical configuration along two dimensions when the scaling graph is oriented to the axes of the principal component graph. (The Gower fit between the two measures is very good at .328.) Since we have some notion of what the two dimensions are in Figures 5 and 6 from Table 2, the clusters can be interpreted as follows. The horizontal axis shows the relationship of systems along the dimension of ethnic group and plantation orientation—positive scores indicate high percentage of Indians, nonplantation orientation, and low concentration of wealth; negative scores indicate the opposite. The three southern lowland (primate) systems cluster to the left, and top-heavy Totonicapan with several feeder systems cluster to the right. The regular

---

[18] Here and elsewhere I have defined certain systems as "unviable." This simply means that the local economies must export labor to meet a subsistence level of income.

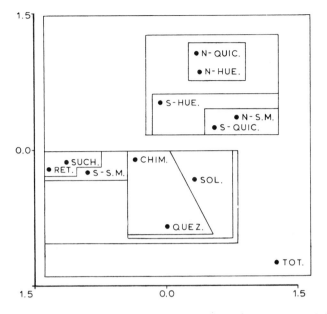

Figure 5.   The 12 systems plotted on the first two principal components of the economic variables.

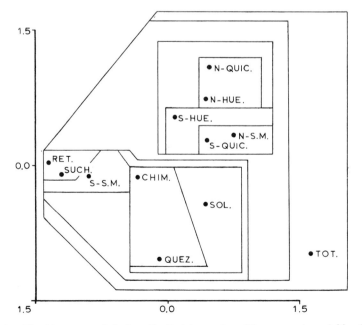

Figure 6.   The 12 systems plotted on the first two scales of the economic variables. The two-dimensional scale is rotated to the axes of Figure 5.

systems of Chimaltenango, Solola, and Quezaltenango fall in the middle. The vertical axis shows the relationship of systems along the dimension of economic alternatives, with negative scores indicating diverse opportu-nities, specialization, high wages, and the like, and positive scores indicat-ing strong subsistence (agricultural) orientation or labor migration. Along this dimension, the two primary central area systems of Totonicapan and Quezaltenango show the closest association in the direction of good eco-nomic alternatives, while the five peripheral area (feeder) systems show the closest association in the direction of poor economic alternatives. The three southern lowland primate systems, together with Solola and Chi-maltenango, fall in the middle.

The economic groupings differ from the central-place groupings in basically two ways: Southern Quiche is now grouped with the feeder systems, whereas before it was grouped with the regular central area systems; and the relationship between the regular central area systems and the primate southern lowland systems is closer than to the feeder systems, whereas before (in terms of central-place function and structure) the opposite was true. Yet basically there is a strong relationship between the two sets of local system clusters. This relationship can be measured by taking the two dimensions of the central-place variables and rotating them to the best fit with the two principal components of the economic varia-bles. In a sense this is a test of the fit of one matrix of variables with another matrix of different variables. Figure 7 shows the results of this

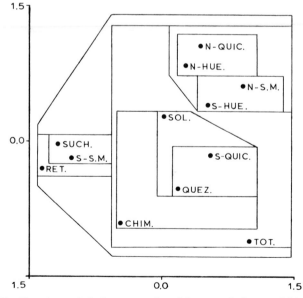

Figure 7. The 12 systems plotted on two scales of the central-place variables, rotated to the principal components of the economic variables.

procedure. The Gower fit of 2.26 is extremely good, given that two entirely different sets of variables are related to each other here. (Figure 7 should be compared to Figure 5 for an eyeball test of goodness of fit, since the central-place variables are rotated to the principal components of the economic variables.)

The results of the grouping procedures show rather clearly that the local systems of western Guatemala fall into distinctive types and that these types co-vary with certain economic variables. The next step will be to relate the system types and the economic variables to the irregular central-place models developed earlier.

TESTING THE MODELS

From the formal grouping procedures described, it is now possible to select four local system groups that may be characterized as similar along both central-place and economic dimensions. These groups will be described and contrasted with particular attention to system variability both within and across the groupings. The primary objective will be to show how central-place characteristics in western Guatemala are determined by certain economic variables and how these central-place characteristics in turn affect certain aspects of the economy. After showing how local economic conditions in western Guatemala co-vary with the types of central-place organization, a specific causal model will be tested.

1. *The southern lowland systems—primate type (Suchitepequez, Retalhuleu, and southern San Marcos).* The three lowland systems are clearly and distinctly grouped by all procedures. The central-place characteristics of these systems are as follows: (1) The predominant type of market is a retail–terminal market, where little or no bulking takes place; (2) the development of rural infrastructure is moderate to low, while the development of urban infrastructure is high; and (3) central-place primacy (dominance by single centers) is the norm. The basic economic characteristics of the three primate systems are these: (1) They are highest on the Ladino–plantation dimension, which means that they are dominated by plantations and Ladino enterprises, are relatively highly urbanized, and have good roads, highly concentrated landholdings, and a low level of labor migration. (2) They are intermediate with respect to economic alternatives, which in this case means that while wages are relatively high, nonagricultural opportunities are low and craft–trade occupations virtually nonexistent. Given the dominance of plantations in these systems, together with highly concentrated landholdings, economic alternatives for nonurban, non-Ladino people are poor. The relationship between these variables is best illustrated by Figure 8.

This specific Guatemalan model can be translated into the general

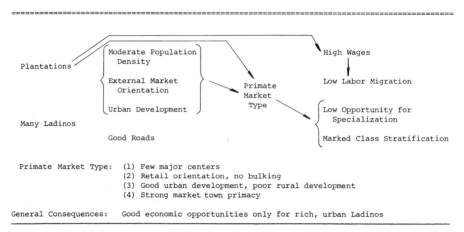

Primate Market Type: (1) Few major centers
                        (2) Retail orientation, no bulking
                        (3) Good urban development, poor rural development
                        (4) Strong market town primacy

General Consequences: Good economic opportunities only for rich, urban Ladinos

Figure 8.   Model of primate central-place systems: causes and consequences.

model for primate systems. Plantations are the best index of concentrated landholdings, since there are very few owners of plantations. Plantations also signify low production diversity and export market orientation. It is hypothesized that these conditions lead to primate systems and that primate systems lead to highly stratified societies with few economic alternatives available to nonrich, nonurban people. In this particular case, wages paid to unskilled labor are relatively high, so that labor migration is low. However, highland laborers usually do return home after a season of work. They migrate to the lowland systems only because plantations are the only businesses in the region that have an unsaturated demand for unskilled labor. Moreover, the high wage figure is somewhat misleading, since plantation labor cannot be supplemented with other sources of income for those who live in these systems, unlike work that pays wages outside the plantation area. Unfortunately, I have no variable that directly measures the amount of class stratification in the local systems. However, most Guatemalan experts would agree that the three lowland systems have the highest degree of class stratification in the region.

2. *The peripheral area systems—feeder type (northern Quiche, northern Huehuetenango, southern Huehuetenango, and northern San Marcos).* The four peripheral area systems are almost as clearly and distinctly grouped by all procedures as the southern lowland systems. The central-place characteristics of these systems are as follows: (1) The predominant type of market is a retail-oriented market, where some bulking takes place; (2) the development of both urban and rural infrastructure is low; (3) there are few major centers and no primate centers; and (4) there are a large number of very small, nonviable (hamlet) marketplaces. The only significant exception to this characterization occurs in southern Huehuetenango, where a single large Ladino town is prominent. In this case, however, the

Ladino town is so isolated from the Indian rural area that it has little effect on the other aspects of market structure; this system has even more small nonviable centers than the others. The economic characteristics of these feeder systems are as follows. (1) They are moderate to low on the Ladino–plantation dimension, with southern Huehuetenango being most deviant in this regard; this means that there are a few plantations and a relatively large number of Ladino enterprises, but very low levels of urbanization and road development, a very high rate of labor migration, and moderately concentrated landholdings. (2) These systems are the lowest on the economic alternatives dimension, which means here that wages are very low, nonagricultural opportunities few, and craft–trade occupations very limited. Moreover, few Indians own any economic enterprises (trucks, shops, warehouses) of significance. In these systems, therefore, economic opportunities for all residents—Indian and Ladino—are relatively poor, despite the fact that population density is low and size of peasant landholdings high. The relationship between these variables is shown in Figure 9.

Each one of these feeder systems sends some 30 to 50 percent of its labor force for seasonal work on the plantations, and so external dependence on outside sources of income is high. There is no lack of local production resources—peasant landholdings are larger than in any other systems and the farmland is of good quality. But the local marketing organization does not provide adequate channels for disposing of surplus or specialized agricultural goods, so local resources for obtaining cash are very poor. Hence the necessity of seeking outside sources of income. This income is spent in the many small retail marketplaces of these systems, provisioned by traders from the more developed systems—particularly from the top-

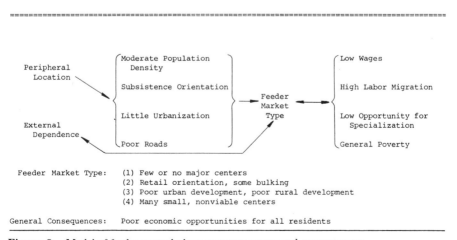

Feeder Market Type: (1) Few or no major centers
(2) Retail orientation, some bulking
(3) Poor urban development, poor rural development
(4) Many small, nonviable centers

General Consequences: Poor economic opportunities for all residents

Figure 9. Model of feeder central-place systems: causes and consequences.

heavy system of Totonicapan. Thus, a vicious circle of dependency is formed.

Part of the reason for this state of affairs is that these particular systems are in the northern periphery of the region, far from both the major administrative capitals and the developed plantation area. Their moderate population density and good land resources allowed subsistence farming for a long period of time, so that marketplaces were slow to develop. Marketing developed first when an influx of nonfarming Ladinos who required regular food provisioning came to the area. Later, with alienation of much land, many local peasants required more for subsistence than their own lands could produce. The only recourse was seasonal plantation labor. Marketplaces grew up to provision this area on the basis of this external source of income, monopolized by traders from other areas, themselves seeking income that their small landholdings would not provide. Their own trade orientation had developed under less desperate circumstances, and they had the advantage of already developed capital. [See Smith (1972a) for documentation.]

All of these circumstances conspired in the evolution of feeder systems in the northern periphery of western Guatemala. In consequence, economic opportunities remain extremely limited in these systems for both Indians and Ladinos.

3. *Totonicapan—top-heavy type (Totonicapan).* Totonicapan stands as a unique system by all grouping procedures. The central-place characteristics of this system are as follows: (1) The predominant type of market is a large bulking market where wholesaling is pronounced; (2) the development of rural infrastructure is good, while the development of urban infrastructure is low; (3) there are no primate centers and very few small, nonviable centers; and (4) there is a large bulge in the middle range of the central-place pyramid—that is, more intermediate-level centers than in regular systems. The economic characteristics of Totonicapan are these: (1) It is the lowest system on the Ladino–plantation dimension, which in this case means that there are few Ladino enterprises of any kind, no plantations, a rather poor level of urbanization, only fair roads, and the most equal land distribution in the region. (2) It is also the highest system on the economic alternatives dimension, which means that wages are high, craft and trade specialization is the norm, and there is very little labor migration; moreover, rural enterprises are well developed in the domestic sector, and Indians own many trucks, shops, warehouses, and the like. In brief, economic opportunities for rural Indians are very good in this system—but probably poor for urban Ladinos. This system is modeled in Figure 10.

The unusual development of the Totonicapan system must be related to the poor development of its surrounding systems—both in the southern lowlands and in the northern periphery. The overmany and overlarge

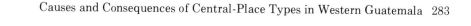

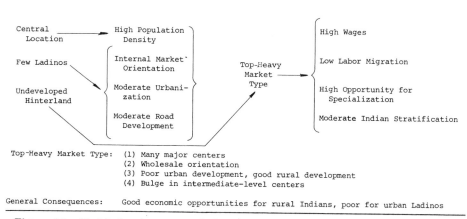

Top-Heavy Market Type: (1) Many major centers
                        (2) Wholesale orientation
                        (3) Poor urban development, good rural development
                        (4) Bulge in intermediate-level centers

General Consequences: Good economic opportunities for rural Indians, poor for urban Ladinos

Figure 10. Model of top-heavy central-place systems: causes and consequences.

bulking centers of Totonicapan exist to serve these areas. Certain other special features of Totonicapan may be unique to it and therefore unrelated to the general model. For instance, the high percentage of Indians and low numbers of Ladinos are probably responsible for the low level of urbanization in this system. Were there many Ladinos with high incomes and purchasing power here, this system might exhibit more primacy than top-heaviness. Service to the undeveloped systems would then come from a single major center rather than from many large intermediate-level centers. In western Guatemala the presence of a large Ladino population is a fairly good indicator of monopoly: Where numerous, the politically powerful Ladinos can usually control all the major income-producing activities, using cheap Indian labor in their enterprises. Totonicapan has few Ladinos and little monopoly, and it is undoubtedly the most competitive system in the region. Consequently, there are many large centers, not just one. But the absence of many individuals with external sources of income—from administrative positions of various kinds—means that government-related infrastructure, with the wealth that it creates, is also largely absent from this system.

Central location has been critical in the development of Totonicapan, for it is not only central with respect to an undeveloped hinterland, but central to all the major administrative centers of western Guatemala. Thus, its market development to feed those centers was early and strong. From this early-developed base it was in a good position to service the feeder systems and rural areas of the primate systems when demand was sufficient in them. Totonicapan has overdeveloped on the base of those underdeveloped systems. The consequences are that economic alternatives in Totonicapan are good—wages are high, and many Indians are relatively wealthy. Another consequence, however, is that Indian communities in

Totonicapan are more stratified than elsewhere and the class interests of rural Indian peasants highly fragmented. Wealthy Totonicapan Indians see as much class difference between themselves and poor Indians as between themselves and Ladinos.

4. *Other central area systems—regular type* (*Quezaltenango, Solola, southern Quiche, and Chimaltenango*). While this group of systems is similar in central-place characteristics, they differ rather widely in their economic characteristics. Most of these differences stem from the land tenure situation. I will not attempt to characterize them with respect to central-place characteristics, but only with respect to economic characteristics, showing how even their differences do not violate the assumptions made about the causes and consequences of irregular systems. Totonicapan will be included in the discussion as a point of reference.

On the Ladino–plantation–road dimension, the five systems have the same ranking as on the market function dimension (see Table 3). This indicates that the independent (environmental) variables of plantations, Ladinos, and land concentration are consistent predictors of market function and that the central area systems are fairly diverse with respect to those characteristics—varying from close similarity to the primate systems to close similarity to the top-heavy system.

On the second market dimension of rural central-place development, the same general ordering pertains except that the position of Totonicapan reverses from last to first and Solola sinks to the lowest position. The ordering on economic alternatives seems unrelated (see Table 4).

On the economic alternatives dimension, Quezaltenango groups with Totonicapan, even though it has quite different environmental and market characteristics. I attribute this to the fact that Quezaltenango and Totonicapan are the two primary central area systems and thus share the same kinds of trade opportunities in the region as a whole. Totonicapan has the

TABLE 3

Ordering the Four Regular Systems and Totonicapan on the First Principal Component of Table 1 and the First Principal Component of Table 2

Ladinos, Concentration[a] $\longrightarrow$	Market Function[b]
1. Chimaltenango (+)	1. Chimaltenango (+)
2. Quezaltenango (0)	2. Quezaltenango (0)
3. Solola (−)	3. Solola (0)
4. S. Quiche (−)	4. S. Quiche (−)
5. Totonicapan (−−)	5. Totonicapan (−)

a. *High to low.*
b. *Retail to wholesale.*

TABLE 4

Ordering the Four Regular Systems and Totonicapan on the Second Principal Component of Table 1 and the Second Principal Component of Table 2

==

Rural Development[a] →	Economic Alternatives[a]
1. Totonicapan (++)	1. Quezaltenango (+)
2. Chimaltenango (+)	2. Totonicapan (+)
3. Quezaltenango (+)	3. Solola (+)
4. S. Quiche (+)	4. Chimaltenango (0)
5. Solola (−)	5. S. Quiche (−)

a. *High to low.*

major rural bulking center of the regional system, while Quezaltenango has the major Ladino market town, and the two systems are very closely related in market trade. The two systems differ in market features because Totonicapan expresses the rural Indian aspect of development, having many craft specialists, long-distance traders, and well-developed bulking centers. Quezaltenango also has a well-developed central-place hierarchy, but one that is much more urbanized and Ladinoized; here, town development and trucking predominate, and there is some tendency toward primacy. In both systems the nonagricultural alternatives for rural Indians are quite good, wages are high, and labor migration is low. But only in Quezaltenango are there urban and Ladino enterprises as well.

Solola and southern Quiche form another cluster on most dimensions. Both systems have few plantations and Ladinos, very poor roads, and little urban development, and both systems have wholesale-oriented marketing systems and similar central-place orders, although Solola has many more very small centers than Quiche, indicating poor rural development. (I attribute this last feature to the fact that Solola is crossed by the major volcanic mountain range, divided by a major lake, and generally cut up into small areas of difficult access, unlike the flatter Quiche system.) Yet while rural central-place development is generally superior in the Quiche system, Solola rates considerably higher in economic alternatives.

A similar kind of reversal occurs with Chimaltenango, which rates highly on rural development (second in 12) and which has a regular central-place hierarchy, but which rates poorly on economic alternatives. In this case and that of southern Quiche, I think a third dimension of population size and density would be useful. For Chimaltenango and southern Quiche, otherwise quite different, have relatively low population densities, large peasant landholdings, and good level land. Consequently, while they have developed rural central-place functions, their primary orientation remains toward agriculture—and within the local system (that is, labor migration to plantations is low). So while the market structure in these systems would allow specialization and diverse economic alternatives, the agricultural situation is good enough that they have not developed. Solola, on the other hand, has high population density, poor land, and few agricultural resources, so it has oriented its market system to wholesaling, allowing trade and craft specialization. (The fact that these are not particularly successful in and of themselves is reflected in Solola's low rating in rural development.) Like Solola, Quezaltenango and Totonicapan have also been pushed into developing nonagricultural alternatives by high population density. But for them, these alternatives have become real opportunities, leading to a high level of rural development. The difference between Solola and the two primary central area systems is probably related to their relative positions in the regional trade system.

Chimaltenango is an unusual system in that it evinces both highland and lowland characteristics. It is in the highlands but in the temperate zone, where plantation crops can be grown. Consequently, it has a high percentage of its land in plantations, but being near the original highland centers of the Indian civilizations, it has a large percentage of Indians. The rural area and lower-level central places are well developed, and there is no market or town primacy. Yet with respect to some functions, Chimaltenango resembles the southern lowland systems, for its markets are oriented primarily to terminal–retail functions. This stems from a similar cause, much of Chimaltenango's rural product being shipped directly out of the system by major producers to Guatemala City. In addition, roads are good, and urbanization is advanced. Within this configuration, economic opportunities are good for both urban Ladinos and landed peasants, but probably poor for peasants without land.

In the southern lowland systems Indian peasants own little if any land—their only significant economic alternative is to work on the large plantations. Moreover, land ownership is highly concentrated, and urban development evinces strong primacy, so that economic alternatives are mainly open to a few wealthy Ladinos. All in all, monopoly concentration in both land and commerce is a striking characteristic of the southern lowland systems.

Finally, the four peripheral area systems are characterized by relatively low population density, good land, and few Ladinos or plantations. Yet these systems are poorly situated in the regional trade system such that the market for their goods is limited. As a result, the local economies are nonviable, and much of the population must gain a living by exporting labor to the plantations. Their local central-place hierarchies are a consequence of the local economies—most of their centers are too small to be viable for providing alternative economic opportunities.

Figure 11 gives a simplified summary of the basic causes of the local system central-place types. It is based on the several kinds of grouping analyses described in the previous section as they are broken down into the basic causal dimensions in this section. An important new variable in this model is the location of the local system in the region. As it happens in western Guatemala, location is a good proxy variable for generalized imperfect competition in the region because most economic wealth and power are concentrated in the center of the region (in political centers) and domestic trade is oriented toward urban rather than rural interests. Since most economic activity is concentrated in and around political centers, rural areas located near these centers are in a position to reap the advantages of specialization and trade. (In western Guatemala these rural areas include the central area local systems, particularly Quezaltenango and Totonicapan; they do not include the southern lowland systems because the rural areas around their political centers are owned by plantations.) The complicated variable of differential ethnic group economic opportunity and political power plays a significant role here. In essence, the region is colonized by a few powerful and wealthy Ladino families concentrated in a few urban (political) centers. The location and power of this small group lie behind the uneven distribution of economic opportunity and thus behind the irregular central-place organization of many systems.

This model will be tested in two ways. The first test examines whether or not the consequences for central-place organization predicted by the four independent variables in Figure 11 are true. The consequences predicted are these: (1) A high percentage of Ladinos leads to good urban development; urban development is measured by the number of different

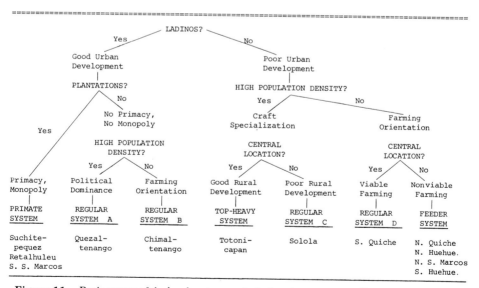

Figure 11. Basic causes of the local system central-place types, western Guatemala.

urban functions in the system. (2) A high percentage of plantations leads
to primacy; primacy is measured by the size difference between the largest
and second-largest centers. (3) High population density leads to specialization and market diversity. And (4) good location in the regional system
leads to rural development. Location is a variable in western Guatemala
that determines whether or not a system has government-developed economic infrastructure. The best numerical indicator of this is road development—centrally located systems have good roads, the southern lowland
systems have fair roads, and the northern peripheral systems have poor
roads. (The measure for road development is described in the appendix to
the chapter.)

The relationship between the independent and dependent variables was
tested by Pearson rank–order correlation, where N is equal to the 12 local
systems. The results are shown in Table 5.

The same variables were then used in a regression analysis to see if they
predicted type of central-place organization. The more important question
addressed in the regression analysis is this: Does central-place organization have an independent effect on the economic alternatives of a system?
Specifically, the regression will show whether or not a central-place type of
variable has a significant relationship to certain economic opportunity
variables in an equation in which the central-place type of predictor variables are also correlated with the dependent variables.

The models of central-place organization developed so far have stated
that the type of organization in a system will have important economic
consequences, particularly for economic opportunity. But it might be that
the variables I term economic opportunity variables are determined
simply by the same variables that determine type of central-place organization—that population density, percentage of Ladinos, percentage of
plantations, and location determine *both* central-place type and economic
opportunity. Most specialists on the Guatemalan economy assume that

TABLE 5
*Pearson Rank-Order Correlations between Independent and Dependent
Variables Shown in Figure 11[a]*

Variables		
Independent	Dependent	r
Ladinos	Urban development	.72
Plantations	Primacy	.90
Population density	Market diversity	.87
Roads[b]	Rural development	.82

a. *All are significant at the .05 level.*
b. *Roads is a proxy variable for location.*

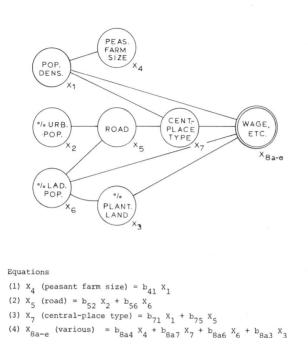

Equations

(1) X_4 (peasant farm size) = $b_{41} X_1$

(2) X_5 (road) = $b_{52} X_2 + b_{56} X_6$

(3) X_7 (central-place type) = $b_{71} X_1 + b_{75} X_5$

(4) X_{8a-e} (various) = $b_{8a4} X_4 + b_{8a7} X_7 + b_{8a6} X_6 + b_{8a3} X_3$

Figure 12. A model of market and economic opportunity determinants for western Guatemala. Equation X_{8a-e}: X_{8a} = wage; X_{8b} = labor migration; X_{8c} = craft specialization; X_{8d} = peasant capital; X_{8e} = agricultural occupations.

these environmental variables are the most significant determinants of economic opportunity and have taken very little account of market or central-place development. My hypothesis is that market and central-place development do affect economic alternatives and that there is a complex causal chain between basic environmental variables, market and central-place development, and indicators of economic alternatives or opportunity. My concern is not to show that central-place organization is the only important variable affecting economic opportunity, but that it is a significant variable that does not "wash out" when the more "basic" environmental variables are put in the same equation. The model that I propose, based on the irregular central-place models and the previous analysis, is shown in Figure 12.[19]

[19] The test of the model will utilize path analysis as described by Duncan and Blalock in Blalock (1971). In this case, however, the objective is not to determine causal paths so much as to determine if central-place type is a significant variable affecting the dependent variables—that is, if it retains some causal independence from the environmental variables that affect it.

The model states that the economic opportunity variables are a direct function of four variables: central-place type, population density, percentage of land in plantations, and percentage of Ladinos in the system. Central-place type is determined primarily by population density and road development (road development is also a proxy variable for location). And road development is determined largely by percentage of urban population and percentage of Ladinos in the population. There should be a strong interrelationship between percentage of plantation land and percentage of Ladinos, so no one-way causality is indicated.

The measure that will be used for central-place type is the market function dimension, taken from the principal component analysis of central-place characteristics (see Table 1). This dimension was a very good predictor of central-place types as measured by the pyramidal structure of central places in a system. A high value on this dimension indicated many intermediate-level centers in the system; a low value indicated few or no important intermediate-level centers. The regular central area systems, together with Totonicapan, rated highest on this dimension, and the irregular feeder systems of the northern periphery rated lowest; the primate systems of the southern lowland area were intermediate. The dependent economic variables examined are wage, labor migration, craft-trade specialization, peasant capital investment, and percentage of labor engaged in nonagricultural occupations. (As measures of economic alternatives, I consider these variables rough indices of economic opportunity.) A correlation matrix of all variables used in the model is shown in Table 6.

Results of this analysis are shown in Figure 13. By and large, the hypothesis is supported. Central-place type is a significant determinant of all economic opportunity indicators except for craft–trade specialization—the only equation in which population density is a significant variable. (The significance tests[20] show that in all cases two of the four explanatory variables explain much of the variance in the dependent economic opportunity variable.)

On the basis of these tests and the previous grouping analyses, I consider the models of irregular central-place systems presented at the beginning to be generally validated for western Guatemala. Various kinds of imperfect competition in western Guatemala have led to particular types of irregular central-place systems. The kind of imperfect competition that leads to primacy is concentration of wealth in a few hands and in a few export-oriented commodities. This is easily measured in Guatemala by percentage of lands in plantations—few people own plantations, and all

---

[20] The beta coefficients in a standard regression analysis are path coefficients. If the βs are at least twice their standard error, they are statistically significant and are asterisked in the path diagram (Figure 13).

TABLE 6

Correlation Matrix of Regression Variables Used in Figure 13[a]

	X_1	X_2	X_3	X_4	X_5	X_6	X_7	X_{8a}	X_{8b}	X_{8c}	X_{8d}	X_{8e}
X_1	--											
X_2	.49	--										
X_3	.57	.48	--									
X_4	-.75	-.43	-.21	--								
X_5	.23	.49	.73	-.42	--							
X_6	.12	.25	.70	-.18	.77	--						
X_7	.62	.44	.54	-.23	.80	.53	--					
X_{8a}	.34	.52	.84	-.47	.43	.65	.85	--				
X_{8b}	-.57	-.65	-.67	.57	.39	-.40	-.85	-.90	--			
X_{8c}	.59	-.07	-.58	-.27	-.28	-.54	.09	-.15	-.08	--		
X_{8d}	.44	-.32	-.57	-.32	-.34	-.60	.12	-.20	-.10	.85	--	
X_{8e}	-.65	-.06	.20	.48	-.16	.20	-.47	-.29	.38	-.86	-.73	--

a. X_1 = population density; X_2 = percent urban population; X_3 = plantation area; X_4 = peasant farm size; X_5 = road condition; X_6 = percent Ladino population; X_7 = central-place type (F-1 in Table 1); X_{8a} = wage (paid to agricultural labor); X_{8b} = labor migration; X_{8c} = craft-trade specialization; X_{8d} = Indian capital ownership; X_{8e} = percent agricultural occupations.

plantations are dedicated to a few export-oriented crops. Plantations are most characteristic of the southern lowland systems, which are primate in type. The kind of imperfect competition that leads to feeder systems is lack of access to politically controlled economic infrastructure, seen most clearly in the number and extent of roads that are planned by government officials; and dependence on external sources of income (measured by labor export) and external sources of supply (measured by percentage of nonlocal traders in a system). These characteristics mark the systems in the northern periphery, which are feeder in type. The kind of imperfect competition that leads to top-heavy systems is monopoly of trade in regions with undeveloped hinterlands. Totonicapan monopolizes much of the long-distance trade and craft production in the region, with which it services the undeveloped primate and feeder systems, and Totonicapan is top-heavy in type. These irregular central-place types in turn lead to an uneven distribution of economic opportunities in the region, those systems

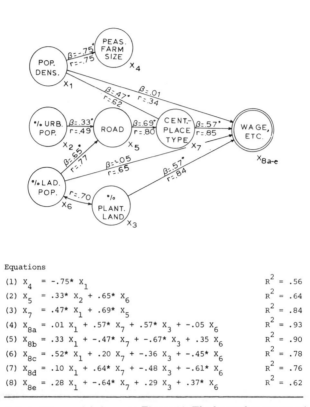

Equations

(1) $X_4 = -.75* X_1$ $R^2 = .56$

(2) $X_5 = .33* X_2 + .65* X_6$ $R^2 = .64$

(3) $X_7 = .47* X_1 + .69* X_5$ $R^2 = .84$

(4) $X_{8a} = .01 X_1 + .57* X_7 + .57* X_3 + -.05 X_6$ $R^2 = .93$

(5) $X_{8b} = .33 X_1 + -.47* X_7 + -.67* X_3 + .35 X_6$ $R^2 = .90$

(6) $X_{8c} = .52* X_1 + .20 X_7 + -.36 X_3 + -.45* X_6$ $R^2 = .78$

(7) $X_{8d} = .10 X_1 + .64* X_7 + -.48 X_3 + -.61* X_6$ $R^2 = .76$

(8) $X_{8e} = .28 X_1 + -.64* X_7 + .29 X_3 + .37* X_6$ $R^2 = .62$

Figure 13. A test of the model shown in Figure 12. The betas that are asterisked are statistically significant at the .05 level. All R^2's are significant at the .001 level. The dependent variables (X_4 through X_{8e}) are defined in Figure 12.

with many of the important intermediate-level centers in their central-place pyramids having good opportunities, and those without them having poor opportunities.

CONCLUSIONS ABOUT THE REGION

The basic integrating feature of the western Guatemalan economy is trade. Since most people are heavily involved in trade, at least as consumers, there is relatively full participation throughout the region in the trade system. The type of trade system varies considerably by local system, but all systems are commercially integrated by the redistributive role of the rural bulking centers and long-distance traders in the domestic exchange system and by the trade and transport ties between the major Ladino market towns in the import–export exchange system. The southern lowland plantations are also a major factor in the integration of the region. While the plantations are not oriented toward domestic commerce, they do provide an important market for regional products and labor. As both regular demand markets and regular sources of cash incomes for laborers, the plantations undoubtedly contribute to the relative self-sufficiency of the region. Finally, the region is integrated politically by a regional system of political centers, hierarchically organized and interrelated by Quezaltenango.

But in order to achieve the integration of a territory characterized by considerable commercial and political diversity, the regional organization of trade and politics is centralized, concentrated in relatively few hands in relatively few centers. Systems that are distant from the major centers of power and wealth are essentially isolated, tapped only for the products and labor that will feed the major centers. Isolation of the many local systems, rather than producing several central-place systems that are well integrated at the local level, seems instead to have produced irregular and poorly developed local systems. The relationship between isolation and poor development of central-place orders is clearly seen in the local systems of the periphery, both north and south. Characteristic of these systems are many very small market centers, poorly articulated with one another and with larger local centers. In many cases these small centers have more contact with centers in the distant central area (via long-distance traders) than with their own higher-level centers. Thus, we do not find a Christallerian nesting of large and small centers at all levels of the region, but instead an inverted central-place system, wherein major centers are closer to one another than they are to many of the smaller centers that they presumably service.

This kind of regional central-place organization maintains the economic differences of its 12 constituent local systems. There is a negative or deviation-amplifying feedback loop between the irregular organization of many local central-place systems, the basic ethnic division of the region, uneven rural development and underdevelopment, and political inequality in the region. The Ladino centers that integrate and control the region are the seats of Ladino political (and commercial) power. And while these centers integrate the region, they also maintain the political and economic separation of Ladinos and Indians, together with the monopolistic position of Ladinos. There are many indicators of the monopolistic position of Ladinos, among them: (1) Ladinos own more than 70 percent of the town establishments and trucks (and nearly 100 percent of the major business firms) in the region, although they are only some 30 percent of the population; (2) more than 70 percent of all commercial establishments in the region are concentrated in the seven major political (Ladino) centers; (3) the only good roads in the region are those that connect the political (Ladino) centers; and (4) all major political decisions are made by the Ladino residents of the major political centers. Local system diversity depends primarily on variability in the distribution of Ladinos, Ladino enterprises (such as plantations), and Ladino political centers. For these variables determine trade orientation, urban and road development, and central-place organization. Thus, the regional organization of central places is heavily biased by political and ethnic variables, economically expressed in ownership of resources, development of market infrastructure, and location of purchasing power in the region.

The pattern of local system diversity suggests the following about developmental processes in the region: (1) Central-place evolution has proceeded from the top levels downward. The political centers established by the Spanish conquerors (the seven major political centers today) were probably the first major market centers in the region; the location of these centers formed the first local systems and determined the subsequent organization of the regional system. Peripheral areas, both north and south, relatively unpopulated at the conquest, were to receive all commercial and political stimulation from the central area, functionally set apart by the location of the political centers. (2) Commercial development of the central area systems, stimulated by the commercial needs of the Spanish, produced regular central-place hierarchies and viable local (domestic) economies. (3) Introduction of a plantation–export economy in the southern lowlands (about 300 years after the conquest) led to urban, market, and transport development in the three lowland systems. But these systems, which could be fed domestic products and labor from the central area, continued to exhibit signs of their dependency by developing only a few major exchange centers that were more closely tied to centers outside the region than to their own rural areas. Both land and commerce were concentrated in a few hands, and development opportunities in rural areas were poor. Hence the development of primate systems. (4) In the northern periphery there were few market centers of any kind until population increase coupled with plantation labor demand provided for some cash inflow. As population increase rendered subsistence-oriented economies inadequate, people from the northern local systems began purchasing central area products with cash obtained from plantation work. Many small retail centers were established, provisioned by long-distance traders from the central area. Thus, the development of feeder systems in the northern periphery and of a top-heavy system in centrally located Totonicapan.

In summary, the thrust of central-place development in western Guatemala has been in the direction of intensification and involution, no reorganization of trade infrastructure accompanying growth. I attribute this kind of evolutionary process to the dominance of political factors in central-place development. Political forces have created an environment of imperfect competition, which has produced the irregular central-place organization of many local systems.

CONCLUSIONS ABOUT
CENTRAL-PLACE THEORY

Like all perfect or ideal market models, central-place theory is based on the assumption of perfect competition. And like all perfect or ideal models, it fails to predict market organization when that assumption is violated. Because of its stringent assumptions, central-place theory is frequently accused of being unrealistic and therefore not useful for explaining and predicting the market organization of real systems. In this paper I have taken the position that the only unrealistic assumption of central-place theory as a model of marketing in western Guatemala is the assumption of perfect competition; and I have tried to show that with market models that assume *imperfect* competition of some particular type, the marketing systems of western Guatemala can be explained and certain features of their organization predicted.

I believe that my efforts have been largely successful for the Guatemalan systems. The next step is to test these models against other regions where the particulars of the economy differ but the general character of competition is similar. If it can be shown that these special models of central-place organization have wide applicability, a major step toward making central-place theory flexible and "real" will have been taken. Such a finding would also have important implications for economic development programs. For if the types of irregular central-place systems described here *generally* have some of the economic consequences suggested for western Guatemala, much more attention should be directed toward marketing systems. Imperfect competition is not that easily eradicated. But imperfect or irregular market structure is much more easily changed, particularly when the causes and consequences are known.

ACKNOWLEDGMENTS

I would like to thank Henry Harpending for his considerable help with the formal analytical techniques. All of the grouping techniques used here utilized programs written in APL by Harpending. I would also like to thank Christina Gladwin for her assistance in designing the regression analysis, and Hugh Gladwin for his general suggestions about formal methods. Stuart Plattner, William O. Jones, and Ronald Smith also made useful suggestions about the regional model. Maps and figures were prepared by Ronald Smith, and computer time was furnished by a small grant from the University of New Mexico.

APPENDIX

Central-Place Variables[21] *(N = 20)*

1. *Percentage of bulking markets* ($\bar{X} = 24.3$, $s = 19.2$). The percentage of viable market centers whose primary function is to bulk local goods for redistribution.

2. *Percentage of other-system traders* ($\bar{X} = 48.1$, $s = 29.9$). The percentage of major traders in all local markets who are from other local systems.

3. *Percentage of producer–sellers* ($\bar{X} = 19.1$, $s = 8.3$). The percentage of sellers in all local markets who are selling goods produced by themselves.

4. *Percentage of terminal markets* ($\bar{X} = 30.3$, $s = 34.9$). The percentage of market centers in the local system that have been classified as terminal. These are simple retail centers without any bulking or redistributive functions.[22]

5. *Percentage of craft sellers* ($\bar{X} = 13.6$, $s = 4.8$). The percentage of sellers in all local markets who are selling craft goods. (Crafts are the only major nonfood item other than manufactured merchandise found in marketplaces.)

6. *Variety index* ($\bar{X} = 46.3$, $s = 8.2$). An index that reflects the variety of commodities found in the average marketplace in the local system.[23]

7. *Town market correlation* ($\bar{X} = 767.2$, $s = 143.2$). The simple correlation coefficient between town and market functions in the local system.

8. *Percentage of major sellers* ($\bar{X} = 53.4$, $s = 17.1$). The percentage of sellers in all local markets who are major (full-time) merchants.

9. *Market concentration* ($\bar{X} = 61.5$, $s = 20.4$). The amount of centrality (derived from a market centrality index[24]) that is taken up by the major market center in the local system.

10. *Rural truck index* ($\bar{X} = 3691.2$, $s = 2512.9$). A per capita index of trucks (population/trucks) found *outside* the major central place.

11. *Average market days* ($\bar{X} = 2.0$, $s = .61$). The number of market

---

[21] All measures are relatively independent of population size and areal extent of the local system because they are measures per capita or per central place, or they are percentages.

[22] There are six major types of market centers in the region, based on seller-type composition. These types are defined in Smith (1972a: Chapter 4).

[23] In the process of deriving a centrality index for marketplaces, I measured the variety of products found in marketplaces in the region. This measure is more fully defined in Smith (1972a: Chapter 3).

[24] The market centrality indices are based on seller–commodity counts of market centers in the region. This measure is more fully defined in Smith (1972a: Chapter 3).

days per market center in the local system; a measure of market periodicity.

12. *Rural town development* ($\bar{X}$ = 43.5, s = 24.7). Average centrality index[25] of rural towns (those other than the major local town) in the local system.

13. *Town establishment index* ($\bar{X}$ = 319.6, s = 138.0). A per capita index of town establishments (population/establishments) found in the local system.

14. *Percentage of major markets* ($\bar{X}$ = 19.0, s = 9.7). The percentage of level 3 or higher market centers in the local system. (In the regional system, there are five orders of market centers.)[26]

15. *Trader origin index* ($\bar{X}$ = 12.6, s = 3.7). An index that reflects the number of different places (*municipios*) represented by sellers in the average local system marketplace; by its nature it is a measure of parochialism.

16. *Percentage of viable markets* ($\bar{X}$ = 62.9, s = 17.8). The percentge of viable[27] market centers in the local system. Where the percentage is low, there are many very minor market centers in the system.

17. *Town concentration* ($\bar{X}$ = 62.5, s = 17.7). The amount of centrality (derived from a town centrality index) that is found *outside* the major town center in the local system.

18. *Major town size* ($\bar{X}$ = 39.2, s = 19.1). The number of central functions that the largest town in the local system has.

19. *Average market size* ($\bar{X}$ = 406.5, s = 112.3). The average number of sellers found per market center in the local system.

20. *Average population/market center* ($\bar{X}$ = 12,295.2, s = 3273.6). The average population dependent on a viable market center in the local system.

Causal Economic Variables (N = 5)
(Imperfect Competition)

1. *Ladino population* ($\bar{X}$ = 28.2, s = 19.7). The percentage of Ladinos in the local system population, based on the 1964 census figures.[28]

----

[25] The town centrality index is based on number of different commercial functions in towns and number of town establishments; the method used follows Marshall (1969).

[26] In establishing market orders, the full regional market system was considered.

[27] Viable market centers would be similar to Skinner's (1964) standard market towns. They provide for most basic retail and wholesale needs of peasants, unlike minor markets, which are similar to Skinner's "greengrocer" markets. In a number of cases, measures are taken of all centers because interest rests on minor market development; in other cases it is more useful to consider only the standard market centers (as in variable 20).

[28] The 1964 Guatemalan census is the latest census and is reputed to be reasonably accurate.

2. *Plantation areas* ($\bar{X} = 21.9$, $s = 23.4$). An estimate of plantation area taken from lands registered to absentee owners in the agrarian census, 1964, Part I, Guatemala.[29] The measure is percentage of all registered land owned by absentee owners; the amount is probably low but accurate relative to local systems.

3. *Percentage of Ladino land* ($\bar{X} = 51.0$, $s = 26.5$). This measure is taken directly from the agrarian census, 1964, Guatemala.

4. *Ladino town control* ($\bar{X} = 70.7$, $s = 19.2$). The measure is based on my town establishment censuses, where ethnic group of owner was noted. The measure is the percentage of Ladino establishment owners.

5. *Land concentration* ($\bar{X} = 89.2$, $s = 14.8$). This measure is percent of total land owned by the first 10 percent of the landowners; that is, it is a measure of a Lorenz curve, taken from the 1964 agrarian census.

Consequential Economic Variables (N = 5) (Economic Opportunity)

1. *Wage* ($\bar{X} = 57.2$, $s = 20.0$). Wages paid to agricultural labor, based on my township questionnaires. The amount used here is the aggregate of all townships in the local system.

2. *Labor migration* ($\bar{X} = 26.4$, $s = 25.6$). The percentage of the total population that migrates annually for seasonal work on the plantations. The number used here is based on my township questionnaires and is the mean of all townships in the local system.

3. *Percentage labor in agriculture* ($\bar{X} = 76.4$, $s = 16.3$). This measure is taken from the 1964 census. Most people not in agriculture in western Guatemala are either in commerce or in civil positions.

4. *Craft–trade specialization* ($\bar{X} = .67$, $s = .75$). This measure is taken from my township questionnaires, checked against a census by the Instituto Indigenista. Townships that were highly specialized in terms of percentage of population in the industry, and the required division of labor, rated 3; townships without specializations rated 0; and lower levels of specialization fell in between. The number used here is the mean of all townships in the local system.

5. *Indian capital ownership* ($\bar{X} = 369.1$, $s = 251.3$). This is a per capita index of Indian owners of trucks or town establishments. The numbers are based on my township questionnaires and give a mean for the local system.

---

[29] The 1964 agrarian census is based on a 5 percent sample and is reputed to be fairly inaccurate. It is, however, the only information available on such matters.

General Economic Variables (N = 5)
(General Environment)

1. *Population density* ($\bar{X} = 79.7$, $s = 43.8$). Persons per square kilometer per local system, based on the 1964 census.

2. *Road condition* ($\bar{X} = 1.7$, $s = .5$). A local system rating based on roads to each market center, where no roads rate 0.0, seasonal dirt roads rate 1.0, all-season dirt roads rate 2.0, and paved roads rate 3.0. The final number is the mean value for local system market roads.

3. *Motor vehicle index* ($\bar{X} = 369.1$, $s = 251.3$). A per capita index of vehicle owners per local system, based on 1964 registration figures.

4. *Urban population* ($\bar{X} = 17.7$, $s = 8.4$). The percentage of the population that lives in any township center, regardless of size.[30]

5. *Indian farm size* ($\bar{X} = 4.1$, $s = 1.9$). The average farm size (in manzanas[31]) per Indian farmer, based on the 1964 agrarian census.

REFERENCES

Adams, Richard N.
    1970 *Crucifixion by power.* Austin: Univ. of Texas Press.
Berry, Brian J. L.
    1961 A method of deriving multifactor uniform regions. *Przeglad Geograficzny* **33**: 263–279.
    1967 Grouping and regionalizing: An approach to the problem using multivariate analysis. In *Quantitative geography. Part I: Economic and cultural topics.* Studies in Geography No. 13, Northwestern Univ. Pp. 219–251.
Berry, Brian J. L., and W. L. Garrison
    1958 Recent developments of central place theory. *Proceedings of the Regional Science Association* **9**: 107–120.
Berry, Brian J. L., and F. E. Horton
    1970 *Geographic perspectives on urban systems.* Englewood Cliffs, N.J.: Prentice-Hall.
Blalock, Hubert M. (Ed.)
    1971 *Causal models in the social sciences.* Chicago: Aldine.
Bromley, R. J.
    1971 Markets in the developing countries: A review. *Geography* **56**: 124–132.
Carmack, Robert M.
    1973 *Quichean civilization.* Berkeley: Univ. of California Press.
Christaller, Walter
    1966 *Central places in southern Germany.* Translated by C. W. Baskin. Englewood Cliffs, N.J.: Prentice-Hall.
Crissman, Lawrence W.
    1973 *Town and country: Central-place theory and the Chinese marketing systems.* Unpublished Ph.D. dissertation, Cornell Univ.

---

[30] I considered all township center dwellers urban because even in very small centers they tend to be either shop owners or bureaucrats and thus contrast with the rural population. As can be seen, the urban population measured thusly is still very small.

[31] A manzana is 1.72 acres.

Fletcher, L., E. Graber, W. Merrill, and E. Thorbecke
  1970 *Guatemala's economic development: The role of agriculture.* Ames: Iowa State Univ. Press.
Gower, J. C.
  1971 Statistical methods of comparing different multivariate analyses of the same data. In *Mathematics in the archeological and historical sciences,* edited by F. Hodson, D. Kendall, and P. Tautu. Edinburgh: Edinburgh Univ. Press. Pp. 138–149.
Harpending, Henry, and T. Jenkins
  1975 Genetic distances among southern African populations. In *Method and theory in anthropological genetics,* edited by M. Crawford and P. Workman. Albuquerque: Univ. of New Mexico Press.
Johnson, E. A. J.
  1970 *The organization of space in developing countries.* Cambridge, Mass.: Harvard Univ. Press.
King, Leslie J.
  1961 A quantitative expression of the pattern of urban settlements in the United States. *Annals of the Association of American Geographers* **51**: 222–233.
Kruskal, J. B.
  1964a Multidimensional scaling by optimizing goodness-of-fit to a nonmetric hypothesis. *Psychometrika* **29**: 1–27.
  1964b Nonmetric multidimensional scaling: A numerical method. *Psychometrika* **29**: 115–129.
Lösch, August
  1954 *The economics of location.* Translated by H. Wolglom and W. F. Stolper. New Haven, Conn.: Yale Univ. Press.
Marshall, John U.
  1969 *The location of service towns in southern Ontario.* Toronto: Department of Geography, Univ. of Toronto.
McBryde, Felix W.
  1947 *Cultural and historical geography of southwest Guatemala.* Washington, D.C.: Smithsonian Institute of Social Anthropology.
Skinner, G. William
  1964 Marketing and social structure in rural China: Part I. *Journal of Asian Studies* **24**: 3–43.
  n. d. The city in Chinese society. Unpublished manuscript, Stanford University.
Smith, Carol A.
  1972a The domestic marketing systems of western Guatemala. Unpublished Ph.D. dissertation, Stanford Univ.
  1972b Market articulation and economic stratification in western Guatemala. *Food Research Institute Studies* **11**: 203–233.
  1974 Economics of marketing systems: Models for economic geography. *Annual Review of Anthropology* **3**: 167–201.
  1975 Examining stratification systems through peasant marketing arrangements: An application of some models from economic geography. *Man* **10**: 95–122.
Tax, Sol
  1953 *Penny capitalism: A Guatemalan Indian economy.* Washington, D.C.: Smithsonian Institute of Social Anthropology.
Webber, M. J.
  1971 Empirical verifiability of classical central place theory. *Geographical Analysis* **3**: 15–28.
Webber, M. J., and R. Symanski
  1973 Periodic markets: An economic location analysis. *Economic Geography* **49**: 213–227.

Section D

ECONOMIC CONSEQUENCES OF REGIONAL SYSTEM ORGANIZATION

This final section of the volume shows how a regional analysis might be used to answer specific kinds of economic questions. The questions asked by Jones and Skinner are quite different ones, but both show how regional system organization affects individual economic behavior.

William O. Jones, a distinguished economist, has conducted marketing research in Africa for many years. His primary concern has been to elucidate the specific conditions necessary for a well-integrated economy and to see how well certain African economies meet those conditions. Here he discusses his findings with regard to the space economy. On the basis of price behavior in different commodities, he developed two market models, a redistributive and a two-level system. The first shows quick and efficient price response, the second sluggish and erratic price response. The two price systems have their analogues in the spatial systems that deliver the commodities, the first showing a well-integrated hierarchy of central places, the second showing an immature system of centers with only two levels. Jones argues that because both systems operate for different commodities in the *same regional system,* the overall organization of the regional system gives one insufficient information for predicting economic behavior. This may be too strong a conclusion; for while the way in which traders for particular commodities will utilize a system is not fully dependent on the existing system for other commodities, the actual spatial system utilized for the distribution of any commodity has definite and specific effects on price and economic behavior. This should at once sound a cautionary note to those (like myself) who like to draw grand conclusions from the organization of a central-place system, and a hopeful note to those who seek to explain the behavioral consequences of a particular kind of space economy. If Jones' model fits other systems, an analysis of the markets used by any set of traders should explain a great deal about their economic constraints and their resulting trade policies and systems of organization.

The study provided here by G. William Skinner, whose earlier work laid a foundation for many of the essays in this volume, has equally important implications. Skinner describes the way in which the economic central-place system and the administrative central-place system meshed in traditional China, and he uses this information to describe certain types of local and regional systems: some purely economic, some purely administrative, some mixed. He then uses this typology, together with the location of the system in question, to explain mobility opportunities and strategies in the different parts of traditional China. What Skinner hypothesizes is that the organization of a local or regional central-place system has direct effects on the people who live there, independent of a host of other factors. And what he finds supports his hypothesis for China. Chinese bureaucrats and traders did not come from a random assortment of places, but rather from local systems that had distinctive urban characteristics. Other types of Chinese specialists were also residents of, if not sojourners in, distinctive types of regional systems. This finding suggests that analysis of the organization of a regional system may give clues for explaining behavioral and cultural systems for which we previously had no explanations: why the class mobility rate in China was exceptionally high for an agrarian society; why a special urban trader class developed in Peru but not in Guatemala; why the Welsh ethnic movement has never had the unity of the Irish ethnic movement. The studies in Volume II address such questions with a regional approach, few with the sophistication and explicit locational methodology of Skinner's study, but all with the same kinds of hypotheses. Thus, Skinner's study both shows a result of regional system organization relevant to students of economic behavior and introduces the kinds of questions taken up in Volume II.

Chapter 9

Some Economic Dimensions of Agricultural Marketing Research

William O. Jones
Stanford University

Five studies of the economics of staple food marketing in tropical Africa that were carried out under the supervision of the Food Research Institute in 1965–1967 raise troublesome conceptual and methodological issues concerning the boundaries and the integration of marketing systems.[1] They challenge the appropriateness for market research of the geographer's concepts of market hierarchies and of the economist's perfectly competitive model. They offer alternative models of possible interrelationships among markets, and they demonstrate the utility of certain elementary kinds of price analysis. The studies also illustrate again the insights to be gained and the errors to be avoided by viewing economic activities through the eyes of the participant.

FARM MARKETING IN TROPICAL AFRICA

For more than 20 years, the Food Research Institute has devoted a major research effort to problems of agricultural development and food

[1] Four studies were financed by the United States Agency for International Development (Alvis and Temu 1968; Mutti and Atere-Roberts 1968; Thodey 1968; Whitney 1968). A fifth parallel study was carried out by E. H. Gilbert (1969) as his doctoral research.

supplies in tropical Africa. In the early 1960s the role of the marketing system in stimulating and facilitating agricultural development and in assuring the availability of foodstuffs to urban populations and to farm populations that specialized in production for sale became a matter of increasing concern. Farmers will not increase production unless they have an attractive market for their product, and they cannot adopt new productive techniques except as the marketing system provides the funds and the necessary inputs. Marketing is an integral part of production. On the efficiency with which it is performed depends agriculture's willingness to supply the wants of the society.

Although economic exchange among African communities was much more common in the precolonial period than was once thought, under the traditional economic order the individual's sphere of economic action was limited essentially to his home community.

> Production was carried on by thousands of small, unitary economies, each of which endeavored to satisfy almost all of its own needs by its produce. . . . These were island economies, in some ways more isolated from one another by warfare and by manners than by space. They were small and they were nearly closed [Jones 1961:13].

The task facing the new African states was to knit together these highly fragmented societies that formed their base, and eventually to transform them into integrated national economies that could be expected to respond to the decisions and actions of policy makers at the center.[2]

An interest in regional science or regional economies that equates region with nation is sharply different from the concept expressed in the recent United Nations publication (1972) on regional socioeconomic development, which identifies regional with subnational development analysis and planning. It is equally in conflict with the supranational concepts of regional development that are usually employed by the United States Agency for International Development (AID).[3] But it alone identifies "region" with a political decision unit; this seems sufficient justification for fostering it.

Concern over the development of nation–states is not the only, or perhaps even the primary, reason for examining the spatial aspects of economic development. Any careful student of economies like the African ones must become keenly aware of the high cost of creating space utility and of the strong relationship between reduction of this cost and increased

---

[2] It is part of the problem of the new African states that the economic imperative of creating a highly articulated production and distribution system frequently comes into head-on collision with the political imperative of preserving the nation–state.

[3] This concept of regions, of course, is also in total conflict with the old cultural area notions of anthropologists, like those embodied in Herskovits' mapping of the cultural areas of Africa and, in particular, his view of the East African cattle complex.

total output of economic goods and services.[4] Concerns about space and location lie at the very heart of all economics and particularly of those branches that treat of development. Commerce—trade over distances— was at the center of the economics first propounded in *The Wealth of Nations*. It is the development of devices for generating space utility at lower cost that makes it profitable for a man "to apply himself to a particular occupation, and to cultivate and bring to perfection whatever talent or genius he may possess for that particular species of business [A. Smith 1937:215]." Many of the greatest increases in productivity in the past have come from the specialization in production made possible by trade and, to a considerable extent, by interregional and international trade. These opportunities for increased productivity by better allocation of productive resources are far from exhausted. Expansion of the market generally makes it possible to move productive resources into higher uses.

No producer ever plans to have a surplus over and above the amount he can consume or exchange, although he may occasionally experience windfall surpluses. It is probably safe to say that *all* economies at *all* times experience shortages. To reduce these shortages, farmers produce crops in excess of their own needs, hoping to exchange them for goods of which they are short.[5] It is anomalous that efforts to increase output without concern for effective demand often impair the conditions of life rather than enhance them. Successful campaigns in parts of Sudanic Africa to overcome animal diseases of rinderpest and bovine pleuropneumonia, for example, have sometimes resulted in increased supplies of cattle that cannot easily find their way to market and that simply increase the demands on an already strained local feed supply.[6]

Marketable surpluses come into being because there is an expectation on the part of producers that commodities they may produce beyond their own requirements can be exchanged for commodities they lack. The great agricultural surpluses of the 1930s and 1950s in the United States arose because the federal government provided such an assurance to farmers and, furthermore, undertook itself to employ this added production in filling grain elevators and in making relief and subsidized shipments to overseas consumers.

A dominant theme of the economic history of tropical Africa during the

---

[4] The marketing economist is equally interested in utility of form and of time. From the standpoint of regional analysis, however, it is primarily space utility that matters (see Jones 1970).

[5] On the other hand, Margaret Hay reports in her study of the Luo that periods of shortage were a powerful stimulus to trade. She says, "Up until 1920, marketplaces remained primarily famine-related phenomena, and the principal motives for engaging in trade were either to acquire grain through the sale of stock to compensate for a local food shortage or to profit from famine in other areas by exchanging surplus food for stock [1972:175]."

[6] Those who wish to find analogies between this situation and human populations in some parts of the world may do so.

past century is the increase in exports resulting from the response of African suppliers to increasingly attractive overseas markets, first for products of the forest, later for products of the farm.[7] This great increase in economic production depended upon the assembling of produce in lots of commercial size from thousands of widely dispersed producers that was "made more difficult, particularly in the earlier periods, by deficiencies in transport and roads, and even today many farmers must head-load their produce over footpaths for 10 miles or more before they can reach a buyer [Jones 1972:25–26]." Just as impressive as the physical achievement was the economic one of developing a complex marketing chain that enabled merchants to offer prices high enough to call forth the desired (surplus) produce and to sell it at prices low enough to attract foreign buyers.[8]

It might have been expected that the expansion of effective consumer demand resulting from the flow of new purchasing power into tens of thousands of African households would in turn have called forth increased African production of a wider variety of goods and resources, but this did not often prove to be so. To what extent defects in organization of the system for marketing agricultural products helped to retard the development of domestic manufacturing and economic services cannot be determined without further study.

Any student of the history of tropical Africa or any student of West African agriculture is familiar with the story of the development of the cocoa industry in Ghana as it has been reconstructed by Polly Hill (1963). The growth of cocoa production makes vivid the impact that a rapidly expanding and very attractive new market can have on the total economic productivity of a society. Development of cocoa growing and marketing in Ghana is almost a model of how such an export crop industry should come into being, not only from the standpoint of efficiency but also from the standpoint of equity and maximum impact on the residents of the producing country. It is frequently cited as an example of how the opening of trade can generate forces leading to economic development. Unfortunately, the Ghana cocoa success story, as told by Polly Hill, turns out in fact to be only the prologue to a record of economic failure. The powerful developmental forces mobilized by a rapidly expanding cocoa industry did not spark similar developments in other sectors of the economy, so far as we have been able to determine.

The linkage or lack of linkage between the cocoa industry and other industries may be explained partly by the structure of markets in Ghana

[7] The attractiveness to African producers of markets for such commodities as rubber, palm oil, and cocoa was due in part to the greatly reduced attractiveness of the market for slaves.

[8] A. G. Hopkins, in the opening pages of *An Economic History of West Africa,* predicts that "Research into production and exchange in the domestic economy will probably become the chief preoccupation of economic historians of Africa during the 1970s [1973:3]."

and their performance; it must also have been affected by the special role that space always plays in the primary agricultural industries.

It is possible to hold in our minds a picture of how economic activities are, might be, or should be organized over space so as to optimize their productivity under a given state of the arts.[9] We can also have a mental picture of how such activities will, might, or should move to a new optimum when the state of the arts changes. One such picture was presented very crudely in an article in 1970 to suggest the interrelationships between the society's spatial organization, the nature of its response to changes in its spatial relationships with other societies, and the continuing interaction between initial stimulus and response. It classifies agricultural marketing systems into six types, listed here in the order of their sophistication (Jones, 1970:179–180):

1. In the least articulated situation each household or community is sufficient unto itself, with only the very fewest articles obtained by occasional contact with other communities. This might be thought of as the Highland New Guinea Stage.

2. Increasing contact with other communities leads to more frequent exchanges for a larger range of commodities, but the products "exported" result more from windfalls than from planned production.

3. There is a conscious and more or less regular effort to assemble the products of the hunt and of gathering in anticipation of the visit of foreign buyers, sometimes only after the buyers have appeared. We could call this the Elephant Tusk, or the Wild Rubber, Stage.

4. A most profound change occurs when some members of the community plant trees or annuals to produce crops primarily for export sale, but without reducing the customary output of food crops. . . . I am inclined to call this the Gold Coast Stage.

5. The fifth stage begins when rural producers find themselves willing to buy a substantial part of their staple food requirements in the market, thus freeing them to concentrate their productive . . . efforts on the most profitable crops. Let us call this the Yoruba Stage. It is neither necessary nor sufficient that the restraint of subsistence production be removed to enter the next stage,

6. When farmers free themselves of all postharvest operations, i.e., the first stage of processing, and also employ the products of the town in crop production. The ultimate development in this stage, when the farmer hires every productive input, including land, labor, and working capital, I shall call the Salinas Valley Stage.

In order to realize the advantages such division of labor can offer, a steadily increasing burden is placed on the marketing system, both to achieve the most productive allocation of all resources and to combine insurance against untoward events that the old subsistence household economy afforded with the risk-spreading possibilities of an integrated national economy.

---

[9] "State of the arts" seems to be a more satisfactory term than "technology," which has such heavy engineering and technocratic overtones.

THE AREAS OF STUDY

The studies were undertaken to obtain, by direct observation and inquiry, an understanding of the extent to which existing market systems in tropical Africa afford an efficient and low-cost outlet for staple food products, to identify inefficiencies when they exist, and to determine their causes, in the expectation that such knowledge would provide a firmer basis for policies to improve market performance.

Enough was known about tropical African societies to recognize differences in the development of their marketing systems, and the field research was designed to sample marketing behavior in three major types of economies: one of the more highly developed western African marketing systems such as are to be found from Abidjan to the Cameroon border; a poorly developed marketing system on the west side, of which there are many; and one of the countries of eastern Africa where the received wisdom insisted that economic and social conditions were quite different. In the event, one study was carried out in Kenya, one in Sierra Leone, and one study in each of the three regions of Nigeria. Most agricultural marketing in Kenya is closely regulated by official marketing boards, whereas the marketing of foodstuffs is relatively free in Sierra Leone and Nigeria.

CONCEPTUAL FRAMEWORK

Primary interest was in the marketing system, the complex network of economic exchange that makes possible the integration of productive activities performed by a variety of economic entities that may be widely dispersed over time and space—the economic element in distribution as opposed to the more visible technical elements of transporting, storing, and processing. Most marketing economists regard the physical acts of transforming the commodities as a part of marketing, but the heart of the problem is the optimum allocation of goods and services over time, space, and form.

Efficiency

Efficiency of the marketing system was thought of in terms of how closely it approximated the perfectly competitive market. This was to be measured in terms of both how well the conditions for such a market are met[10] and how well the behavior of prices conforms to that expected in a

---

[10] Essentially that each participant buy or sell only a "trifling fraction" of total transactions, that participants act independently, and that there is "complete knowledge of offers to buy and sell [Stigler 1968:181]."

perfect market, where prices at any time reflect all information in the system about supplies and requirements.

Mapping

There are spatial dimensions both in the definition of conditions for a perfect market and in the measurement of its performance. They relate to the location of production and consumption—that is, to place utility of a commodity[11]—and to the location of stocks held off the market to enhance their time utility.

The perfect market concept in its purest form is without time and space. In examinations of agricultural marketing systems, both dimensions enter strongly—time because crops are produced only at certain times of the year but their products may be consumed throughout the year, and space because production occurs over extended areas that are spatially distinct from the places of consumption. Consumption may or may not be similarly distributed over space; one of the consequences of market development is to achieve more concentrated production and more dispersed consumption.

The temporal dimension of an agricultural market implies storage; the spatial dimension implies transportation, and this too occurs over time. These physical aspects are of great interest in themselves, and their technical solution affects the economic analysis. But the engineer concerned with storage and transport requires a different map of space, and probably of time, than does the investigator who is solely concerned with the economic problem as we have defined it. The transportation engineer needs to know the location of production—of the field, pasture, or orchard. He will be concerned about how far it is from field to barnyard to the first stage of processing and about the kind of surface and the means by which the crop is carried this distance. He will also want to know the location of other processing activities, of points where the nature of transport and roadbed change, of the amounts and locations of storage, and of the location of consumers.

Some of the same features may occur on the economic map as it is defined here, but the principal features are not points where some physical act is performed on the commodity, but rather exchange points where rights of individuals over the commodity are transferred—where title changes—whether they be in the field, at the farmstead, along the

[11] Not to be confused with the utility of a place to an individual. In marketing terminology, "place utility" of a commodity is the utility or value that a commodity acquires because it is at a particular location, as opposed to utility of time and of form. Place utility as used in regional science is defined by Julian Wolpert as "the net composite of utilities which are derived from the individual's integration at some position in space [1972:405]."

roadside, or in a marketplace, a shop, a coffeehouse, or an organized commodity exchange. It was so that the marketing maps for the five studies were conceived.

The research procedures were designed on the assumption that exchange points would be linked together in patterns like those G. W. Skinner (1964, 1965) found among Chinese market towns. This is more or less what has sometimes been called a redistributive system (Jones 1972:108–115); it bears kinship to what specialists in produce marketing have called a "Covent Garden system," in which all merchandise is traded through one central market at some time in its flow from grower to consumer. The systems were also expected to be characterized by "levels" of exchange at each of which merchants first assembled produce into larger and larger lots (bulking), and then divided it into smaller and smaller parcels (breaking bulk), and that goods could only move between markets of the same level (order) through the intermediation of markets of a higher order.[12] This concept was borrowed from central-place theory and specifically from Skinner and accepted unquestioningly. When various members of the teams reported, after 2 or 3 months in the field, that they were not able to find the kind of market hierarchies postulated by central-place theory, it was assumed that this was simply because they had not looked hard enough or had not been asking the right kinds of questions. As it turned out, this was not so.

Boundaries

The areas of study were defined so as to permit the investigations to be as exhaustive as possible. There seemed to be little merit in undertaking the study of national systems, primarily because it was clear that articulation of the national marketing economies was extremely imperfect. On the other hand, there appeared to be evidence (see Jones 1974:18–19) that many regions contained several spatially distributed smaller marketing systems, each surrounding a major city. The geographical areas of study were accordingly defined as the staple food supply hinterlands of five major African cities: Nairobi, Freetown, Ibadan, Enugu, and Kano.

It was also necessary to bound the commodity space, remembering that marketing tends to be commodity-specific, but keeping in mind the need to conserve limited research resources. This was done by limiting the number of commodities to be studied to four or five and by selecting first those that made the largest contribution to the total food energy of the country. This dictated concentration on the starchy staples, although domestic foodstuffs of major economic importance were included when possible (Table 1).

[12] A. M. Hay and R. H. T. Smith (1969) base their model of "strands" of trade on a similar concept.

TABLE 1
Cities and Commodities

Nairobi	Freetown	Ibadan	Enugu	Kano
Maize		Maize	Maize	Sorghum
	Rice	Rice	Rice	Rice
Potatoes	Manioc (fufu)	Manioc (gari)	Manioc (gari)	Millet
Bananas	Palm oil	Yams	Yams	
Beans	Peanuts	Cowpeas	Cowpeas	Cowpeas

The kinds of information to be collected by the teams were implied by the conceptual framework. An attempt was made to collect prices weekly in a principal market in a central city; prices were also to be collected in rural markets whenever members of the teams visited them.

The principal task of the teams in the field was first to gain a fairly clear knowledge of the marketing chains regardless of whether they passed through markets in the central city or not and to identify all points where title to the goods was transferred. It was expected that this would provide a basic map of the marketing system. Estimates were also made of the volume of merchandise flowing through each one of the transfer points and the direction of flow.

EFFECTIVENESS OF THE METHODOLOGIES

Because of the broad scope of the inquiry, the findings cover a wide range of characteristics of the markets. Those relating primarily to policy issues are reported in *Marketing Staple Food Crops in Tropical Africa* (Jones 1972). The insights gained from the study that are presented here bear on conceptualizations underlying the methodologies that were employed. They have to do mostly with boundaries, efficiency and integration, and levels and hierarchies.

Boundaries

It was, of course, obvious that if the spatial boundaries of the studies were described as the supply hinterlands for four or five distinct com-

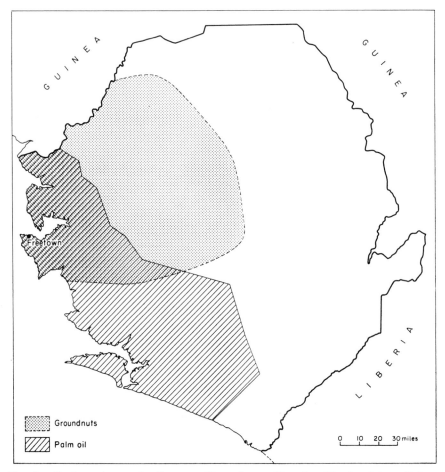

Map 1. Food supply area for Freetown, Sierra Leone. [Based on Mutti and Atere-Roberts (1968:13).]

modities, this would be likely to result in several different areas for each study. This is best illustrated by the crudely drawn boundaries of the supply hinterland for Freetown, particularly the distinctly different areas supplying palm oil and peanuts (see Map 1). This was not a matter of great concern in studies focused on commodities; it could present serious problems if an attempt were made to describe a region using a similar approach. And it provides the first clue to a difficulty that was to recur throughout because commodity-specific investigations were being carried out on the basis of concepts derived from studies of generalized markets in which a wide variety of goods and services are traded. [Some of the same incompatibilities are evident in Carol Smith's (1972) Guatemalan studies.]

Another problem, also deriving primarily from the commodity

approach, was that the supply areas for certain products, specifically cow-peas in the Enugu and Ibadan studies, were so distant that they could not—by any stretch of the imagination—be thought of as forming part of the hinterlands of these cities. This is more troublesome than it seems at first. Cowpeas move in a long-distance, redistributive trade, but not an international trade. At present, they move from one region to another, but if enough goods travel and enough transactions take place over these distances, the trade will cease to be interregional, for the "region" will embrace all of Nigeria. S. O. Onakomaiya, in a study of Nigerian interna-tional trade in "delicacy foodstuffs" (kola, oranges, onions, and dried meat and fish) that was carried out in 1969, makes a comment that embodies the difficulty: "Local (intraregional) distributional channels for oranges tend to have an average of two exchanges between grower and consumer, while longer-distance interregional channels have an average of between four and five exchanges [1970:63–64]." Is a region then to be defined as an area in which the market chain is short, so that any chain that is long must be interregional? Perhaps, but it requires some reconsideration of previous ideas.

A distinct surprise was the discovery in the western Nigerian study that Ibadan's staple supply hinterland wound around and leaped over the sup-ply hinterland of neighboring cities (see Map 2a). There is a suggestion in

Map 2a. Staple food supply sheds of the major urban centers of western Nigeria. [Based on Thodey (1968:VII-2).]

Map 2b. Schematic representation of urban staple food supply sheds, western Nigeria. This diagram more or less ignores topography, roads, and canoe routes. Some cities shown on Map 2a do not appear, and others have been added for tidiness. All cities shown actually exist. Empty areas in the eastern and southeastern parts of western Nigeria are presumably tributary to cities in the Midwest and Northern Regions.

the mapping that supply sheds for each of the Yoruba cities were once arranged like tiles across the landscape with each little city surrounded by its farmlands, from which came its basic food supply (see Map 2b).[13] When the rapid growth of Ibadan created demands for foodstuffs its traditional hinterland could not meet, merchants could not obtain suppliers from wholesalers located in Ibadan's sister cities and were forced to break out into new areas lying beyond their supply sheds. This phenomenon is related to the two-level marketing system discussed later.[14]

[13] The interested reader will find extremely informative Gloria Marshall's "Women, Trade, and the Yoruba Family" (1964).

[14] Peter R. Jones, in a letter of December 15, 1974, informs me that the location of Ibadan's supply hinterland is exactly what a gravity model would predict, although he is careful to point out that no one really knows why gravity models work. He writes: "the [migration] hinterland for Los Angeles snakes around the hinterlands of San Francisco, Portland, and Seattle, and . . . engulfs the hinterland of Denver. This is as predicted by the gravity model. The gravity model for the supply shed of Ibadan can be tested against your hypothesis. . . . It is a characteristic of the gravity model that smaller cities will be on the 'windward' side of their supply areas (with respect to a wind blowing out in rays from the dominant city). . . . Now, eyeballing your Map 2a, I list towns according to whether or not they seem to be on the windward side of their supply areas with respect to Ibadan." Eleven of the 17 towns seem to be so located. Lagos is one of those that is not, and it may be dominant over Ibadan. All but 2 of the 17 towns (including Ibadan) are on the windward side with respect to Lagos.

Efficiency and Integration

The concept of the conditions for a perfectly competitive market is use-ful in determining how a market is inefficient, but it is not very helpful in determining how inefficient a market is. It provides no mechanism for estimating the cost of an imperfection; it does not indicate whether causes of the imperfection lie within the area of investigation or outside it; and it provides no clue for identifying those imperfections that are in effect introduced by market participants in order to correct other imperfections that are beyond their control.

Certain imperfections that have received a great deal of attention in the literature seem in fact to provide slight obstacles to smooth functioning of the markets. In Nigeria public market information services were generally lacking, and crop forecasting was almost nonexistent. Nevertheless, wholesalers and assemblers seemed to have no difficulty in learning about prices in the markets where they customarily traded, and they frequently also knew what prices were in other markets.[15] Similarly, there was a tremendous variation in units of volume, very little use of weighing scales, and no standardized measures of quality. This situation creates serious problems for the statistician, but apparently much less difficulty for merchants and their clients.

In some ways the measurement of market performance as manifested by the behavior of prices was more satisfactory than that based on identi-fying imperfections. The problem, of course, is to obtain records of prices in enough places and over long enough periods of time to permit useful analysis. Such data do exist for Nigeria in the form of monthly reports on retail prices of major domestic foodstuffs for up to 68 cities, beginning in 1952. These data are not of high quality, but they stood up rather well when tested against known seasonal variation in supplies, and they seem to represent reasonably well the varying patterns of seasonal price move-ments of the different crops.

On the whole, seasonal rises in prices, as measured by indexes of seasonal variation, were consistent with current rates of interest, which range around 36 percent a year, and with very low storage costs and losses for cereals, high costs for yams. The seasonal behavior of prices of cowpeas was important in explaining the nature of spatial arbitrage in this crop.[16]

---

[15] J. O. C. Onyemelukwe reports that in the early 1960s wholesalers of gari, rice, and beans in the Onitsha market were increasingly using a "waybill" system for obtaining supplies. A trading partner in the rural area sent supplies on request by truck, accompanied by a "waybill" to his partner in the city. The urban wholesaler in turn sent payment back by truck. The "waybill," in the form of a letter, advised the consignee of the size of the shipment and the amount due to the trucker. These letters also provided the Onitsha wholesaler with information about market conditions in the supply area. In fact, "a kind of regular trade cor-respondence between an Onitsha wholesaler and a trader in the source area is commonly maintained [1970:196, 213–214]."

[16] Analysis of the Nigerian price series is described in detail in Jones (1972, 1974).

The series made it possible to identify 8 or 10 market areas in the Northern and Eastern Regions alone, based on whether staple foodstuffs were moving in or out, being "imported" or "exported." These market areas matched up rather well with the regions of food surplus and food deficit that Kenneth Baldwin had found in a study based on the 1950–1951 sample census of Nigerian agriculture (Nigeria Northern Region Ministry of Agriculture 1958).

These earlier tests of the Nigerian price series suggested that they might be used to advantage as well to test the performance of arbitrage over time and space.

The principal method used to determine quantitatively the effectiveness of arbitrage over space was simple bivariate correlation of actual prices among pairs of markets. Coefficients of correlation among actual prices are, of course, likely to be much higher than among first differences, especially when strong secular, cyclical, or seasonal forces are present. Secular measurements are not apparent in the Nigerian series, although some episodic movements, apparently connected with political change or civil unrest, did cause at least two nationwide oscillations. Seasonal movements are apparent in most series, but in fact those price series displaying the strongest patterns also showed the weakest intermarket correlations.

The correlation coefficients appear to be low (Table 2). Certainly they are when compared with the values Uma Lele obtained for cereal markets in India (1971). But there is no real standard with which to compare them, and whether on the whole they show strong or weak spatial arbitrage is a matter of personal judgment; reasons set forth in *Staple Food Crops* (1972) and in "Market Structure" (1968) suggest that arbitrage for most commodities is weak. It is quite clear, however, that intermarket relationships for some commodities—cowpeas and gari specifically—are much higher than they are for others. Cowpeas figure prominently in long-distance trade, but so does rice. Cassava is grown throughout the southern part of the country, but gari production tends to be concentrated spatially, and a certain amount moves over long distances.[17] At the other extreme, maize is widely grown, and probably only a relatively small share of the harvest is stored for more than a few months.

The intermarket price correlations were used to construct correlation maps for each commodity at the highest value of the correlation coefficient that showed any significant pattern of interconnections.[18] (An example of one of the maps, that for cowpeas in northern and western Nigeria, is

[17] Onyemelukwe states that there was a major concentration of gari production in the Midwest and that by 1966 that region was shipping gari to Aba, once a major supply center. Wholesalers in Onitsha obtained supplies from the Midwest to be railed north (1970:271–273).

[18] Cowpeas and gari, for example, show clear patterns of relationships of prices among markets at $r = .80$; yams and maize show no clear pattern at $r = .65$.

TABLE 2
Bivariate Correlation between Prices for Each Commodity: All Pairs of Markets[a]

r^b	Gari	Cowpeas	Rice	Sorghum	Yams	Millet	Maize
.95+	.3						
.90-4	4.7	1.0					
.85-9	10.7	4.9	.1				
.80-4	19.7	5.9	.2	.6		1.0	.7
.75-9	17.7	8.1	.8	1.4	.3	3.2	.7
.70-4	18.0	9.9	2.4	2.4	1.1	3.0	.7
.65-9	11.7	13.8	5.3	6.3	3.3	3.9	1.0
.60-4	7.0	12.6	6.9	8.4	4.9	4.4	3.0
.55-9	5.3	11.3	9.6	9.5	8.1	3.7	3.5
.50-4	2.3	9.4	10.9	10.3	7.5	5.4	3.7
.0-.49	2.6	22.9	61.4	56.2	71.6	64.8	75.1
< .0		.2	2.4	1.9	3.2	10.6	11.6
Total	100.0	100.0	100.0	100.0	100.0	100.0	100.0
Number of markets	25	29	57	43	30	29	35
Number of pairs	300	406	1596	903	630	406	595
Q_1	.80-4	.70-4	.55-9	.55-9	.50-4	.45-9	.35-9
Q_2	.75-9	.60-4	.40-4	.45-9	.35-9	.35-9	.25-9

a. Reprinted from Jones (1968:111).
b. Figures are given as the percent of r's that have the values indicated in this column.

shown as Map 3.) A fairly strong interconnectedness is displayed in northern Nigeria, with a link to the south through the city of Zaria. Zaria appears as the major northern link for cowpeas and sorghum, although it is not the major point of origin of shipments of either. Kano probably is, but it does not so appear on any of our maps. The most reasonable explanation of this phenomenon, and probably the correct one, is that Zaria is a center of market information and that this information is reflected in prices quoted in the Zaria market, even though the volume transacted there is rather small.[19] Qualitative information tends to confirm this, as does a map of the major rail and road routes from north to south (see Map 3).

Differences among commodities in the degree of market integration as

---

[19] This is not a unique phenomenon in commodity markets. For years the New York auction market for eggs, which remained open for only 30 minutes each day and on which only a few hundred cases were traded, set the prices for all of the northeastern United States.

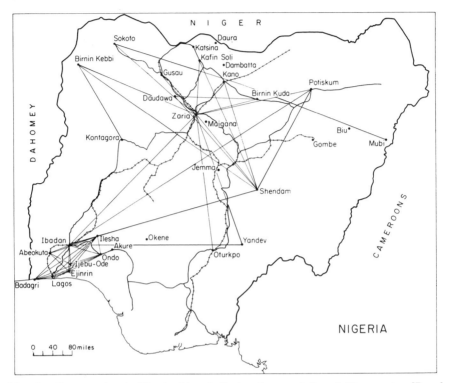

Map 3. Cowpea prices in Nigeria. Lines indicate price correlation of .80 or greater. [Based on Jones (1972:144).]

measured by price correlations implied that there were differences in the organization of their trade. These could arise from physical characteristics of the commodities themselves, of the societies in which they are most important, or of the way in which trade had developed. The search for explanation led to the formulation of four models of marketing systems that are compatible with field observations and with the differences in integration. Only one of these bears much resemblance to marketing models derived from central-place theory.

The simplest model starts with a von Thünen type of state and then places another beside it, without weakening the isolation of either. For a long period of time, each center may receive all of the supplies it needs without encroaching on the supply hinterland of the other. This condition will continue until one place or the other experiences a severe shortage of an essential foodstuff.[20] It may then seek supplies directly from the other or from the other's hinterland. While the two states are isolated; prices in each may fluctuate modestly as supplies do; prices in the two states will

---

[20] Hay's history of the Luo provides an example (see note 5).

only move together when shortage is severe—that is, when the price movement is large. The consequence would be weak, but positive, correlation of prices between the two places.

Something like this may actually have prevailed in parts of Nigeria at an earlier time and may still be found in parts of tropical Africa where marketing is weakly developed. It is consistent with the pattern of settlement in Yorubaland (Map 2b). It is likely that not too long ago, empty uncropped lands bordered the territory of each city–state. It is not so now, but a variant of the simple model, to which the name "gold-point" model has been given, may approximate reality in some localities.

The gold-point model takes its name from the days when gold was the international monetary standard and each country defined its currency as a specific quantity of gold, establishing a "mint parity." If the price of gold in one country fell, it would be shipped out; if it rose, it would be shipped in. The prices at which gold moved were the "gold points" and were determined by shipping costs. Before World War I, for example, the dollar value of the pound sterling defined in weight of gold was $4.8664, the mint parity, plus or minus about 2 cents, which was the cost of shipping an amount of gold worth £1 between New York and London (Bernstein 1968:17). Something similar could happen in commodity trade. The model is set forth in Jones (1968:116–117):

> Consider first markets A and B, each of which produces and consumes commodity Y. Assume that trade in Y is possible and customary between A and B, determined only by cost of transport and by prices in the two markets. Now clearly the price in A can be above or below the price in B by an amount equal to the cost of transport between them, i.e., it can vary by as much as *twice* the cost of transport without affecting the price in B. Can we find anything analogous to this in Nigeria? Perhaps we can. Maize is grown over a very wide area in the south, there is very little tendency toward specialized areas of production, and farmers customarily sell only part of their crop, holding the rest back for their own needs. Imagine that A and B draw from the same generalized producing area, which has its own generalized reservation demand. Consuming center A can expand its requirements considerably, drawn primarily from supplies otherwise destined for its own consumption, before it impinges on supplies going to B. The converse also is possible. Under these circumstances an approximation of the gold-point situation might be reached, and prices in A could be relatively insensitive to prices in B over a rather wide range.

Examination of prices of sorghum in Sokoto and Kano in northern Nigeria suggests that a situation something like this may have prevailed between these two cities in the 1950s and the 1960s.

Kano was reported to have a population of 295,000 in 1962, and Sokoto 90,000. These ancient cities are about 240 miles apart as the crow flies, but the circuitous all-weather road that connects them adds another 100 to

150 miles and took 10 hours to traverse by truck in the 1960s. Sokoto was the "capital" of the Hausa–Fulani empire, and Kano the capital of an important emirate. The two cities are linked culturally, politically, and by commerce, but each depends primarily on the farmlands that surround it for its supplies of food grains—millet and sorghum. Sokoto is not a regular supply center of these cereals for Kano, nor is Kano a supply center for Sokoto, but when the difference in prices becomes great enough to pay the cost of transport, sorghum may move from Sokoto to Kano or from Kano to Sokoto. The correlation of prices for sorghum in the two cities over the period 1952 to 1965 was .68; that is, 46 percent of the variation of sorghum prices could be explained by fluctuations of sorghum prices in the other.

Comparison of sorghum retail prices over this period reveals 9 years when annual average prices were higher in Kano and 4 when they were higher in Sokoto, all before 1959. The amount by which averages prices varied ranged from .01 pence per pound in 1963 to .51 pence per pound in 1958, with no clearly marked central tendency or time trend. Where differences in monthly retail prices are examined, their distribution is similar to that which the gold-point model might generate (Table 3). Positive and negative differences are almost equal in number, and 60 percent of the time the price spread was less than .50 pence per pound. If the average cost of moving sorghum between these two cities was about .5 pence per pound, then during 6 months out of 10 the spread was not large enough to

TABLE 3
Distribution of the Amount by Which Monthly Retail Prices of Sorghum in Kano Exceeded Those in Sokoto, July 1953 to December 1965[a]

Negative	Price Differential[b]	Positive
29	.10 to .29	18
15	.30 to .49	23
22	.50 to .69	13
8	.70 to .89	5
2	.90 to 1.09	4
5	1.10 to 1.29	2
1	1.30 to 1.49	
	1.70	1
1	2.10	
83 Total		66 Total

In 13 months prices were the same in both markets.

a. See Jones (1972:121-122) for source and description of price data.
b. Pence per pound.

lead to shipments.[21] During these months there would be no correlation between price movements in the two centers. The correlation of gold prices in New York and London .before World War I was close to 1.00 because cost of shipment was small relative to value—the largest difference that could occur was less than 1 percent of mint parity.[22] If it in fact cost as much as .5 pence per pound to ship sorghum from Kano to Sokoto, or 20 percent of the average value during the period, the largest difference that could occur without causing sorghum to move from one market to the other would be 40 percent of the average value. It would not be surprising, then, if correlation coefficients were low.[23]

A third model provides for a situation in which supplies still move directly from the producing area to the consuming area, but the supply hinterlands of the various centers are contiguous, as in Maps 2a and 2b. This seems to be true of the trade in maize and yams in Yorubaland and is probably also true of cocoyams[24] and fresh cassava (manioc). Gilbert reports similar relationships among some of the northern cities with regard to millet and sorghum.

Under these circumstances, commodities still move through a two-level marketing system—that is, they move simply from supply point to consuming point—but the various consuming centers are continuously linked together through the supply areas. The relationship is shown graphically in Figure 1. Information about supplies moves through this system from supply point to consumption center to supply point. Merchants know the supply situation in their own city and in the particular area in which they buy.[25] A change in supplies in the country, say at S_5, is reflected in a change in supplies in C_3 a day or two later, when the trucks return. Alteration of the supply situation in C_3 affects supplies in S_4 and S_6 another day or two later. By this means, the shortage or surplus in S_5 eventually affects supplies and prices throughout the system, but ever more weakly. The new information can travel through the system only as rapidly as trucks travel back and forth from consuming to supplying centers. When markets in the rural areas are periodic, meeting only every 4 days as they do in most of Nigeria, the spread of new information is even slower.

In this sort of two-level system, all prices in the system may influence

---

[21] Data are not available on cost of transporting sorghum between these two cities during the period to which the prices apply. Onakomaiya gives a price of .86 pence per pound for transporting perishable kola nuts the 490 miles from Shagamu to Kaduna in 1965.

[22] That is twice the shipment cost, or 4 cents divided by the dollar value of 4.8665.

[23] See Jones (1968:117) for a description of an apparent gold-point situation between the Los Angeles and San Francisco egg markets.

[24] Cocoyams include both *Colocasia esculenta* (taro) and *Xanthosoma sagittifolium.*

[25] It is characteristic of all staple food marketing in Nigeria that each wholesaler tends to get his supplies in one place, frequently from only one supplier.

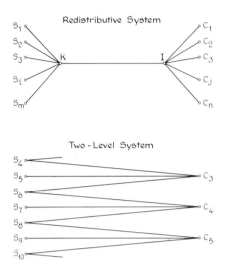

Figure 1. Redistributive and two-level systems. [From Jones (1968:118).]

all other prices, but they do so only after much delay. This delay in itself weakens the allocative efficiency of the system and probably places stubborn barriers in the way of measures to improve marketing efficiency that are based on models derived from central-place theory. the problem is complicated by the fact that there seems to be a multitude of lesser two-level systems supplying lesser centers within hinterlands of large cities like those shown in Map 2b. The location of crops held in store for sale later in the crop year further handicaps merchants in achieving appropriate prices and efficient allocation. As a consequence, a large part of the marketed produce does not move through markets in the central city (Table 4).

As is to be expected in countries where food farmers rely on their own production for a major part of their own consumption, at least in terms of calories, most starchy staples are stored in the countryside, and the timing of sales during the course of the year depends on a complex of factors (see Gilbert 1969:218–219). As a consequence, although the average seasonal price rise tends to approximate the cost of storage, and farmers and consumers do not experience excessive seasonal price fluctuations from postharvest to preharvest over the years, the upward movement of prices during the season is not at all smooth, and the seasonal pattern in any particular year may vary substantially from the average pattern. Furthermore, it is difficult for merchants to know with any accuracy just how big the crop was and where the largest potentially marketable stocks are to be found. Location of storage, therefore, impairs arbitrage from year to year and over space. Farm storage also contributes to the prevalence of a two-level system, thus further impairing the spatial allocation of stocks.

For a number of the starchy staples, conspicuously millet, sorghum, maize, and yams, trade appeared to be organized almost entirely on the

TABLE 4

Estimated Flow of Marketed Maize in Supply Hinterland of Ibadan, Nigeria, 1960s[a]

| | Buyer | | | | |
Seller[b]	Assembler[c]	Wholesaler	Retailer	Consumer	Total
Farm, Roadside, Silo, or House in Village					
Farmer	30	5	5		40
Assembler			5		5
Retailer				5	5
Rural Market					
Farmer	35	10	10		55
Assembler	25	10	15		40
Retailer				20	20
Town					
Farmer		5			5
Assembler		20			20
Wholesaler[d]			30	10	40
Retailer				40	40
Central City					
Assembler		15			15
Wholesaler			20	5	25
Retailer				20	20
Total Transactions, All Locations					
Farmer	65	20	15		100
Assembler	25	45	20		90
Wholesaler			50	15	65
Retailer				85	85
Total	90	65	85	100	340[e]

a. Based on A. R. Thodey (1968, Vol. 2: VII-16, 17, 23). Magnitudes estimated to be less than 5 percent are not shown.

b. Percent of total market.

c. Assemblers are merchants normally resident in the producing area who buy in small quantities, such as by the olodo (pan holding about 8 pounds of maize) or basket, and sell in larger quantities. They are bulkers, do not sell from a stall, but may sell through an agent.

d. Wholesalers normally live in the town and have a permanent selling facility there. They deal in large quantities, bags of two hundredweight or kerosene tins holding about 28 pounds, and sell mostly to other merchants. Some may in fact be agents for assemblers who do not themselves take title to the produce they sell.

e. 340/100 or 3.40 measures average number of transactions between producer and consumer.

basis of a two-level system. Typically, the commodity moved from the producing center to the consuming center without any change of title between
the two. The phenomenon also shows up very clearly for some of the commodity flows mapped by Carol Smith (1972:216–223). A different kind of
system is used to carry cowpeas from producer to consumer, and probably
gari and rice as well. It is denominated as redistributive and is shown in
the upper part of Figure 1. It resembles closely the hierarchical model of
Skinner.

Most cowpeas are produced in the drier northern part of Nigeria, but
they find an important market in the south. In earlier times a considerable quantity was railed from Kano to the south, and much still is, but the
greater part probably travels by truck. Supplies are bulked in the
countryside and carried to major centers like Kano for shipment south.
Ibadan appears to be a major distributive point for the south, and supplies
move out from it to lesser centers. The same may be true of Lagos,
although it resembles more a terminal market, and Onitsha in the east.
Most cowpeas move into commercial channels shortly after harvest and
travel south early in the crop year. Under these circumstances, supplies
can be estimated with some accuracy by merchants in the north. Similarly, wholesalers in Ibadan and Onitsha have a good notion of the requirements of the southern centers. The consequence is the relatively high correlation of cowpea prices and the efficient allocation of cowpeas that these
coefficients imply.

GENERAL IMPLICATIONS

That there are considerable differences in the marketing patterns of
specific commodities is in no way a new discovery. Commodity economists
are well aware of the wide ranges of characteristics—biological, technical,
social, cultural, and economic—that determine the marketing system for
each commodity. It is important in the present context because it implies
that knowing a general system of markets and their hierarchies will not
necessarily make it possible to describe the marketing of any one commodity, and because regions as they may be built up by aggregating individual commodity studies can be quite different from those arrived at by
methods of anthropologists and geographers. The concept of hierarchy of
central places stands up well in Nigeria, as A. L. Mabogunje (1968)
demonstrates, but it may be a poor guide to the structure of marketing of
an individual commodity. The rank of a city is determined by a complex
of services, and no one commodity need flow up and down each level of the
hierarchy.

The foregoing account of problems and difficulties—and failures—in
five African marketing studies illustrates how some of the concepts

developed in regional science research and in marketing research may be useful, and also how they may mislead. It probably could be demonstrated that researchers were mislead when they overlooked some of the assumptions underlying the models they were using. But in many instances more precise examination of the extent to which basic assumptions were satisfied would not have helped because theory frequently does not predict the consequences of lifting assumptions. When this is so, all that the investigator can do is plunge ahead and see what happens. It is extremely important, though, that he keeps his wits about him and realize how far the situation he is examining departs from those postulated in the models.

ACKNOWLEDGMENTS

A rather different version of this paper was published as "Regional Analysis and Agricultural Marketing Research in Tropical Africa: Concepts and Experience" in *Food Research Institute Studies* (Vol. 13, No. 1, 1974). I am indebted to Carol A. Smith for her warm encouragement as I prepared the first version of this paper and for her constructive editorial suggestions. I must also acknowledge the thoughtful criticisms by my colleagues, Scott R. Pearson and Omar L. Davies.

REFERENCES

Alvis, V. Q., and P. E. Temu
    1968 *Marketing selected staple foodstuffs in Kenya.* Morgantown: Department of Agricultural Economics and Office of International Programs, West Virginia Univ.

Bernstein, E. M.
    1968 International monetary organization. *International Encyclopedia of the Social Sciences* **8:** 16–26.

Gilbert, E. H.
    1969 The marketing of staple foods in northern Nigeria: A study of the staple food marketing systems serving Kano City. Unpublished Ph.D. dissertation, Stanford Univ.

Hay, A. M., and R. H. T. Smith
    1969 A theory of the spatial structure of internal trade in underdeveloped countries. *Geographical Analysis* **1:** 122–136.

Hay, Margaret Jean
    1972 Economic change in Luoland: Kowe, 1890–1945. Unpublished Ph.D. dissertation, Univ. of Wisconsin.

Hill, Polly
    1963 *The migrant cocoa farmers of southern Ghana: A study in rural capitalism.* Cambridge: Cambridge Univ. Press.

Hopkins, A. G.
    1973 *An economic history of West Africa.* New York: Columbia Univ. Press.

Jones, William O.
    1961 The food and agricultural economies of tropical Africa: A summary view. *Food Research Institute Studies* **2:** 3–20.
    1968 The structure of staple food marketing in Nigeria as revealed by price analysis. *Food Research Institute Studies* **8:** 95–123.
    1970 Measuring the effectiveness of agricultural marketing in contributing to economic development: Some African examples. *Food Research Institute Studies* **9:** 175–196.
    1972 *Marketing staple food crops in tropical Africa.* Ithaca, N.Y.: Cornell Univ. Press.

1974   Regional analysis and agricultural marketing research in tropical Africa: Concepts and Experience. *Food Research Institute Studies* **13:** 3–28.

Lele, Uma J.
1971   *Food grain marketing in India: Private performance and public policy.* Ithaca, N.Y.: Cornell Univ. Press.

Mabogunje, A. L.
1968   *Urbanization in Nigeria.* London: Univ. of London Press.

Marshall, Gloria A.
1964   Women, trade, and the Yoruba family. Unpublished Ph.D. dissertation, Columbia Univ.

Mutti, R. J., and D. N. Atere-Roberts
1968   *Marketing staple food crops in Sierra Leone.* Urbana–Champaign: Department of Agricultural Economics, Univ. of Illinois.

Nigeria Northern Region Ministry of Agriculture
1958   *Movement of local foodstuffs,* Kaduna, Nigeria.

Onakomaiya, S. O.
1970   The spatial structure of internal trade in dietary foodstuffs in Nigeria. Unpublished Ph.D. dissertation, Univ. of Wisconsin.

Onyemelukwe, J. O. C.
1970   Staple food trade in Onitsha market: An example of urban distribution function. Unpublished Ph.D. dissertation, Univ. of Ibadan.

Skinner, G. William
1964   Marketing and social structure in rural China: Part I. *Journal of Asian Studies* **24:** 3–43.
1965   Marketing and social structure in rural China: Part II. *Journal of Asian Studies* **24:** 195–228.

Smith, Adam
1937   *An inquiry into the nature and causes of wealth of nations,* edited by Edwin Cannan. New York: Modern Library.

Smith, Carol A.
1972   Market articulation and economic stratification in western Guatemala. *Food Research Institute Studies* **11:** 203–233.

Stigler, G. J.
1968   Competition. *International Encyclopedia of the Social Sciences* **3:** 181–186.

Thodey, A. R.
1968   *Marketing of staple food in western Nigeria.* (3 volumes.) Menlo Park, Calif.: Stanford Research Institute.

United Nations
1972   *International social development review, No. 4.* New York: Department of Economics and Social Affairs, United Nations.

Whitney, Anita
1968   *Marketing of staple foods in eastern Nigeria.* East Lansing: Department of Agricultural Economics, Michigan State Univ.

Wolpert, Julian
1972   Behavior aspects of the decision to migrate. *Papers of the Regional Science Association,* 1965 **15:** 159–169, as reprinted in *Man, space, and environment: Concepts in contemporary human geography,* by P. W. English and R. C. Mayfield. New York: Oxford Univ. Press.

Chapter 10

Mobility Strategies in Late Imperial China: A Regional Systems Analysis

G. William Skinner
Stanford University

This paper[1] focuses on the export of specialized human talent as a maximization strategy pursued by territorially based social systems in late Imperial China.[2] Specialization in the export of local products was, of course, commonplace, and many localities became renowned for a specific product, at least within the relevant commercial system. The identification of the locality name with the product served many of the functions of brand names in our own economy. I concentrate here on a comparable specialization in human talent whereby particular localities cultivated specific occupational skills for export. When the strategy was successful,

[1] A preliminary version was delivered at the symposium "Regional Systems in Agrarian Societies," held during the annual meeting of the American Anthropological Association, Mexico City, November 1974.

[2] I draw here on three research projects. One is an empirical study of the development of social structure on the landscape within the regional-city trading system of Chengtu (Szechwan) in the Upper Yangtze region, from the seventeenth century to the present. The second is a comparable study of the adjacent regional-city trading systems of Ningpo and Shaohsing (Chekiang) in the Lower Yangtze region, from the thirteenth century to the present. That study is jointly pursued within the Ning-Shao Project, and I acknowledge with gratitude the work of my colleagues Yoshinobu Shiba, James H. Cole, Susan Mann Jones, and Stevan Harrell. The third is a study of urban development in late Imperial China as a whole, the firstfruits of which may be seen in Skinner (1976a, 1976b).

the specialist's provenance branded him as the real thing: whether he was
a magistrate's private secretary from Shao-hsing prefecture, a general
from Ning-hsia prefecture, a banker from Ning-po prefecture, a stonecut-
ter from Chia-ying *chou,* a mechanic from Nan-hai county, or a male pros-
titute from Lin-ch'ing *chou.* Just as the possibilities for product specialization and export were constrained by location with respect to urban
markets, sources of supply, and transport routes, so the possibilities for
occupational specialization and the export of talent were constrained by
location with respect to urban opportunity structures, institutional
resources, and transport routes.

CENTRAL PLACES AND
REGIONAL SYSTEMS

For this reason, I must briefly characterize the overall structure
whereby local systems were cumulated and articulated to constitute
regions and provinces.[3] Two hierarchies of central places and of associated
local/regional systems must be distinguished, one given shape primarily
by economic and social transactions, the other given shape primarily by
administrative and political transactions.

To start with the former, basic-level market towns, of which there were
27,000–28,000 in late Ch'ing times, were but the bottom rung of a
hierarchy of economic central places that had seven or eight levels,
depending on the region. In ascending order I have termed these centers
standard market towns, intermediate market towns, central market towns,
local cities, greater cities, regional cities, regional metropolises, and central
metropolises (see the row labels in Table 1).[4] Place in this hierarchy was
associated with economic function. Centers at any given level were distinguished from those at the next-lower level by (1) the presence of (or a
greater number of) firms offering more specialized retail goods and
services, (2) more complex arrangements for extending credit and supplying retailers, and (3) more differentiated organizational forms such as
guilds and same-line business associations. In general, as one ascended the
hierarchy, commerce, industry, credit, storage, and transport were increasingly differentiated from one another, and within each of these functional
spheres occupational differentiation, product specialization, and institutionalization steadily increased. Economic centers at each ascending level
must also be seen as the nodes of ever more extensive and complex territorial economic systems. Such systems at any one level were articulated

[3] A more detailed presentation may be found in Skinner (1976b).

[4] The terms used here for central places at the lower levels of the economic hierarchy in
China were introduced in Skinner (1964:6–9).

TABLE 1

Distribution of Central Places by Level in the Administrative and Economic Hierarchies[a]

Level in Economic Hierarchy	Level in Administrative Hierarchy					
	Imperial	Provincial[b]	Prefectural	County	Non-administrative	Total
Central metropolis	1	3	1	1		6
Regional metropolis		15	4	1		20
Regional city		1	41	13	8	63
Greater city			95	86	19	200
Local city			69	498	102	669
Central market town			17	580	1,722	2,319
Intermediate market town				106	7,905	8,011
Standard market town				12	27,700	27,712
Total	1	19	227	1,297	37,456	39,000

a. Agrarian China except Manchuria and Taiwan, 1893.
b. Includes Nanking, "secondary" imperial capital and seat of the governor-generalship of Anhwei, Kiangsi, and Kiangsu.

329

with those at the next-higher level through a complex network in which one center—say, a standard market town—might be oriented to one, two, or three centers—say, intermediate market towns—at the next-higher level. A significant feature of the overall structure was that systems at each higher level overlapped a number of systems at the next-lower level and completely enveloped several systems of the level below that.

For obvious reasons, the hierarchy of nested economic systems was sharply constrained by the structure of river systems, topography, and other physiographic givens. I have shown elsewhere (Skinner 1976a) that the hierarchical structure of economic systems culminated in some 26 metropolitan trading systems, many of whose limits were defined by mountain barriers, and that these in turn formed eight great economic systems, each essentially coterminous with one of China's physiographic macroregions. These macroregions are shown in relation to river basins on Map 1. Each region was characterized by the concentration of resources of all kinds—arable land, population, capital investments—in a central area and a thinning out of resources toward the periphery. An indication of where regional resources were concentrated, Manchuria aside, is given on Map 1, where each region's area of highest population density is shaded.

It will be noted that these regional "cores" are—with the exception of Yun-Kwei's—river-valley lowlands, which almost by definition enjoyed higher levels of agricultural productivity and crucial transport advantages. Ecological processes, natural (for example, the transfer of fertility through erosion) as well as technological (for example, irrigation and the application of fertilizer), boosted agricultural fertility in the lowland cores. Because of the low unit cost of water as against land transport, navigable waterways dominated traffic flows in all regions except Yun-Kwei and the Northwest, and even where rivers were unnavigable, their valleys typically afforded the most efficient overland routes. The less rugged terrain of the core areas made it relatively inexpensive to build roads and canals. These are the chief reasons why the major cities of each region grew up in the core areas—as shown on Maps 1 and 2, all but 2 of the 26 metropolitan cities were situated in macroregional cores—and why the various cities within a physiographic region developed hierarchical patterns climaxing in one or more major cities in the regional core. Transactions between the centrally located cities of one region and those of another were minimized by the high cost of unmechanized transport and the great distances involved. Significant interregional trade was limited to the water routes linking the Lower Yangtze region with its immediate neighbors. Even there, however, the magnitude of interregional transactions was insufficient to link these regional systems of economic central places into a single integrated urban system.

By contrast with the hierarchy of economic central places, the functionally distinct administrative hierarchy had a single apex, the imperial capital, and was far simpler in structure.[5] There were three levels in the bureaucratic field administration below the national capital—provincial, prefectural, and county. The imperial capital, Peking, and each of the 19 capitals of provinces or governor-generalships also served, along with 227 other cities, as capitals of prefectures and other prefectural-level administrative units. At the next-lower level, these 247 cities plus some 1300 others served as capitals of county-level units. For the purpose at hand, central places below county-level capitals may be considered nonadministrative centers.

Did a city's level in one hierarchy normally correspond to its level in the other? In considering the alignment of central functions in this sense, it is important to realize that in both hierarchies, higher-level centers normally also served as system nodes at lower levels. In the administrative system every provincial capital also served as capital of a prefecture and of at least one county. Thus, a provincial capital had three concentrically nested administrative umlands. An analogous structure characterized territorial economic systems. Each central market town was the center of three concentric commercial umlands: a standard marketing system (the minimal hinterland), an intermediate marketing system, and a central marketing system (the maximal hinterland). In some instances the lower-order functions of a town were compartmentalized in time and/or space from its higher-order functions through complementary market schedules and differentiated marketplaces. Higher levels of the economic hierarchy saw a departure from this general pattern in that it was not the city per se that served as the center of low-level marketing systems but rather the various marketplaces located at the city's major gates. Thus, a large city might have four central marketing systems arrayed sectorally around it. Nonetheless, at adjacent levels the general principle normally held without distortion; thus, a regional city was the center not only of a regional-city trading system but also of a greater-city trading system and of a local-city trading system.

Turning now to Table 1, which shows position of central places in both hierarchies, we see a gross correlation overall. Most regional metropolises were provincial capitals and vice versa. A plurality of greater cities were prefectural capitals and vice versa. County-level capitals were for the most part either local cities or central market towns, and the great majority of

[5] The system of field administration was, however, rather more complex than is suggested here. With regard to levels: (1) Some but not all provinces were grouped to form governor-generalships, which thus constituted an embryonic administrative level. (2) Most prefectural-level units were grouped into *tao* "circuits," whose administrative functions were, however, sharply circumscribed. (3) A few counties contained subdistricts whose "capitals" were towns where subdistrict magistrates (*hsün-chien*) served, but subdistricts were never considered a regular administrative unit at the subcounty level, and their number was repeatedly reduced during late imperial times. The distinctions among different types of prefectural-level units and among different types of county-level units are spelled out in Skinner (1976a).

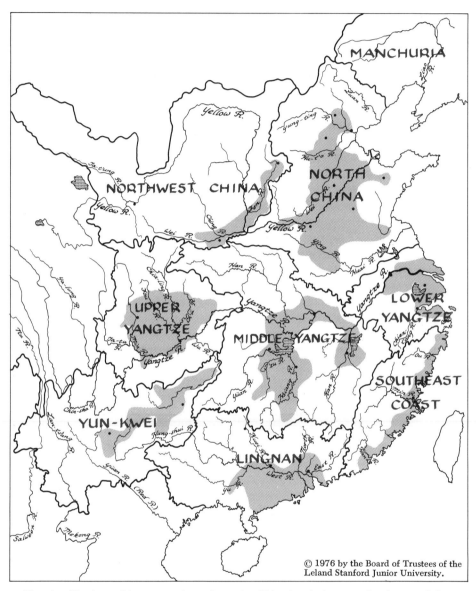

Map 1. Physiographic macroregions of agrarian China in relation to major rivers and show-
ing regional cores. [This map will appear in the forthcoming book *The City in Late Imperial
China,* edited by G. William Skinner, and is reproduced here with permission of Stanford
University Press.]

nonadministrative centers were intermediate or standard market towns.
The fact that the economic hierarchy had more levels than the administrative accounts for much of the variation in economic level among capitals at
the same administrative level. Thus, county-level capitals whose economic
position was that of local city (498 cases) or central market town (580
cases) are properly seen as differently aligned rather than misaligned.

Map 2. Physiographic macroregions in relation to provinces and showing metropolitan cities, circa 1843. [This map will appear in the forthcoming book *The City in Late Imperial China,* edited by G. Willaim Skinner, and is reproduced here with permission of Stanford University Press.]

Instances of true misalignment in the county-level column of Table 1 would be the 101 cases whose level in the economic hierarchy was that of greater city or higher and the 118 cases that were merely intermediate or standard market towns. Even in this strict sense, however, Table 1 reveals considerable misalignment: some 235 instances (deviant cases, if you will) of cities whose economic central functions overshadowed their administrative central functions, and some 205 instances of central places whose administrative status far outweighed their economic importance. The data arrayed in Table 1 also make it possible to single out for special attention central places whose level was high (or low) in *both* hierarchies. For instance, the number of cities that served as capitals of prefectures (247, the sum of the first three figures in the total row) was similar to the number that served as the nodes of greater-city trading systems (289, the sum of the first four figures in the total column), but of these only 161 cities were at once the capital of a prefecture *and* the center of a greater-city trading system.

Whereas an economic center was normally oriented to two or three centers at the next-higher level of the economic hierarchy, an administrative capital was dependent on only one higher-level capital. Moreover, unlike their economic counterparts, administrative units at the same level were wholly discrete. Thus, by the very nature of the two structures of territorial systems—the uniform discreteness of the one, the indiscrete overlapping of the other—administrative boundaries did violence to natural economic systems. While alignment of *centers* could be reasonably close, alignment of *systems* above the basic level was necessarily grossly imperfect. It is not possible to provide here the maps that would demonstrate this point for local economic and administrative systems, but Map 2, which shows economic–physiographic regions in relation to provinces, indicates the degree of system misalignment at the macro level.

A major proposition of this paper is that the maximization strategies followed by particular local systems were strongly conditioned by location in this overall structure. Since higher-level central places were the nodes of two or more concentric systems, it is critical in considering a particular local system to ascertain the position of its central place in the relevant hierarchy. Was the node of a given central marketing system a central market town, a local city, or a still higher-level economic central place? Was a given county just another county, or was it the metropolitan county of a prefecture or of a province—that is, did its capital also serve as a higher-level capital? The administrative level of an economic central place is no less significant. Was the node of a central-marketing system a county capital or a nonadministrative center? Did the capital of a county rank in the economic hierarchy as a greater city, a local city, or a mere central market town? Finally, it is important to note whether the local system in question was located in the core of a region near to a great metropolitan city or in the more remote periphery and, if in the periphery, whether or not it had access to interregional transport routes. These locational and functional characteristics of local systems determined within limits whether the cultivation and export of human talent would figure importantly among the maximizing strategies of a given local system and, if they did, narrowed the range of likely specializations.

SOJOURNING AND MOBILITY

The export of cultivated talent is, of course, a form of migration, but it is migration of a very special type. It must be distinguished in particular from permanent emigration from one territorial system to another. China's long history has been characterized by sporadic extensions of the frontier and by recurrent cycles of devastation and development within already settled regions, and the largest migrations during the imperial era were those associated with the colonization of landscapes newly opened for cultivation or reopened in the wake of devastation.[6] It can be argued that in arranging to ship off its surplus population as permanent migrants, a local system maximized—or at least adapted—by improving its man–land ratio. But this is just one of the many types of maximization strategies not under consideration here. Emigration to pursue specialized callings elsewhere differed from emigration for colonization in several ways. The occupational skills involved were nonagricultural, and the general direction of movement was from hinterland to node within a given system, from less urbanized to more urbanized local systems, and from lower- to higher-ranking central places. Furthermore, it was normally individual persons who moved rather than intact families, and the expectation of all concerned was that the emigrant would eventually return to his native place.

In traditional China large numbers of persons pursued their occupational calling away from home; if we leave aside the vast majority of the population who derived their livelihood from tilling the soil, sojourners in the sense just specified were commonplace. Whereas an ambitious man was likely to leave his local community to work or study elsewhere, his family's residence normally remained unchanged. I draw a distinction here between residence and abode. Residence was maintained in one's native place, and one's native place was in the short run of generations virtually an ascribed characteristic; abode, by contrast, was impermanent. Although a man's abode could vary in the course of his career, his residence perdured. Moreover, membership in one's native local system (that is, the community of one's residence), and hence in the higher-order local and regional systems of which that community formed a part, persisted even when a sojourner was upwardly mobile. It was precisely because those who left could be counted on to return that a man with aspirations to get ahead could expect support from members of his local system beyond the limits of family and lineage.

A preliminary word is in order concerning the metaphor of local-system maximization by means of mobility strategies. This admittedly flam-

---

[6] For an analysis of regional development cycles, see Skinner (n.d: 10-30). For the standard treatment of mass migrations in the wake of devastation, see Ho (1959: Chapters 7, 10).

boyant terminology, a useful shorthand for complex phenomena, has the virtue of emphasizing precisely those aspects of mobility processes in traditional China that seem to me to have been underplayed if not in fact unrecognized in the relevant literature. One ought not to imagine, however, that the mechanisms of specialization on the part of local systems—which term refers not only to villages and marketing communities, towns and townships, but also to counties and even prefectures—involved anything like popular assemblies at which explicit decisions are made concerning the type of specialists to be cultivated for sojourning careers. To the contrary, insofar as conscious decisions were involved, they were made by leadership councils and had to do with the allocation of resources. A local-system specialization could arise in many ways, ranging from collective decisions (for example, to open a local school) to wholly fortuitous events (for example, the business success of a sailor who jumped ship in a distant port and began recruiting employees from his native place). It was manifested as a viable career alternative and a belief on the part of the local people that they had a good thing going for them that was peculiarly theirs. In this sense, sojourner strategies became part of the local subculture. The feedback mechanisms involved will, I trust, become clear later.

ACADEMIC AND ADMINISTRATIVE TALENT

The most prestigious status symbols in late Imperial China were graduate degrees obtained by passing high-level academic examinations held every three years. The *chü-jen* degree was obtained by passing examinations administered at provincial capitals, the superior *chin-shih* degree by passing the metropolitan examination held in the imperial capital. It was from the pool of *chü-jen* and *chin-shih* degree holders that officials in the upper and middle strata of the imperial bureaucracy were appointed, and holders of these degrees dominated the highest stratum of the traditional class structure. There were several possible routes to the examination sheds in the provincial capital and hence a variety of possible strategies whereby a young man might bid for the lower graduate degree. In the "regular" or orthodox examination route, an aspiring scholar sat first for an examination in the capital of his native county and, if successful there, was eligible to sit for subsequent examinations in the capital of his native prefecture. Those who passed the prefectural examination could go on to examinations in the provincial capital, and the successful there could proceed to the metropolitan examinations in Peking (Chang 1955: Part III). Thus, ascent up the regular academic ladder recapitulated the structure of the administrative hierarchy, and the four stratified status groups created by the examination process—*t'ung-sheng* at the bottom, *sheng-yüan, chü-jen,* and *chin-shih*—were the result of successful competition within successively more inclusive administrative units. The manifest function of the examination system was to cultivate and identify talented men for recruitment to government service, but the system also enabled the government to define and monopolize the most important status symbols in the society at large and to control their significance and distribution by setting quotas, fixing the academic content of the examinations, canceling or adding examinations, and denying certain groups access to the examination sheds (cf. Chang 1955:197–202).

Under these circumstances a common mobility strategy in Imperial China, and certainly the most orthodox, was to groom young men for academic success. In the paradigmatic case a local system selected the most academically promising of its boys and provided the resources to support them through the early years of study in a bid for academic degrees and bureaucratic office. The odds were long, but the rewards of success—placing a native son in office—were overwhelming and comprehensive. The benefits returned included power with which to protect the local system and further its interests, wealth to enhance its living standards and productivity, and, above all, prestige, which, by enhancing the community's reputation, yielded specific payoffs for families throughout the local system.

A critical first step in the cultivation of academic talent was the identification of the bright boys in the community, a process that required investment in subsidized elementary schools (*she-hsüeh* or *i-hsüeh*) typically made by lineages, or by gentry families within villages and marketing communities, or by merchant and gentry associations in cities (Ho 1962:210–212; Hu 1948:70–72). Any previous success in the scholar-official track was blatantly publicized by erecting *p'ai-lou* (ceremonial gateways) to honor successful native sons, by establishing community temples where tablets of past higher-degree holders were kept, and by flying in front of a successful candidate's residence or lineage hall a vermillion flag on which the name of the graduate degree was emblazoned in gold (Ho 1962:90–91). These symbolic manipulations served not only to diffuse prestige throughout the community but also to instill and maintain ambition of such intensity that peasant families could be motivated to endure privation and hardship to keep a son in school for several years. We know that in some localities at least, the system worked reasonably well. An informant from Kao-an *hsien,* the metropolitan county of Jui-chou prefecture in Kiangsi,[7] recorded that in his native place

> The boys who take up studying in order to attain an official position are not always well-to-do. If a first- or second-degree student were hard up he could go even to men outside the *tsu* [lineage] who were wealthy and had themselves

---

[7] Ch'u Wei-ao. Mr. Ch'u's description is reproduced as Appendix 10 in Hu (1948).

attained a fairly high status through imperial examinations, and borrow money from them. This was called *ta-pa-tzu*—"to shoot at the target." Knowing that the young man would soon make his way up to the administration, these men were willing to help.

The Li lineage in Chen-hai, a coastal county in Ning-po prefecture, Chekiang, consisted for the most part of poor families who made a living by extracting salt from sea water. Nonetheless, the lineage's charitable estate supported a school with four classes, each with its own teacher; "The intelligent among the members of the *tsu* are chosen to be instructed there [Hu 1948: Appendix 46, pp. 166–167]. Every educated person could recite true-life stories in which young men from the families of peasants and petty tradesmen rose via the examination system to become great officials; the case of Hsü Kao, prime minister in the 1580s, was a great favorite (Ho 1962:274–276).

One beauty of cultivating human talent in the orthodox fashion—that is, for upward mobility via the scholar–official track—was that since each level in the hierarchy of local systems stood to benefit from success, a bright and ambitious scholar could expect subsidization all the way. Virtually every local lineage pursuing this strategy provided for cash grants to cover expenses of those traveling to their county or prefectural capital to sit for the imperial examinations.[8] Some higher-order lineages and clans maintained hostels in prefectural and provincial capitals for degree candidates,[9] and sojourners from particular counties and prefectures commonly organized clubs in their provincial capital, and even in Peking, to provide moral and financial support in addition to free housing for aspiring candidates.[10] Elite organizations of counties and prefectures (in reality, as often as not organizations of local-city or greater-city trading systems) took as one of their major activities the subsidization of all "local boys" taking examinations for graduate degrees. In some localities and counties, endowments for this purpose were administered by the leading local academy (see Grimm 1976), whereas in others an elite committee administered a

[8] Hui-chen Wang Liu (1959:126) analyzed the regulations of 75 Ch'ing and early Republican lineages, and of these 40 provided cash grants toward the expenses of schooling and taking imperial examinations, and 19 provided cash rewards or lineage-financed celebrations for successful candidates. For examples in the regulations of particular lineages, see Hu (1948:144, 155, 163, 166).

[9] A number of such clans with halls in Canton encouraged scholarship by providing examination study rooms and, less frequently, by paying stipends to those attempting the provincial exams, and rewards to those passing them. See Baker (1976).

[10] A rare manuscript owned by the late Niida Noboru and now in the collection of the Institute of Oriental Culture, Tokyo University, lists for Peking a total of 598 institutions, including *hui-kuan* and temples, that served as headquarters for native-place associations. There were institutions representing particular administrative units at all levels from the county to the province, as well as some representing conventional combinations of contiguous units at the same level.

trust fund, the income from which went toward grants to local scholars regardless of the academy attended (Ho 1962: 203–209). Because of the vested interest of higher-level territorial systems, then, a local lineage, village, or standard marketing community that succeeded in imbuing its young men with scholarly ambitions, in identifying the brightest among them, and in providing these few with a sound elementary education could reasonably view its initial investment as seed money.

Another reason why the orthodox strategy was popular despite the heavy odds against placing a native son in the bureaucracy was that each of the more modest achievements up the orthodox ladder yielded rewards for the local system. Even the undergraduate *sheng-yüan* degree added appreciably to the local reputation of a standard marketing community or a village lineage and increased its clout in the parapolitical structures that inhered in economic local systems in the lower levels of the hierarchy. A *chü-jen* degree holder, even one who had never held office, was a powerful man in the eyes of a county magistrate. Moreover, the *sheng-yüan* who failed to pass subsequent examinations could often find employment in government offices as a subofficial, private secretary, or clerk. If all else failed, he could take a job as a tutor or establish a private school, if not in a major center then in a remote market town. Thus, local systems that specialized in the production of scholars and thereby produced a surplus of *sheng-yüan* served as a source of supply for schools in other localities where scholarship was not pursued as a means of upward mobility. The cultivation of academic talent was by no means an all-or-nothing strategy.

The possibilities in this regard are graphically illustrated by Shao-hsing, a prefecture in Chekiang province, where an extraordinarily comprehensive strategy was developed for exploiting opportunities in official yamens.[11] Already in Southern Sung times (1127–1280), lineages in the rich agricultural area west of the prefectural capital were avidly pursuing the orthodox strategy, and by the Ming period (1368–1644) the success rate of the two metropolitan counties of the prefecture had outstripped all others in the province (that is, in the examination given at Hangchow, the provincial capital) and quite possibly throughout the empire (that is, in the metropolitan examinations). The prefecture as a whole, comprising eight counties, produced nearly 1000 *chin-shih* during the Ming period, placing it second only to Chi-an, a somewhat larger prefecture in Kiangsi also famous for its scholarship (Ho 1962:246). Precisely because Shao-hsing was phenomenally successful in winning graduate degrees for its native sons and placing them in bureaucratic office, it had to contend with a massive number of scholars who had failed to obtain graduate degrees— massive because the success rate for the critical examination yielding the

[11] I draw here primarily on the research of James H. Cole. This summary, necessarily oversimplified, does not begin to suggest the richness of the data presented in Cole (1975: Chapter 1).

chü-jen degree was less than 2 percent on the average. Employment opportunities for this reservoir of ambitious, educated youth were systematically built up, first in Peking itself and then, by means of control exercised at the imperial capital, throughout the Chinese field administration. The first step was the introduction of Shao-hsing natives into the Central Board of Revenue, doubtless engineered by Shao-hsing officials, apparently through a deliberate strategy of developing mathematical expertise.[12] By the end of the sixteenth century, Shao-hsing clerks dominated the Board of Revenue and had begun to extend their employment in others of the Six Boards as well. An envious official from another Chekiang prefecture complained early in the seventeenth century that "when you enter the yamens [of the Central Boards] you are surrounded by Shao-hsing people. The officials in charge are like puppets on a string."[13]

Meanwhile, back in Shao-hsing, competition in the prefectural examination (which, it will be recalled, yielded the undergraduate *sheng-yüan* degree) grew ever fiercer, largely because of population increase and the growing popularity of the orthodox strategy coupled with a somewhat diminished quota. To circumvent the *sheng-yüan* bottleneck, Shao-hsing candidates at least as early as the seventeenth century began traveling to Peking, where they purchased a degree that entitled them to sit for the "provincial" examination in Shun-t'ien, the directly administered metropolitan prefecture. The status of Shun-t'ien prefecture resembled that of a province in that it administered examinations leading to the *chü-jen* degree and in that nonnative *sheng-yüan* were barred from taking it; it was unique, however, in admitting as examination candidates holders of nonorthodox degrees from throughout the empire. Since the pass rate was markedly higher in the Shun-t'ien examination than in the Chekiang provincial examination, the strategy taking advantage of this loophole quickly spread among those Shao-hsing lineages and communities that could afford it.

The net result was that the colony of Shao-hsing sojourners in the Peking area grew to include not only Central Board clerks, officials employed at the capital, and Shun-t'ien *chü-jen* waiting to take the metropolitan examinations, but also hundreds (eventually thousands) of candidates who had failed the Shun-t'ien examinations for the *chü-jen* degree. The latter typically found employment of two kinds. Many took jobs as assistants to veteran Central Board clerks, with whom they spent an arduous apprenticeship lasting 10 years or more, so that when vacancies occurred among regular clerks they would not fail to qualify on the basis of relevant merit. By the late eighteenth century it was claimed that regular

---

[12] The beginnings are moot, and Cole (1975:54) suggests alternative strategies that may have been followed in gaining a power base in the Board of Revenue.

[13] Shen Te-fu, a native of Chia-hsing prefecture. Quoted in Cole (1975:58).

clerkships in several of the Six Boards, those of the Revenue and Civil Office in particular, had become the specialty of failed examination candidates from the two metropolitan counties of Shao-hsing prefecture. Other failed examination candidates sought low-ranking and unranked posts in yamens of the field administration. It was possible to purchase most of these posts directly—a process effectively controlled by clerks in the Board of Revenue—and the remainder could be obtained by recommendation and appointment—a process directly influenced by clerks in the Board of Civil Office. In these circumstances it is not difficult to imagine how it was that Shao-hsing natives gained a lion's share of suboffical posts (for example, registrars, and subdistrict magistrates, and jail wardens) in metropolitan Shun-t'ien and a sprinkling of such positions (between 10 and 40 per province) throughout the empire.[14]

The final chapter in the Shao-hsing saga concerns yet another specialized role within field-administrative yamens: the private secretaries employed by prefects, magistrates, and other top yamen officials. Secretaries with special expertise in fiscal and legal affairs had become virtually indispensable by the mid-nineteenth century, if for no other reason than that the average population of county-level administrative units had very nearly trebled during the preceding two centuries. Experienced Central Board clerks and suboffcials with a solid academic background constituted the most obvious pools from which private secretaries could be recruited. By the nineteenth century, when it had become "as natural for a Shao-hsing man to be a *mu-fu* [private secretary] as it was for a Shansi man to be a banker [Folsom 1968:46; Shansi bankers are discussed later]," not only Shao-hsing natives in Peking who had failed the Shun-t'ien examinations but also *sheng-yüan* who had traveled from Shao-hsing directly to Peking in search of employment favored career patterns that led from clerkships and/or suboffcial posts to prestigious and high-salaried jobs as private secretaries. Through it all, Shao-hsing natives, many now formally registered in their provincial capital, Hangchow, or in Peking, continued to capture a highly disproportionate share of graduate degrees and hence of high-ranking official posi-

---

[14] Data culled by Cole (1975:21–31) from the 1885 edition of the *Shun-t'ien fu chih* enable one to compute for the period 1662–1875 the proportions of all incumbents in particular types of posts throughout the metropolitan prefecture accounted for by Shao-hsing natives. Shao-hsing men constituted 13.2 percent of assistant county magistrates (rank 8A), 14.5 percent of registrars (rank 9A), 15.7 percent of subdistrict magistrates (rank 9B), and 23.5 percent of jail wardens (rank 9B and unranked). Ranks 8A through 9B together constituted the lowest stratum of officialdom, and, as Cole himself points out, the proportion of Shao-hsing natives rose with decreasing rank; their proportion of other unranked posts, for which data are not available, may well have been higher still. It is notable that 75 percent of the Shao-hsing incumbents in these four categories of posts were natives of the two metropolitan counties of Shan-yin and K'uei-chi, the remainder being natives of the other six counties within the prefecture.

tions (Cole 1975:50–52, 67; Ho 1962:236, 247, 253). Well before the end of
the Ch'ing period, Shao-hsing natives in government had another feedback
loop going for them: Their organizational network within and between
yamens led officials to seek out Shao-hsing men to hire as secretaries,
subofficials, and clerks *in order* to expedite the flow of business.[15] In short,
by late Ch'ing times, Shao-hsing's success had assumed the proportions of
a takeover of imperial administration. It is instructive to recall that a
development of such moment, empire-wide in its significance, all began
several centuries earlier with the cumulation of mobility strategies on the
part of a few dozen lineages in the immediate hinterland of the prefectural
capital. To the very end of the imperial era, natives of the prefecture's two
metropolitan counties constituted a clear majority of all Shao-hsing
officials, subofficials, and clerks, and probably of private secretaries as
well (Cole 1975:67).

The Shao-hsing case suggests that in pursuing the orthodox strategy, success tended to breed success. More native sons serving in lucrative yamen
posts meant more wealth flowing back to the local system, and one of the
critical feedback loops was the investment of this extra capital in scholarship—and in the mechanisms for identifying, motivating, and training the
academically gifted. Successful communities and counties were in a position to hire more tutors per capita, support more schools and academies,
bring in highly trained headmasters by means of higher salaries, establish
more and better libraries, maintain more and larger educational trust
funds, and even underwrite scholarly publication. In these circumstances,
less favorably endowed communities found it difficult to break into the
competition. For this reason above all, only a minority of local systems
pursued the orthodox strategy.

Available evidence indicates that these academically successful
localities were heavily concentrated in the local-city trading systems of
cities that were at once greater- or higher-level cities in the economic
hierarchy *and* prefectural or higher-level capitals in the administrative
hierarchy. Notable cases in the Lower Yangtze region include the
immediate environs of Soochow, Hangchow, Nanking (all regional
metropolises), Yangchow, Ningpo, Shao-hsing-fu (all regional cities), and
Chia-hsing-fu, Hu-chou-fu, and Ch'ang-chou-fu (all greater cities).[16] Rich,
well-fertilized paddy land surrounded such large cities, merchant capital

---

[15] One source (Hsü K'o, comp., *Ch'ing pai lei ch'ao,* 1917) comments that Shao-hsing
private secretaries "are ensconced in all yamens, from those of governors-general down to
those of county magistrates. They work with one another, communicating readily among
themselves. . . . The reason why officials must use them is their ability to deal effectively
with higher-level yamens [quoted and translated in Cole (1975:70)]."

[16] It is interesting to note that it was natives of the metropolitan counties of Ch'ang-chou
prefecture, Kiangsu, who first challenged Shao-hsing's dominance of private-secretary
posts—this in the second half of the nineteenth century (Cole 1975:69).

available for investment was concentrated in their highly commercialized trading systems, and the assemblage of powerful, high-ranked, and high-living bureaucrats in prefectural and provincial capitals heightened the ambitions of those in the immediate vicinity. Extrapolation of available statistics indicates that of the 950-odd local-city trading systems in all of agrarian China, the 161 whose node was at once a greater- or higher-level city in the economic hierarchy *and* a prefectural- or higher-level capital (17 percent of the total) accounted for between one-half and two-thirds of the *chin-shih* degree holders produced during the Ch'ing period.[17]

ENTREPRENEURIAL TALENT

Despite the lower prestige of business in comparison with academic achievement and bureaucratic service, the cultivation of specialized business talent for export was also a widespread maximization strategy. Trading specializations often arose in connection with the special product of a local system. A case in point is the rice wine produced by the central marketing system whose node was Mien-chu, a county capital in Mien *chou*, Szechwan province. Its quality was much appreciated throughout Chengtu's regional-city trading system, and in many towns of that system wine shops were operated by tradesmen from Mien-chu. At a higher systemic level, Shao-hsing wine was famous not only throughout the Lower Yangtze region but in most of the surrounding regional economies as well, and as a result cities and towns with wine shops owned by natives of Shao-hsing were much more far flung. Hokkien traders and merchants from local systems along the coast in Chang-chou and Ch'üan-chou prefectures (Fukien province) originally established their foothold in port cities elsewhere in China in connection with the export of their regional specialties and of exogenous goods brought to the port of Ch'üan-chou by Arab and Southeast Asian traders. It would appear that most extra-regional merchant colonies in China's commercial centers were founded in connection with the import of products from the merchants' native area.

The case of Hui-chou prefecture in Anhwei province, an area long famous for the export of successful traders and merchants, illustrates this point and several others of generic significance. Unlike the homelands of trading groups dominant in coastal and riverine commerce, Hui-chou is a

---

[17] Some of the relevant data are presented in Ho (1962:246–254). Chekiang may be taken as an example. In the 1840s, 10 of the province's prefectural capitals served as greater cities or higher-level economic centers, and the counties in which these 10 cities were located accounted for approximately 65 percent of the entire province's production of *chin-shih* during the Ch'ing period. The metropolitan counties in question (14 out of a provincial total of 79 county-level units—14 because 4 of the 10 cities each served as the capital of two counties) may be taken as roughly coterminous with the cities' local-city trading systems.

landlocked area far from the seacoast or major waterways. In fact, it straddles the mountain crest separating the Middle Yangtze region from the Lower Yangtze. The physiographic heartland of the prefecture is an upriver basin of a tributary of the Chien-t'ang River, which flows into the sea near Hangchow (a regional metropolis in the Lower Yangtze region; see Map 2), and prominent among Hui-chou's early exports was lumber floated downstream to Hangchow (Shiba 1975:40). By the Southern Sung (1127–1280), hilly areas in two counties of the prefecture were cultivating a highly prized species of cedar, while another county had invested heavily in the cultivation of paper mulberry—and in the production of paper from its bark. Another county, Ch'i-men, was famous for its high-quality tea, whose major market lay to the west in the Kan basin of the Middle Yangtze region, dominated by the city of Nanchang. Exports to western markets were shipped out via a river that flows from Ch'i-men into Po-yang Lake, whence all major cities of the Middle Yangtze region were accessible by navigable waterways. By the thirteenth century, then, Hui-chou had achieved a highly commercialized local economy oriented to two metropolitan trading systems, Hangchow's to the east and Nanchang's to the west.[18] The prefecture's traders subsequently gained access to markets in yet a third metropolitan trading system, that of Nanking (see Map 2), when a highway from Nanchang to Nanking was constructed that traversed the Hui-chou basin.[19]

As I have already implied, traders from Hui-chou established themselves elsewhere in connection with the export trade of their local specialties, and it is hardly surprising that it was in the three metropolitan trading systems already specified that Hui-chou traders first achieved dominance. By the sixteenth century, Hui-chou merchants had extended their economic power to all regional trading systems of the Lower Yangtze region and achieved commercial preeminence in the salt-monopoly district whose headquarters were in Yangchow. By the seventeenth century, they had preempted important specializations in the trade between the Lower Yangtze and its neighboring regions—dealing not only in salt and Hui-chou's traditional products but also in rice, cotton, silk, and Ching-te-chen porcelain (Fujii 1953: Part I). During the seventeenth century, they

[18] The prefecture's downriver exports included laquer, wax, and dyes in addition to lumber, paper, and tea; its imports were chiefly foodstuffs, fish and cattle from the Middle Yangtze, salt from the Lower Yangtze, and rice from both regions (Shiba 1975:39–40).

[19] It goes without saying that with an economy so closely geared to external trade, responsible leaders within Hui-chou were seldom reluctant to commit local resources to keep trade routes operating efficiently. Waterworks designed to tame or bypass rapids and maintain shipping channels in the two rivers flowing out of Hui-chou date back to the ninth century, and in all recorded instances local merchants contributed heavily to the expenses of these public works (Shiba 1975:39–40). I have not been able to obtain data on the role played by Hui-chou merchants in routing and constructing the Nanking–Nanchang highway, but it is clear that its maintenance within Hui-chou was a local responsibility taken seriously.

extended their operations to finance and foreign trade.[20] Meanwhile, even as expatriot Hui-chou merchants were extending their control of interregional trade, the mechanisms whereby the prefecture's traders had originally consolidated their commercial hegemony were being recapitulated from one generation to the next. Informants of the Hu lineage[21] provide a classic description of how young men from the area were apprenticed to Hui-chou traders for a lifetime of sojourning.

> When a family in our region has two or more sons, only one stays home to till the fields. The others are sent out to some relative or friend doing business in some distant city. Equipped with straw sandals, an umbrella and a bag with some food, the boy sets out on the journey to some place in Chekiang or Kiangsi, where a kind relative or friend of the family will take him into his shop as an apprentice. He is about 14 years old at this time. He has to serve an apprenticeship of three years without pay, but with free board and lodging. Then he is given a vacation of three months to visit his family, who in the meantime have arranged his marriage for him. When he returns to his master he leaves his wife in his old home. Every three years he is allowed a three months' vacation with pay which he spends at home.

Locational factors analogous to those shown to have shaped the rise of Hui-chou merchants are also important in understanding the specialization of certain local systems in Shansi first in the interregional trade and then in the remittance banking of northern China.[22] The three contiguous counties involved—T'ai-ku, Ch'i *hsien,* and P'ing-yao—lie athwart the mountains separating the two great regional economies of Northwest China and North China. In T'ang times (618–907), the major highway connecting Taiyuan with Sian, then the imperial capital, ran east of the Fen River (see Map 1, where the river is shown, and Map 2, where the cities are labeled) and passed through the three counties in question. In the tenth century a new highway was constructed linking Taiyuan with Kaifeng, which had been chosen by Sung dynasts as their imperial capital and had quickly grown to become the central metropolis of the North China macroregion. This road, which ran south through an important pass in the T'ai-yüeh Mountains, branched off the older highway in T'ai-ku county and passed through Ch'i *hsien* and P'ing-yao as well (Aoyama 1963:30–33, map facing p. 50). Taking advantage of their location with respect to these long-distance trade routes, entrepreneurs in the three-county area were led to specialize first as transport brokers and com-

---

[20] The expansion of Hui-chou merchants during the Ming period is well documented in Fujii (1953: Part II).

[21] Hu Shih and Hu Tun-yüan. Their description is reproduced as Appendix 4 in Hu (1948).

[22] The summary treatment here does gross injustice to the rich secondary literature on the Shansi merchants and bankers. Major studies include Ch'en (1937), Kao (1937), Saeki (1971), and Terada (1972).

mercial middlemen and later as traders. The extent to which local products played a role in their expansion is not clear to me, but by the beginning of the twelfth century traders from the three Shansi counties were established in nearby commercial centers of both North and Northwest China.

The traumatic invasions of North China during the twelfth and thirteenth centuries brought Kaifeng's central role to a decisive end, and North China's regional economy was eventually restructured with Peking as the central metropolis. In consequence, the Taiyuan–Kaifeng trade route that passed through the three Shansi counties was almost entirely eclipsed by another that ran east from Taiyuan across a pass north of T'ai-ku to Cheng-ting-fu and on to Peking. Thus, stimulated initially by a situation that attracted commercial activity to their homeland, Shansi traders were subsequently frustrated by realignments that deprived them of any situational advantage. The somewhat paradoxical consequence was that Shansi merchants from the three counties became more aggressive and expansionist than ever before. Available evidence suggests that they moved to shut out traders who were now favorably situated by closing ranks and drawing on their combined capital resources to meet competition in particular cities as needed. It appears likely that one aspect of the successful expansion of Shansi merchants during the Ming period was the relatively heavy capitalization of their firms coupled with generally conservative financial policies, and another was the tight organizational control that enabled firms to counteract the centrifugal tendencies of branches in distant cities. By early Ch'ing the dominant position of Shansi merchants in the interregional trade of North and Northwest China was on a par with that of Hui-chou merchants in the interregional trade of the Lower and Middle Yangtze.

There is no need here to detail the story of how Shansi merchants came to collaborate with the Manchu conquerors of China and eventually to become virtual fiscal agents of the Ch'ing dynasty (see Saeki 1971). Shansi import–export firms began converting to remittance banks early in the Ch'ing, and by the mid-nineteenth century they had achieved a near monopoly of remittance banking in cities throughout North and Northwest China and a dominant position in most cities of the three Yangtze macroregions.[23] As of the 1890s, they had made serious inroads in the Southeast Coast region as well; by then, for instance, five of the six remittance banks in Foochow, the regional metropolis, were branches of Shansi firms. Shansi banks remitted funds for merchants, for officials as private parties, and for the government. They sent funds to Peking from those purchasing degrees, and they lent money to expectant officials, who were more or less obligated to return the favor when in office by giving the bank

[23] The description here of Shansi banking in the nineteenth century is drawn primarily from King (1965:92–94).

official patronage. In capital cities where branches were maintained, they held government funds on deposit and disbursed them on instruction of the local official. The larger banks had branches in up to 30 major cities, and the various firms in a given city cooperated when faced with a local financial crisis. There appears to have been no recorded failure of a Shansi bank, at least through the nineteenth century, and their reputation was such that interest rates on deposits were consistently lower than those of local competitors. Shansi banks naturally worked in concert whenever their interests were threatened and opposed the entry of new banks into the remittance business.

To the very end, this vast financial network was owned and manned almost entirely by natives of the three counties initially favored by Northern Sung trade routes. The entire capitalization of each Shansi banking firm was derived from the resources of its owners, usually a consortium of kinsmen, who had unlimited liability. Employees were normally hired from the owning family's local system. "The branch managers, who were responsible to the owners for the conduct of business during their three-year appointments, were paid on a profit-sharing basis. . . . Payment, however, came only after a full accounting had been rendered [King 1965:94]." Meanwhile, back in Shansi, the manager's family was temporarily "adopted" by the owner, an arrangement described by one source as de jure captivity (Yang 1952:83–84). There is no basis for estimating the number of households in T'ai-ku, Ch'i hsien, and P'ing-yao whose livelihood was dependent on extralocal banking, but the proportion in the nineteenth century must have been considerable.

As a final example of maximization involving the cultivation and export of business talent, let me give brief notice of the famed Ningpo merchants and financiers [Jones 1972 (and the literature cited therein), 1974; Shiba 1976]. This specialization arose in conjunction with the development in the eighteenth century of ch'ien-chuang, a new type of formal banking institution that issued notes and used a clearing house. The comparative advantage of these banks led to their spread throughout the maximal trading system of the city and provided training and experience for many young men. In the late eighteenth century ch'ien-chuang banks were established in Shanghai by migrants from the Ningpo area, who appreciated the significance of that city's growing importance as an entrepôt of the Chinese coastal trade. By the 1840s, Ningpo people had achieved dominance of banking and credit in Shanghai. The Taiping Rebellion, which marked the end of the Soochow cycle of development in the Lower Yangtze region, initiated a new cycle of development with Shanghai recast as the central metropolis. From their base in Shanghai, Ningpo merchants and financiers from the 1870s on extended their operations throughout the Lower Yangtze region, and eventually to major commercial centers in other regions as well.

For the most part, Ningpo merchants and financiers came not from the city itself but from a few clusters of local systems, the largest of which lay south of the city in Yin *hsien,* with other important clusters in Chen-hai and Yü-yao. Young men from the participating local systems were typically apprenticed to *ch'ien-chuang* or shops in market towns, while whose who proved themselves were eventually promoted to responsible jobs in Ningpo city. The best talent was then sent off to manage banks and stores in Shanghai and other cities farther afield. It is notable that participating local systems were encompassed not by Ning-po prefecture, the administrative unit, but by Ningpo's regional-city trading system. Local systems exporting this specialized talent through Ningpo city included several in those portions of Yü-yao and Shang-yü that fell within Ningpo's economic hinterland, even though those two counties belonged to the neighboring prefecture of Shao-hsing.

Much of the impetus for outreach on the part of Ningpo entrepreneurs was Ningpo's decline as an entrepôt in favor of Shanghai. As Shiba (1976) has argued, until the mid-eighteenth century entrepreneurial talent in the Ningpo area was largely absorbed with the internal development of the regional economy, and the port's trade was dominated by "alien" economic specialists, including most notably Hokkien and Hui-chou merchants. However, even as the region's "internal frontier" receded, the city's foreign trade expanded, and this combination of developments drew native entrepreneurs into interurban shipping, trade, and finance. Flourishing trade during the eighteenth century was followed by the gradual stagnation and decline of Ningpo's entrepôt functions during the nineteenth, culminating in the city's total commercial subordination to Shanghai after both cities were opened as treaty ports in the 1840s. Thus, once again, we observe a sequence in which native entrepreneurial talent that had developed in response to favorable local circumstances was directed to opportunities in higher-level cities when the local economy stagnated or declined.

Business fluctuation is, of course, more often the rule than the exception, and I have argued elsewhere (n.d.:27–28) that cycles of economic prosperity and depression in traditional China were poorly synchronized from one region and subregion to the next—a symptom not only of imperfect economic integration but also of the restricted impact, in so large a country, of political and military events that stimulate or depress economic activity.[24] If this view is valid, then one may expect the challenge of local adversity in the wake of economic stimulation to have had general significance for the type of sojourner mobility strategies that concern us here. A particularly dramatic illustration of this effect is provided by the Chang-Ch'üan region in Fukien, whose native Hokkien

---

[24] In view of the differential impact of dynastic policy and end-of-dynasty rebellions and invasions on the various macroregions, I would now reformulate the model presented in Skinner (1971) in terms of regional cycles of development and decline rather than of dynastic cycles per se.

merchants have already been mentioned. In each of the recurrent business macrocycles within this subregion, a heyday of economic activity, stimulated by a booming foreign trade that was initiated by overseas merchants, was followed by declining trade and a general economic depression. In each cycle the flourishing trade fostered entrepreneurial talent among native traders, whose eventual expansion to cities outside the region got underway during the period of economic heyday and was accelerated during the subsequent eras of decline and depression (Skinner n. d.:18–25).

The first such heyday came in the twelfth and thirteenth centuries, when Ch'üan-chou-fu, or Zaitun, as it was known to Arab merchants, attracted traders from ports throughout Southeast Asia and the Indian Ocean. The maritime trade began to decline early in the fourteenth century, largely in response to a swing in imperial policy whereby foreign trade was first restricted and then prohibited, but also because of an upsurge in pirate activity and of foreign developments that adversely affected overseas markets and freedom of the seas. A prolonged depression was broken in the third decade of the sixteenth century when Portuguese traders began holding markets near Chang-chou-fu, and the subsequent trading boom lasted from the 1560s, when Ming opposition to maritime commerce was largely abandoned, to the 1630s, during which period Hokkien merchants were particularly active in the trade with Japan and the Philippines. The subsequent depression was deepened in the mid-sixteenth century by the attenuated Ming resistance to Manchu rule. Resistance leaders in the Chang-Ch'üan area commandeered all available shipping, and for a decade the pro-Ming leader Cheng Ch'eng-kung controlled the subregion from a base near Amoy. The Ch'ing rulers eventually had recourse to a scorched-earth policy, which, while effective in denying mainland resources to Cheng's Taiwan regime, broke the back of local prosperity. Early in the seventeenth century, Chinese were forbidden once again to trade overseas, and in 1757 the fate of the whole Southeast Coast region, Chang-Ch'üan included, was sealed for nearly a century when Canton was designated by the Ch'ing court as the sole legal port for foreign trade. The heyday of yet a third macrocycle of development followed the disintegration of the Canton system in the 1830s and the opening of Amoy as a treaty port in the 1840s. Under the stimulus of British and other Western traders, the region's foreign trade expanded once again. This boom, however, was even shorter lived than its predecessor, primarily because of the small market for exogenous imports in Amoy's hinterland (that is, the limited size of the physiographically defined subregion) and the poor access it provided to larger regional economies. Amoy, like Ningpo and all other less favorably situated east-coast ports, eventually lost out to the three cities that monopolized access to macroregion-sized markets: Canton (together with Hong Kong) in Lingnan, Shanghai in the Lower Yangtze, and Tientsin in North China.

Cycles of emigration from the Chang-Ch'üan subregion were associated with each of these three macrocycles of economic development such that out-migration rose, peaked, and declined as the economic cycle moved from its upper turning point (that is, the peak of prosperity) to its lower turning point (that is, the depth of the depression). On closer analysis, migration of the sojourner type, in particular the export of commercial talent, predominated during the early stages of decline, as we have been led to expect, while migration of the colonization type predominated during the later stages. With each migration wave, Hokkien merchants expanded their role in interregional and foreign trade and increased the number of ports where their trading firms were established. By the end of the eighteenth century, they had achieved dominance among overseas Chinese merchants throughout Southeast Asia and in Korea and Japan. As of the early twentieth century, Hokkien merchants were well established in major commercial centers of all but two of China's eight macroregional economies.[25]

CRAFT AND SERVICE SPECIALIZATIONS

Local-system specializations in the export of craftsmen, semiprofessionals, and the purveyors of services were probably more widespread than those involving either the scholar–official or the merchant–financier tracks. The potential for spectacular success was, of course, more limited, and most such specializations were focused on opportunities within a particular city or the market towns and cities of a circumscribed subregion. In Hangchow, for instance, carpenters and cabinetmakers hailed from various local systems in Ning-po prefecture, tailors and bankers from Chu-chi, and most of the blacksmiths and beggars from still other peripheral counties in Shao-hsing prefecture. In general, no one area supplied artisan or service specialists for more than a few cities within a macroregion. Hangchow's wood-carvers came from Yin *hsien,* Hu-chou-fu's wood-carvers from Chu-chi.[26] Even Peking, the imperial capital and China's largest city, appears to have drawn its artisan and service specialists only from the North China region—for example, dyestuff workers from a cluster of local systems in Shansi, water carriers from another cluster in Shantung. Most came from Chihli, the metropolitan province (Burgess 1928:73, 129).

Just as the type of trader specialist exported by a local system might reflect its exported products, so the type of artisan specialists could reflect a local system's craft specialties. Thus, Ningpo, a traditional center for the

---

[25] For the ubiquity of Hokkien merchants in commercial cities of China proper, see the evidence on geographic distribution of merchant *hui-kuan* (same-native-place associations) in Ho (1966a, 1966b).

[26] These particular instances are mentioned in Cole (1975:16) and Cloud (1906:9–10).

manufacture of fine furniture, exported to Hangchow not furniture, a bulky product priced out of the Hangchow market by the cost of transport, but cabinetmakers. But for the most part, craft specializations—and a fortiori service specializations that involved little skill—appear to have developed in serendipitous fashion. The success of even one native son in a distant city could initiate the chain migration that eventually led to dominance of the occupation in that particular city. If one can generalize from the situation that prevailed within the trading system of Chengtu in the late 1940s, few of the craft or service specialists established in any given market town were natives of the marketing system in question. In Kaotien-tzu, where I did research, the great majority of economic specialists in the town, and virtually all of the itinerants, were natives of other local systems within Chengtu's metropolitan trading system.

An instructive case of specialist export is provided by the Hakkas of southeastern China. Their homeland, an extensive area encompassing the upper reaches of several river systems, straddled the watersheds that define the junction of three great macroregions—the Middle Yangtze, the Southeast Coast, and Lingnan. From strategically located native places in this area, Hakka itinerants penetrated the several regional trading systems as peddlers and artisans. In time, they were established in lowland market towns, where they gained a virtual monopoly of certain artisan services, most notably barbering, blacksmithing, and stonecutting (Lechler 1878:359; Vömel 1913:598). Their success was due in some degree to the lowly status of their calling, for certain lineages among the lowland populations (Cantonese, Teochiu, or Kan, as the case may be), eager to protect their elitist standing, forbade their members to engage in such demeaning occupations as barbering, leaving an occupational niche to be filled by outsiders. Thus, sojourning abroad came to be a way of life for Hakka barbers and blacksmiths from Chia-ying *chou,* who worked in lowly market towns around the periphery of great economic systems, no less than for Hui-chou merchants, whose heavily capitalized stores were located in such metropolises as Nanchang and Nanking.

MISCELLANEOUS SPECIALIZATIONS

It remains to mention one other important category of specialized talent, namely military specialists. Local systems exporting soldiers and other military specialists tended to be situated around the remote periphery of physiographic regions, especially along China's inner Asian frontiers. It is in such inaccessible areas that romantic-rebel countercultures thrived, banditry was endemic, and young men as a matter of course became proficient in the martial arts. Moreover, the Chinese court traditionally drew its military men disproportionately from local systems stretched along the steppe frontier, where Hui (Chinese Muslims) and other less-than-wholly-Han ethnic groups with more robust traditions were concentrated. Since the military examinations stressed physical prowess rather than literary attainment, young men from local systems with a martial tradition could, if they chose, achieve upward mobility in the military via the orthodox examination route. Others began their careers as bandits or rebels and achieved rank in the regular armed forces either through co-optation or, every century or so, through the happy circumstance of fighting for the winning side as the Mandate of Heaven shifted (Ho 1962:215–219).

It should be emphasized that low respectability of a calling was no necessary barrier to local-system specialization. Reading between the lines of official reports, one glimpses local systems located around the periphery of regions far from the major trade routes, or along the seacoast away from open ports, that thrived on smuggling, and some of these apparently exported experienced smugglers to serve reputable trading firms elsewhere. Just as some successful military men began their careers as bandits, so some successful merchants began theirs as smugglers. Nor should we be surprised to find despised occupations monopolized by particular local systems. Yamen runners, a demeaned calling in imperial times, were typically dominated by sojourners from a particular local system. Those in the county yamen in Chang-hua, Taiwan, for instance, were natives of Chin-men *hsien* (Quemoy) from the time of its establishment until well into the nineteenth century.[27]

It does come as something of a shock to students of Chinese society, however, to come across references to local-system specialization in the production of Buddhist monks and of eunuchs. By social definition, a monk or eunuch betrayed his ancestors by failing to continue his descent line, and yet within the Buddhist hierarchy great worldly success was possible, and the careers of numerous eunuchs are among the most spectacular cases of upward social mobility on record. As Mitamura (1970:68) wryly notes, while a cultured man had only to pass an imperial examination in order to attain high position, some among the lower classes, denied the means to prepare for examinations, chose eunuchism as an alternative road to power. The official history of the Ming period records that in certain areas lower-class families "competed by having their children or grandchildren castrated out of a desire for wealth and rank." The number castrated in one village during the Cheng-te reign (1506–1522) was reported to have exceeded 100 despite official prohibition of the practice (Mitamura 1970:70). As for monks, their production for export is recorded for subregions of the Southeast Coast as early as the Sung,[28] and in the

---

[27] *Chang-hua hsien chih* (Chang-hua County Gazetteer), 1833. Reference courtesy of Donald R. DeGlopper.

[28] Wang Ying-chen wrote of Fukien in the twelfth century: "When there are three adult males in a family, generally one or even two of them will abandon secular life and enter a Buddhist or Taoist monastery [Shiba 1970:185]."

Ch'ing a portion of northern Kiangsu was known as the "cradle of monks" (Welch 1967: mapped on endpapers). The explanation of the paradox is not hard to find. Despite all, some monks and many eunuchs could be counted on to use the wealth, influence, and power gained in their careers to serve the interests of kinsmen and their native local systems. One of the dozen or so Chinese villages that have been ethnographed in English turns out to have been founded in the fifteenth century when the retired eunuch Wang Yen bought a large tract of land on which he built a temple and settled two of his nephews (Gamble 1963:144).

It should be clear that success in strategies of the kind described in this paper depended very much on the socialization and selection of the mobile. With regard to socialization, it was thought by many of those involved that the system would break down if young boys were reared in the "softer," more urbanized milieu of their father's abode. For one thing, living standards were generally somewhat higher in cities, and for another successful sojourners often felt constrained, if only for professional reasons, to live in some style. It was also considered difficult in an urban environment to ensure proper associates for one's children without at the same time overprotecting them and giving them airs. Thus, homiletic family and lineage instructions usually inveighed against the comforts, extravagance, conspicuous consumption, and dissipation of urban life. A typical view is the following, written by a sixteenth-century Ch'ing official (Wang Ch'i, quoted in Ho 1962:143).

> It is a good thing if they [one's sons and grandsons] are content with coarse clothes and straw shoes and refrain from going to the cities. . . . While being brought up in their fathers' official residences, they are subjected to various tempting traps laid by bad associates and flattering servants. . . . Besides, their fathers are . . . so occupied as a rule that they . . . have no time or energy to supervise their children. Even though the youths acquire bad habits, no one dares speak frankly about it to their fathers. . . . Fortunately, [my brothers and I] were sent back to our ancestral home, thus avoiding such traps and bad environmental influences.

Comparable attitudes were even more strongly held by businessmen. Thus, even in cases in which a succcessful sojourner brought his wife to the city or took a second wife there, the children were normally sent back to the family residence to be reared. This meant that despite a tendency for specialties to be continued from father to son,[29] specific skills were infrequently passed on in the family context. In many cases very little of the training associated with the specialized skill took place even in the young man's native place, narrowly defined. If he was headed for the

[29] For instance, despite regulations to the contrary, clerkships and more lowly posts within field-administrative yamens tended to become hereditary (Ch'ü 1962:36, 63–64). Cole (1975:54–55) cites evidence suggesting that by the late eighteenth century a son's claim to his father's clerkship had become recognized as a de facto right.

scholar–official track, his real training began after he enrolled in an academy in a local city or, if headed for the business track, after he left home and was apprenticed to an experienced sojourner (who might be his father or kinsman) from his local system. Childhood socialization in one's native place was seen as imparting attributes more important to success than skill alone, namely, industriousness, frugality, discipline, and above all ambition.

On the side of selection, it is apparent that local-system specialization in the export of human talent proceeded in a framework of same-native-place particularism. Yet elements of universalistic selection were present throughout the career cycle. To begin with, for reasons that are obvious to students of Chinese society, "only sons" seldom emigrated; sojourners were selected from sets of sons, and there can be no doubt that relevant criteria—ambition, venturesomeness, intelligence—played a role in deciding which should go. In addition, upward mobility in any sector involved testing and tempering sojourners in a context of competition with their same-native-place fellows. In the long run, relevant merit played a major role in success.

CONCLUSIONS

In conclusion, I focus on those aspects of mobility strategies that relate specifically to local or regional systems as defined at the beginning of this paper, in particular to their hierarchical structure and the urban systems that served to articulate them. In these concluding observations certain points heretofore left implicit are developed in the context of tentative propositions.

Let me first summarize empirical tendencies that illustrate the manner in which the importance and type of sojourner strategies were affected by the local system's location within the overall structure of territorial systems. Specializations in disparaged occupations were normally followed by peripheral local systems targeting cities at some remove—within striking distance, as it were, but not so close that those from neighboring local systems were likely to go there. Thus, the yamen runners of the Chung-hua county yamen in Taiwan were supplied by an offshore island across the strait in Fukien; barbers in Hui-chou-fu, Kwangtung, were mostly Hakkas from the northern periphery of the physiographic subregion that corresponded to that capital's regional trading system; actors were exported to Peking by local systems in Anhwei in the southern periphery of the North China region; and kidnappers were exported to Shanghai by local systems in Ch'eng *hsien,* on the southern periphery of the Lower Yangtze region (Cole 1975:15).

In general, localities specializing in craft and service occupations sent their sojourners to a single large city or to a particular urban subsystem consisting of a city and its dependent market towns. When the exported business talent was commercial, sojourners were likely to ply their trade within a system of central places. The more widespread and successful was the mobility strategy within a local system, the higher the level and the more extensive the urban system encompassed within its traders' network. Outstanding success was marked by control of wholesaling of selected commodities in all the higher-level cities in a subregional or even macroregional urban system. The potential for success in business specializations was largely a function of the local system's location with respect to cities at different levels in the economic hierarchy and to the transport routes linking the cities within an urban system. Local systems disfavored on both counts were simply in no position to maximize by exporting business talent of any kind. Such disadvantaged systems were in a clear majority in every region, with the possible exception of the Lower Yangtze.

Turning now to occupational specializations of significance beyond the bounds of a single macroregion, I have already noted the relative concentration in Northwest China of localities specializing in the export of military specialists. In the Lower Yangtze and Southeast Coast regions, there was a similar concentration of localities specializing in the export of Buddhist priests (cf. Welch 1967:412–419). Holding these macroregional specialties constant, one discerns a general tendency for local systems with these specializations to be peripheral within regions. Quite apart from the association of military prowess and religious heterodoxy with the less accessible and mountainous terrain of regional frontiers, there was a tendency for the peripheral counties within a prefecture to produce proportionately more military than civil degree holders and for peripheral areas within a macroregion to produce proportionately more "religious" specialists than orthodox scholars. In part at least, this spatial pattern reflects the Confucian bias that pervaded Chinese values.

"Big-time" sojourning was practiced with greatest success by local systems in resource-rich regional cores. Specialization in the cultivation of academic talent and of officials and their private secretaries was most prevalent among local systems clustered in the immediate vicinity of high-level capitals. Specialization in the cultivation of commercial and financial talent was most likely within the local-city trading systems of cities high in the economic hierarchy. In fact, as we have seen, local systems pursuing the orthodox academic mobility strategies were most heavily concentrated in the vicinity of large cities whose level was high in both the administrative and the economic hierarchies. And it is no accident that the great trading groups of traditional China were associated with prefectures (Hui-chou, Ch'üan-chou, Ning-po, and so on) and that the economic centers in which their talents were perfected and from which they emigrated were prefectural capitals. We are left with the paradoxical conclusion that great success in the scholar–official track was often coupled with great success in the merchant–financier track in the same favorably situated areas.

This leads me to a second set of propositions concerning the interrelation of specialties at the local-system level. In view of the superior prestige and power of the scholar–official, one might expect the historical record to show a predominant tendency for commercial success to be transformed into academic success in the long run. There is much evidence in support of the proposition that an increment of commercial wealth at the local level was in fact normally invested in the ingredients of academic success. Shiba (1975:40–41) has shown that the economic development of Hui-chou and the associated export of sojourning merchants, a process begun in the ninth century, was reflected during the Sung period in a steadily rising rate of academic success. During the Southern Sung (1127–1280), the prefecture produced *chin-shih* at a phenomenal rate, and academic success was heavily concentrated in the same two counties that most successfully pursued the export of business talent. In an analysis of the consequences of economic prosperity during the heyday of the second (that is, late Ming) developmental cycle in the Chang-Ch'üan subregion, Rawski (1972:88–94) has shown that during the sixteenth century the counties most closely connected with the booming foreign trade registered a sharp increase in the number of *chin-shih* degrees won. On the other hand, one discerns no tendency whatsoever for either Hui-chou or Chang-Ch'üan to shift all or even most of its eggs to the academic basket. To the contrary, as Ping-ti Ho (1962:85, 246) has demonstrated, Hui-chou successfully pursued both strategies throughout late imperial times; while its production of graduate degree holders remained phenomenally high, it could hardly be said to have surpassed the prefecture's business achievements during the same centuries. In Chang-Ch'üan academic success was less marked during the Ch'ing than in the Ming, although business success, overall, was greater in Ch'ing than in Ming times (Ho 1962:249–251). One can even point to instances of an unambiguous contrary trend: While Ning-po prefecture was extraordinarily successful in producing scholar–officials throughout late imperial times, its academic success rate declined somewhat during the eighteenth and nineteenth centuries as its business expansion gained momentum (Ho 1962:253).

The situation at the local level was unquestionably complex, but I think we can catch a glimpse of the relevant dynamics. Case studies by Ping-ti Ho (1962: Chapter 4) and others have documented the difficulties faced by any given family or even a lineage in maintaining a high rate of academic success generation after generation. Downward mobility out of the bureaucratic elite was the eventual fate of every successful family, if only because one could never count on having sons bright enough to pass the critical examinations. In these circumstances, diversification was only prudent. A fifteenth-century *chin-shih* described the strategy in his ancestral home as follows (Wang Tao-k'un, quoted in Ho 1962:73).

Hui-chou, with approximately one scholar for every three merchants, is a highly cultured area. . . . It is not until a man has been repeatedly frustrated in his scholarly pursuit that he gives up his studies and takes up trade. After he has accumulated substantial savings he encourages his descendants, in planning for their future, to give up trade and take up studies. Trade and studies thus alternate with each other, with the likely result that the family succeeds either in acquiring an annual income of ten thousand bushels of grain or in achieving the honor of having a retinue of a thousand horse-carriages. This can be likened to the revolution of the wheel, with its spokes touching the ground in turn. How can there be a preference for any one profession?

One can also approach the matter from a somewhat different direction. Rural lineages that pursued the orthodox strategy were typically those that controlled rich agricultural land in the vicinity of important cities. As a matter of course, their wealthier families "diversified" by providing an advanced education for the one or two brightest sons while socializing another to manage the family farm. Wealth achieved through bureaucratic service was ideally used to enlarge the family's landholdings, thereby ensuring the continuity of prosperity and schooling during the intervals between academic successes. As Ping-ti Ho (1962:76) has pointed out, this basic strategy was symbolized in one of the names commonly used for ancestral temples: Keng-tu T'ang (Hall of Plowing and Studying). Thus, the difference between local systems pursuing the academic but not the business strategy and local systems pursuing both was that the latter had yet another string to their bow in the struggle to maintain elite status.

It must also be realized that within counties favorably situated for the pursuit of both academic and business mobility strategies, not all lineages or villages or marketing communities commanded the resources needed to compete in the scholar–official track. The situation in the New Territories of Hong Kong was probably not atypical in this regard. There, five higher-order lineages together occupied most of the first-class land, including nearly all of that suited for double-cropping rice; and these lineages, each of which maintained a school, monopolized academic success in the area (Baker 1966:31–33; Freedman 1966:12 and passim). In the nineteenth century other lineages simply had no recourse to sojourner strategies. With the rise of Hong Kong as a major entrepôt, however, the relatively small and poor lineages in the New Territories found themselves in a position to pursue maximization strategies involving business and service sojourning (cf. Watson 1975: Chapter 4). This example suggests that the enduring across-the-board success of certain favorably situated counties in late imperial times rested in part on the fact that business opportunities associated with the nearby city made it possible for almost all local systems to settle on a sojourner strategy that fell within its means.

My third set of conclusions relates to the distribution of sojourners in central places of different types. We have seen that mobility along the

scholar–official track involved advancement up the hierarchy of administrative central places and that the process gave expression to the system
hierarchy itself through competition within successively more inclusive
administrative units. An analogous point can be made with respect to the
merchant–financier track, in that upward mobility often involved progress
up the hierarchy of economic central places and competition with businessmen drawn from successively more extensive marketing or trading
systems. However, this general picture should be qualified in several ways.
First, the image of hierarchical ascent must be supplemented by another
of downward movement to the cities dependent on a given higher-level
city. It is clear that in building up a commercial hegemony, regionally
based entrepreneurs often moved up the hierarchy to a strategically
situated commercial city and then consolidated their position throughout
its trading system by expanding their operation to lower-level dependent
central places. Similarly, the progress of Shao-hsing natives within the
imperial administration involved consolidating their position in Peking
and then extending their operations to less exalted capitals.

Another qualification relates primarily to the upwardly mobile who
made it into the "big time": Many interregional traders and most high-
ranking officials actually worked in cities outside the hierarchy to which
their own native place belonged. In the bureaucracy this followed from
avoidance rules designed to protect officials from particularistic demands,
most notably those from same-native-place fellows, whereas in the spatial
economy it followed from the necessity to ground long-distance economic
transactions in the trust and accountability that same-native-place bonds
assured. The full implications of this somewhat paradoxical situation are
pursued elsewhere (Skinner 1976a).

One must qualify in a different direction the implication that the
scholar–official track related solely to the hierarchy of administrative
capitals while the business track related solely to the hierarchy of economic centers. In fact, the mobility paths and destinations of officials
were influenced by the economic level of capitals, and those of merchants
were influenced by the administrative level of commercial cities. Field-
administrative posts at the county and prefectural levels were officially
graded according to "importance" and to the nature and volume of
transactions in the yamen, and these classifications were in large part a
function of the capital's place in the hierarchy of economic central
places.[30] Thus, it was clearly perceived as a promotion when a magistrate
was transferred from a county whose capital was a local city to another

---

[30] The top administrative post of each county- and prefectural-level yamen was categorized
according to four binary variables, yielding 16 possible designations. Posts were also assigned
to one of four categories according to importance (Ch'ü 1962:15). See Skinner (1976a) for an
analysis of the relation between the designations of a capital's yamen(s) and (1) the capital's
rank and level in the administrative hierarchy, (2) its level in the economic hierarchy, and
(3) its location with respect to macroregional cores and peripheries.

whose capital was a greater city in the economic hierarchy. Similarly, merchants recognized clearly enough that the conduct of business in cities at the same economic level had to be quite different according to their administrative rank—say, prefectural capital, county capital, or nonadministrative. Among the critical variables were likely to be the efficiency of taxation, vulnerability to customary exactions, and the composition of one's clientele.

My earlier discussion concerning the significance of the disparity between the economic and administrative functions of a central place (focused on the data in Table 1) is relevant here. It would appear that in general both merchants and officials preferred to sojourn in cities whose economic central functions overshadowed their administrative importance (that is, the cases near the upper right of Table 1) and avoided whenever possible cities whose administrative level was disproportionately high in relation to their economic importance (that is, the cases closer to the lower left of the table). In a city where the imbalance favored economic centrality, the ambitious bureaucrat had everything to gain. Opportunities for extraofficial income were great, for he could tap the resources of an economic system more extensive than the unit he administered, and by the same token he could more readily chalk up a laudable record as a tax collector. More generally, the challenge of a busier, larger yamen provided ample opportunity to prove himself to superiors. Other things being equal, the businessman, too, was favorably situated in such a city. By virtue of the city's high level in the economic hierarchy, he could reap the economic rewards of scale, agglomeration, and diversification.[31] Moreover, whereas the bureaucratic take was absolutely large for a capital at that level, it was proportionately small for an economic center of that functional importance, and in any case the loss could be spread among a larger number of proportionately wealthier firms. A city near the other typological extreme—that is, a capital whose rank was high in relation to the city's economic functions—was something of a backwater for bureaucrat and businessman alike. The marketing system whose commercial wealth could be effectively tapped, whether to fill government coffers or the sleeves of officials, was typically smaller than the administrative unit in question. As for the businessman, the scope for entrepreneurship and profit was limited by the center's low position in the economic hierarchy. More important, while the bureaucratic take would be absolutely small for capitals at that level, what was skimmed off would amount to a larger cut of the profits of the smaller and less prosperous business community.[32]

My fourth set of conclusions concerns the manner in which the hierarchy of local systems was expressed in sojourner alliances and organi-

---

[31] Mera (1973) musters evidence in support of the general proposition that economic productivity increases with city size, particularly in the case of less developed countries.

[32] While there is considerable anecdotal evidence supporting the generalizations in this paragraph, they are advanced tentatively as propositions requiring empirical verification.

zations. The general model of segmentary opposition (cf. Smith 1956) holds that lower-level units ally as necessary to counter external threat or to take advantage of external opportunity; both motivations were evident in Chinese sojourner alliances. Time and again, sojourners from local systems within a trading system or an administrative unit joined forces at that level in the hierarchy which was necessary to claim the prize in a distant city and to deny it to other similar alliances elsewhere. Thus, among Shao-hsing private secretaries, those from Hsiao-shan and Chu-chi were resentful of the advantages enjoyed by their more powerful and numerous colleagues from the metropolitan counties of Shan-yin and K'uei-chi, but they were all as one in competitive situations involving secretaries from other Chekiang prefectures. And in the face of competition from secretaries whose native prefecture was Ch'ang-chou (Kiangsu), they would combine with secretaries from throughout Chekiang. In a given city, sojourners normally organized themselves formally on the basis of common origin. The inclusiveness of membership was, of course, a function of the relative numbers of sojourners from various local systems as well as of the competitive situation. Relevant units for cumulating native-place ties ranged from subcounty townships-cum-marketing-communities up to conventional groupings of provinces. The relevant point here is that membership was always defined in terms of contiguous territorial units and that, despite discrepancies and inconsistencies in organization names, the de facto membership and distribution of power reflected the hierarchy of local and regional systems of the immigrants.

Finally, I want to underline the importance of sojourner mobility strategies for China's spatial integration. It is now generally recognized that "career mobility systems," as they have been termed in the anthropological literature, may be an important means of articulating levels in complex societies (cf. Adams 1970 ; Leeds 1964). A critical form of such articulation in Imperial China was the upward mobility of scholars via the imperial examinations, for that process forged an effective link between the imperial bureaucracy and the leadership of local parapolitical systems below the county level of administration. However, this point is well understood, at least by China specialists, and it is in any case more appropriate here to emphasize the role of mobility strategies in China's economic integration.

Interurban transactions are normally critical in integrating spatial economies, and so it was in traditional China. If the Lower Yangtze constituted a regional economy, it was in no small part a function of the flow of information, goods and services, money and credit, and economic specialists among the region's principal cities. It is these flows above all that enable us to identify Soochow, Nanking, Hangchow, and Shanghai together with the many lesser cities in their hinterlands as a *system* of cities. Moreover, the indicators of an emergent national economy or domestic market in late Imperial China were precisely the interurban flows—trade and other economic transactions—between commercial cities in one region and those in others.

It was a special feature of interurban transactions in traditional China that a high proportion involved entrepreneurs who shared a common origin (that is, *t'ung-hsiang*, same-native-place ties). A Cantonese firm in one city exported goods to a Cantonese firm in another. Shao-hsing breweries shipped their product to Shao-hsing wholesalers in Hangchow. Couriers carried market and price information from the Hui-chou gild in Nanking to the Hui-chou gild in Hankow. Remittances went from a Shansi bank in Chungking to another Shansi bank in Tientsin. There are many reasons for expecting long-distance economic transactions to make use of *t'ung-hsiang* bonds whenever possible, but in the last analysis it came down to a matter of trust and accountability, on the one hand, and of reliable business competence, on the other. On the one hand, fellow natives could trust one another because both were socially grounded in, and would eventually return to, the same local system, in which the reputations of their families, lineages, and particular native places were at stake. On the other hand, the skills and knowledge specific to particular lines of business were developed through experience, cumulated within local systems, and perpetuated through established practices of business recruitment, selection, and socialization. On both counts, then, the risks of long-distance business transactions were minimized by keeping within *t'ung-hsiang* alignments.

Interurban transactions within subregions rested on scores of local-system specializations, those within macroregions on hundreds. Yet a certain few of these were of special importance to the integration of regional urban systems in that multibranch enterprises, organizational and business affiliations, and the sheer weight of business transactions within a single "common origin" group linked together all the major commercial cities within the region. Interurban business transactions between macroregions, the riskiest of all, were dominated by entrepreneurs from a very few regional systems, and theirs was a vital role in the articulation of China's semiclosed regional economies. My final point is that the interurban economic transactions that underlay China's economic integration rested in a fundamental sense on mobility strategies whereby local systems sought comparative advantage in the export of specialized human talent. The potential for such strategies, their realization, and their consequences were all constrained and shaped by the structure of China's regional systems.

REFERENCES

Adams, Richard N.
    1970 Brokers and career mobility systems in the structure of complex societies. *Southwestern Journal of Anthropology* **26**: 315–327.

Aoyama Sadao
  1963　Tō Sō jidai no kōtsū to chishi chizu no kenkyū (Transport and communications in
        the T'ang and Sung periods and contemporary maps and gazetteers). Tokyo:
        Yoshikawa kōbunkan.
Baker, Hugh D. R.
  1966　The five great clans of the New Territories. *Journal of the Hong Kong Branch of the
        Royal Anthropological Society* **6:** 25–48.
  1976　Extended kinship in the traditional city. In *The city in late Imperial China,* edited
        by G. William Skinner. Stanford, Calif.: Stanford Univ. Press.
Burgess, John Stewart
  1928　*The guilds of Peking.* New York: Columbia Univ. Press.
Chang, Chung-li
  1955　*The Chinese gentry: Studies on their role in nineteenth-century Chinese society.*
        Seattle: Univ. of Washington Press.
Ch'en Ch'i-t'ien
  1937　*Shan-hsi p'iao chuang k'ao lüeh* (Researches on Shansi banks). Shanghai: Shang wu
        yin shu kuan.
Ch'ü, T'ung-tsu
  1962　*Local government in China under the Ch'ing.* Cambridge, Mass.: Harvard Univ.
        Press.
Cloud, Frederick D.
  1906　*Hangchow: The "City of Heaven", with a brief historical sketch of Soochow.* Shan-
        ghai: Presbyterian Mission Press.
Cole, James H.
  1975　Shaohsing: Studies in Ch'ing social history. Unpublished Ph.D. dissertation, Stan-
        ford Univ.
Folsom, Kenneth E.
  1968　*Friends, guests and colleagues: The Mu-fu system in the late Ch'ing period.*
        Berkeley: Univ. of California Press.
Freedman, Maurice
  1966　*Chinese lineage and society: Fukien and Kwangtung.* London: Athlone Press.
Fujii Hiroshi
  1953–1954　Shin'an shōnin no kenkyū (A study of Hsin-an merchants). *Tōyō gakuhō* **36,**
        Parts 1–4.
Gamble, Sidney D.
  1963　*North China villages: Social, political and economic activities before 1933.*
        Berkeley: Univ. of California Press.
Grimm, Tilemann
  1976　Academies and urban systems in Kwangtung. In *The city in late Imperial China,*
        edited by G. William Skinner. Stanford, Calif.: Stanford Univ. Press.
Ho, Ping-ti
  1959　*Studies on the population of China, 1368–1953.* Cambridge, Mass.: Harvard Univ.
        Press.
  1962　*The ladder of success in Imperial China.* New York: Columbia Univ. Press.
  1966a *Chung-kuo hui kuan shih lun (A historical study of hui-kuan in China).* Taipei:
        Hsüeh sheng shu chü.
  1966b The geographical distribution of hui-kuan (Landsmannschaften) in Central and
        Upper Yangtze provinces. *Tsing Hua Journal of Chinese Studies* **5:** 120–152.
Hu, Hsien Chin
  1948　*The common descent group in China and its functions.* New York: Viking Fund.
Jones, Susan Mann
  1972　Finance in Ningpo: The "Ch'ien Chuang," 1750–1880. In *Economic organization in*

Chinese society, edited by W. E. Willmott. Stanford, Calif.: Stanford Univ. Press. Pp. 47–77.

1974 The Ningpo *pang* and financial power at Shanghai. In *The Chinese city between two worlds,* edited by Mark Elvin and G. William Skinner. Stanford, Calif.: Stanford Univ. Press. Pp. 73–96.

Kao Shu-k'ang
1937 Shan-hsi p'iao hao ti ch'i yüan chi ch'i ch'eng li nien tai (The origins and formative years of Shansi banks). *Shih huo* **6:** 24–35.

King, Frank H. H.
1965 *Money and monetary policy in China, 1845–1895.* Cambridge, Mass.: Harvard Univ. Press.

Lechler, R.
1878 The Hakka Chinese. *Chinese Recorder* **9:** 352–359.

Leeds, Anthony
1964 Brazilian careers and social structure: An evolutionary model and case history. *American Anthropologist* **66:** 1321–1347.

Liu, Hui-chen Wang
1959 *The traditional Chinese clan rules.* Locust Valley, N.Y.: Augustin.

Mera, Koichi
1973 On the urban agglomeration and economic efficiency. *Economic Development and Cultural Change* **21:** 309–324.

Mitamura Taisuke
1970 *Chinese eunuchs: The structure of intimate politics.* Translated by Charles A. Pomeroy. Rutland, Vt.: Tuttle. (Originally published as *Kangan: Sokkin seiji no kōzō,* 1963.)

Rawski, Evelyn Sakakida
1972 *Agricultural change and the peasant economy of South China.* Cambridge, Mass.: Harvard Univ. Press.

Saeki Tomi
1971 Shinchō no kōki to Sansei shōnin (Shansi merchants and the rise of the Ch'ing dynasty). In *Chūgokushi kenkyū (Studies in Chinese history),* Vol. II. Kyoto: Tōyōshi kenkyūkai. Pp. 263–322.

Shiba, Yoshinobu
1970 *Commerce and society in Sung China.* Translated by Mark Elvin. Ann Arbor: Center for Chinese Studies, Univ. of Michigan. (Originally published as *Sōdai shōgyōshi kenkyū* 1968.)

1975 Urbanization and the development of markets in the Lower Yangtze valley. In *Crisis and prosperity in Sung China,* edited by John W. Haeger. Tucson: Univ. of Arizona Press.

1976 Ningpo and its hinterland. In *The city in late Imperial China,* edited by G. William Skinner. Stanford, Calif.: Stanford Univ. Press.

Skinner, G. William
1964 Marketing and social structure in rural China, Part I. *Journal of Asian Studies* **24:** 3–43.

1971 Chinese peasants and the closed community: An open and shut case. *Comparative Studies in Society and History* **13:** 270–281.

1976a Cities and the hierarchy of local systems. In *The city in late Imperial China,* edited by G. William Skinner. Stanford, Calif.: Stanford Univ. Press.

1976b Regional urbanization in nineteenth-century China. In *The city in late Imperial China,* edited by G. William Skinner. Stanford, Calif.: Stanford Univ. Press.

n.d. Urban development in Imperial China. Unpublished manuscript, Stanford Univ.

Smith, M. G.
  1956   On segmentary lineage systems. *Journal of the Royal Anthropological Institute* **86,**
         Part 2: 39–80.
Terada Takanobu
  1972   *Sansei shōnin no kenkyū* (A study of Shansi merchants). Kyoto: Tōyōshi
         kenkyūkai.
Vömel, Johann Heinrich
  1913   Der Hakkadialekt. *T'oung pao* 2e série **14:** 597–696.
Watson, James L.
  1975   *Emigration and the Chinese lineage: The Mans in Hong Kong and London.*
         Berkeley: Univ. of California Press.
Welch, Holmes
  1967   *The practice of Chinese Buddhism, 1900–1950.* Cambridge, Mass.: Harvard Univ.
         Press.
Yang, Lien-sheng
  1952   *Money and credit in China: A short history.* Cambridge, Mass.: Harvard Univ.
         Press.

Index[1]

[1] Scholars are indexed only if their works are discussed. For references readers are referred to
the individual reference lists at the ends of chapters.